SEGREGATION'S SCIENCE

CARTER G. WOODSON INSTITUTE SERIES
Deborah E. McDowell, Editor

SEGREGATION'S SCIENCE

Eugenics and Society in Virginia

Gregory Michael Dorr

University of Virginia Press   *Charlottesville and London*

University of Virginia Press
© 2008 by the Rector and Visitors of the University of Virginia
All rights reserved
Printed in the United States of America on acid-free paper

First published 2008
First paperback edition published 2018
ISBN 978-0-8139-4149-3 (paper)

1 3 5 7 9 8 6 4 2

The Library of Congress has cataloged the hardcover edition as follows:

LIBRARY OF CONGRESS CATALOGING-IN-PUBLICATION DATA
Dorr, Gregory Michael, 1965–
Segregation's science : eugenics and society in Virginia / Gregory Michael Dorr.
p. cm. — (Carter G. Woodson Institute series)
Includes bibliographical references and index.
ISBN 978-0-8139-2755-8 (alk. paper)
1. Eugenics—Virginia—History. 2. Eugenics—Study and teaching—Social aspects—
Virginia—History. 3. Virginia—Race relations—History. I. Title.
HQ755.5.U5D67 2008
363.9'209755—dc22
2008017074

For Fiona, Sophia, Sabrina, Chris,
and especially Holly

Contents

Acknowledgments   ix

INTRODUCTION: "You *Are* Your Brother's Keeper!"   1

1   "The Sacrifice of a Race"
Virginia's Proto-eugenicists Survey Humanity   21

2   "Rearing the Human Thoroughbred"
Progressive Era Eugenics in Virginia   48

3   "Defending the Thin Red Line"
Academics and Eugenics   70

4   "Sterilize the Misfits Promptly"
Virginia Controls the Feebleminded   107

5   "Mongrel Virginians"
Eugenics and the "Race Question"   137

6   "A Healthier and Happier America"
Persistent Eugenics in Virginia   167

7   "They Saw Black All Over"
Eugenics, Massive Resistance, and Punitive Sterilization   195

CONCLUSION: "I Never Knew What They'd Done with Me"   221

Notes   231

Bibliography   269

Index   289

Acknowledgments

M ANY INDIVIDUALS AND INSTITUTIONS contributed to this book. The following account is necessarily partial. Those unmentioned share my thanks with those named.

I am grateful to the archivists who helped me uncover the facts about Virginia eugenics, especially the University of Virginia's interlibrary loan department, Edward Gaynor, Margaret Hrabe, and the archivists in Special Collections, and Joan Echtenkamp-Klein and Joby Topper at the medical school. Archivists at Randolph-Macon College, the College of William and Mary, the Hampton Institute, Howard University, and the Library of Congress Department of Manuscripts all eased my research. Jodi Koste at the Medical College of Virginia assisted and, along with Joan Klein, promoted my research.

The Spencer Foundation, the American Philosophical Society, the University of Virginia's Graduate School of Arts and Sciences, the Institute for Law, Psychiatry, and Public Policy, and the History Department financed the dissertation from which this work grew. David Jones, director of MIT's Center for the Study of Diversity in Science, Technology, and Medicine allowed me time to complete the book. The late Harold and Cora Lindquist helped underwrite my graduate work. George and Mary Lindquist assisted in countless ways—attempting an accounting would be futile. They have my heartfelt gratitude.

My intellectual mentors have my abiding appreciation. Dr. William J. Jacobs predicted that I would become a professional historian. Margaret Darrow and Ted Mitchell provided guidance at Dartmouth. Paul Lombardo of the University of Virginia Law School suggested this study. Paul taught me about the nuts and bolts of research, convincing me never to say die. Paul coached multiple drafts into articles, chapters, a dissertation, and a book. Words fail to express my thanks for his intelligence, integrity, and friendship. Joseph Kett of the history department also led by example. His penetrating questions clarified my muddy thinking and elicited better work. Edward Ayers, Lenard Berlenstein, Reginald Butler, Alon Confino, Grace Hale, Ann J. Lane, Nelson Lichtenstein, and Chuck McCurdy all shaped my thinking. My graduate school comrades—Hayley Froysland, Lodge Gillespie, George Grattan, Matt Iden, Zak MacNamara, Alberto Mosquera, Rolland Murray, Ben Riddell, and Chris Rieber—have my thanks, too.

At the University of Alabama, John Beeler, Kari Frederickson, Howard Jones, Larry Kohl, Michael Mendle, George Rable, George Williamson, and especially Larry Clayton, provided advice and encouragement. Maarten Ultee pushed me toward medical history. Without Paul Hagenloh this book would not exist. Hasan Kwame Jeffries improved my analysis of race. Lisa Lindquist Dorr read large portions of the draft dissertation. Her input refined my first two articles. Our conversations about history, writing, and teaching—not to mention current events and parenting—have enriched me as a scholar and a person. Dr. Jill Martin kept me sane.

Scholars of eugenics and disability—Gar Allen, Elof Carlson, Christina Cogdell, Ian Dowbiggin, Wendy Kline, Steven Noll, Johanna Schoen, Steve Selden, and Alex Stern—gave me their time and constructive criticism.

At the University of Virginia Press, Dick Holway demonstrated the patience of Job shepherding this manuscript and its irascible author through the publication process. He has my abiding thanks. Susan Brady performed a copyediting miracle, especially with the documentation. Alan Lessoff of the *Journal of the Gilded Age and Progressive Era* exemplified the best of academic editing and provided encouragement at a crucial moment.

Folks outside the academy supported this work. Among the Lodge Boys, Chris Bates, Gus Conrades, Mark Curnin, Peter Dammann, Greg Gilbert, Dan Hanifin, Jeff Martz, Greg McGowan, Jim Murphy, Dan Offit, Bill Rexford, Scott Schorer, Paul Simpson, and Scott Whelehan deserve special mention. Chris, Dan, and Paul hosted me during my month in Philly. Batesy's buddy Dan Katz graciously hosted a near-total stranger. David E. "Dewey" Winebrenner V accompanied me from grammar school through college, embodying friendship. Dewey, Mark, Greg McGowan, and Scott Schorer smoothed the roughest patch of my adult life—there are no words to express my appreciation.

Among the gymnastics community, Coach Isidore Battino, Steve DiTullio, Steve Infante, and Steve Thompson employed me and modeled great coaching. Vinny Pozzuoli taught me philosophy, art, and artistic gymnastics. Peter

Jeffrey, Jason Melbourne, Emma Alpert, Shelby Barscelou, Kim Streng Collins, Kathy Girouard, Linda Thompson Drowne, Laura Kannaird, Amy Balkite Rantilla, and Jen Recine provided gales of laughter. The McKiernan family has been in my corner since kindergarten. Robert J. McKiernan Sr. and his wife, Elvira, were surrogate parents; their sons, Bob, Chris, and Mark, are my brothers. In different ways, they taught me about perseverance, caring, and integrity.

My hometown produced some remarkable individuals who sharpened my thinking and scholarship. Henry Frazer Herbert Jr. has challenged me since grammar school while remaining a steadfast friend. Lori Graham Brady and I trekked from junior high through Dartmouth; while in Virginia's engineering faculty she offered encouragement and good advice. Rob Jazwinski has lifted me when I have been down, time and time again.

My family deserves the greatest measure of thanks. James Richard Dorr, the finest physician I have ever known, gave me a thirst for knowledge, a belief in the necessity and attainability of social justice, and my Dartmouth experience. My brothers, Chris and Jeff, have stood in front of me as models of intelligence and determination; beside me as staunch supporters; and behind me as a relentless cheering section. Best friends, Chris and I muddle through life in kilts, on skis, at concerts, and on the phone, laughter always at the ready. A fabulous surgeon and a graceful writer, my wife, Holly, read and edited the manuscript thrice, excising intellectual cancers and resuscitating a moribund work. Her contributions are so significant that—were it not for fear of embarrassing her with my remaining errors—I should name her coauthor. My love and gratitude know no measure and here find weak register.

Finally, my daughters, Fiona, Sophia, and Sabrina, provide joy and balance, keeping academic and scholarly nonsense in perspective—trivial pursuits compared to loving family. Following their example, this book is dedicated to them, my brother Chris, and, always, my love, Holly.

SEGREGATION'S SCIENCE

I N THE EARLY TWENTIETH century, America witnessed the emergence of a new faith. The rise of empirical science had a profound impact on cultural practices and social structure. Scientists' increasing understanding of and control over the natural world became the focus of intense public interest. Laypeople began turning toward scientists in many disciplines for solutions to the problems created by the swiftly changing currents of modern life. The life sciences (biology, medicine, public health) and the social sciences (economics, sociology, psychology, and educational theory) contended for status. Each field hoped to be voted "most likely to be of service" by reformers determined to create a more just world. Social validation promised scientists personal, professional, and political power as avatars of modernity.

As new discoveries launched the life sciences to a prominence they have commanded ever since the turn of the twentieth century, one science sought to unify the others in the service of humanity. Eugenics—the study of self-directed human heredity and breeding—promised to raise the general welfare by reproducing better individuals. Humans might reach near-millennial perfection by rationalizing their procreation, propagating beneficial inborn traits, and thereby controlling their own evolution. Equating public health with the *"health of the race,"* eugenicists believed that America might lead the world toward "that Utopia of which More wrote, and the Kingdom of

Heaven on Earth of which Christ spoke." As one prominent Virginia anatomist proclaimed, mixing traditional religious rhetoric with the new eugenics creed: "You *are* your brother's keeper! Your brothers are the human race.
Even patriotism should move you to want to make the American race the best
and most virile of history. Wherever you go, whatever your profession in life
may be, racial conservation, the eugenic ideal, needs your guiding counsel,
your valiant help." Fourteen years later, after U.S. Supreme Court Associate
Justice Oliver Wendell Holmes Jr. ruled that "three generations of imbeciles
are enough," a twenty-year-old woman would be wheeled into a Virginia operating room and sterilized—the first of over eight thousand constitutionally
sanctioned eugenic sterilizations to occur in Virginia (and over sixty thousand
nationwide) between 1927 and 1980. Meanwhile, Virginia's Bureau of Vital
Statistics policed births and marriages in an effort to safeguard the "racial integrity" of the Old Dominion's white citizenry. Virginia's eugenically inspired
Racial Integrity Act—which forbade interracial marriages—would survive
until struck down by the U.S. Supreme Court in 1967. Virginia's amendment
and eventual repeal of the eugenic sterilization law in the 1970s, coupled with
the notification of sterilization survivors in the 1980s, seemed to sound the
death knell of segregation's science.[1]

The ghosts of eugenics continue to haunt Virginia at the beginning of the
twenty-first century. In 2002, the General Assembly issued a statement of
"profound regret" for Virginia's eugenics program; the governor formally
apologized to survivors. Nevertheless, five years later—forty years after the
Racial Integrity Act's demise—Virginia's General Assembly passed a measure
calling for the Department of Mental Health, Mental Retardation and Substance Abuse Services and the state attorney general to study "the feasibil-
ity of the use of physical castration as a treatment option" for the "condi-
tional release of civilly committed sexual [*sic*] violent predators." Over one
hundred years before, Virginia's earliest eugenicists viewed the castration
of rapists as a progressive, humane, and economic therapy. Castration not
only ensured that the perpetrator could not commit similar crimes, but also
that there would be no similarly criminally disposed progeny. Both the old
and new efforts sought to prevent crime, release the incarcerated after rendering them nonthreatening (thereby humanely increasing their freedom),
and save the state money. Both attempts ended inmates' procreative potential. In the past, lobbyists were explicit about trying to eradicate allegedly
inherent criminal genes through a compulsory procedure; overtly eugenic
intent and compulsion appear absent from the modern iteration. Nevertheless, the striking parallels have raised the hackles of prisoners' rights advo-

cates. These events remind us that while history never repeats itself, it often rhymes.[2]

The reach and durability of eugenics in Virginia demonstrates how it provided a quasi-religious, quasi-scientific, but ultimately flexible intellectual matrix for channeling long-standing cultural imperatives into both modern social policy and the defense of traditional mores. The eugenics movement explained southern rural poverty (resulting from a shiftless, "unfit" population); the apparent rise of mental illness with urbanization (the marginally unfit, who may have survived in a rural areas, went mad under the pressures of urban life); economic failures during the Depression (the crash resulted from the drag of the unfit on the economy); African American civil rights militancy ("mixed breed" mulattoes suffered hereditary psychic conflict and became "uppity"); and many whites' resistance to desegregation (desegregation would result in miscegenation and the destruction of civilization)—all were allegedly functions of heredity. Whether the facts sustained these explanations is immaterial. What is important is that in America generally, and in the twentieth-century South particularly, eugenics justified a concrete sociopolitical agenda that favored various forms of segregation: the sick from the well, black from white, male from female, able from disabled, and the so-called "fit" from the "unfit." Eugenic segregation offered hope for a modern, scientific, and peaceful solution to endemic social tensions.

Today, the word "segregation," in an American context, evokes images of the Jim Crow South. One seldom thinks of segregation as a scientific term, although it has a definite scientific meaning. Beginning with Gregor Mendel, the Catholic monk who first described the basic laws of genetics, the word "segregation" has been used to describe the hereditary process. Mendel's belief that hereditary traits "segregated" independently and randomly in the process of sperm and egg cell formation built upon a long tradition of using the language of separation to describe the living world. The notion of segregation—distinguishing types—has structured the biological sciences since the Swedish naturalist Carolus Linnaeus first developed his Latinate system of classification dividing the living world into orders, families, species, and "races."[3] From Linnaeus forward, naturalists—and their descendants the biologists and geneticists—have parsed life according to ever more refined systems of analysis. There is nothing inherently invidious in the act of classification. Still, emphasizing the differences between, rather than the similarities among, organic life-forms created a discursive and theoretical matrix susceptible to reorganization on hierarchical lines. Ostensibly value-neutral observations could then be recast to support claims of "inferiority" and "superiority," a tendency that appeared in the works of early biologists, and came to characterize the practices of many later biologists, geneticists, and theorists in other fields who built on earlier work.[4]

Neither fate nor the internal workings of empirical science determined that Mendel's law should be known as the "Law of Segregation." The European scientists Carl Correns (German), Eric Von Tschermak (Austrian), and Hugo DeVries (Dutch) rediscovered Mendel's work and named his "Law of Segregation" in 1900, during the period when institutional racial segregation appeared in the American South, and European colonization of Africa (particularly by Germany, Austria, and the Netherlands) was creating racially stratified societies and, eventually, the apartheid regime in South Africa. That these biologists' language mirrored the contemporary political discourse was not coincidental. Biologists and anthropologists had become interested in hereditary difference as "white" nations became concerned with racial difference. Even as investigators sought to segregate biology into discrete but related subfields, disciplinary boundaries remained blurry. Yet botanists, zoologists, geneticists, cytologists, anatomists, physiologists, and others described the separation of discrete genetic "racial" traits as segregation; politicians used the same word to denote the physical and social separation of the races. The correlation in time and discourse did not consign all these investigators to careers marred by racist research and conclusions. Still, it helps to explain how the assumed barrier between "objective science" and "biased politics" often gave way, yielding scientifically justified racist conclusions. It also underscores the fallacy of thinking about "good biologists" and "bad eugenicists." The categories of biologist and eugenicist overlapped almost completely in the early twentieth century, when both modes of inquiry were considered viable science.

At the time, the concept of segregation seemed eminently objective and powerful. Biologists no longer believed that offspring expressed a homogenous "blend" of parental traits that could not be separated, the "bad" from the "good." Instead, offspring received traits as discrete units that segregated by parent and by parental gamete. Thus, understanding genetic segregation pointed the way toward human life free from genetic "defect." If scientists could identify the trait, and the parent from which it came, one could promote or retard the trait's expression. All that stood between humanity and utopia was the identification of "bad" traits, followed by careful breeding to eliminate them. As Charles Benedict Davenport, America's pioneering geneticist and foremost eugenicist, put it, "The law of segregation of traits, the disproof of the blending hypothesis [that traits from each parent merged in

Harry H. Laughlin and Charles B. Davenport posing before the new main building of the Eugenics Record Office in Cold Spring Harbor, Long Island, ca. 1913. (Courtesy of Truman State University)

the offspring], is of the utmost importance since it shows how a strain may get completely rid of an undesirable trait."[5]

Early American geneticists unanimously championed the modern faith in the ability of scientific inquiry to improve society. Genetic law, these scientists believed, could be applied through eugenics to smooth the transition to modern living. Did this concurrence of thought condemn all geneticists to bigotry? No. A few, like Edward Grant Conklin, resisted racism. But Conklin joined his racially biased colleagues in allowing social and scientific beliefs to merge into a conviction that some genes (and the people who harbored them) were superior to other genes (and the people who harbored them)—and this justified efforts to eliminate deleterious traits. The scientific consensus evolved from conflating eugenic "fitness" and "unfitness" with race, class, and gender biases, to reflecting contemporary notions of ability or disability, regardless of an individual's race, class, or gender. Invidious biases never disappeared; over time, fewer mainstream investigators held them or expressed them publicly.

Yet the notion of fitness as defined by disability, and potentially corrected by eugenic intervention, persisted.

The seductive power this genetic panacea held for many educated Americans—cutting across lines of race, gender, and class—should not be underestimated. Although vocal critics like William Jennings Bryan, Walter Lippmann, and eventually the Catholic Church assailed eugenic doctrine, it would take decades before the majority of life scientists admitted the various biases inherent in their eugenic pronouncements. It would take even longer for the public, once won over to the eugenic creed, to recognize this change in scientific opinion. Value judgments and politics created a time lag between theoretical change and practical application.

The practice of empirical science and the belief in its inherent value-neutrality, especially in biology, has often led to a dangerous syllogism: science is objective, objective beliefs are moral beliefs, therefore science is moral. This syllogism affects scientists, and to an even greater extent laypeople, eliding skepticism and inverting the scientific process. To paraphrase Thomas Lacqueur, "Seeing is believing" often becomes "believing is seeing." Put another way, scientists tend to discover precisely what they expect to find. Lay observers, mystified by scientific authority, often uncritically accept the tentative findings of science as irrefutable fact. This dynamic helped to establish the broad appeal of eugenic ideas and their subsequent instantiation in public policy during the twentieth century. It also continues to have serious implications today; many scientists, engineers, journalists, advocates, and laypeople still insist that science and technology can solve society's problems.[6]

Far from advocating genetic Luddism, this book applauds today's genetic science by drawing into sharp relief the differences between contemporary genetics and earlier eugenics. Nevertheless, this examination of eugenics illuminates how the reflexive relationship between science and social context conditioned the past and continues to influence the present. While present-day geneticists excoriate eugenics as a pseudoscience, many of them still research and teach about genes connected to alcoholism, breast cancer, sexual orientation, and aggression as if the experiments that "discovered" these genes occurred in a culture that is not overly concerned with issues surrounding substance abuse, epidemiology, morality, and violence. This is not to say that the intent of these scientists is nefarious. The point is that social culture influences the science we fund, the questions scientists ask, the experiments they devise, and the conclusions they draw—historical context conditions science.

Population genetics, recombinant DNA technology, and the emerging fields of cloning and "germinal choice" all propose different paths to various utopias of health and longevity—goals that, in themselves, are laudable. Yet these technologies also offer a "back door to eugenics."[7] As our power to diagnose the genetic basis for variations and diseases evolves, our definition of "defect" changes, too. Presently, many people agree that genetic disorders like Huntington's chorea and Tay-Sachs disease—which doom sufferers to short lives and horrid deaths—are diseases to be avoided by genetic screening and the termination of afflicted pregnancies until genetic therapies are discovered. Yet where is the line between irredeemable defect and survivable disability to be drawn?[8] Assuming gene therapies become available, they will doubtless be costly for a long time—who should be able to access those therapies? If only the rich receive treatment, does not that raise the dysgenic pressure on the poor? Will the current vogue for tracing one's racial ancestry through genetic markers associated with geographic populations result in the "molecularization of race," rebiologizing race, a category that for the past fifty years has been understood by scholars and scientists to be cultural, not biological?[9] Coupled with disparities in health, intelligence, education, or wealth can this not lead to claims of genetic inferiority and superiority of given populations? If we are to avoid engaging in segregation's science ourselves, we need to understand how our context shapes our science and the programs derived from scientific knowledge. We need to remain vigilant that what begins as "objective" research does not, intentionally or unintentionally, slide into a biased campaign to stigmatize individuals or groups. Understanding past eugenic experience may allow us better to discern the meanings and implications of present science.

What follows is not just "another" state-level study of eugenics. The distinctive interaction between science and society in Virginia, which resulted in powerful social policies, merits sustained, fine-grained analysis. Unlike other histories of eugenics in the South, this portrait of Virginia's eugenics movement reveals how Virginians used eugenics to navigate between the extremes of New South "modernism" and Old South "traditionalism." By maintaining traditional race, class, and gender hierarchies, eugenics facilitated the southern embrace of positivist science and industrial economics in a state otherwise opposed to such innovation. Voluminous source material—including correspondence, professional papers and books by Virginia eugenicists, newspaper articles, course syllabi, lectures, and student term papers—exists to document the web connecting elite Virginians to the state and national eugenics movement. Two things emerge from the sources. The first is a sense of the persistent power of eugenic thought throughout the twentieth century. The second is the powerful role education played in converting Virginia's educated elites to the eugenics creed. In the minds of white Virginians, the mixture of eugenics and context precipitated an elastic belief system apparently responsive to all social problems. The step from good ideas to good institutional policy was short, indeed.

Scientific hereditarian thought first entered Virginia's institutions during the eighteenth century, gravitating from the "soft" environmentalism of acquired characteristics to the "hard" genetics of Mendel's law. By the turn of the twentieth century, educators and propagandists had spread hard hereditarianism throughout Virginia society, prompting some elite Virginians to locate the causes of social problems in the bodies and genes of "lower" and "darker" citizens. By the early 1900s, hard heredity converged with apparently rising social unrest to create specters threatening society. In short order, Americans confronted the "menaces" of feeblemindedness, immigration, the so-called "Negro problem" and "girl problem," as well as contagious diseases like tuberculosis, syphilis, and gonorrhea.

Even as some scientists used hard hereditarian theories to justify social inequality, others used the same theories to explain social disruption. In light of racial and ethnic intermixture, American eugenicists recharacterized the American "melting pot" as "race suicide." Careless breeding across racial and ethnic lines, and the apparent propensity of poor people to give birth to more children than did wealthy people, convinced eugenicists that the "best stocks" faced extinction. The melting pot was yielding a weak amalgam instead of a strong racial alloy. Eugenicists sought to halt the damage through eugenic education and legislation that would mandate the breeding of a sound American race. Virginia scientists adopted these new doctrines, taught them to their students, acted upon them in medical practice, and lobbied for the passage of eugenically informed social policy. Although the language of eugenics was new, the desire for racial purity was not.[10]

From Thomas Jefferson's *Notes on the State of Virginia* to the Civil War, Virginians used ideas about hereditary difference to shape society. After Emancipation, Jefferson's intellectual descendants deployed these notions to constrain African American liberty. In the Progressive Era, eugenics harmonized with the reform impulse that swept through Virginia's educational and political institutions, depositing accretions of eugenic ideology in its wake. Academics converted to the eugenics creed taught it to elite Virginians who were destined to mold public policy in an era of social reform. In 1924, the state General Assembly enacted eugenic sterilization and marriage restriction laws. The U.S. Supreme Court upheld Virginia's sterilization law in the

1927 decision *Buck v. Bell.* Virginia subsequently sterilized more people than any other state except California. Thus, Virginia remained at the forefront of applied eugenics throughout the twentieth century. Indeed, in 1962 Virginia became the first state to pass a law allowing "voluntary" sterilization as a birth control measure.

Then the tide turned. In the 1967 case *Loving v. Virginia,* the Supreme Court struck down Virginia's eugenic antimiscegenation statute. In 1980, *Poe v. Lynchburg* brought to light the legacy of eugenic sterilizations. In 1997, Virginia established America's first database of "DNA fingerprints"—genetic samples for use in criminal investigations. This effort revamped a bankrupt eugenic goal of identifying "born criminals" by using bona fide genetic technology to inculpate or exculpate alleged offenders without a priori character judgments. The 2002 expression of "profound regret" from the General Assembly and the governor's "sincere apology" for Virginia's eugenics program sparked a national reconsideration of America's eugenics past. Oregon, California, North Carolina, and South Carolina quickly followed Virginia's lead and issued apologies. Georgia and Indiana have recently joined their ranks.[11]

While they never exerted the hegemonic influence they sought, elite Virginians who favored eugenics created a durable ideology that influenced social policy and public opinion for much of the twentieth century. Virginia's eugenics movement provides a case study in eugenical organizing. Evidence demonstrates the links among education, political mobilization, and public policy, as well as the connection between local and national eugenicists. Educators and other eugenics supporters instilled their beliefs in their students, who emerged from the formal educational process, in many cases, anxious to enact eugenics in public policy. Virginians' experience passing and enforcing eugenic laws highlights this dynamic. Moreover, because Virginia's eugenics movement resulted in two significant U.S. Supreme Court decisions, *Buck v. Bell* (1927) and *Loving v. Virginia* (1967), marking the beginning and the end of constitutionally sanctioned hereditarian social engineering, Virginia's experience illustrates the national public policy ramifications of eugenics, from the perspective of those who considered their state on the cutting edge. Understanding the adoption and implications of these ideas depends upon knowing the origins of eugenics.[12]

———

Eugenics is at least as old as Plato; the modern iteration of the notion, however, is commonly attributed to Sir Francis Galton.[13] In 1883, Galton, an English scientist and cousin of Charles Darwin, coined the word "eugenics" to describe "the science of improving the stock." The proposed improvement, Galton believed, tended "to give the more suitable races or strains of blood a better chance of prevailing speedily over the less suitable than they otherwise would have had." Eugenic intervention took "positive" and "negative" forms. Positive eugenics encouraged procreation among the "best" stock. Negative eugenics sought to "cut off defective germ-plasm" by curtailing procreation among the so-called "worst" stock. Negative measures ranged from immigration and marriage restriction to institutional segregation during the procreative period, to compulsory sterilization, birth control, and even euthanasia.[14]

While Galton and his English followers relied on statistical correlations between body form and social traits, American eugenicists deployed the emerging sciences of particulate heredity and psychometrics to crack the mystery of racial difference. The rediscovery of Mendel's theory presumably clarified the identification of and breeding method for hereditary traits. Intelligence tests, especially in the American environment, purported to measure inborn, hereditary intelligence. A shotgun wedding between Mendelian genetics and intelligence tests seemed to provide scientists with the basic information necessary to begin breeding improved human beings. Since social mobility, not class hierarchy, underpinned the American cultural mythos, the rugged individual, the "self-made man," stood at the center of the American cultural landscape in memory if not in reality, providing a model for eugenic breeding.[15]

Mendelian genetics and intelligence testing allowed American eugenicists to explain social mobility as a function of genetics, while simultaneously normalizing established class and racial hierarchies. Correlating genetic studies and IQ tests "proved" what scientists long suspected: heredity produced qualitative differences between races that transcended class, culture, or environment.[16] The coincidence of "favorable" genes from otherwise "inferior" parents accounted for the careers of American "self-made" men *and* the existence of "superior strains" within races. Thus, opportunity for class mobility, fostered by proper breeding, existed under the American eugenic scheme. Whiteness, however, even more than class status, became the first marker of genetic fitness. Americans emphasized race, a hierarchy most wanted maintained, while they deemphasized class as a concession to democratic tradition.[17]

Eugenic appeals to racial integrity and "Nordic" superiority emanating from elite northern universities echoed white southern rhetoric regarding racial purity and Anglo-Saxon supremacy.[18] Fears of miscegenation—white intermarriage with inferior immigrant "races" or blacks—alarmed northern-ers and buttressed southern concerns about both African Americans and the eugenically tainted "shiftless, ignorant, worthless class of anti-social whites of the South."[19] American eugenicists, North and South, advocated racial pu-rity, using theories about race mixing to shape public policy. Southern eugeni-cists often drew analogies between racial segregation and northern efforts for immigration restriction, institutionalized segregation of mental patients, and restrictive marriage laws.[20] This study demonstrates how eugenics eased the merging of Virginians' regional identity with a new overarching identity of "pure," "100 percent Americanism."

Virginia, a state with an established history of control by "enlightened" elites, embraced both the progressive and eugenics movements. Confronting the tensions between "Old South" traditions and "New South" dislocations, eugenics mediated between "progressive" liberalism and the self-consciously "backward" Agrarian reaction.[21] This "middle passage" allowed Virginians to adopt ideas that many southerners derided as "northern," like economic lib-eralism, industrialization, and urbanization. Indeed, Virginians' embrace of eugenics and evolutionary biology set them apart from every other southern state. University of Virginia president Edwin Anderson Alderman success-fully rallied progressive Virginia educators in defense of academic freedom, evolution, and the separation of science and religion. As a result, Virginia was the only southern state to avoid legislative consideration of an anti-evolution bill in the 1920s.[22] Thus, eugenics empowered Virginians to dodge the north-ern characterization of the South as "a section stubbornly dissenting from—and sometimes defying—the nation's progressive achievements and ideals."[23]

Eugenics provided educated Virginians with a modern solution for tradi-tional southern social problems—dispensing with poor white trash and the "Negro question"—while ushering in "modern" liberal-industrial society in one motion.[24] Conserving traditional southern social hierarchies on a modern basis, eugenics legitimized long-standing social prejudices with apparently objective, scientific observations.[25] Eugenic theories eventually persuaded many otherwise resistant southern whites to support the invasive state in-terventions favored by progressive reformers.[26] In the Deep South, eugenic theory found strong early support among scientists and physicians, but not legislators. By contrast, the most progressive Upper South states, Virginia and North Carolina, moved rapidly from theory to practice, enacting powerful eu-genics laws at a relatively early date. Eugenics allowed elites in these states to embrace progressive liberalism without adopting racial liberalism, something those in the Deep South acknowledged only after traditional institutions for racial control—lynching, the convict-lease system, and the chain gang— became national embarrassments.[27] Although eugenic legislation challenged traditions of local control, it sounded many of the major chords of southern society: white supremacy, paternalism, and the myth of a predatory, atavistic African American population. This scientific stance allowed elite Virginians to claim that they represented the vanguard of modern social engineering, ushering in a future that looked suspiciously like the past. Eugenics also provided Virginia elites with a new creed that fused liberal Protestant religion with positivist science to explain social inequalities as the logical expression of natural—and hence moral—law. The explanatory power of the eugenics creed created generations of Virginians who believed in the scientifically verified, hereditary inequality of individuals and races.

Language has always occupied a central position in the construction of racial and gender identities, and how those identities embodied power relationships. Eugenics appealed to Virginians because it drew on a familiar idiom.[28] To promote their views, eugenicists developed and deployed a specific rhetorical construction, the "eugenic metaphor."[29] The eugenic metaphor melded elements of political, economic, scientific, medical, and popular discourse. If society was indeed analogous to a living organism (the "body politic"), then the next logical step was to construe social problems as equivalent to physical illnesses.[30] Social intervention by government paralleled the therapeutic interventions physicians used to cure patients. Eugenicists reduced the philosophical problem of perfectionism from a moral to a physical plane. Human perfection, and hence salvation, would result not from religious teaching alone. Instead, eugenic breeding would increase all those traits that made individuals more moral, better citizens increasingly susceptible to religious inculcation and an acceptance of God's saving grace. While this position remained anathema to most Christian fundamentalists, who asserted the inherent sacred equality of all human life, for more theologically liberal Christians—disproportionately represented in the ranks of progressive reformers and legislators—this stance seemed to reconcile a belief in God's efficient creation with the inefficiency of human free will. Put another way, if humans simply procreated according to genetic laws—a proxy for divine injunction rather than their passionate whims, they could help bring on the millennium by creating a more morally educable, perfect race.

Using the familiar language of genealogy, breeding, and illness/health, the eugenic metaphor facilitated the redefinition of citizenship—who was and who was not "fit" to be a full member of the polity. In the process, eugenicists created an imagined community—the "American race"—and sought to

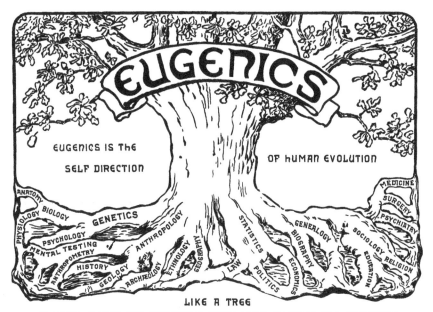

This logo, from an award certificate from the Second International Congress of Eugenics in 1921, replaces the biblical tree of knowledge with the "Eugenics Tree." Eugenicists believed their science represented a monistic philosophy melding all other intellectual endeavors into an organic whole. (Courtesy of the American Philosophical Society)

substantiate its existence by an appeal to biology. Genealogists and animal breeders blurred the distinction between human and nonhuman life by using phrases like "blood lines" and "pedigree" in tracing the "heritage" and "heredity" of individuals over time.[31]

Americans, particularly those in Virginia, maintained a deep fascination with issues of genealogy, kinship, and "bloodlines." To be of "good blood" meant approximately the same thing as being "eugenic"—both individuals were considered "well born." Similarly, to be of "bad blood," or to possess a mixture of "good" and "bad" blood, relegated one to a lower, subhuman level similar to what eugenicists termed "dysgenic" or "cacogenic." This ancient notion of "blood" as the vehicle for heredity demystified genetic science even as it obscured the complexity of genetic operation.[32]

The term "germ" compounded this obfuscation by facilitating the convergence of agricultural, medical, and genetic language. Originally the term for a plant's seed, "germ" came to denote both pathological bacteria and, slightly modified to "germ-plasm," the matter responsible for heredity. Moreover, early geneticists appropriated "germ" at almost precisely the same time that medicine began to describe microscopic pathogens as "germs" in the 1870s and 1880s. The familiar word "germ" took on new, more precise and technical meanings when invoked by scientists. These "refurbished" words never lost their original meanings; new meanings were merely grafted onto the old ones, which maintained a certain intuitive homology with the phenomena scientists wished to describe. These familiar images resonated with the "common knowledge" and "conventional wisdom" among both educated and uneducated people. Thus, laypeople remained linguistically attuned and connected to the new science.[33]

The separation between experts and lay observers remained incomplete because experts refused to use the new nomenclature to the exclusion of the older terminology. Thus, biologists often used familiar terms like "family" and "race" interchangeably with the more esoteric words "genus" and "species." Similarly, although William Bateson coined the word "genetics" in 1905 to describe the study of particulate heredity, geneticists continued to use older words derived from agriculture.[34] In action, this language created a popular consensus fostering the acceptance of eugenic programs, although many in the public remained ignorant of the full implications of eugenic policy. This common understanding allowed eugenicists to refashion memory and sustain the imagined community.

Redefining citizenship allowed eugenicists to create their own "origins myth" explaining the biological superiority of the "American race." According to eugenicists, the American race descended from "Old Stock" Americans— those pioneers who founded the first colonies at Jamestown and Plymouth. Through fortuitous breeding these intrepid settlers created a new, superior race. As the twentieth century advanced, individuals claiming descent from "Old Stock" like the "Virginia Cavaliers" and "Boston Brahmins" ascribed their social status to now-measurable genetic qualities passed down through the ages. Biology thus made the ineffable material, identifying those entitled to full political and legal privileges, as well as those individuals and groups in need of control.

In the Virginia context, the eugenic metaphor's ability to recast memory reinforced traditions of elite control. Paradoxically, the eugenic metaphor made complex biological phenomena readily accessible to laypeople, while masking the eugenicists' social control agenda. Poor farmers could wander through the eugenics exhibition at their state fair, see the displays of stuffed guinea pigs explaining heredity, and make the connection between animal breeding and human procreation. These same farmers could then see the charts depicting the heredity of "defectiveness" and, based on their own experience with animal breeding, agree with the eugenicists that "culls"—inferior individuals, whether human or animal—should be eliminated. Many of these individuals participated in the "Fitter Families Contests," allowing themselves to be evaluated like animals. Yet these same farmers, because eugenics resonated strongly with their own common sense, might never realize that their failure to win a Fitter Families Contest medal might indicate that they fell into the category of the "unfit," potentially subject to eugenic culling. Their facility with eugenic terminology and their self-identification as "not one of them" allowed such people to applaud efforts to control the "obviously" unfit while remaining oblivious to the implications eugenics held for their own social position.[35]

The language of the eugenic metaphor thus used science to render transparent the biases of both the eugenicists and their audience. Eugenicists invoked familiar terminology of the halcyon past, extolling "America's pioneer stock" when discussing such alarming phenomena of modern life as "race suicide." As a 1935 biology textbook written by a Virginian noted, collapsing the old into the new, "blood will tell, or rather to put it more scientifically, '. . . the chromosomes will tell the story.'" Students were led to believe that the old aphorisms now had scientific backing; old beliefs, in modern parlance, offered solutions to social problems. The eugenic metaphor's reliance on genealogy, breeding, and medicinal cures made both present tumult and the unknown future seem controllable—by understanding the "trend of the race," people could shape the genetic destiny of their offspring, and hence society. Eugenical pronouncements gained cultural force because many laypeople believed that eugenic programs derived from a purportedly objective, scientific study of conditions, not political legerdemain. Thus the eugenic cure would be permanent, whereas the traditional political nostrums lasted only as long as the ruling regime.[36]

By invoking the eugenic metaphor, eugenicists appropriated the physician's gaze—which both perceived and constructed the world in terms of health and illness—and viewed the world through a new lens that merged biology, genetics, and medicine. Just as medical discourse normalized health and pathologized illness, eugenical discourse defined and identified genetically normal humans. It also valorized genetically exceptional individuals and demonized the genetically abnormal. This new function allowed eugenicists, like physicians, "not only to distribute advice as to healthy life, but also to dictate the standards for physical and moral relations of the individual and of the society in which he lives." By normalizing this hierarchical understanding of human genetic worth, eugenicists adopted more than the clinician's therapeutic gaze; they also appropriated the physician's cultural authority. Eugenicists emphasized prevention, and borrowed heavily from the lexicon of public health. Hard hereditarianism left little room for environment to change destiny. "You can't keep a good man down" became a rallying cry of eugenicists. Similarly, the only way to stop genetically "unfit" or "bad" people from degrading society was to curtail their procreation. In eugenic terms, the public health ultimately depended on human breeding, not mere environmental sanitation. Borrowing the language of progressivism, eugenicists trumpeted the "social efficiency" to be achieved through such genetic selection.[37]

As the first decade of the twentieth century gave way to the second, and eugenics became a common subject for discussion in newspapers, periodicals, literature, movies, and academic journals, the eugenic metaphor reflected the growing preoccupation with "efficiency." Progressive Era thinkers, whether in business, politics, science, or social reform, all emphasized the necessity of using scientific expertise to make life more pleasant by making living more efficient. In the medical field, which lacked almost all of today's powerful therapeutic interventions, this focus on efficiency translated into a conviction that the best way to treat disease was to prevent morbid conditions from developing. Practically, this impulse led to the organization of schools of public health, the reorganization of the federal and state public health services, and a fixation on public sanitation and personal hygiene. Not surprisingly, mental health experts redefined their quest as "mental hygiene," and emphasized prevention as much as therapy. Eugenicists joined this efficiency and prevention vogue, linking the Taylorite quest for rationalized, efficient business to the pro-active, preventive ethos of public health.[38]

Increasingly, the eugenic metaphor emphasized the economic savings that could be realized by preventing the procreation of the "unfit." Arguing from the barnyard and biblical aphorisms that "like begets like" and that one could not "gather figs from thorns or grapes from thistles," eugenicists conflated religion and science while arguing that the best way to solve persistent social problems was permanently to interrupt the reproduction of problem populations. To eradicate crime, one could segregate criminals for the duration of their reproductive life. Or, one could sterilize criminals, rendering them unable to reproduce "their kind," and saving society the expense of building prisons and maintaining inmates. The second option seemed intensely "efficient," from both an economic and an epidemiological standpoint. Eugenicists applied this same reasoning to other institutional populations, including the tubercular, the insane, and the mentally retarded (known then as the "feebleminded," a capacious designation embracing a constellation of "antisocial" traits). The most extreme eugenicists touted capital punishment and euthanasia as the most efficient eugenic interventions.[39]

In analyzing eugenics in Virginia, one runs the danger of casting the interaction of science and society in dichotomous terms: a battle between "biased" politics and "objective" science, as if one could or has ever existed without being influenced by the other. Moreover, periodizing the ascent, apogee, and descent of the American eugenics movement is a complex task, yet it is essential to understanding the movement's intellectual history. This effort depends on the definition of eugenics and where one locates the impetus for change. The benchmark study of American eugenics argued for a 1930 turning point, after which "the course of eugenics was rapidly downhill," accelerated mostly by the internal advances of genetic science.[40] Many subsequent investigators adopted this scheme but became increasingly sensitive to the persistence of certain strains of eugenic thought. All, however, agreed that by the 1930s eugenics had split into "good" and "bad" or "reform" and "mainline" wings. What characterized these polar groups was that the good/reform group (now known as geneticists) adhered to the canons of "objective" science, while the bad/mainline group (the eugenicists) stood mired in the pseudoscientific claims of a biased ideology based on antiquated science.[41] The evidence, however, refutes this dichotomy. Many men lionized as reformers hewed to mainline eugenics' belief that "good" and "bad" genes exist and that mankind can be improved.[42] This impulse persists today in the Human Genome Project and the assurances the most visionary genomists give the public that genetic therapies will, someday, make humans impervious to disease. Although the obvious eugenic effect of germ cell therapy has made it a relatively taboo area of research, somatic cell therapies would still have a quasi-eugenic effect. Thus, advances internal to genetic science have merely qualified eugenic thinking without ever abandoning the hope for genetically improved human beings.

The triumphalist history of "objective" genetics overcoming "biased" eugenics is flawed beyond repair. Such a narrative obscures the dynamic process of belief formation, rejection, transformation, and persistence that this book hopes to elucidate. Understanding the fallacy of the triumphal narrative helps to clarify how eugenics persisted among academic scientists in Virginia and elsewhere. Unlike in the Deep South, where eugenics arrived late as a flash in the public policy pan, in Virginia eugenics devolved as the result of a gradual "changing of the guard" rather than a rapid repudiation of eugenic premises. Ultimately, the breakdown in the overtly racist eugenic consensus was "rooted in political, and not scientific events. . . . [T]he role played by events internal to science was indirect and largely unrelated to the discovery of new facts or the development of new theories."[43]

While not formally divided in two, the book's organization falls into two large sections. The first three chapters detail the intellectual and institutional history of eugenics in Virginia. Chapter 1 develops the prehistory of Virginia eugenics and hereditarianism by examining the careers of Thomas Jefferson, James Lawrence Cabell, and Paul Brandon Barringer. These Virginians' theorizing about hereditary racial inequality set the stage for the acceptance of eugenic thought in the Old Dominion.

The rise of eugenic ideology at the University of Virginia between 1900 and 1919 forms the focus of chapter 2. The crusade for the progressive restructuring of Virginia's secondary and higher educational systems linked education and social engineering. The University of Virginia hired Harvey Ernest Jordan and William Henry Heck to help modernize the schools of medicine and education, respectively. These men introduced the "first wave" of formal eugenic thinking to the University of Virginia, building the foundation for an imagined community of hereditarily superior "Old Stock" Virginians.

Discussion of the "second wave" of eugenicists, flooding Virginia's colleges between 1915 and 1930, forms the bulk of chapter 3. Teaching biology, psychology, sociology, education, and medicine, these men imbued thousands of professionals with a desire to recapture the memory of the Old Dominion's golden age of superior citizen-leaders. This hereditarian outlook pushed Virginians to pursue applied eugenics in the name of conserving the old "Cavalier" stock. Additionally, this chapter examines the teaching of eugenics in women's colleges and historically black institutions, highlighting the ideological flexibility of eugenics and the eugenic metaphor. These marginalized groups were able to hone eugenics into a scientifically justified program that cut against the status quo. So, even as elite white men sought to use eugenics to buttress traditional forms of segregation, other Virginians sought to "fight fire with fire" by using eugenics to argue for different social and cultural balances.

The second part of the book documents the ways in which educators became activists, militating behind the scenes for eugenic public policy. These chapters demonstrate how continuing professional education reinforced ideas first encountered in the state's secondary schools and colleges. The efforts to pass eugenic sterilization and segregation laws to control the "feebleminded," "delinquent," and "defective delinquent" classes are examined in chapter 4. Eugenicists co-opted medical authority to convince legislators that eugenic sterilization could resolve the "menace of the feebleminded." Virginia's Racial Integrity Act, the focus of chapter 5, used eugenics to protect the purity of the "American race" from the menace of miscegenation.

Chapter 6 traces the persistence of eugenic teaching, research, and enforcement in Virginia from the 1930s to the early 1950s. The chapter follows the rise of anti-Semitism and antiradicalism in 1930s Virginia and relates this development to the rise and fall of fascist eugenics in Nazi Germany. Virginia sped up its sterilization program amidst the fear that the Germans were "beating us at our own game" and potentially breeding a race superior to Old Stock Virginians.[44]

Chapter 7 considers the slow demise of eugenics between the 1950s and the 1970s. It establishes the connections between eugenics and Massive Resistance in Virginia through the 1955 antimiscegenation case *Naim v. Naim*. It also examines the laws proposed in 1962 and 1964 that promoted the sterilization of Virginia's "welfare mothers." A brief analysis of the failure of these legislative initiatives, and the U.S. Supreme Court's ruling striking down Virginia's Racial Integrity Act, reveals how the dissonance between eugenic ideology and historical context led to the failure of eugenics as a rationale for public policy. Without segregation, eugenics—segregation's science—lost a major portion of its reason for being.

The conclusion considers the ongoing repudiation of mainline eugenics in Virginia since the 1979 cessation of eugenic sterilization and the 1980 lawsuit *Poe v. Lynchburg*, a class action brought against the state by survivors of Virginia's eugenic sterilization program. In a political environment that has rejected most forms of legalized segregation, the science of innate human difference can no longer command broad assent. Ironically, given its past embrace of segregation's science, Virginia became the first state to apologize for its eugenics program. Just as it took time for eugenic ideology to supplant older rationales that had justified these forms of segregation, so, too, it took time for newer ideologies to supersede eugenics. The eugenic grail of fitter, longer-lived, more socially adaptive human beings nevertheless remains an underlying, unspoken goal of both modern genetics and Virginia social policy.

1

"THE SACRIFICE
OF A RACE"

*Virginia's Proto-eugenicists
Survey Humanity*

I N February 1900, Dr. Paul Brandon Barringer—chairman of the faculty at the University of Virginia and professor of medicine—took the stage before the Tri-State Medical Association of Virginia and the Carolinas. His task was to explain what he, and many other whites of the era, considered to be "the rapid increase of the negro and his relatively greater increase in crime." According to Barringer, rigid hereditary determinism held dire consequences for African Americans because it predetermined the absolute limit of blacks' social advance. African Americans' "generic tendency" to "savagery" doomed them to revert to the "primitive" and "barbaric" status of their African ancestors. The controlled environment of slavery had artificially raised slaves beyond their lowly evolutionary niche. Yet, Barringer asserted, "the fifty centuries of historically recorded savagery . . . can not be permanently influenced by one or two centuries of enforced correction if the correcting force [slavery] be withdrawn." With emancipation came reversion to "savage" status, creating a new, degenerate black generation that could not possibly survive in contact with civilized white society. Recapitulation and reversion thus accounted, in Barringer's mind, for the apparent surge in black criminality that terrified whites in the two decades surrounding the turn of the twentieth century.[1]

Barringer's argument proceeded from the axiom that "sociological problems are in most cases biological problems," and therefore any attempt to solve racial tensions must recognize the biological laws governing race relations. To set his address on the appropriate scientific foundation, Barringer cited the doctrine of recapitulation formulated by the German biologist Ernst Haeckel: that every organism retraces all the evolutionary stages that its ancestry passed through to assume its present form. Comparative anatomists had traced human development from fertilized egg to multicellular structure to a fetus that appears similar to the fetuses of less complex life-forms—from fish through birds to mammals—before becoming distinctly human. As Barringer framed recapitulation, "the life history is the repetition of the race history . . . a terse expression of the force we call 'heredity' in life." According to recapitulation theory, heredity dictated the life course of "an individual from the fertilized ovum to the grave, and declares that throughout all this period the child shall tread the path his fathers trod; and this tendency to repeat is not only structural," Barringer averred, "but physiological and psychic as well."[2]

Invoking the specter of the "born criminal," Barringer continued: "The young negro of the South, except where descended from parents of exceptional character and worth, is reverting through hereditary forces to savagery. . . . It is the nature that makes the criminal and imperils a civilization, not the language, the skin or the clothes." The percentage of blacks genetically endowed with "exceptional character" was too small to save the black race. Without white intervention, Barringer condemned free African Americans to a life of barbarism where "tuberculosis and syphilis vie for each other to be 'first in at the finish' which is the potter's field." Worse still, in Barringer's view, this whole degraded existence would be lived, "even down to the last, at the white man's expense," bankrupting white civilization.[3]

Barringer's title, "The American Negro: His Past and Future," was misleading. Posing as a champion of the "hereditary" salvation of the black race, Barringer's primary concern was "to save the white man of the South from barbarism by reclaiming the savage to whom he is inseparably tied." Solving the "Negro problem," Barringer held, echoing the concerns of an earlier Virginia intellectual—Thomas Jefferson—"rises above a question of altruism and becomes a question of self-preservation." White civilization faced a racial apocalypse. Either white retribution for alleged incidents of black-on-white rape would spark "race war," or black-white miscegenation—resulting from rape or white intermarriage with blacks "passing" for whites—would pollute the white gene pool. Barringer decried black criminality not because crime is inherently evil, but because of the effect it had on whites, particularly white women. Barringer, like many white males intent on maintaining both black and white female subservience, conjured images of the "black beast rapist."

Paul Brandon Barringer, M.D., Chairman of the Faculty, University of Virginia, and proto-eugenicist. (Courtesy of the Albert and Shirley Small Special Collections Library at the University of Virginia)

For Barringer, these spectral images of "savage" black men embodied the genetic expression of ineluctable scientific "fact."[4]

Barringer proposed a tripartite solution: political disfranchisement, transferring responsibility for African American education from black to white teachers, and training blacks to be "law abiding laborers and artisans." Disfranchisement would, according to Barringer, "bring again the old relations in feeling that existed between the races at the close of the war," by depriving "the ignorant negro of the political liberty, which he now uses for license." Placing black education in white hands would ensure that the type of education offered to blacks would comport with their inborn capacities. To educate blacks like whites would fail, Barringer claimed, because "the phylogenies of the two races are so divergent that the results of experience with one are not safely applicable to the problems of the other." Blacks should not be trained to be "ladies" and "gentlemen," because "these ambitions are absolutely unattainable . . . and result in a soured and vindictive generation." So Barringer fell back on inculcating class and race subservience, making "the next generation of negroes in the South honest, law-abiding laborers and artisans, with an ambition for the respect of the better class of their own people and of the whites." Anything less would result in disaster for "even the lower [white] classes of the South are of pure Saxon blood," and, if forced to recapitulate their own Saxon phylogeny, "will put an end to the negro problem, because it will be the end of the negro," presumably through extermination in a genetically programmed pogrom.[5]

"The American Negro" was so well received that, overnight, Barringer became America's most visible, learned, and "scientific" southern expositor on the "Negro problem." The Tri-State Medical Society unanimously voted to print the paper and send copies to all southern medical societies. The *Central Presbyterian* ran a laudatory synopsis, commending Barringer's "scientific acumen." Letters poured in from professionals and laymen, North and South. Holland Thompson, a professor of political science at Columbia, called Barringer's address the "best statement of the difficult Southern question that I have ever seen." The rector of the University of Virginia effused: "what you have said is so luminous, so convincing, so historically, scientifically, and socially exact as to exclude all negation. I wish every politician, philanthropist and negrophile from Massachusetts Bay to San Francisco could read it." The secretary of the state board of health attempted to raise money to publish the address. Virginia's secretary of education wrote, "Any man who now contends that the Negroes are making substantial progress in moral, mental, or material development simply shuts his eyes to the actual state of things." Another supporter wrote, "your biological axiom and structure is expert." Echoing Barringer's racial rhetoric, this correspondent reemphasized the probability of racial cataclysm: "The Anglo Saxon, and the Southerner is the most perfect Anglo Saxon, was *never* known to move out, as a race, in front of any other race except to *drive off and destroy* the other race." The only equivocal response came from the president of Western Reserve University, but even he asked Barringer for extra copies and offered to suggest "names of people in the north who would be more than glad to receive it." Barringer's words reverberated across the state and nation, establishing his authority and serving to unite northerners and southerners who viewed the "problem" in the same light.[6]

Long before he mounted the rostrum to deliver "The American Negro," Paul Brandon Barringer had combined his deep southern roots with his training in scientific medicine to become one of the most influential Virginians at the turn of the twentieth century. His independent politics, direct personality, love of a "darkey" joke, and his ideas concerning the proper solution of the so-called "Negro problem" informed the opinions of men like Edward A. Ross and Theodore Roosevelt, as well as those of Virginia politicos and social and business leaders. Barringer's addresses on race married the progressive, modernist impulse motivating "New South Boosterism"—the desire to lift the South into the mainstream of national development—to the "fraternal unity that the creed of the Old South had furnished."[7] Old enough to remember life with slavery, yet young enough to be at the height of his professional power in 1900, Barringer facilitated the ideational shift from the splenetic racism of the Redemption Era to the scientific racism of the Progressive Era. His hereditarian ideas promoted sectional rapprochement by scientifically legitimating the subordination of women, immigrants, the sick, poor, and people of color in precisely the same way that northern intellectuals used science to justify the repression of these groups. This biological marginalization provided justification for many forms of legal and social segregation. Barringer alloyed a curious belief system—an amalgam of traditionalism with regard to social structure, progressivism with regard to the political economy, and a positivist, liberal Christian theism uniting science and religion as the motive force behind human progress. Building on this ideological foundation, later theorists lobbied for ever more coercive laws that traduced individual civil and human rights in the name of national unity and progress.

Other major figures in Virginia's intelligentsia—notably Thomas Jefferson and James Lawrence Cabell—preceded Barringer in linking ideas about biologically determined inferiority and superiority to issues of public health, government, and survival of the social order. Jefferson had confronted the two central—and most explosive—questions of human biology: did all humankind descend from a common ancestral pair, and could variation in human physical traits and abilities be squared with both religion and Enlightenment universalism? Jefferson sidestepped the first issue, aware that it was theological dynamite. Rather than stake a claim for common or disparate creation, Jefferson asserted that all humans had an equivalent inborn "moral sense." Jefferson's theorizing about human intellect—which uniformly concluded that African Americans were inherently inferior—clashed with his Enlightenment faith that "all men are created equal," opening a Pandora's box of scientific, theological, and political questions. Nevertheless, the observations of the Sage of Monticello set the foundation for all subsequent investigations. Dr. James Lawrence Cabell, the third professor of medicine at Jefferson's University of Virginia, refined the founder's racial conclusions. In the process, Cabell anticipated Charles Darwin's evolutionary theory, upheld his own devout Christian beliefs, and provided scientific legitimation for slavery. Now science and religion converged in assigning superior status to whites and inferior status to blacks. All men, despite their common creation, were not created equal.

Weaving together dominant strands of social, political, and religious thought within the tapestry of scientific naturalism, Cabell created a new "hereditary creed" to cloak his a priori bias. Generations of students learned his doctrines that, ultimately, found their basis in Jefferson's thought.[8]

Examining the works of Jefferson, Cabell, and Barringer highlights the continuities in scientific and racial thought in Virginia and America. All three men believed they were objective investigators. All three agreed on black inferiority. And all three located the cause of that inferiority in black biology. Perhaps the most striking dynamic revealed is how all three of these men engaged in "normal science." Normal science is "predicated on the assumption that the scientific community knows what the world is like" and is willing "to defend that assumption, if necessary at considerable cost," often by suppressing "fundamental novelties because they are necessarily subversive of its basic commitments." Enmeshed in both cultural and disciplinary contexts that constrained their thinking, what science told these men was "true" about the world often matched their preconceptions, despite countervailing evidence. Each man encountered situations that undermined his theories—for example that Benjamin Banneker, a black man, was an accomplished scientist (Jefferson); that whites and blacks could mate and produce fertile offspring (Cabell); and that not all black men regressed to the savage state of rapist (Barringer). Nevertheless, these men's normal science dismissed such instances as anomalies, successfully aligning professional research and personal expectation. As a result, their "objective" scientific observations ultimately supported traditional social hierarchies. This dynamic would continue into the twentieth century, despite the massive expansion in biological knowledge, providing a stage on which Virginians' imagined community of superior individuals played out their lives. The real "paradigm shift" in scientists' conceptualizations of race—when race would be seen as having no basis in physical, genetic reality—remained far in the future.[9]

Framing the Debate over Racial Biology:
The Legacy of Thomas Jefferson

Hereditarian thinking in Virginia, like many other traditions in the Old Dominion, traces its lineage to Thomas Jefferson. Anyone attempting to understand the history of hereditarianism and scientific racism in Virginia and America must begin with Jefferson. His views were "more widely read, in all probability, than any others until the mid-nineteenth century," and they were embedded in the scientific tradition.[10] Jefferson's judgments set the pattern for later racial and eugenic scientists. He created the mythic "American race" later defended through eugenic public policy. His ruminations on inherent African American inferiority "framed the terms of debate still carried on today." Jefferson was the epitome of Enlightenment rationalism in America, and his obeisance to the ideals of "natural law" characterized all his thinking, whether social, economic, political, or scientific. The dissonance between Jefferson's idealistic statement that "all men are created equal" and his pronouncements on black inferiority has presented an enduring conundrum, earning Jefferson the sobriquet "American Sphinx."[11]

Watching his slaves on Monticello, Jefferson identified and catalogued apparent racial differences. In his considered philosophical opinion, blacks lacked beauty, emitted "a very strong and disagreeable odor," were "in reason much inferior," and "in imagination they are dull tasteless, and anomalous," being locked in an existence that "appears to participate more of sensation than reflection." The cause of blacks' many infirmities was not their enslaved condition. While Jefferson avowed that, "it will be right to make great allowances for the difference of condition, [slavery and its disadvantages]," he still marveled that, "never yet could I find that a black had uttered a thought above the level of plain narration; never see even an elementary trait of painting or sculpture." This obtained despite many African Americans' having "availed themselves of the conversations of their masters" or being "liberally educated... and [having had] before their eyes samples of the best works" of white artists and intellects. Clearly, nature—not environment—accounted for black inferiority.[12]

Jefferson's conclusions stemmed from his observations of what he and others agreed were concrete phenomena.[13] His conclusions excited much comment precisely because others recognized them as scientific. Yet, Jefferson seemed ambivalent about his findings and reluctant to make a final determination. He stated: "The opinion, that they are inferior in faculties of reason and imagination, must be hazarded with great diffidence. To justify a general conclusion, requires many observations, even where the subject may be submitted to the Anatomical knife, to Optical glasses, to analysis by fire, or by solvents." Some historians have construed these statements as Jefferson's tacit admission that his analysis was flawed.[14] A more fruitful interpretation is that Jefferson *believed* in his conclusions, but to state them absolutely risked alienating the scientific community for methodological reasons, and infuriating the religious community for ontological ones.[15] He was too savvy to do either.

Thus, Jefferson could espouse the political equality of all men, yet make qualified but invidious distinctions among "types" of men—and still remain

consistent within the framework of natural law and the epistemology of natural philosophy. Political equality did not mean biological identity. He could
"acknowledg[e] the nationhood of enslaved Africans and the legitimacy of
their claims to freedom and independence" and still remark, "It is not against
experience to suppose, that different species of the same genus, or varieties of
the same species may possess different qualifications."[16] It is *because* Jefferson
adhered to natural law idealism in *both* his "sciences" that his political and
natural philosophies formed a circular logic that convinced and compelled
subsequent generations. This conflation of science and politics characterizes
Jefferson's argument for a biological national identity—an imagined community of Americans, people preternaturally fit for democracy—based upon a
new "racial" identity.[17]

Jefferson turned to the hereditary ancestry of the colonists to substantiate his claims for independence and a new American nationality grounded
in race. Just as the colonists' "Saxon ancestors," in emigrating to Britain, had
acted upon their "right which nature has given to all men of departing from
the country in which chance, not choice, has placed them," so too did the colonists act on this natural right when moving to America. Their autonomous action, construed as a protogenetic ancestral birthright, differentiated American colonists from the "people" who remained in Britain. Jefferson's emphasis
on "action"—both in terms of mobility and then in the imagery of his vigorous
agrarianism—prefigured "romantic and racialist constructions of national
identity in the nineteenth century." This racialized identity fostered nativism
and racism throughout the nineteenth and twentieth centuries.[18]

Jefferson, like his intellectual descendants, worried about the assimilation
of immigrants and feared the purported hypersexuality of nonwhite races.
His apprehension about foreigners stemmed from two sources, both of which
had hereditary undertones.[19] First, since immigrants would be coming from
monarchies, they would "bring with them the principles of the governments
they leave, imbibed in their early youth. . . . These principles, with their language, they will transmit to their children," rendering them unassimilable.
Worse still, immigrants might "infuse into" the government "their spirit,
warp and bias its direction, and render it a heterogeneous, incoherent, dis-
tracted mass." Twentieth-century eugenicists feared immigrants because they
brought with them their genes, the biological substructure for their "manners
and principles," which they might "infuse" into the American gene pool. Just
as Jefferson felt that "a degeneracy in these [manners and spirit] is a canker
which soon eats to the heart of [a republic's] laws and constitution," later
eugenicists feared that introducing "inferior" genetic stock would undermine

the republic by creating a population unfit for democracy. During committee hearings about the 1924 Immigration Restriction Act, the eugenicist Harry Hamilton Laughlin claimed: "The character of our future civilization will be modified by the 'blood' or the natural hereditary qualities which the sexually fertile immigrant brings to our shores. . . . We should therefore make the possession of desirable natural qualities one of the conditions for the admission of sexually fertile immigrants." Both Jefferson and later Virginia eugenicists, however, viewed the large number of unassimilable African Americans in the South as an even greater threat than northern white ethnic immigrants.[20]

Like those who followed, Jefferson proposed two ways to acculturate foreigners, one social and the other biological—education and intermarriage. For Jefferson, as for the later generation, education could equip both foreign elements and younger generations for their republican responsibilities. Education's acculturative effect, however, depended upon the ability of those exposed to it to benefit from it. Jefferson's storied educational system used merit to create a hierarchy that reinforced class structure and purported hereditary "endowment." All Virginians were entitled to three years of education in Jefferson's primary schools. Those who wished their children to attend longer must pay for their schooling. Annually the school's "visitor" would "chuse the boy, of best genius in the school, of those whose parents are too poor to give them further education, and send him forward to one of the grammar schools." After another winnowing process, with "twenty of the best geniuses" being "raked from the rubbish," a final cut would send half of this cohort off to become schoolteachers. The other half, "chosen for the superiority of their parts and disposition," would attend William and Mary College.[21]

Jefferson's plan democratized education as compared to contemporary standards. Still, it was a meritocracy in name only. Those who could pay for school could continue to attend. Only a tiny percentage of poor children gained access to higher education, ostensibly on the basis of their inborn abilities. Although Jefferson's plan implied inborn capacities, his stated purpose for educating the poor relied on a notion of equality among whites, regardless of economic class. Not denying the inborn inequality of "talents" among white men, Jefferson suggested that heredity transcended class distinctions, often the most visible and insuperable of late-eighteenth- and early-nineteenth-century social boundaries. Of course, Jefferson's ideal educational system was for white men only—he never set out a system for educating blacks or women "according to their geniusses." Notwithstanding Jefferson's numerous equivocations, his actions demonstrate that he believed African Americans were intellectually inferior to all whites—or at least too inferior for citizenship.[22]

Despite the achievements of black exemplars like Phillis Wheatley, Igna-
tius Sancho, and Benjamin Banneker, Jefferson believed that blacks could not
be educated to the point of assimilation. "The improvement of the blacks in
body and mind, in the first instance of their mixture with the whites, has
been observed by every one, and proves that their inferiority is not the effect
merely of their condition of life," Jefferson argued, constructing his brief for
black hereditary inferiority and negating the role of slavery in suppressing
black achievement. The children of black-white mating benefited from genetic "leavening" that increased their cognitive power. Since additional miscegenation would fail to raise the level of the mixed-race offspring to that of
"pure" whites, Jefferson averred that blacks should be "brought up, at the public expence, to tillage, arts or sciences, according to their geniusses" and then
expatriated to an all-black colony. Eugenicists and hereditarians extended
Jefferson's analysis and conclusions in a self-conscious attempt to substantiate his "suspicions" about black racial inferiority.[23]

Jefferson viewed any attempt to assimilate blacks within the American
polity as a greater threat to the integrity of the republic than naturalizing immigrants. Politically and biologically, Jefferson constructed blacks and whites
as "two distinct peoples whose natural relation . . . was a state of war." Americans faced a choice between two unpalatable solutions: expatriation of blacks
and the loss of slave property, or "convulsions which will probably never end
but in the extermination of one or the other race." Assimilation of blacks
through intermarriage with whites was also out of the question. Not only had
Virginia law and custom barred intermarriage since 1691, natural law also
seemed set against such unions. While it was known that blacks and whites
could interbreed, many natural philosophers felt that since "like begets like,"
nature had placed certain barriers between the mating of divergent forms.
Building an analogy between humans and animals, some theorists argued
that "mulattos," the offspring of black-white crosses, suffered from reduced
fecundity or "relative sterility," just as in mules resulting from horse-donkey
crosses.[24] Other theorists suggested that the geographic separation of "races"
indicated a divine or "natural" desire to keep the races distinct. Another barrier, according to many scientists, was what Jefferson termed "the real distinctions which nature has made," differences in physiognomy or physiology that
would cause each group to be repelled by the other. Later eugenicists would
draw these ideas into harmony with new discoveries in genetics, reproductive
biology, and intelligence to circumscribe black citizenship.[25]

According to Jefferson and later eugenicists, American whites and blacks
could not mate "without staining the blood" and increasing "this blot in our

country." Acknowledging his qualified belief that blacks might represent a "variety" of the human species, Jefferson nevertheless inveighed against racial mixing. "Will not a lover of natural history then," Jefferson wrote, "excuse an effort to keep those in the department of man as distinct as nature has formed them?" Although marriage between immigrants and native-born white Americans might facilitate acculturation, intermarriage with blacks was "a dangerous, unnatural transgression"—both politically and biologically. These pronouncements seem ironic in light of Jefferson's probable relationship with Sally Hemmings. By granting freedom to the Hemmingses after his death, perhaps Jefferson tacitly acknowledged their white heritage and suitability for freedom, if not full citizenship.[26]

Unlike black-white intermarriage, Jefferson could countenance white unions with Native Americans. Still, he also felt that very few "pure" Native Americans remained in Virginia, most having interbred with blacks. The best way to preserve natural differences was not merely through categorization, but through what would come to be known as "racial integrity"—efforts to stop miscegenation. Later racial theorists would adopt this logic regarding the "varieties" of humanity and the desire to prevent racial mixing. And, in a nod to Jefferson and all "whites" who claimed descent from John Rolfe and Pocahontas, Virginia's 1924 eugenic antimiscegenation statute would recognize as white all those who had "not more than one-sixteenth the blood of the native American"—that is, one "pure" Indian great-great-grandparent and fifteen pure "white" ones.[27]

For both Jefferson and later eugenicists, "racial purity and national identity were inextricably linked." Jefferson, like his intellectual descendants down to the present, saw only two outcomes: segregation or amalgamation. Indeed, "sex and war converged" for Jefferson and later eugenicists. Both activities could result "in the extermination of the one or the other race" through physical (war) or biological (miscegenation) genocide. Jefferson's theoretical efforts helped to shift race from a "legal" notion derived from the mother's "political" status toward a "hereditary," biological conception. Instead of defining blackness as congruent with slavery, as a function of descent from an enslaved mother, blackness precipitated from the intermixture of genetic material. By the twentieth century, "one drop" of black "blood" caused a genetic reversion from whiteness to blackness.[28]

Regardless of *his* intent, Jefferson set the stage; those who followed collapsed any subtle distinctions he intended. He established the barn-to-bedroom analogy from which all later eugenic schemes extended. Citing both Johann Friedrich Blumenbach's taxonomy and animal husbandry, Jefferson wondered aloud why "the circumstance of superior beauty, is thought worthy attention in the propagation of our horses, dogs, and other domestic animals; why not in that of man?" His advocacy of racial hierarchy and "scientifically managed breeding" indeed "reduced 'man' to the level of 'domestic animals,'" and did more than point "ominously toward the eugenic theories of later generations of scientific racists." Jefferson paved the way for later eugenicists by providing a rationale that harmonized their theories with democratic political ideology. Just as Jefferson argued that "self-preservation was [the nation's] highest moral imperative," and that "'self-preservation' was the first law of nature," later Virginia eugenicists sought to deprive the personal and procreative liberties of blacks, poor whites, and the "mentally defective" to prevent their destroying the *lives* and *people* of Virginia through genetic pollution.[29]

Jefferson forged links among reason, religion, social planning, and medicine that characterized later eugenic thinking. He expected religion to reflect the scrutable regularity of God's natural laws. This early articulation of "science as religion" became a hallmark of the later eugenics movement, which tried to create a "secular creed" where biological imperatives took on religious significance. Jefferson and later eugenicists excoriated "the mobs of great cities" that "add just so much to the support of pure government, as sores do to the strength of the human body." Jefferson's emphasis on the rhetoric of "commonwealth," and the metaphor of the "body politic" as afflicted by disease, anticipated later ideas of public health and visions of a society beset by actual disease. He applauded the congruence of protobiological reform and the public weal in Virginia law, which sought "the preservation and improvement of the races of useful animals . . . the extirpation of those which are noxious . . . [and] the guarding [of] our citizens against infectious disorders, by obliging suspected vessels . . . to perform quarantine, and by regulating the conduct of persons having such disorders within the state." These same concerns would be invoked by later eugenicists to justify social policies meant to prevent the birth of "persons having such disorders" or those susceptible to them.[30]

Changing scientific ideas in the nineteenth century did little to alter the fundamental social goals expressed by Jefferson. Instead, scientific advance sharpened the edge of the legislative scalpel, and increased the precision with which it dissected pathological agents from the body politic. This medicalization of the rhetoric hardened to dogma throughout the nineteenth and twentieth centuries as the "advance" of science—particularly the advent of Darwin and the rise of experimental biology—allowed experts to speak with greater authority about biological phenomena. Indeed, Social Darwinism, derived from Herbert Spencer's conscious adaptation of Darwinism to social processes, destroyed any remaining barriers between the biological and the political.

Before this melding of paradigms gained popular currency, with both society and individuals being discussed in evolutionary terms, the nagging issue concerning the origins of humanity had to be resolved. It is perhaps not surprising that one of the most coherent expositions in favor of the specific unity of humanity emanated from the crown jewel of Jefferson's educational structure, the University of Virginia. It is even less surprising that, in demonstrating the common creation of humankind, Dr. James Lawrence Cabell would distinguish "permanent varieties" of humans that, despite their equal moral sense, might vary absolutely in their native intellect. Often overlooked by historians, Cabell's treatise represents the next articulation of Jefferson's racial logic. As a result, the University of Virginia's medical school became a seat for hereditarian and eugenic theorizing during the second half of the nineteenth century.

Diversity from Unity: Reconciling Inequality and Common Creation

Jefferson viewed the University of Virginia as the fruit of his intellect and one of his greatest accomplishments. If Jefferson was the university's father, then certainly the South—in land, custom, and myth—was the university's mother. The institution, in turn, became the alma mater for generations of Virginia, southern, and national leaders. In this way, Jefferson created an institutional "womb" for the propagation of his intellectual "germ" across time. Writing in 1919, as America and Virginia neared the pinnacle of popular interest in heredity and eugenics, the historian of the University of Virginia remarked: "No biography can be accepted as complete which fails to scrutinize the qualities of the parentage of its subject. The laws of heredity are equally applicable to the University of Virginia, for all its principal characteristics . . . derived from the moulding hand of Jefferson."[31]

Jefferson founded the university intent on providing locally trained professionals in all the arts and sciences needed for Virginia's public welfare. The university's medical school embodied Jefferson's desire to apply science to society, and it became associated with concepts of heredity and public health early in its history. Two of the medical school's giants, James Lawrence Cabell and Paul Brandon Barringer, did much to convince Virginians and Virginia medical school students of the importance of public health, considering it one of the physician's primary responsibilities. Cabell trained Barringer; Barringer then directed the modernization of the school of medicine, the construction of the university hospital, and the training of two future surgeons general, an assistant surgeon general, and a number of other U.S. Public Health Service (USPHS) physicians. This association between the University of Virginia and the USPHS solidified throughout the twentieth century and had a direct effect on the course and character of public health provision in the South, including the now-infamous Tuskegee syphilis experiment. Such would be the fruit of the seed planted by Cabell and Barringer, the first professors to cross hereditarianism and public health in proto-eugenical fashion.[32]

James Lawrence Cabell proved himself a precocious scholar. Born in Nelson County, Virginia, in 1813, he earned the University of Virginia's most prestigious degree, the master of arts, in 1833. The next year, he earned a medical degree from the University of Maryland, and went on to postgraduate study in France. Cabell gained the chair of Anatomy, Physiology, and Surgery at the University of Virginia in 1837, becoming "the most distinguished professor of this medical school" from then until the twentieth century. Only the third man to hold the chair of medicine in Mr. Jefferson's university, Cabell began serving as chairman of the faculty in 1846. Like Jefferson, Cabell cast a long shadow over Virginia and southern medicine.[33]

Cabell maintained a keen interest in the most progressive medical ideas and techniques and became an innovator in his own right. After witnessing the horrible hospital mortality rate as a chief surgeon in the Confederate army, he became a proponent of aseptic cleanliness as early as 1867. He then founded Virginia's first State Board of Health in 1872. He was a charter member, in 1878, of the American Public Health Association, becoming its president the next year. Cabell gained such stature in the field that he was appointed the first president of the first National Board of Health from 1879 to 1883. Cabell held his chair at the University of Virginia until he died in 1889, teaching hundreds of young men who entered the medical profession. Not surprisingly, Cabell inspired many of his students to champion public health—including Walter Reed (famed for vanquishing yellow fever) and Paul Brandon Barringer. Barringer did not achieve Reed's lasting fame. Yet, for a time at the turn of the century, Barringer was one of the two most recognized southern physicians (along with Dr. Hunter McGuire, president of the American Medical Association). Barringer's later ideology depended, in large measure, on the notions presented in Cabell's 1859 book, *The Testimony of Modern Science to the Unity of Mankind.*[34]

Cabell's *Testimony* sought to resolve the heated debate among natural philosophers regarding the origins of humanity that had simmered since Jefferson's time. Specifically, Cabell digested all available scholarship in an effort to decide whether all humans descended from a common ancestor (monogenism), or if the various races each had their own distinct ancestral pair (polygenism). The answer to this question held deep ramifications for Christian theory, Enlightenment philosophy, and American social structures, particularly slavery. Polygenism denied the biblical account of humanity's descent from Adam and Eve. This heresy facilitated the "scientific," hierarchical ranking of races. It also reinforced slavery and undercut Enlightenment natural-rights egalitarianism. Monogenism, in contrast, upheld Christian and Enlightenment doctrine, but it *seemed* to undermine chattel slavery by highlighting the immorality of holding divinely created equals in bondage. Most slaveholders, however, considering themselves faithful Christians, wanted nothing to do with the polygenist defense of slavery, relying instead on biblical justifications.[35] The task remained then, to show that monogenism could uphold both the Christian equality of the races and their secular inequality—the basis of slavery. Cabell exploited shifts in philosophical and scientific ideas to create a modernist logic that supported slavery: if the science of origins upheld the theology of origins, and if the science of origins upheld racial inferiority, then slavery was both theologically and scientifically justified.

For Cabell as for Jefferson before him, the truths revealed by science complemented the truths revealed in the Bible; nature accurately reflected God's will. Cabell, like Jefferson, was willing to segregate the metaphysical from the physical world, allowing each to operate independently, yet claim a common origin in natural law. Following Jefferson's belief in the economy of nature, Cabell envisioned a single creation with various "permanent varieties" arising from a common ancestor. Cabell argued that "certain *acquired* peculiarities are often reproduced with perfect regularity so as to give rise, within the limits of a single original species, to '*varieties*' marked by characters as '*permanent*' as those which distinguish the species itself." Environmentally guided genetic selection, passed down through families, exerted a profound effect on individual organisms. Yet, unlike strict environmentalism, which proposed a population constantly changing in response to environmental conditions, Cabell envisioned the creation of stable groups. New anatomical traits "may then be perpetuated by hereditary transmission, under the law of assimilation between parent and offspring, even though the causes which originally determined the variation from the primitive type have ceased to operate." Environment prompted the change, while heredity propagated and stabilized it, regardless of further environmental change. Cabell came to these conclusions without knowledge of Darwin's revolutionary *Origins of Species,* six years before Gregor Mendel would prove the particulate inheritance of characteristics (and forty-one years before its famed rediscovery), and a decade before Francis Galton would describe ancestral heredity. Cabell thus enhanced the Jeffersonian framework undergirding the construction of an imagined racial community.[36]

As prescient and "progressive" as Cabell's analysis was, it ultimately served a conservative purpose. His system of permanent varieties comported with Scripture and recast Jefferson's ideas about the natural (biological) basis of human nature and intellect—without altering any of Jefferson's racial conclusions. According to Cabell, since all humanity stemmed from a single Divine creation, all individuals, regardless of apparent biological differences, were open to God's saving grace, but that did not make them equal in the physical world. Cabell asserted that the unity of humanity "is not inconsistent with the idea of permanent differences among the races," and he justified his position "by referring to the analogous case of different children of the same parents. 'If two men, the offspring of the same parents, can be the one a dunce, the other a genius, why cannot different races, *though descended of the same stock*, be different also in intellectual endowments?'" Nevertheless, morality stemmed from the education of equal inborn moral dispositions, leaving all people equal potential access to salvation, not equality in the here and now. His religious scruples reconciled with his science, Cabell next needed to square his science and religion with chattel slavery. Cabell advanced a materialistic explanation for the existence and permanence of "a most decided inferiority in intellect, and in the capacity of social improvement" in "certain races." Such inferiority, he argued, proved nothing about the unity or diversity of racial origins, just as differences between siblings failed to deny their common parentage.[37]

As a slave owner, Cabell had a vested interest in preserving the peculiar institution. Cabell minced no words in laying the groundwork for differentiating the races, pointing out that "the great difference between the cranium of domestic swine and that of the primitive wild boar" was a variation "quite equal to that which has been observed between the skull of the Negro and the European." Analogizing humans and animals, Cabell created a hierarchical relationship between race and civilization. Environment created the conditions for "domestication" and "civilization," which heredity fixed as "racial traits" in animals and humans. Obviously, whites were genetically civilized while blacks were naturally savages.[38]

Cabell had to defend his explanation against the obvious counterargument, that removing an organism from one environment to another should cause change. Using the oft-cited example of skin color, Cabell argued:

The fact that dark-skinned people do not lose their characteristic hue by living for many successive generations in temperate climates, is not at all inconsistent with the supposition that this hue might have been originally acquired as the effect of climatic or other external conditions. For a positive mark once acquired, is apt to be perpetuated by hereditary transmission, and is, therefore, not lost by the mere withdrawal of the influences under which it was originally formed.

Assuming that Western civilization marked the apex of development, Cabell implied that whites were permanently "civilized," since they had developed and lived under the "highest" form of social organization for the longest period of time. By extension, enslaved African Americans were only temporarily civilized. They had lived in the environment of slavery that exposed them to a level of development far "above" that of their "barbaric" relatives in Africa. By implication, enslaved African Americans would revert to their "primitive" and "barbaric" tendencies without the "salutary" influence of slavery—just as domesticated swine might revert to feral boars. Contact with whites under the "benign" institution of slavery may have been "intended, in the merciful and wise providence of God, as the only means of extricating [blacks] from their otherwise inevitable 'destiny,' and of bringing them under the tutelage of a superior race without danger of becoming 'extinct before' such a higher race." Cabell's theory thus extended Jefferson's assertion that the environment of slavery did not cause black inferiority. Indeed, Cabell's science effectively preserved the status quo of chattel slavery in the name of saving blacks from barbarism, extinction, and damnation. Just as southern politicians had shifted from viewing slavery as a necessary evil to identifying it as beneficial, so had southern scientists.[39]

Southern social context regarding slavery changed dramatically between the 1787 publication of Jefferson's *Notes* and the 1859 release of Cabell's *Testimony*. Slavery was now advocated as a positive good for whites and blacks, instead of characterized as a "blot in our country."[40] Indeed, Cabell's science— and he was a leading authority and respected practitioner, not some backwoods crank—now used the same invidious racial distinctions Jefferson made to buttress an institution the Sage of Monticello had hoped to destroy. Jefferson opened the field to the scientific exploration of race and social structure in America. Cabell, following Jefferson's lead, used science to resolve theological concerns, attempting to quiet the political debate surrounding race and slavery. Cabell's ideas, however, did not help forestall the Civil War, in some ways the great racial cataclysm presaged by Jefferson. Although the Civil War ended slavery, Cabell propounded his ideas about racial subordination until his death in 1889. A later generation developed Cabell's thought, in conjunction with the incipient science of genetics, to maintain a "scientific" justification for racial hierarchy. Long before he died, Cabell met the young man he would eventually choose to succeed him. It would be this youngster who, as chairman of the faculty at the University of Virginia, would give Cabell's ideas their widest public airing.

Dr. Cabell attended to Paul Brandon Barringer when the lad fell ill during his first year at the university. Cabell became a "guiding influence" in the young man's life. Barringer, like Cabell before him, would pursue the practical application of scientific medicine for the public health. He would also champion the consonance of science and religion. Barringer believed in both the power of heredity and the biological differences between the races. On the surface, his convictions did not distinguish him from many other southerners of his era. Barringer's scientific training and authority, his prominence among southern educators, and his enduring influence upon his students—largely children of Virginia elites—put him in a position of great power. His ideas influenced generations of Virginians by modernizing their cultural prejudices and placing them on a foundation formed by the most recent science. Jefferson and Cabell limned the outline of modern racial theorizing. Barringer filled in the sketch and prepared the blueprint for Virginia's twentieth-century eugenic edifice.[41]

Racial Science Meets Public Policy

As is evident from Barringer's address "The American Negro: His Past and Future," quoted at the beginning of this chapter, Barringer constructed himself as a "scientific Redeemer." His appeal to the Tri-State Medical Association—to use science to confront "race suicide" and defend against atavistic blacks—resonated with larger social and scientific concerns about the future of American civilization. This approach, in turn, made the "Negro problem" implicitly and explicitly a public health problem threatening the biological and political survival of the "American race." Barringer's alarmist tone ensured that his ideas would reach a wide audience. His other major addresses hammered the same themes, increasing his dependence on genetic and proto-eugenic ideologies. Barringer's career exemplifies the creation of "normal science," as culture and the scientific method merged in mutually reinforcing fashion.[42]

Barringer's progressive convictions prompted him to use his position within the University of Virginia to advance the New South cause. First, he dragged the university's medical school into the modern age by endorsing laboratory training in bacteriology, the clinical training of students under the tutelage of established practitioners, and a lengthened course of study. Second, Barringer founded the University of Virginia's hospital, rebelling against "those who would apparently keep the old school just as Jefferson built it, even if the University had to shrivel as a consequence in the competition of a modern world."[43]

Despite his avowed interest in progressive causes, Barringer maintained a strong sense of traditionalism regarding the southern social fabric. Indeed, Barringer may have been the first Virginian and southerner to use the new science of Mendelian heredity to substantiate his belief in the innate inferiority of African Americans. At least in Virginia, this rationalization of prejudice attenuated the extreme racial tensions that rocked America at the turn of the century. In the end, Barringer, presented arguments that reinforced the political and social disfranchisement of African Americans by criminalizing and pathologizing their bodies. His cultural background, his historical context, and science forged his opinions on religion, race, and the public health into an ideological trammel that fettered African Americans' civil rights.

Paul Barringer was born into a family whose roots stretched back to colonial Virginia. His great-grandfather "Pioneer Paul" Behringer emigrated from Germany in 1743, becoming "a man of consequence and a large landholder." Barringer's grandfather served as a brigadier general in the War of 1812, while his father commanded Confederate cavalry during the Civil War. After the war, Barringer's father served prominently in North Carolina's "Redeemer" government, helping to install white supremacy as the de facto and de jure law of the land. The patriotic and martial exploits of his ancestors, slaveholders all, left a deep impression on young Paul Barringer. Ancestry became a clear marker of one's potential and worth; it also delineated one's social responsibilities. That his elders fought again and again for "their Southland" and their way of life imbued Barringer with a passion for preserving his southern heritage and family honor. Barringer mourned the tragedy of the "Lost Cause." As a youth he lived with his aunt, wife of Confederate General Thomas Jonathan "Stonewall" Jackson; he also met Jefferson Davis near the war's end. Then, Barringer wrote, "a great catastrophe occurred for me, the first end result of the war, the leaving of almost all our negroes." Writing almost seventy years later, Barringer echoed former slaveholders' disbelief that "their" former slaves had not enjoyed bondage, and that slave "loyalty" was only as strong as the threat of the whip. Barringer harbored a lifelong image of African Americans as inferior subservients. His academic training rationalized his ideas about racial hierarchy, giving them a sophistication and a justification beyond antebellum nostalgia.[44]

Barringer prepared for college at the Kenmore School in Amherst, Virginia, under Professor H. A. Strode, the father of Aubrey E. Strode, who would later figure prominently in establishing Virginia's eugenic sterilization statute. On a trip from Kenmore, Barringer decided to attend the University of Virginia. At Virginia, Dr. Cabell became Barringer's personal hero, who "shaped my life profoundly." Citing his "increasing veneration for Dr. Cabell," Barringer enrolled in medical courses and blossomed, taking his degree in 1877. He then received another medical degree from the University of the City of New York while interning at Bellevue Hospital, "the center of all things medical." It was in New York that Barringer discovered the sweeping changes overtaking American medicine as William Henry Welch established America's first department of scientific, research-based pathology at Bellevue Hospital in 1878.[45]

While Barringer just missed working under Welch, he saw Welch's star begin to rise as he pioneered colossal change by advocating rigorous scientific training, public health, and eugenics. Barringer sought to emulate Welch's example. In 1879, Barringer "considered the possibility of entering the Marine Hospital Service (the forerunner of the public health service)" after his stint in Manhattan. His father dissuaded him, however, supporting him for eighteen months of medical study in London, Edinburgh, Dublin, Paris, and Vienna. Barringer became "an ardent exponent of Pasteur and of preventive medicine," hoping to adapt scientific medicine to the specific needs of the South. A belief that the South was sick and needed the therapeutic intervention of its best sons—its physicians—drove the remainder of Barringer's career.[46]

Returning to the United States in 1883, Barringer addressed the Medical Society of North Carolina. Not above a bit of showmanship, he gave the first-ever demonstration of the laboratory microscope in the South, then presented a lecture titled "Constitutional Syphilis and its Diagnosis." Barringer—perhaps in an arrogant display of his European studies—asserted that all physicians had a "fair knowledge of the therapeutics and pathology of syphilis," and pronounced himself astonished by "the indifference and ignorance displayed [presumably by his audience] on this subject, the best known perhaps in all medicine."[47]

Barringer described syphilis in epidemic and protogenetic terms, stating, "By inheritance and contagion, (mediate and intermediate) syphilis is now becoming one of the most common of diseases." Such a situation raised the specter of a public health disaster because "the prostitute and the rake . . . are not the only sufferers. . . . The unoffending as well as the offender often suffer together, for some of those who go down to the slums come from the sanctity of the marital chamber." Barringer declared that "a disease like syphilis, laying aside its heredity, must increase in proportion to its basis of contagion, and spreading from a class in which its propagation is, with the majority, a business, who can see the end, unless it be checked by some appropriate legislation."[48]

Barringer's invocation of "inheritance" and "heredity"—which he construed as both the congenital transmission of the disease from parent to child, as well as the constitutional (genetic) susceptibility to the disease—was meant to impress his audience by alluding to cutting-edge science. By "laying aside" the hereditary aspect of the disease, however, Barringer appealed to their fears of "accidental" contagion; they, themselves, might acquire the disease either through sexual "dalliances" or the presence of infected household "help." Thus, Barringer rallied doctors to the defense of civilization against diseased, unfit degenerates in their midst.[49]

Barringer's rhetoric relied upon class, moral, and racially charged imagery—prostitutes inhabited slums while unscrupulous "rakes" brought the contagion back to "the sanctity of the marital chamber"—to allow his audience to identify who constituted public health "menaces." Barringer excused "respectable" white men for their sexual peccadilloes, despite the social cost of philandering, apparently preferring to control men and women of low class and dark skin. Just as Jefferson decried "mobs" as "sores" and "cankers" on the social organism, Barringer stigmatized very definite race, gender, and class groups for contaminating society, drawing analogies between various classes and pathological organisms, between sick individuals and a sick society. For Barringer, there was but one remedy: eradication of both the affected classes and the disease through enactments by "legislative bodies" enforced by "sanitary boards." The state should intervene in the name of public health.[50]

Since the only solution for this plague preying on the morals, health, and productivity of the South involved anti-Jeffersonian government intervention, progressive boosters like Barringer believed that these policies should be determined by "disinterested," expert authorities. Should elite physicians fail to act, Barringer predicted a dire fate for all whites: "This yearly increasing addition of infected blood cannot fail to have its influence upon the stamina of the race or fail to affect, however remotely, all the constitutional ills of its subjects." Considered a racial poison, syphilis threatened the very existence of white society and civilization. Only scientifically trained physicians, committed to protecting the public health (and implicitly the white race), could halt the scourge. Barringer eventually met his own challenge by training numerous "public-spirited" physicians who enlisted in the United States Public Health Service (USPHS). This address launched his career.[51]

Upon his retirement in 1888, James Lawrence Cabell nominated Barringer as his successor. Barringer recapitulated his mentor's career. While Cabell produced Paul Barringer, Walter Reed, and a number of other men who entered the USPHS, Barringer trained surgeons general Rupert Blue and Hugh Cumming; assistant surgeon general and director of the Division of Venereal Disease Taliaferro Clark; and many other members of the USPHS corps. Like Cabell, Barringer had a profound effect on his students. Surgeon General Cumming remembered Barringer as a favorite among the students, and regarded him as "one of the most brilliant intellects I have known." Barringer, like Cabell, attained immense stature at the university, becoming chairman of the faculty from 1897 to 1903. Renewing old ties between the university and organized public health, Virginia's Governor McKinny appointed Barringer president of a revived State Board of Health during the cholera outbreak of 1893. As innovative as his mentor, Barringer tirelessly lobbied state and university officials for the construction of the university hospital, opened in 1901. Although Edwin Anderson Alderman displaced Barringer to become Virginia's first president just two years later, Barringer continued to advise the new president on matters of hiring and modernizing the medical school. This influence affected the tenor of the teaching at Virginia's medical school for generations. Hired in part on Barringer's recommendation, an enlarged faculty took their place and surrounded themselves with like-minded physicians and scientists.[52]

While Cabell and Barringer taught their students a respect for public health, they taught with greater intensity about the power of heredity over human destiny. Faculty and students investigated, and presumed to prove, the biological differences separating the "races" of mankind. Paul Barringer began this trend in public with "The American Negro: His Past and Future," and two other published addresses that appeared between February 1900 and March 1901. Over the ensuing years, Barringer, like Jefferson and Cabell before him, developed his own conception of the organic relationship among religion, science, race, and social policy. Barringer's influence peaked at a historical moment conducive to infusing his updated, "progressive" hereditarian ideas into public policy and the conventional wisdom.[53]

The acclaim Barringer's first address received catapulted him to prominence as the South's most scientific and learned expositor on the race problem. In May 1900, the noted southern progressive Edgar Gardner Murphy gave Barringer his next opportunity for wide publicity before a Montgomery, Alabama, conference titled "A Southern Society for the Consideration of Race Problems in Relation to the Welfare of the South." Though the conference promised Barringer a bully pulpit, Murphy had to assure him that, "No negro is upon the program, or a member of the Society, and those who may be present will be assigned separate seats in the gallery of the auditorium." Barringer announced that his speech would be titled "The Sacrifice of a Race."[54]

Booker T. Washington, principal of the Tuskegee Institute, perhaps alerted to Barringer's forthcoming speech by Murphy himself, sought to convince the powerful Virginian to visit Tuskegee before going on to the conference. Possibly one of Washington's diplomatic efforts to defuse a potential adversary by convincing him that Tuskegee was no real threat, the entreaty fell on deaf ears; Barringer declined. Noting that "in dealing with racial matters I speak of the *race* and not of individuals," Barringer affirmed that his conclusions resulted from his understanding of black biology, not personal antipathy. He delivered a left-handed compliment to Washington: "The very generic tendencies which you have to combat makes the assumption of the position of worth and prominence among men the more to be appreciated." The "you" in the sentence remained sufficiently vague; it might refer to the entire black race, to Washington, or to both—since generic, in its biological sense, meant "familial" or hereditary. Barringer, who prided himself on clever wordsmithing, no doubt intended the construction as a jab at Washington. Barringer's address would amplify the "scientific" judgments he first propounded in "The American Negro."[55]

"The Sacrifice of a Race" again argued that any attempt to solve America's race problem without attention to the "racial history" of African Americans would fail. "Amendments to the Constitution count as naught when pitted against the inexorable laws of nature," Barringer wrote, dismissing the Civil War amendments. Since emancipation, African Americans had "already gone back to original racial tendencies." The only other solution to the "negro problem" would be "euthanasia" unless the "soul and the hand" of black America were educated "more than the mind." Writing just five years after Booker T. Washington's Atlanta Compromise speech, Barringer sought to use science permanently to circumscribe black socioeconomic opportunity. Although Washington envisioned blacks' role as "hewers of wood and drawers of water" as temporary, Barringer concluded that blacks were hereditarily unfit ever to rise above this menial station.[56]

According to Barringer, the benevolence of white slave owners had "saved" blacks, improving their meager racial stock at the same time. Slaves had benefited from eugenical breeding that "was the first and only application of intelligent hygiene to a special race," which established "the vigor and prepotency" of a race otherwise destined for indolence and extinction. He argued that enslaved African Americans were "allowed to multiply, but this under a careful selective process of breeding that outstripped nature itself," creating a "purified" slave population of which white Virginians—who boasted of selling "bad" slaves down South—were proud. With emancipation, blacks reembarked on their path toward extinction in America, their end hastened by their reversion to irrational procreation, which exacerbated their genetic susceptibility to disease and criminality.[57]

Marshaling reams of statistics, Barringer substantiated his case that blacks were becoming unhealthier and more criminal as a function of heredity. The high incidence of tuberculosis, syphilis, and typhoid fever among African Americans indicated nothing to Barringer about their environment. Instead, the occurrence of these diseases proved the genetic unfitness of "a markedly criminal race." Until that race died out, then, they posed a massive public health threat; the "public," of course, was implicitly construed as white. Thus the "Negro problem" was more than a political problem; it was a social disease of massive proportions.[58]

Instead of posing as the savior of the black race, Barringer used his authority as "a Southerner and a physician . . . familiar with the physicians of the South" to sound the death knell for African Americans. If whites represented the survival of the fit, then blacks embodied the complementary axiom, "the death of the unfit." Revealing just why he avoided Washington's invitation, Barringer proclaimed: "The wealth of the Indies could not give this entire race technical training. . . . Industrial training should be reserved for a more industrious people." Extinction loomed; unable to reintroduce slavery, the artificial conditions most likely to "save" the black race, Barringer claimed that nothing—not even medicine or education—could stop "this grand but ghastly tragedy—The Sacrifice of the Race."[59]

Speaking before the Southern Educational Association in Richmond, Virginia, on December 28, 1900, Barringer asserted African Americans' innate intellectual inferiority in "Negro Education in the South." Since African Americans comprised 40 percent of the southern population, white southerners must take an interest in the fate of black folks because "if this forty per cent., the negro race, improve, the South to that extent will improve; if it go backward, it will either carry the South with it or, failing in this, it will demand as the price of progress an expenditure of energy on the part of the whites which no people can endure." The only solution, according to

Barringer, was to restrict black education to manual and industrial training. Barringer argued that, "every negro doctor, negro lawyer, negro teacher, or other 'leader' in excess of the immediate needs of his own people is an anti-social product, a social menace." Appealing to natural law like Jefferson, Barringer reasoned that, "Nature made the white man and the black, it made the natural and unalterable prejudice between the two races, and hence the crime lies at the door of him who knowingly attempts the impossible." Biology, not society, ultimately dictated racial aversion. Social context could exacerbate or attenuate these tensions; it could not eradicate them. America's foremost educational authority, Professor Nicholas Murray Butler of Columbia University, pronounced Barringer's address "the most statesmanlike contribution since the [Civil] War."[60]

Barringer's three addresses formed an ideological triptych joining hereditarian notions of race, educability, and public health. The speeches encapsulated widely held, Progressive Era views regarding the "management" of the "race problem." They also revealed the statist approach to problem solving favored by both white supremacists and public health officials. After a generation of decrying the exercise of centralized federal power over southern social conditions, Barringer and other scientific Redeemers and New South boosters were more than anxious to use the same type of governmental intervention—provided it was under the "local," state-level control of educated, elite whites. Barringer's rhetoric appealed to deep racial fears and hatreds, prompting agreement among many southerners. One supporter wrote, "When the old darkey [African Americans raised under slavery] passes away the young ones will be so worthless that I am afraid much hemp and lead will be required to keep them in bounds." Barringer sold his scientific rationale as a civilized alternative to lynching.[61]

Barringer made one other address in 1900, and in it he established the creation myth for Virginia's version of the new "American race." Invited by the Merchants Club of Chicago to address "the race question in America," Barringer, former president Benjamin Harrison, Chinese Minister Wu, and Booker T. Washington all presented their opinions on racial tensions in America. Barringer squared off against all "barbaric" races—the red, yellow, and black—and lauded the white race as the epitome of strenuous masculinity. The fight for survival against the "savage" Native Americans "forced upon [Anglo Saxons] a necessary appreciation of manhood" that, in time, "grew into a national trait." Native Americans, destined to die out in front of the conquering "Aryans," nevertheless provided the conditions that "moulded the Aryan" into a new, superior "American race." African Americans, in contrast to Native Americans, posed a substantial threat to the American race creating "sectional hatreds" that would "deluge the land with the blood of kinsmen." Paradoxically, supposedly inferior Native Americans provided the catalyst for the American race while the mere presence of allegedly inferior blacks had the power to destroy superior civilizations. Nevertheless, Barringer sarcastically consigned blacks "to the soil," either in labor or death, as the solution to racial and sectional tensions.[62]

Barringer's words drew the approval of many educated elites. Hermon Butler, the organizer who invited Barringer, later wrote of this address that, "it was probably the most important debate since the historical one between Douglas and Lincoln that has taken place in this country in the last fifty years." Describing the crowd, he continued:

> We sat in our seats, spellbound, until quarter before twelve, and the guests were stirred deeply by the presentation given. Dr. Barringer had very much the hardest side of the proposition. His treatment was scientific and skilled . . . like a marble statue in its perfection and beauty. I could have but wished that Mr. Washington was absent so that Dr. Barringer would have been freed from any possible restraint, which he seemed to think necessary, owing to the presence of the representative of the race discussed.

Though Barringer himself faded from the national stage, his ideas carried on in the writings of G. Stanley Hall, who would teach a generation of early psychologists and sociologists about the racial inferiority of blacks. In 1905, Hall asked Barringer for copies of any "pamphlets which you have published . . . on the racial question."[63]

What Barringer achieved with his addresses, then, was an early enunciation of the ideas that would dominate discussions of southern educational reform. Northern philanthropists accepted increasingly national and "scientific" ideas about the inferiority of blacks. This allowed them to concede that southern advance would be a "whites-only" affair. Southern whites would determine and oversee the "appropriate" education for blacks, while remaining free from northern interference in managing the race problem.

Although his career tapered off, Barringer extended his influence in subtle, but far-reaching ways. Leaving the University of Virginia in 1907, Barringer held the presidency of Virginia Polytechnic Institute, where he continued to teach and lecture. Following his retirement in 1914, Barringer moved back to Charlottesville and resumed his relationship with the university and its students. He often drew a rocking chair up under a favorite oak tree, "constantly in touch with a group of young students, medical and otherwise, who daily stopped by for a chat about their problems or some angle of development in thought or experiment that Dr. Barringer might suggest"—including race and health. In his spare time he wrote poetry filled with racist and eugenical imagery. In 1924, at the height of American eugenics and eugenically motivated immigration restriction, Barringer wrote a poem advocating birth control to "stop the heathen / from crowding Christian [*sic*] lands / And underliving lighter folks / And making fool demands." Simultaneously, Barringer sought to develop a "natural history of religion" that reconciled religion and science. And he lobbied for Virginia's eugenic laws and the national Immigration Restriction Act. He continued these activities until his death in 1941.[64]

Long before his death, Barringer recapitulated his own history. Before leaving the University of Virginia in 1907, he concurred in the hiring of Harvey Ernest Jordan, educated at Lehigh University, Columbia, and Princeton, as professor of anatomy. Jordan would eventually become dean of the University of Virginia School of Medicine. Throughout his tenure, he advocated and taught eugenics and facilitated the appointment of eugenicists to the medical school faculty. By 1930, no fewer than seven professors engaged in medical training were outspoken eugenicists.

The incipient sciences of racial biology and racial anthropology, propounded by Jefferson and developed by Cabell, held immediate relevance for the social, political, and religious debates preoccupying Virginians from the late eighteenth through the nineteenth century. That each generation brought its most advanced technology—however flawed it may seem from our standpoint—to bear in attempting to resolve intractable social problems, only stands to reason. That each generation's historical and social context informed their science, only itself to be modified by scientific ideas in an endless ideological feedback loop, is a commonplace of historical interpretation. The salient issue is not the "objectivity" or "empirical veracity" of these early scientific beliefs. What is important is that people invested authority in theories backed by scientific warrants. In so doing, they established a syllogism that related science and moral behavior: science is objective, objective beliefs are moral, therefore science is moral. Extending this logic, scientists and educated elites assumed that any public policy based on scientific principles constituted the most moral course of action. Such logic motivated the intellectual heirs to the Virginia tradition established by Jefferson, Cabell, and Barringer.

2

"REARING THE HUMAN THOROUGHBRED"

Progressive Era Eugenics in Virginia

F ROM ITS JEFFERSONIAN FOUNDING, the University of Virginia commanded immense respect in the South. For a time in the nineteenth century, Virginia's master's degree, which required a student to pass every course
offered at the university, was considered one of the most difficult degrees in
American higher education. At the turn of the twentieth century, Virginia was
the largest school in the South, with a reputation for an elite, hard-drinking
student body. Despite its place in regional myth and memory, by 1900 Virginia's administrators were feeling the pressure to maintain pride of place and
the institution's national profile.[1]

Awash in the maelstrom of New South change, with its single-minded emphasis on "efficiency," the University of Virginia's Board of Visitors jettisoned
the traditional position of "chairman of the faculty" in favor of the modern
office of university president. Paul Barringer, nurturing political aspirations
and aware of the visitors' desires, removed himself as chairman of the faculty in 1903. Edwin Anderson Alderman, one of the South's most nationally
prominent progressive educators, became president—charged with steering
the university between the twin shoals of traditional reaction and "modernist"
radicalism. Henceforth, the university's administration reflected the organi-
zational hierarchies of America's commercial giants.[2]

The shift from Barringer to Alderman signaled the final separation of the "better sort" of southern leaders from the gut-level, Redemption Era racism that marked Barringer's theorizing. Now, Progressive Era scientific racism with its cooler, rational tone and national outlook would condition elite discussions of the "race problem." This transition helped resolve tensions between "Old South" traditionalism and "New South" progressivism. Southerners no longer faced a Hobson's choice between "modern" political and economic liberalism and self-consciously "backward," antimodern agrarianism. Instead, progressive southerners reconciled regional tradition and modern innovation by promoting centralized, bureaucratic social reforms as the way to "democratize" southern life. Such programs increased access to the benefits of modern living, public health, and public education. By promoting rational, scientific management as the watchwords of social organization in both sections, progressives offered an "enlightened" elitism as the new matrix for democratic governance. The commonweal became a surrogate for individual success, as a rising tide lifts all boats. Reformers in both sections "spoke the same language" and shared the same concerns about their social status. Many would turn to eugenics to reify their preferred imagined community of "Old Americans."[3]

Alongside political disfranchisement, industrialization, and educational reform, hereditarian and eugenic ideas enabled white southerners to control social boundaries and to subvert northern self-righteousness regarding the "Negro problem." Southern eugenicists announced that the South approached the "problems" posed by blacks and "poor white trash" in the same scientific, rational—and hence objective, moral, and acceptable—fashion as the North confronted the "immigrant problem." This new ideology collapsed the dichotomies facing southern progressives. Eugenic thinking correlated modernity *and* racism, white advancement *and* social stability, uplift *and* subordination, progressivism *and* agrarianism. Eugenic theories promised to elide southern "distinctiveness" without losing southern identity. Science thus reinforced the imagined community by erasing outdated political rationalizations for hierarchy and reinscribing transformed class, gender, and racial boundaries on the basis of "objective fact" and "expert" authority.

These new ideas attenuated tensions arising from the attempt to create a monolithic white identity and collective memory amidst the increasing strain of white class consciousness. The new ideology allowed whites to feel superior to blacks and justified upper-class whites in their exploitation of lower-class whites, presumed to be eugenically inferior. At the same time, eugenics

muffled protest from the "unfit." Laboring under the treble burdens of socioeconomic oppression, educational deprivation, and scientific stigmatization, the people marginalized by eugenics had a difficult time challenging the
experts. Moreover, any protest was deflected by the propaganda of "popular
eugenics." Contests promoting "fitter families" and "better babies," and mail-
ings from the Virginia Bureau of Vital Statistics, allowed everyone to imagine
themselves as "fit" and rightful heirs to the collective memory of Old Virginians and the Cavalier tradition.

Southern Progressivism, Education, and the Rise of Expert Authority

After 1900, progressive southern educators built on the ideas expressed by
men like Paul Barringer, tempering his rhetoric and amending his solutions
to social problems. For Virginia's educated white males, the eclipse of liberal
arts humanism by professionalization changed their approach to the "white
man's burden" from noblesse oblige to bureaucratic paternalism. University-
trained experts would deftly steer society toward utopia. Popularizing eugenics through southern universities exploited the tendency of education to
inculcate conservative social traditions.[4]

The importance of education could not be overstated. As the famed southern educator Samuel Mitchell said, "Education represents a structural process in society . . . the South has found in the school the latent potency that
will create industries, uplift the masses, adjust racial differences, and regain
political prestige." When applied to women, poor whites, and blacks, this
pedagogical and social ideal emphasized segregated education that fit each
group for its appropriate, subordinate slot in the social order. Blacks would
be educated for manual labor, poor whites for industry, and women as nur-
turers, caregivers, and helpmeets. Southern educational progressives focused
on disciplinary reform through "adjustments" that would calibrate the social
balance.[5]

Alderman's progressive restructuring of Virginia "included no basic al-
teration of social, racial, and economic arrangements." A native North Carolinian who had spearheaded that state's educational reform effort, Alderman came to Virginia from the presidencies of Tulane University and the
University of North Carolina. A seasoned crusader, he was well prepared to
propel Virginia's educational flagship against the currents of traditionalism
and penury swamping the university. Even as Alderman and the Board of
Visitors committed Virginia to becoming a modern research institution, they
self-consciously attempted to maintain the school's southern character and its

place in the van of southern higher education. They agreed that the university should increase its already powerful ability to shape social conventions.

Using the University of Wisconsin as a model, Alderman reorganized Virginia, placing increased emphasis on the instruction of professionals. As Alderman put it, the job of the university was to "get close to the life of the people and to serve that life practically," especially by offering correspondence courses, facilitating "debate and public discussion," and conducting research in areas of "community and State importance." Alderman sought a symbiosis between schools and society, writing: "the Southern scholar must forego his office of prophet and seer and become ruler and reformer. Southern universities and colleges must do the work of social regenerative forces, reaching out directly into the life of the people, making known how much better light is than darkness." Favoring this movement of academics from the periphery to the center of social power, faculty members applauded Alderman's initiative and joined the fight to advance the South.[6]

As Alderman begged for appropriations, politicians embraced his promise of economic advance and increased social stability through higher education. The Old Dominion's distinctive political structure partially explains Alderman's success. Virginia, with its history of elite political domination, never underwent the Populist tumult that swept states like North and South Carolina in the late nineteenth and early twentieth centuries. Elites defused pressures for popular reform with minor accommodations and concessions—like marginally increased funding for education—that undercut protest.[7]

Alongside his campaign for public school reform and the professional education of teachers, Alderman demanded state funds to improve Virginia's medical school and the university hospital. Alderman believed that, "there is no more practical servant of the State than the doctor," because "his greatest function in our civilization is not only to cure and restore to economic efficiency those who are sick but to keep the community at large in a normal condition of health." By 1917, Alderman could boast that the university had spent over $600,000 dollars expanding the hospital, medical faculty, and staff. Physicians, dressed in their "pure" white lab coats, and armed with the technology of modern science, became the iconic representation of southern progressivism. For a region in need of therapy—wracked with hookworm, pellagra, tuberculosis, and syphilis—physicians offered hope.[8]

The public also recognized the relationship among institutions of higher education, science, and society. The *Charlottesville Daily Progress* expressed the popular faith in university-trained experts, writing: "Nothing is more evident than the fact that modern life ... finds its basis in science. ... The scholar versed in the great achievements of the past and possessing exact and extensive knowledge of modern science, can interpret modern life as no one else is able to do." This ideal fit the Progressive Era ethos of scientific positivism.[9]

Alderman applied the same rationale to the "Negro problem." Like most "liberal" southern progressives, Alderman favored white expert management of race relations. The "progressive" social policies of segregation and disfranchisement isolated the volatile ingredients of racial politics, allowing southern elites to perform a "scientific" analysis of the problem. Disarming the explosive issues surrounding black education and social uplift would allow southerners to cultivate "a scientific habit of investigation" that would yield answers. After all, as Alderman wrote, "the right adjustment of relations between the white man and the colored man in American life, still remains perhaps our most complex and momentous public question." It was time that "patient, wise, scientific, just men should labor at the problem and seek to place it where it belongs among the great economic and sociological questions of the time." His use of bloodless phrases like "the right adjustment" of race relations revealed his faith in expert control. Rather than hoping for a solution, Alderman believed that Americans "should be grateful for the fact that the negro has somehow gotten off the southerner's nerves and out of the northerner's imagination." This studied deliberation regarding the "race question" placed Alderman squarely in the ranks of the "racial accommodationists" who labored to maintain a segregated society while arguing that black economic advance and racial cooperation would benefit the white South, too.[10]

In spite of his "liberal" attitude toward black improvement, Alderman was no racial equalitarian. Writing in 1906, Alderman advocated universal public schooling, provided that "the children of the white and black races shall be taught in separate schools." In 1908, he again argued for the "absolute social separateness" of the races if both were to advance. Alderman's racial views betrayed the effect of hereditarian ideas and "reform Darwinism" on the intelligentsia of the South. Darwinian evolutionary theory, Spencerian rhetoric about the "survival of the fittest," eugenics, and the application of these ideas to society became guiding scientific principles within Virginia's progressive curriculum.[11]

Medical Eugenics: True Belief, Biological Inequality, and Public Health

Identifying medicine and the public health infrastructure as the surest agencies for promoting southern progress, Alderman inherited an institution crying out for modernization. The advent of Mendelian genetics in 1900 co-

Harvey Ernest Jordan, Ph.D., anatomist, eugenicist, and Dean of the University of Virginia School of Medicine. (Courtesy of the Albert and Shirley Small Special Collections Library at the University of Virginia)

incided with Paul Barringer's crowning achievement, the construction of the university hospital. The promise of eugenics captivated many of the best and brightest physicians and biologists of the day. The medical faculty Alderman hired, beginning most notably with Harvey Ernest Jordan, looked to genetic and eugenic technologies for solutions to medical and social problems. While genetics provided the theory for analyzing social issues in biological terms, eugenics provided the practical rubric for applying that theory to populations.

Harvey Ernest Jordan, born in 1878 to a Pennsylvania farmer's family, would become one of the most respected medical educators in the New South. On his way to becoming dean of the University of Virginia medical school, Jordan achieved an impressive record as a researcher in histology, embryology, genetics, and eugenics. His personal bibliography lists 177 journal articles and three books. Jordan was trained and befriended by two of American embryology's giants, Edmund Beecher Wilson and Edwin Grant Conklin.[12]

Jordan also established close associations with many nationally prominent eugenicists, among them Charles Benedict Davenport (founder of the Eugenics Record Office [ERO]); Harry Hamilton Laughlin (superintendent of the ERO); Conklin (member, Eugenics Research Association [ERA]); Robert Cook (member, ERA; president, American Genetics Association); Clarence C. Little (member, ERA; president, University of Michigan, University of Maine); David Starr Jordan (member, ERA; chancellor, Stanford

University); and Paul Popenoe (eugenics popularizer). Through these connections, Jordan joined the organized eugenics movement. He did his share
as researcher, author, and lecturer to advance and popularize the eugenics
creed in Virginia and nationally.[13]

While the card-carrying membership of the eugenics movement was relatively small—a few thousand at most—that cohort encompassed most academic biologists and many physicians, as well as a large number of social reformers. Although the movement was strongest in the Northeast, the Upper
Midwest, and California, Virginia was its southern clearinghouse, exporting
ideas farther south. Jordan's ties to professional organizations like the American Eugenics Society, the ERO, the ERA, the American Genetics Association,
and the American Association of Physical Anthropologists facilitated the
expansion of Virginia eugenics. Jordan alerted national-level eugenicists to
research possibilities in Virginia. He also organized like-minded Virginia scientists and laypeople in support of eugenics education and social policy. In
many ways, Jordan's career links the protogenetic racial beliefs of Paul Barringer to the Progressive Era race thinking of Edwin Alderman and other
Virginia intellectuals. Jordan's tenure as professor and then dean of Virginia's premier medical school ensured that generations of Virginia physicians,
nurses, and state health-care institution administrators learned and acted
upon the tenets of the eugenics credo.[14]

Jordan wrote that as a boy in rural Coopersburg, Pennsylvania, he "was
impressed with the importance of heredity, while playing about the barns"
of a local corn and horse breeder. Graduating from Keystone State Normal School in 1897, Jordan entered Lehigh University, where he earned his
bachelor's (1903) and master's (1904) degrees, the latter in bacteriology and
organic chemistry. He then became a teaching assistant in histology at the
Cornell University Medical College from 1904 to 1906. During the academic
year 1905-6, Jordan simultaneously taught at Cornell's medical school and
studied cytology as a "special student" at Columbia under Edmund Beecher
Wilson. The following year, Jordan attended Princeton, where he finished his
training under Conklin.[15]

At elite universities and field stations, students like Jordan met the leading cadre of scientists studying medicine, cellular biology, evolution, genetics, and eugenics. Through these guiding lights, young scientists garnered
research appointments at prominent "field stations." Bench assignments at
Massachusetts's Woods Hole Marine Biological Laboratory (MBL), the Carnegie Institution's Station for Experimental Evolution (SEE), and the Brooklyn
Institute of Arts and Science's Biological Laboratory (BIBL) (the latter two in

Cold Spring Harbor, Long Island) established close personal and professional friendships among the rarefied biological community. Moreover, this group formed the nucleus of the American eugenics movement. Indeed, the founder of American eugenics, Charles Benedict Davenport, directed the latter two laboratories. The more moderate eugenicist, Edwin Grant Conklin, directed the former. Harvey Jordan availed himself of these opportunities, spending the summers of 1905, 1906, and 1908 at Woods Hole with Conklin. Jordan spent the summer of 1907 in Cold Spring Harbor, soaking up genetic and eugenic ideas from Davenport and others. The small classes, familiar instructors, and cramped quarters fostered a professional network among investigators. Thus, Jordan left Cold Spring Harbor to become professor of anatomy at the University of Virginia well acquainted with, and well regarded by, some of the most important figures in American biology, eugenics, and medical education.[16]

Jordan began teaching in the medical school of the University of Virginia during the fall of 1907. By 1910, however, Jordan's time in Virginia had convinced him the state was in need of reform. Having just read Davenport's book *Eugenics*, Jordan gushed, "It contains just such facts as I have been searching for in preparation of a thirty minute address on 'Heredity as a factor in the improvement of social conditions' before a meeting of the State Society of Charities and Corrections." Jordan turned to eugenic reform after "noting the distressing racial conditions in our colored population in the South." Not only was Jordan interested in applying eugenics to the American race problem, he also advocated "sterilization in extreme cases of hereditary defects." In the very year the Eugenics Record Office was being founded, Harvey Jordan already possessed well-formulated ideas about eugenical policies, and was spreading the eugenics creed among the wider community.[17]

Noting his proximity to various state hospitals and insane asylums, Jordan entreated Davenport with the plea of a converted believer: "I have been wondering if I could be of service in this great work . . . perhaps in gathering statistics at close range. . . . I should be very glad for an opportunity to help, if my efforts could be of real assistance." This correspondence grew into intimate cooperation that continued for the next four years. Jordan collected skin samples for Davenport's studies on the inheritance of skin color. Jordan's association with the university hospital, and his chairmanship of the Eugenics Section of the American Association for the Study and Prevention of Infant Mortality (AAS&PIM), gave him access to plentiful medical statistics of interest to Davenport, earning him Davenport's esteem. Together, the men collaborated on research projects, exchanged lecture invitations, discussed their views on "race" and eugenics, and developed their ideas about practical eugenics.[18]

Jordan's interactions with Davenport quickened Jordan's eugenic thought, presaging his involvement in more repressive eugenical campaigns during the 1920s. In his public writing, Jordan cast himself as an "objective" scientist. He affirmed the coequality of nature and nurture in shaping the individual. "Heredity and environment go hand in hand," began Jordan's signature formulation. "As absolute essentials they are relatively equally important. . . . Attention to either heredity or environment alone under present economic and political conditions will be largely abortive of telling results." Yet, while he noted environment's power, he always reinforced the primacy of heredity because, "heredity comes first; environment, however necessary, can only follow." Ultimately, Jordan joined mainline eugenicists in believing that, "It is a popular fiction that 'men are born free and equal.' Nothing really is further from the truth. . . . As Davenport puts it, 'Men are born *bound* by their protoplasmic make-up and *unequal* in their powers and possibilities.'"[19]

In a manner reminiscent of Jefferson's equivocation, Jordan's pronouncements can be seen as adhering to the "normal science" of his day. Intuitively, Jordan knew that heredity and environment both affected individual development. He knew he must acknowledge this to sustain professional credibility. But he also knew the potency of heredity from his own casual observations. Typically progressive, Jordan looked for the most "efficient" solution to social problems. Since environmental intervention had already proved to be slow and costly, eugenic policies seemed to offer a quick, permanent, and cost-effective program for social uplift. It is no wonder, then, that his scientific conclusions proved that heredity overawed environment.

Jordan sought to use his status as an objective, moral scientist to convince educated, progressive laypeople of the necessity for eugenic intervention. He addressed the Civic Club of Charlottesville and the State Society of Charities and Corrections on numerous occasions, as well as the Child Welfare Conference held in Richmond in 1911. Davenport, recognizing Jordan as a motivated and articulate spokesman for eugenics, referred speaking engagements to him and provided him with lantern slides to illustrate his talks. Jordan delivered eugenics lectures at the 1912 International Congress of Hygiene and Demography, before the Rensselaer County, New York, Medical Society, before college audiences at Trinity College and Dickinson College, and to "lay" groups in Boston and New York. Davenport also tapped Jordan to deliver lectures under the auspices of Lucy James Wilson, a wealthy eugenics enthusiast. An ardent proselytizer, Jordan assured Davenport, "I shall be glad to give as many of these lectures for expenses, or a little better in certain cases, as my time will permit."[20]

Jordan also advised University of Virginia students to study at the ERO and SEE during the summers. He especially targeted candidates for the Phelps-Stokes Fellowship for the study of the "Negro problem." Jordan stated: "This would be a means of recruiting to the eugenics work in the South some of the best men we have. I believe that effective work as concerns the betterment of negro conditions and the relations between negros and whites must be through a biologic approach; and the various investigations necessary are far preferably done by southern men." Trained southern professionals would institute necessary eugenic interventions.[21]

Jordan convinced Davenport of Virginia's fitness as a locus for eugenical research. Virginia provided ample investigative "material" for studying eugenic and cacogenic families. The descendants of the fabled "First Families of Virginia"—the Lees, Randolphs, Jeffersons, and Lewises, for example—with their long and well-maintained genealogies, seemed perfect for studying the eugenic inheritance of intelligence, leadership, and beauty. Such studies, it was hoped, would provide the prescription for eugenic breeding within the American race. Virginia contained material for studying dysgenic families, too.[22]

The isolated Chesapeake peninsula and the mountains and hollows of the Blue Ridge and western Virginia harbored the "dysgenic" branch of Virginia's family tree, poor whites. Studying family pedigrees in these areas might, eugenicists hoped, explain the hereditary nature of deleterious social traits—pauperism, physical and mental "defect," incest and inbreeding, low intelligence, and diseases like pellagra and tuberculosis that seemed to "run in families." Eugenicists like Davenport and Jordan believed that comparisons between the "best" and "worst" stock would explain class differences as natural biological outcomes for different "strains" of the white race. Experts could then devise social policies that would reduce tensions between the rich and poor, while simultaneously increasing the birthrate among the socially adapted and reducing it among the "unfit." Sanitizing "white trash," however, did little to resolve the pressing southern concern about miscegenation and racial separation.[23]

The presence of blacks, whites, and Native Americans provided excellent conditions for studying whether or not interracial procreation was advantageous or deleterious to "the race." Clarifying the biologically determined differences between races might suggest appropriate social policies. Before deciding policy issues, however, the eugenicists had to settle questions of taxonomy: who was and was not black, white, or Native American. Jordan

and Davenport believed their first collaborative investigations, concerning
the inheritance of skin color in humans, cleared the way for the development
of definite racial categories, with their attendant qualitative hierarchy. Inequalities in society could then be explained as the natural result of biology,
not cultural prejudice. Social policy regarding the "race question" could now
be made in unequivocal conformity with natural law.[24]

Jordan proposed a family study of miscegenation as early as 1911. He
wrote Davenport about a "lost tribe of Indians" about thirty miles from Charlottesville in Amherst County. "The tribe got lost," Jordan explained, "through
intermarriage with negroes. I have thought there ought to be fine material
here for a study in human heredity." Davenport urged Jordan to "take up the
study . . . or put a student on it." Lacking time and funds, Jordan turned the
lost tribe project over to the Civics Club; that group never followed through.
Davenport, however, never forgot the lost tribe of Amherst, Virginia, and
neither did other Virginia eugenicists interested in "racial integrity." In
1923-24, Davenport dispatched ERO fieldworker Arthur Estabrook to investigate the tribe. The resulting eugenic family study, *Mongrel Virginians*,
became a cornerstone of Virginia's eugenic public policy and education. In
the meantime, normal science required that both men maintain a front of
studied diffidence regarding the relative "civic value" of the mulatto population. Davenport and Jordan both believed in the inherent intellectual inferiority of "pure blooded" blacks. Despite this conviction, however, neither man
considered racial interbreeding—miscegenation—a self-evidently dangerous
phenomenon.[25]

In "The Biological Status and Social Worth of the Mulatto," Jordan wrote:
"I admit the general inferiority of black-white offspring. . . . But I emphati-
cally deny that the result is inherent in the simple fact of cross-breeding."
This opinion presented a radical challenge to the accepted wisdom of the
time. Jordan defended his position by invoking the idea of "hybrid vigor"—
that "an unusually fortunate combination of the best racial characteristics of
both races [results] in an extraordinarily endowed human being." Yet, for all
his equanimity, Jordan's language betrayed his bias. A favorable outcome occurred only as the result of "an unusually fortunate combination"—crossing
was most often deleterious. "The reason for the frequently inferior product
of such crosses," Jordan continued, invoking the Jeffersonian notion of inborn biological prejudice, "is that the better elements of both races . . . feel an
instinctive repugnance to intermarriage. Under these usual circumstances a
white man who stoops to mating with a colored woman, or a colored woman
who will accept a white man, are already of quite inferior type." Biology itself

imbued the desire for like to mate with like, black with black, white with white, inferior with inferior. This biological conclusion reinforced southern conventional wisdom, which held that *no* white woman would *ever* accept a black man into her bed—any such congress must, therefore, be rape.[26]

Jordan believed that since the mulatto represented "an advance on the negro," mulattoes constituted "a real national advantage in our efforts to adjust the negro 'problem.'" Jordan wrote: "The mulatto is the leaven with which to lift the negro race. He serves as our best lever for negro elevation." Through eugenic crossings of mulattoes and "pure" blacks, Jordan hoped to effect the moral, mental, and physical uplift of the "naturally handicapped" black race. Jordan claimed that giving superior mulattoes access to the vote, while disfranchising inferior "pure" blacks, would resolve the "negro problem." In Jeffersonian language, Jordan argued that this strategy would heal the "canker of our present political condition" and the "moral sore of a stultified conscience" created by the dissonance between constitutional guarantees and southern disfranchisement. Jordan's eugenics, as applied to southern blacks, would lighten complexion and raise intellect and "civic value." Jordan thus resolved the ancient Jeffersonian fear of a black "nation" within a white "nation" by creating a white and mulatto nation—a polity comprised of more nearly related "races." He ignored the issue of passing—light-skinned blacks pretending to be white and "passing" into the white community.[27]

Ultimately, Davenport and Jordan felt that racial difference could be established only by empirical measurements of intelligence, a characteristic more indicative of social worth than skin color. In 1912, six years before U.S. Army psychologists used intelligence tests to study large groups of men, Jordan proposed testing black, white, and mulatto school children in Charlottesville, a project Davenport considered "of supreme importance." Yet, Davenport added, "I think it is important to get the pedigree of the mulatto, whether the first or second generation of hybrids." Only a precise determination of ancestry could fortify the racial taxonomy by revealing just how much intelligence was lifted by the presence of white genes or "blood." Jordan and Davenport's racial ideas meshed well because they believed they approached the "race problem" from a dispassionate, scientific perspective. Over time, both men would become more extreme.[28]

Like other strident eugenicists, Jordan believed America faced "race suicide" because of the failure of the best people to reproduce. He called for the eugenic education of professionals, especially physicians, and the integration of eugenics into medical therapeutics to improve the quality of the American race. As Jordan's racial convictions hardened, he underscored eugenics' applicability

to southern conditions and promoted eugenics as a quasi-religious creed. Ultimately, Jordan is recognizable as a reflection of Davenport, "a strange mixture
of scientist and advertiser." Although Jordan performed creditable scientific
research that had eugenical applications, his pronouncements about eugenics
far outstripped any evidentiary warrant provided by his studies.[29]

Jordan examined the heredity of left-handedness to bolster eugenics,
Mendelism, and perhaps as a way to predict antisocial behavior. In his first
paper on "sinistry," Jordan averred that, "there is no escaping the conclusion
that left-handedness is at least twice as frequent among colored as among
white families." Since Italian researchers had linked left-handedness to criminality, Jordan's result begged the inference that blacks, therefore, were more
often criminals. A congenial conclusion, particularly in the American South,
this explanation of black criminality could replace the discredited notion of
simple reversion. He concluded hopefully that, although "it seems a far cry
from the inheritance of coat-color [which followed Mendelian rules] to that
of such a subtle characteristic as left-handedness," the gap was "perhaps only
as wide as between [left-handedness] and such apparently still more subtle
characteristics as virtue, justice, temperance, integrity, thrift, sagacity, etc.—
characteristics of prime significance for the future trend of human history—
and if the former gap can be bridged by hereditary formulae, as seems possible, why not the latter?" Jordan remained convinced that, "once the principles
which govern the transmission of these highly desirable human qualities are
known, their 'fixation' in continually increasing numbers of individuals seems
a comparatively easy problem."[30]

Where Jefferson, Cabell, and Barringer could only speculate upon the
meaning of differential disease susceptibility, with the aid of the new genetic
technology Jordan sought to identify and "breed out" inherited susceptibility.
In the case of tuberculosis, Jordan argued that marriage among patients was
"ill advised" and that, "the eugenic bearing is obvious; and restrictive measures clearly indicated in the interests of a final control of the 'white plague.'"
On the basis of five cases, and despite the sure knowledge of the tubercle bacillus's virulence and ubiquity, Jordan decided that susceptibility to infection
was hereditary—without ever considering obvious environmental causes of
predisposition. His "final control" presaged later eugenic "final solutions."[31]

Calling on professional authority, patriotism, and fiscal responsibility, Jordan rallied physicians to the eugenic banner. "Because of the universal deference paid the physician and the consequent great influence he wields, the best
interests of the nation require that he take the initiative in genetic studies of
human pathologic conditions and in a eugenic propaganda with respect to

their eradication." Should these motives not provide sufficient inducement, Jordan highlighted the economics of tuberculosis. Denigrating the effect of sanitary reforms, he claimed that the annual loss from sickness and death due to tuberculosis was estimated to be from $200 million to $300 million, despite $15 million expended annually for environmental improvements. Only eugenic skimming of the gene pool promised a "final solution" to the tuberculosis crisis. Jordan admitted that, "the present generation of tuberculous patients should be cared for as generously and as comfortably as is possible," but they should not be allowed to procreate because, "The eradication of tuberculosis seems at base a problem of establishing a resistant race."[32]

Eugenics offered more than a solution to the "white plague." Jordan felt it could stop another of America's "racial diseases," venereal infection. In 1912, Jordan identified venereal diseases as "extremely pernicious anti-eugenic factors" that, like tuberculosis, could weaken the hereditary constitution of the "American race." Again, Jordan called on physicians to enter the lists against this scourge. Since the commonweal subsumed individual right, Jordan wrote, "no interest can be paramount to that of the race. There can be no loftier motive than that to aid in the production and universal establishment of the highest type of physical, moral and intellectual man within the limits of human protoplasm." Given this communitarian outlook, he felt that in conquering syphilis, "all questions of practicality and constitutionality must give way to *right*. Nothing can be more practical than the elimination of economic and racial inefficiency." Jordan's pragmatic search for efficiency clearly marked him as a progressive reformer. His program remained punitive, arguing for "the legal registration, isolation or detention and prohibition from marriage of certain contagious gonorrhoeal [*sic*] and syphilitic patients."[33]

The targets of Jordan's venereal prohibitions carried other eugenic stigmata. Jordan located the racial poison within a particular race, class, and gender cohort. The venereal-eugenic threat existed "especially among the 'household help' class." Clearly reflecting on his own regional experience, Jordan noted that, "among the colored population, from whom this kind of 'help' is very largely drawn, this condition is unusually prevalent." Infected black domestics, almost entirely female, posed a grave racial threat not because they might carry infection into their own homes, but because, "through carelessness on the part of such 'help' in the performance of household work, in the capacity of nurse or cook or housemaid, infections might readily occur with dire consequences to the members of the employing household." Since white southerners comprised the vast majority of employers, "the serious menace of affected 'help,'" Jordan added ominously, "must thus be apparent." The echoes of Paul Barringer's syphilis address ring out of Jordan's piece. Although the essays are separated by thirty years, the only significant difference between them is the overt invocation of eugenics.[34]

In the era before antibiotics, Jordan believed eugenics offered the only possible therapy for syphilis. Only compulsory registration of those infected, marriage restriction, and segregation would prevent future infant death from "native debility, an inaptitude for life, a lack of what might be termed 'biologic capital.'" Only the passage and enforcement of eugenic legislation could solve what Jordan viewed as "perhaps as much an economic and social as a moral problem." Typically progressive, Jordan's efforts sought to reform society, encouraging economic and social efficiency not through therapeutic intervention, but by controlling the diseased.[35]

Harvey Jordan's response to the "color line," left-handedness, tuberculosis, and venereal disease paints a portrait of a "true believer" in eugenics. Jordan portrayed eugenics as a quasi-religious, patriotic, and pragmatic solution to endemic problems threatening the American race's survival. Following Davenport, Barringer, Galton (and Cabell and Jefferson before them), Jordan sought to collapse science and religion into a new secular creed, eugenics. In fact, eugenics outstripped religion. "An intelligent understanding of the laws of heredity and reproduction would do more toward minimizing vice than much impersonal religious teaching," according to Jordan. He argued: "We want religion to appeal to strength and to health—and we want it to help in the effort to restore racial health. . . . Religion to appeal more universally must become suffused with modern biological teaching." With "criminality, pauperism, degeneracy, idiocy, insanity, and various forms of maladjustment apparently on the increase," Jordan stated that it was "incumbent upon the patriotic, and the strong and intelligent, and especially those in positions of trust, influence, and responsibility to use every means, to search every resource, to make any sacrifice, and to go to any reasonable extent to ameliorate, and if possible to eradicate, this human woe."[36]

Evoking images from his rural childhood, Jordan reaffirmed the practical possibility of the organic improvement of human beings. "There is no issue so vital to this nation today as the rearing of the human thoroughbred," he often wrote. His conviction only strengthened over time. Speaking before a large audience at the University of Virginia's YMCA in 1913, Jordan stated that eugenics "aims to produce a better race by better breeding. It does not aspire to create; it seeks merely . . . to produce a race of thoroughbreds, considered physically, mentally and morally." Even as he invoked "positive" eugenics through salutary mating, Jordan also emphasized "negative" eugenics—the eradication of deleterious genetic traits through marriage restriction, segregation of the unfit, and sterilization.[37]

Jordan termed eugenic marriage, segregation, and sterilization laws, "peculiarly public and racial health measures" that "should form part of the health code, to be administered under the State Police Powers." Eugenics and public health were, for Jordan and almost all eugenicists, identical. Jordan championed eugenic sterilization "for the protection of society against distressing economic and moral burdens and racial decay." Since not everyone, and especially not the degenerate class, was selfless enough to respond to eugenic persuasion, Jordan felt that "some external repressive methods must be instituted" against them. Sterilization was forced altruism, sacrificing the individual's right to procreate for the well-being of the American race. White Americans must overcome their "traditional feticism [*sic*] of 'personal liberty' and 'equal rights,'" and learn to defend "the race."[38]

Mounting this defense would depend on education. "Courses in heredity and applied eugenics in our medical schools and training schools for social service are urgently demanded," Jordan wrote. Progressive physicians would be "more efficient public servants if they approach their work with a eugenic outlook on life," which would allow them to determine which maladies deserved scarce curative therapies, and which deserved eugenic interventions. To make eugenic therapy available, "The future physician must also take a more active part in helping to shape legislation in the interests of race welfare," Jordan told the First International Congress of Eugenics. Transforming doctors and scientists to biological technocrats, Jordan sought to replace natural selection with eugenic public policy.[39]

More significant than his reliance on expert authority, however, was his implicit connection between public health, state power, and eugenics. Jordan called for the creation of a national public health service, as a eugenic measure, two years before Congress reorganized the Marine Hospital Service into the U.S. Public Health Service. Standard sanitation and hygiene counteracted "the working of the principle of selection. . . . Rigidly applied eugenics would accomplish the end in several generations." Ultimately, he believed, "it is more desirable to be able to prevent the production of social inferiors than to raise such elements to physical, mental, and moral par," because prevention was far cheaper than therapy. The progressive impulse was rationalizing medicine, making it "less a curative and more a preventive science." And, as Jordan argued the next year, "just as we are now guarding the *public health*, so it is our yet more clear and sacred duty to guard the *health of the race*, by every humane effective means at our command." Thus, even in public health, heredity and progressive rationalism trumped environment and traditional humanitarianism.[40]

Practical eugenics would advance in lockstep with the eugenic education of those professionals most intimately involved in the life sciences and public policy. Applied eugenics required legislation drafted and enforced by eugenically savvy lawyers and judges. When addressing Virginia undergraduates, Jordan attempted "especially to solicit the interest and aid of the coming legal profession." Echoing educational reformers like Alderman, Jordan wrote, "The public schools also can do a splendid work here in dissipating harmful ignorance and foolish sentimentality by giving well-planned courses in botany and zoölogy." Once students understood the iron dictates of biological law, eugenics would become a self-evident necessity.[41]

Jordan also appealed to women, deploying both feminist and sexist rationales. He linked the feminist demand for a single moral standard to the eugenics creed. Supposing himself a eugenic "minister," Jordan "would give every boy an opportunity to pledge himself to a life of continence until marriage, and every girl to the enforcement of the single standard of morals—not on any mystical or sentimental ground primarily, but for the very practical reason of personal gain in happiness and efficiency and of racial welfare." If fit men and women remained chaste until marriage and accepted only fit spouses, there would be no dysgenic threat from the diseased or unfit. Essentializing women to their biological capacity for motherhood, Jordan co-opted the suffrage movement: "Woman will legislate to properly protect herself as the 'mother' of the race against wanton infection. She instinctively feels more keenly the importance of conserving the greatest national asset—human life—and will bring about proper action for the preservation of the best elements of the race." For the same reasons, women would encourage eugenic laws to curtail venereal infection, and they would "originate and help enforce laws providing for surgical sterilization as a eugenic measure." Women, politically coequal with men, occupied an essential position in the battle for eugenics.[42]

Jordan's vision mixed idealism and pragmatism. The notion that practical eugenics would lead to utopia rings out of his work. "The ultimate ideal sought is a perfect society constituted of perfect individuals," he wrote. In 1912, he declared, "the idea of eugenics, based upon the science of genetics, will work the greatest social revolution the world has yet known." Jordan based this vision on the altruism and "chivalry" that eugenics drew forth from its adherents. In extolling the eugenic creed in 1913, Jordan claimed, "This new emphasis on the claims of the future and the race is awakening a world-wide more intelligent interest in eugenics and its foundations, and promises to convert society into that Utopia of which More wrote, and that Kingdom of Heaven on Earth of which Christ spoke." For Jordan, eugenics reconciled science and religion, rationalism and mysticism, physics and metaphysics into a single ideology aimed at social and racial perfection.[43]

Despite this apparent emphasis on voluntarism, Jordan always returned to the need for legal compulsion to ensure eugenic behavior. Jordan anticipated the rationale that Justice Oliver Wendell Holmes Jr. would use in declaring the constitutionality of compulsory eugenic sterilization. "Exactly as society has a right to protect itself by most rigid safeguards—little recognizing individual and personal comforts and wishes—against smallpox, cholera, and so on," Jordan argued, "so it would seem to have an equal right to protect itself by adequate methods against idiocy, syphilis, and pauperism." Intentionally evoking Jefferson, Jordan declared that, "Man does not have an inalienable right to personal or reproductive freedom, if such freedom is a menace to society." These eugenic convictions provided the bedrock on which Jordan built his worldview.[44]

As more prolific authors raised public awareness, Jordan's proselytizing diminished. With men like former president Theodore Roosevelt, Madison Grant, and Alfred E. Wiggam popularizing eugenics, Jordan localized his activities. He continued to lecture throughout Virginia, and to teach eugenics incidentally through his courses in the medical school. By 1912, however, he was no longer alone in teaching eugenics at Virginia. That year, William Henry "Harry" Heck joined the university's school of education.

Hereditarianism, Eugenics, and Educational Policy

Honoring the Progressive Era's impulse toward efficiency, scientific measurement, and rationalized professional training, Alderman and educators nationwide engaged in a search for the "one best system" of modern education. "Progressive education" evolved into two distinct theoretical schools. The "soft progressive" camp, headed by the philosopher/educator John Dewey and the psychologist John Broadus Watson, viewed cognitive potential as limited only by external circumstance: the quality of one's educational environment. The "hard progressive" wing, promoted by Henry Herbert Goddard, Lewis Terman, and Edward L. Thorndike, believed that cognitive potential was finite and fixed by inborn characteristics; environment could aid in expressing potential, but inborn capacity could not be exceeded by additional training or a more favorable environment. The new technologies of intelligence and "aptitude" testing—known as psychometrics—supported these "hard" progressive theories, generating scientific evidence purporting to document qualitative differences in intelligence.[45]

When Alderman looked to improve the University of Virginia's offerings in education, he sought instructors with two main characteristics: missionary zeal and training in the "hard science" tradition of the new psychometricians. Interested in improving southern public health through education, Harry Heck had both the most advanced "scientific" training, and direct ties to the largest philanthropic organization funding southern educational reforms.

Harry Heck perfectly fit what Alderman desired in a "conservative progressive." A "Tar Heel" like Alderman, Heck was born in 1879 in Raleigh, North Carolina. Thoroughly steeped in southern Methodist culture, Heck attended Wake Forest College, where he earned both his bachelor's and master's degrees in English, in 1897 and 1899. Heck proceeded to Columbia University, intending to pursue a doctorate in English literature. In his second year, however, he encountered educational theory at the new mecca of scientific education, Columbia's Teachers College. Swayed by the "masterful" lectures of Nicholas Murray Butler (erstwhile admirer of Paul Brandon Barringer's racial pronouncements), Heck wrote home that, "the development of the individual (it should not be narrowed to school work), is absorbingly interesting to me." Attracted by Butler, Heck found his formative influence in Edward L. Thorndike.[46]

Recognizing the southerner as a brilliant student, the Rockefeller Foundation's General Education Board (GEB) hired Heck as a field agent to survey the status of southern public education. While serving on the GEB, Heck met the most influential progressive educators, including Edwin Alderman. When the GEB appropriated the funds for a school of education at Virginia in 1905, Heck—given his initial graduate training, his experience with the GEB, and his southern heritage—was a natural candidate for the deanship. Between 1905 and 1919, Heck would become, behind Alderman, the most visible educational reformer in Virginia. He would also begin the first formal course in eugenics at the University of Virginia. Heck's hereditarian and eugenical beliefs revealed Thorndike's impress on his thinking, influencing both his teaching and the educational reforms he championed.[47]

Heck spent the first six years of his tenure at Virginia teaching during the regular and summer sessions, and traveling throughout the state spreading his gospel of progressive education. Heck argued that, "through society are we educated for society." Schools existed to "socialize" students, inculcating social norms and developing the skills necessary to contribute to social progress. Southern schools performed a quasi-religious "mission" vital to southern success. In the mythic terms of the Lost Cause, the South *would* rise again, through education. The year before he arrived at Virginia, Heck wrote: "teachers in the South are called to a mission broader than schoolbooks and class exercises, a mission of social leadership. More than any other part of our nation, the South is looking to its schools for leadership in all phases of its growing life." Heck implored Virginia educators to accept this charge.[48]

Heck's gospel had three major commandments, each directly inspired by Thorndike's work. For students to learn, Heck held, they must study in clean, hygienic schools; they must be taught specific subjects related to their probable life experiences; and their training must be adapted to their innate biological potential as determined by mental tests. Heck mirrored Harvey Ernest Jordan's rating of environment and heredity as coequal essentials, with heredity ultimately deciding the limits of individual potential. Schools should abandon the classical curriculum that was the same for all students, and increase "social efficiency" by teaching specific subjects that prepared students for life. Only then would scholastic training be relevant and effective.[49]

Heck developed this thesis in his 1909 monograph *Mental Discipline and Educational Values*, where he implied the role of heredity in the educational process. "We are . . . doomed to our efficiencies and our inefficiencies by the activities which have made out of our native tendencies whatever we are today." Education could maximize the potential of "native tendencies," but little more. Heck concluded that improvement in thinking was "due not to the subject, but to the original capacity of the individual." Heck viewed curricular specialization—tracking—as egalitarian because it offered students equal opportunity to realize their potential. Equality of education would be judged by how well each track fit its students for their station in life. In the end, Heck's program was little more than a hereditarian justification of the social status quo. Heck's ideology hardened in 1910, when he purchased Charles B. Davenport's *Eugenics*, and again when he returned to Columbia for a year in 1911, under the direction of his erstwhile eugenics mentor, Edward L. Thorndike.[50]

Heck brought more than Thorndike's positivist, hereditarian approach back to the University of Virginia in 1912. In 1910, before his sabbatical at Columbia, he had offered a new course, "Education C1: Principles of Education." Heck described the course as "a summary of present educational theory and practice. . . . Theories of organic evolution are outlined and discussed in their influence on theories of education." Upon returning from Columbia, he offered this course again, retitled to "Education C1: Evolution, Heredity, and Education." After "a detailed consideration of the principles of heredity and eugenics," the course culminated with "the discussion of certain biological and sociological questions, with special reference to education." For the first time, eugenics explicitly entered the University of Virginia's curriculum, shaping students' understanding of education. The *Eugenical News* reported Heck's teaching of eugenics in its 1916 survey of college and university courses in the field.[51]

"As a teacher," one faculty member remembered, "Professor Heck was a pioneer." His course in the biological and eugenic foundations of education "was duplicated in no other university in the United States." Heck was known for presenting both sides of an argument and challenging his students "to constructive and critical thinking for themselves." As a result, his classes did not attract masses of students; however, "those who came in contact with his teaching were always profoundly impressed by it." His students remembered him as "a striking figure in the class-room," "brilliant," with a "fearless devotion to the truth." Lacking the obscuring lens of sentimentalism, Heck "unflinchingly faced facts and the most valid conclusions that could be drawn from them. Neither tradition, nor personal comfort, nor fear of popular disapproval seemed to stand in his way in his pursuit of truth and the presentation of the truth as he saw it. He had the true instincts of a scientist." This description of Heck's dogged pursuit of scientific truth as he saw it reflects the influence of his mentor's philosophy (and the realist rhetoric that other eugenicists used about themselves). It also shows that Heck, too, engaged in normal science. Constantly claiming to be objective, neutral observers of society, Heck and other eugenicists claimed that "facts" and "truth" motivated their "unsentimental" policy nostrums—whether extolling careful mate selection or compulsory sterilization. That these programs conserved the status quo was, to these investigators, the natural outcome of science, not the function of a priori bias.[52]

Heck married public education and public health by emphasizing the role of schools in providing both a sanitary physical environment and student training in eugenic hygiene. In an eminently efficient manner, children could learn the cognitive skills required of good citizens, as well as the necessary hygienic skills to ensure that they would remain healthy "human capital"—stock for the American race.

Ironically, Heck, like millions of others worldwide, fell victim to the great influenza pandemic of 1919. The vigorous young professor died on January 4, 1919, at age thirty-nine. His principles outlived him in the state through the careers of numerous Virginia teachers and school administrators. Within the university, his course "Education C1" would be reconstructed. The year after Heck's death, the hereditarian psychologist George Ferguson offered courses on psychometrics that focused on "the value and amount of differences among individuals and groups due to such factors as race, sex, heredity, environment, maturity. Methods of adjusting school organization to individual capacities." Ferguson would continue to teach eugenic notions through his education and psychology courses, focusing particularly on the relative intelligence of whites and blacks. As a self-contained subject, evolution and eugenics would be taken up by Heck's memorialist, professor of biology Ivey Foreman Lewis, in his course "Biology B5: Evolution and Heredity," which would eventually become "Biology C1: Evolution, Heredity, and Eugenics." Lewis, one of the most outspoken eugenicists in Virginia's history, was chairman of the Miller School of Biology, and President Alderman's close advisor and confidant.[53]

Eugenics offered attractive explanations for social problems that captivated Virginia's elite educators, who then taught generations of students to think about the world along eugenic lines. Virginia's political elites used the "democratic" rhetoric of eugenically informed white supremacy to champion public policy curtailing the individual liberties of blacks, poor whites, women, mental patients, and the disabled, preserving social stability and elite power. As a result, Virginians accepted the culture of segregation as the natural ordering of the world—delineated by biological law, not just cultural prejudice. Eugenics won over professionals and students as a way of justifying their elite social position. To trace this development, one must consider how eugenics permeated Virginia's educational structure. This approach explains the momentum that the eugenics movement gained, and how that inertia would drive Virginians to institute repressive eugenic programs in the name of social uplift.

3

"DEFENDING THE THIN RED LINE"

Academics and Eugenics

"THE DAWN OF PEACE and the new year find the principles of eugenics more strongly than ever entrenched upon the field of science and ready to play their role in national reconstruction," Harry Hamilton Laughlin announced in the January 1919 issue of the *Eugenical News*. "In constructive or aristogenic eugenics," Laughlin crowed, "one after another our colleges are offering instruction in genetics and eugenics." For eugenics to become effective, it had to reach those most likely to shape public policy—college and professional students. In an era when only 40 percent of seventeen-year-olds were in school and only 1 percent of Americans held bachelor's degrees, educational status certified genetic worthiness—even as it opened doors to positions of power. College graduates would defend America's genetic heritage, "that 'thin red line' tipped with genius which is ever growing thinner, and which is all that ever stands between any nation and its doom." The urgent necessity of this mission was not lost on Virginia eugenicists.[1]

The institutionalization of eugenics in Virginia reflects both the national trend and Virginia's particular conditions. Between 1914 and 1928, the number of colleges teaching eugenics skyrocketed from 44 to 376, with an estimated enrollment of almost twenty thousand students. Virginia colleges and universities mirrored this growth. This proliferation tightened the ties between Virginia academics and nationally and internationally renowned eugenicists. Cooperating within Virginia, these individuals established a web of affiliation. Moreover, as eugenics permeated teacher training and teacher continuing education, hereditarian theories seeped into the high schools. The infusion of eugenics into Virginia's educational structure ensured the influence of hereditarian social policy for generations to come.[2]

Mr. Jefferson's Eugenical Village

Edwin Alderman was swept along by the surge of scientific racism that began around 1900 and lasted throughout the 1920s. In 1909, he hosted Stanford University chancellor David Starr Jordan as he toured the South. Discussions between David Starr Jordan and his distant cousin Harvey Ernest Jordan likely alerted Alderman to the relevance of eugenics for southern social policy. Alderman's reformist impulses led him to join a number of groups larded with eugenicists. In 1915, Alderman accepted an offer to serve on the board of the National Committee for Mental Hygiene, joining eugenics supporters Lewellys F. Barker, G. Alder Blumer, Walter Fernald, Irving Fisher, David Starr Jordan, Gifford Pinchot, and William Henry Welch. By 1930, just before his death, Alderman also had ties to the Aristogenic Association. This group of elite Americans believed that, "[white] Race survival and advance depend much on leadership. . . . The study and understanding of the biological characteristics of leaders is therefore of importance." Founders of the Aristogenic Association included Lewellys F. Barker, David Starr Jordan, Albert E. Wiggam, and the ubiquitous Charles B. Davenport and Madison Grant.[3]

Familiar with eugenics through his associations, the press, "highbrow" and "midbrow" journals like the *Literary Digest* and the *American Mercury,* and the books of Madison Grant and Lothrop Stoddard, Alderman moved closer to the mainline eugenics creed. Stoddard sent Alderman a complimentary advance copy of *Re-Forging America: The Story of Our Nationhood.* Stoddard's book argued that the Civil War, immigration, and the "negro problem" all conspired to "destroy our [Old American] ideals, our culture, our very nationhood itself." Throughout his discussion of the "parallel evolution" of the white and black races, Stoddard hammered the same term favored by Alderman in discussing race relations—"constructive adjustment." Alderman thanked Stoddard, assuring him that he had read all Stoddard's works and "found them full of stimulation, suggestion, and thoughtful interpretation of the national movement and the national spirit." In letters of recommendation, Alderman invoked the eugenic metaphor, noting that one woman's father "belongs to the best blood there is in the South and this young woman, both on her father's and mother's side comes of the best stock in this region of America." Alderman's faculty instructed him in eugenics' veracity and utility.[4]

Alderman hired the first professor in a succession that would become the "second wave" of eugenicists at Virginia in 1915. These individuals established the network that would control eugenics statewide. Examining the interactions among this "second wave" at Virginia, and between them and eugenicists elsewhere in the state and nation, reveals the close linkages connecting the Virginia and national eugenics movements. All these advocates presented heredity as the preeminent force guiding human life. Eugenics, therefore, became the most viable human intervention into social conditions.

Biology, Eugenics, and Progressive Education:
The Career of Ivey Lewis

The three strands of educational progressivism, religious liberalism, and social conservatism wound together in eugenics, creating an ideological tether that anchored Ivey Foreman Lewis to contemporary social trends within Virginia and its state university. Lewis would revamp the biology program at the University of Virginia, although his influence in the state began earlier and extended beyond Charlottesville. A North Carolinian like Alderman, Lewis's father had attended medical school at the university under Dr. Cabell. Steeped in southern culture, Lewis—like Alderman—remained wedded to the ideal of preserving the university's southern heritage. Beginning as chairman of the biology department, Lewis rose to the highest levels of the university's administration. Constantly consulted by Alderman (and his successors), Lewis became assistant dean, dean of men, and ultimately dean of the college. Merging his eugenic ideology and his liberal Protestantism, Lewis—like Jefferson, Cabell, Barringer, and Jordan—reconciled science and religion in his approach to teaching, university administration, and life. Natural law and biological law became inseparable; they were also the guideposts to moral behavior and proper social organization. His ideology ultimately made Lewis one of the university's most beloved and most reviled figures during his thirty-eight-year career.[5]

Born in 1882 and reared in Raleigh, North Carolina, Ivey Lewis was immensely proud of his southern genealogy. Lewis matured as interclass tensions rocked the southern white population. Battles over voting rights increased class animosity, fracturing the racial solidarity often presupposed by white supremacists of an earlier era. Disfranchising African Americans and

Ivey Foreman Lewis, Ph.D., Chairman, Miller School of Biology, University of Virginia, ca. 1915. (Courtesy of the Albert and Shirley Small Special Collections Library at the University of Virginia)

instituting Jim Crow segregation became the anodyne across the South. At the same time, however, systematic racism became a *national* phenomenon. America's 1898 victory in the Spanish American War merged nationalism with nativism and racism. These social currents shaped Lewis's development, predisposing him to imagine his family as an exemplary branch of the "American race."[6]

Lewis enrolled at the University of North Carolina, receiving his A.B. and M.S. degrees in biology in 1902 and 1903 respectively. Captivated by biological research, Lewis proceeded to Johns Hopkins, where he studied under the legendary zoologist William Keith Brooks and the animal physiologist William Henry Howell. Lewis completed his Ph.D. in biology, with a concentration in botany, in 1908. His star rose rapidly. After studying abroad and churning out publications, Lewis occupied the prestigious Smithsonian Table at the Stazione Zoologica in Naples, Italy, and then was elected a Fellow of the American Association for the Advancement of Science (AAAS) in 1914. Recognized as an excellent teacher and investigator, Lewis taught botany at the Marine Biological Laboratory, Woods Hole, Massachusetts, from 1910 to 1917, directing the program from 1918 until 1927, when Virginia opened a biological station. At Woods Hole, Lewis, like Harvey Jordan before him, met all the giants of biology and eugenics, including Jordan's mentors Edward Wilson and Edwin Grant Conklin. Lewis also taught at the Long Island Biological Laboratory, where he undoubtedly became acquainted with Charles B. Davenport and the eugenics movement. Lewis's training, and his growing reputation in the world of biology, perfectly fit the role of progressive modernizer that Alderman would ask him to play.[7]

In early 1914, Lewis approached Alderman regarding an opening in Virginia's biology department. Alderman became convinced of Lewis's "splendid fitness for our work." Calling Lewis "alert and progressive," Samuel C. Hatcher, the vice president of Randolph-Macon College, wrote that Lewis "made his department so interesting that our students were enthusiastic for classes under him." Lewis's southern heritage helped, too. "Lewis is a very fine man and being one of our own people [North Carolinian/southerner], I think you would like him better than anybody whom you could get who is not one of us," averred Robert E. Blackwell, the president of Randolph-Macon College. Alderman agreed, writing of Lewis in neo-eugenic terms, "He is a gentleman by birth and breeding, and a cultivated gentleman." Alderman offered and Lewis accepted a hefty starting salary, the department chairmanship, and complete control over the curriculum. With this "progressive modernization" of its biology department, the University of Virginia entered the race toward national preeminence.[8]

Both Alderman and Lewis sought to increase the university's influence on social policy. Lewis sought to ensure that *all* educated Virginians exercised their citizenship informed by a solid understanding of the biological laws determining social organization. Lecturing on the extension circuit and teaching secondary school teachers during the summer, Lewis said, "The primary aim of the Miller School of Biology in recent years has been to establish fruitful programs of research and to relate this to education in the south by wide contacts with teachers from southern colleges and schools." These well-trained experts could then materially contribute to southern social reform.[9]

Lewis adhered to the "gospel of social evolution," and believed it was up to educators to proselytize the polity. The "social organism" evolved like any other; therefore people should look to biological laws to help shape and determine custom, law, and governance. Knotty social problems could best be solved by understanding how biological laws determined their existence. The symmetry between biological and social evolution comported with Lewis's religion, reinforcing his conviction and making his eugenic beliefs more accessible to his students.[10]

To promote his new gospel, Lewis addressed groups in various churches before and after Tennessee's infamous anti-evolution Scopes Trial. With such titles as "Evolution and Religion" and "Science and Religion," Lewis's lectures helped to establish Virginia's progressive stance. For Lewis, science existed as a natural extension of God's goodwill toward humanity: science and religion were complementary, not antagonistic, modes of thought. God allowed humans to discover natural laws in order to improve conditions on earth. Hereditary determinism, a natural law created by God and discovered by science, could be controlled by man through science: eugenics. A society of eugenically "fitter" individuals would operate intelligently and efficiently, easing the strain of survival. An efficient society left time and resources for cultivating morality through religion and education, making society more humane. A eugenically improved population would be better equipped to receive moral instruction, for there would be no "moral delinquents." Humanity could then refine the "higher things in life," such as "courage, honor, a descent [*sic*] reserve, gentleness, magnanimity, pride in ideals." This theme of moral improvement following eugenic advance informed all of Lewis's teaching.[11]

A staunch hereditarian, Lewis believed genes determined individual destiny. As he told Virginia students in a 1924 speech reported by the *New York Times,* "The one clear message that biological investigation has brought as its gift to the thought of the twentieth century is that the idea of environment molding something out of nothing is sheer nonsense." Lewis continued that the notion of a "creative environment . . . the idea of the great American melting pot, into which one can put the refuse of three continents and draw out good, sound American citizens" was "simply and perilously false." The American environment, notwithstanding all its advantages, could do nothing to improve the progeny from poor genetic stock. Education and opportunity could "bring out the best in a man, but what is in him to be brought out is a matter of heredity." Acceding to this "natural law," Lewis backed both eugenic immigration restriction and interracial marriage restriction laws because "the only foundation for an enduring culture," Lewis argued, "is a sound stock of fairly homogeneous races." His insistence on the "fusion of nearly related stocks" harked back to Thomas Jefferson, allowing Lewis to construct notions of fitness that relied upon racial purity. Echoing Jefferson, Lewis noted that immigration of dissimilar people and "prolonged contact with a race which may be considered unassimilable [i.e., African Americans]" presented "two sources of danger" to the American race. Therefore, Lewis told his audience at Jefferson's academy, "it is the duty of every good citizen to support restrictive immigration legislation." Substituting a new "racial contract" for the social contract traditionally believed to be undergirding American democracy, Lewis wrote certain racial categories out of citizenship, enfranchising the imagined American race.[12]

Believing that blacks constituted the "one unsolvable American problem," Lewis claimed that "there are only two solutions: one is miscegenation and the other segregation of the members of the negro race now in this country." Lewis praised Virginia's recently passed eugenic Racial Integrity Act (RIA), which banned intermarriage between whites and anyone with any trace of black "blood," concluding with a shibboleth that has served as a white supremacist touchstone from his era to our own: "The purity of the white race in America we regard as a basal necessity for the maintenance of the heritage which we have received." Any dilution of white "blood" with that of African Americans or other races, including "inferior strains" of the white race, would destroy American civilization.[13]

Comparing Lewis's actions in the 1920s with the opinion he expressed in March 1948 demonstrates the consistency of his beliefs. Responding to a eugenics-based query regarding race relations, Lewis stated:

> There is a lot of sap-headed thinking about it [race as it relates to heredity], mostly based on the silly notion that all men are brothers and therefore alike in their potentialities. Actually, there is no biological principle better established than that of inequality of races, and yet sociologists, especially the Jewish ones, are loud and effective in their denial of any racial differences, even saying there is no such thing as race. They deride and laugh to scorn such books as Madison Grant's "Passing of the Great Race."

Lewis respected authors like Grant, Lothrop Stoddard, and Virginia's own Earnest Sevier Cox. The works of these men became texts for Lewis's course and his personal ideological guides. He displayed little tolerance for individuals or methodologies that denied what he considered self-evident scientific fact.[14]

Lewis traveled throughout Virginia addressing educators. Two main ideas characterized his speeches. First, education should "make good and useful citizens." Second, students' inherent, hereditary inequalities limited educators' ability to achieve the first goal. Regarding education's constraints, Lewis wrote that, "the greatest discovery of the twentieth century is the establishment of the laws of heredity as they relate to human beings." This knowledge dispelled old myths. "Not even the most round eyed believer in the doctrine of equality, even in the nineteenth century when the doctrine ran wild," Lewis intoned, indicting Jefferson and the abolitionists in the same breath, "could imagine that such things as skin color or eye color can be produced by training." Modern science demonstrated that "the laws of heredity hold also for mental traits and . . . human destiny is predetermined to a much greater extent than has been supposed by hereditary factors." Therefore, "the very best education can do is to cultivate and intensify the natural capacities." Lewis advocated education for its socializing aspect—it integrated individuals into society at the level determined by their heredity. His conclusions led Lewis to amend Jefferson's famous aphorism as follows:

> We must reword the bold statement to read that all men are created equal only in the sense that all have a right to equality of opportunity and equality before the law. Actually all men are created unequal in their hereditary equipment and potentialities, in their natures. Given identical training, the same food, the same home environment, the fact remains that people look different, act differently, and are different.

Thus, it seemed essential to Lewis that education target a student's innate potential, as gauged by intelligence tests. Consequently, like Heck before him, Lewis vigorously advocated educational tracking.[15]

Notwithstanding Lewis's avowed belief in eugenics, he may have preached better than he practiced. Lewis suffered from a speech impediment that made him the butt of student jokes. His sister—the fabled editor of the *Raleigh News and Observer*, Nell Battle Lewis—suffered from manic depression, a psychiatric condition eugenicists sought to eradicate. Given his sister's mental illness and his eugenic convictions, that Lewis fathered three children seems a glaring inconsistency. Lewis's eldest daughter was born with a genetic condition that left her completely hairless and without fingernails. With this obvious genetic flaw in his immediate family, Lewis would have had difficulty justifying continued procreation among his children. The University of Virginia cemetery bears mute witness to his paternal and scientific influence. Despite living long lives, all of his children are interred next to their parents, with no indication of marriage or progeny.[16]

Medical Eugenics: Physical Anthropology and Pediatrics

In 1916, the year after Ivey Lewis joined the faculty and assumed responsibility for undergraduate premedical training, the medical school hired a prominent American eugenicist. Robert Bennett Bean came to the university to assume the chair of anatomy, vacated by Jordan as faculty expansion allowed him to concentrate on histology. Bean made it his life's work to substantiate qualitative differences between the races through comparative anatomy. He began by studying crania. Then, while teaching at the University of Manila,

Bean analyzed the physique of Philippine Islanders. Upon his return to America, he focused on the comparative study of white/black anatomy, investigating the "stature" of so-called "Old Americans"—people descended from the original settlers at Jamestown and Massachusetts Bay, the progenitors of the American race. As one of the leaders of American physical anthropology, he was well acquainted with Charles Benedict Davenport and eugenics. American Eugenics Society documents list him as an "active" member during the 1920s. Although times changed and science moved on, Bean never abandoned his quest to prove the significance of racial differences.[17]

Born in 1874, Bean grew up in Botetourt County, Virginia, before beginning a globe-trotting career. Bean's family proudly traced its ancestry to the colonial era in Virginia and Maryland. Bean's mother was a descendant of Thomas Jefferson. His father served in the Army of Northern Virginia as an artillery lieutenant during the Civil War. Bean matured, his son later recalled, "under the most trying circumstances of economic distress in the backwash of the Reconstruction period," and was schooled by a disciplinarian aunt. The Bible became "a strong factor in his life," and Bean remained a devout, lifelong Christian.

Bean entered the Virginia Polytechnic Institute in 1896 at age twenty-two, graduating in 1900. He then entered the Johns Hopkins University School of Medicine, the most rigorous medical training then available in America. At Hopkins, Bean worked under Franklin Mall, the leading human anatomist in America. After graduating in 1904, Bean stayed on as instructor in Mall's laboratory. Bean then became an assistant professor of anatomy at the University of Michigan, before answering the call to direct the anatomical laboratory at the Philippines medical school in Manila. He returned to Tulane University as a professor of anatomy in 1910. Finally, in 1916, he returned to Virginia and Mr. Jefferson's university.[18]

Bean sought to carry "the study of man outward to the macrocosm of type and race rather than inward to microanatomy and the biophysics of the cell." Building on a long scholarly tradition that began with Johann Friedrich Blumenbach, reached its apogee with Paul Broca, and in America was represented by Josiah Nott and George Gliddon, Bean's conclusions about racial difference revealed less about his subjects than they did about his prejudices.[19]

In "Some Racial Peculiarities of the Negro Brain," Bean plotted measurements of brain structures within 152 black and white brains. A striking pattern emerged: the measurements segregated almost perfectly by race. Bean concluded that the structure of black brains explained the purported differences in black and white cognitive ability. He presented telling psychological portraits of the races. "The Caucasian—more particularly the Anglo-Saxon," Bean wrote, "is dominant and domineering, and possessed primarily with determination, will power, self-control, self-government, and all the attributes of the subjective self, with a high development of the ethical and aesthetic faculties." African Americans were:

> primarily affectionate, immensely emotional, then sensual and under stimulation passionate. There is love of ostentation, and capacity for melodious articulation; there is undeveloped artistic power and taste—Negroes make good artisans, handicraftsmen—and there is instability of character incident to lack of self-control, especially in connection with the sexual relation; and there is lack of orientation, or recognition of position and condition of self and environment, evidenced by a peculiar bumptiousness, so called, that is particularly noticeable.

A striking continuity of thought characterizes Jefferson's and Bean's conclusions. Jefferson believed that blacks were inferior in "reason," gifted musically, trainable to "the handicraft arts," and sexually "more ardent after their female: but love seems with them to be more an eager desire than a tender delicate mixture of sentiment and sensation." Jefferson judged blacks unable to produce "high" art. Bean, writing after decades of blackface minstrelsy had popularized notions of black creativity, held a more capacious definition of art, with a surer sense of what "blacks" were really capable of creating. Moreover, as he was writing during the year of the Atlanta race riot (which was sparked by false reports of a black man raping a white woman), it is not surprising that Bean would find the superimposed images of the "black beast rapist" and Zip Coon (the dandified black confidence man) physically inscribed in the black brain.[20]

Bean made pronouncements about gender differences as well, finding that brain structure proved superior male intelligence. So, the rank order of intelligence would be, in descending order, white men, white women, black men, black women. According to Bean, nature had embodied the laws of social hierarchy within the anatomy of the human brain. Moreover, because these differences were structural, training could not hope to alter them. Bean's conclusions provided ammunition for those who sought to limit the social, political, and educational opportunities of African Americans and women.

The very month of the Atlanta race riot, Bean published a "popular" version of his paper in *Century Magazine*. He concluded that racial differences in brain size made blacks and whites "fundamentally opposite extremes in evolution." A month after the riot, Bean published "The Training of the

Negro," writing: "The object to be attained in training the true negro is to cultivate his natural endowments and to fit him for positions that he can fill. The training should be in manual labor of various kinds, useful in the industrial development of the South, and in intellectual pursuits for the production of men of affairs among their own people," under "white male teachers of the highest moral caliber." Bean had pulled a page from Paul Barringer's earlier ideas about black education and capacity. He had also anticipated Harvey Ernest Jordan's article "Eugenical Aspects of Venereal Disease" when he wrote: "The negroes in the South prepare our food, and in this way tuberculosis, or worse contagious diseases [syphilis], may be transmitted. . . . As washerwomen, they contaminate our clothes. They are foci of infection in any community." "For our own preservation and purity," Bean argued, whites had to control black moral and intellectual education. His insistence that "history, investigations, experiments, and existing conditions indicate that the [black mental and moral] traits are hereditary and stable, and that the negro is not capable of mental development in the same way that the Caucasian is" sealed the intellectual fate of blacks in the minds of many whites.[21]

These articles convinced the editors of *American Medicine* that Bean had proved "the anatomical basis for the complete failure of negro schools to impart the higher studies—the [black] brain cannot comprehend them any more than a horse can understand the rule of three." Had politicians known "these anatomical facts when we placed a vote in possession of this brain which cannot comprehend its use," the editors commented, invoking the shibboleth of the "Crime of Reconstruction," America would have avoided lingering sectional animosities. Supporting black disfranchisement, the editors claimed that Bean's study may help "remove a menace to our prosperity—a large electorate without brains." Lashing pervasive racist sentiment, Bean's first major study gained widespread publicity and launched his career.[22]

For reasons that remain unclear, in 1909 Bean's mentor at Hopkins, Franklin Mall, attempted to verify his student's conclusions by an independent analysis of 106 white and black brains. He included in his sample 18 brains in which Bean claimed to have found distinct anatomical variations. Mall, however, made a crucial methodological change. "In order to exclude my own personal equation [bias], which is an item of considerable importance in a study like this," Mall wrote in his rebuttal article in the *American Journal of Anatomy*, "all of the tracings as well as the measurements of all the areas were made without my knowing the race or sex of any of the individuals from which the brains were taken. The brains were identified from the laboratory records just before the results were tabulated."[23]

Mall either knew his student or knew himself very well, probably both; he definitely knew his science. His results demolished those of Bean. When he plotted his measurements, his graph showed no meaningful correlations between brain structure and race or sex. This renunciation of Bean's work came too late. Published after the worst of America's turn-of-the-century race riots had occurred, after disfranchisement had stripped most blacks of the vote, and in a culture more concerned with the advent of aircraft and automobiles, Mall's study drew little attention outside professional circles. Bean had won the day for scientific racism.

Bean continued his quest to parse humanity into hard-and-fast racial categories after joining Virginia's faculty, where he befriended Harvey Jordan, Harry Heck, and Ivey Lewis. Together, Lewis and Bean founded Virginia's chapter of the scientific honor society Sigma Xi in 1923. They brought many of the university's professors of science into the fold, turning especially to Jordan and other eugenics enthusiasts. The society invited prominent eugenicists to address them at their 1924, 1927, and 1928 annual dinners (not coincidentally, during each of these years eugenics was at the forefront of Virginia politics). Thus, these men exposed most of the university's scientific faculty and many of its best students to eugenics. In his courses, Bean insisted that measurable biological differences existed between the races, claiming that his anthropometric investigations "proved" black inferiority. His innocuously titled paper "The Sitting Height" announced that, "Racial differences that remove the Negro further from the remainder of mankind than any other group of people have been demonstrated." In a later paper, Bean went further, claiming, "The negro is probably being bred out and is certainly dying at a more rapid rate than the white in America, due to climate, bad living conditions and neglect, but the physical makeup of the race in America may have more to do with this than we can at present determine." Blacks represented an evolutionary dead end, an unfit variety doomed to extinction. Bean's belief in the "important bearing" of racial differences "in relation to medicine" informed his conception of appropriate medical care.[24]

Bean argued that "human types that represent different degrees of susceptibility to disease may be segregated" and given different medical therapies. Physicians sensitive to racial differences would reach speedier diagnoses, leading to the most effective treatment. Bean lamented that, "the enormous exacerbation of interest in germ diseases following the brilliant studies of

Pasteur as to the role of bacteria in the production of disease" led to the neglect of racial medicine. Like Davenport, Jordan, and Barringer before him,
Bean believed that there existed separate, race-specific pathological reactions
and therapeutic approaches to disease. Thus, in circular fashion, differences
in morbidity revealed the existence of racial types, while racial types determined differences in morbidity. Racial medicine represented a significant di-
vergence from the biomedical notion that germs are the most democratic of
all life-forms. Pathological differences augmented physiognomic distinctions
in separating the races.[25]

At the Second International Congress of Eugenics, held at the American
Museum of Natural History in Manhattan, Bean explained the "sinuosities of
the vertebral column in the negro" and "the great muscular development of
the trunk in the negro" as "due to the attempt on the part of the negro to maintain the erect posture." The "natural" posture of blacks, Bean implied, was
some form of quadrupedia; blacks walked upright as a force of will—perhaps
in emulation of whites—not as a result of natural capacity. Bean ignored the
role of environment. Grueling agricultural labor and heavy lifting seem more
likely causes of the overdevelopment Bean observed. Hard labor is a compelling explanation given that Virginia law allowed medical schools to claim the
bodies of executed criminals, the unclaimed remains of individuals who died
while incarcerated, and the bodies of the indigent. African Americans composed a large portion of the state's unskilled and agricultural laborers, the
criminal "class," and the indigent. Thus, black bodies comprised a disproportionate amount of the "material" dissected in Bean's anatomical laboratory.[26]

During dissection, Bean transformed cultural segregation into scientific
racial taxonomy by highlighting these cadavers' supposed "racial differences"
for his students. While this practice hardened segregationist and racist thinking, it also presented a significant irony. Medical students learned anatomy by
dissecting black bodies, while their instructors underscored black difference.
One wonders how competent the students felt examining white patients, with
their anatomical knowledge derived from black bodies. Nevertheless, on this
foundation, Bean built his definition of the "true" American racial stock.

Bean collaborated with the physical anthropologist and eugenicist Aleš
Hrdlička in describing America's "pioneer" racial stock. Hrdlička, trained as a
physician, was the curator of anthropology at the Smithsonian Institution. He
founded the *American Journal of Physical Anthropology*, and in 1930 he and
Bean founded the American Association of Physical Anthropologists at the
University of Virginia. He was a delegate to the First International Congress
of Eugenics in 1912, a member of the American Eugenics Society's board of

advisors from 1923 to 1935, a member of the Eugenics Research Association, and a frequent contributor to the *Eugenical News* and the *Journal of Heredity.*

In 1917, Hrdlička suggested that Bean work on "Old Virginians"—the genetically gifted Virginians descended from the earliest settlers, a group to which Bean belonged. Hrdlička used Bean's data in his 1925 book, *Old Americans,* which purportedly traced the development of the American race from the original "Nordic" settlers of the colonial era. Not coincidentally, the profile embossed on the cover of the book is that of Thomas Jefferson. Jefferson embodied the ideal "type" of the "American race" that Hrdlička and Bean sought to define and to defend. In 1938, Bean published *The Peopling of Virginia,* an extended eugenical survey of the state's inhabitants, high and low. The imagined community of Old Virginians now had an evolutionary history establishing the biological basis for southern cultural traditions.

Two new members of the university faculty, George Oscar Ferguson and Lawrence Thomas Royster, contributed to Bean's research. Ferguson had taken courses under Harry Heck before going to Columbia to train under Heck's mentor Edward L. Thorndike. He assumed Heck's chair after Heck's death in 1919. Royster, a University of Virginia–trained pediatrician and social reformer, returned to his alma mater in 1923 to head the department of pediatrics. Royster and Bean would collaborate on a number of anthropological/eugenical studies during their tenure at the University of Virginia School of Medicine.

George Oscar Ferguson and the American Negro

Even before his arrival at Virginia, George Ferguson used the newest intelligence tests to establish the hereditary inferiority of African Americans. Convinced of psychometrics' predictive power, Ferguson used intelligence testing to guide students and workers into intellect-appropriate slots. Born in Leesburg, Virginia, and educated at the College of William and Mary, Ferguson maintained a lifelong commitment to improving the state's social conditions. His career hinged on public education and the application of scientific methods to the common schools. Although ensconced at Colgate University, in 1919 an associate wrote, "he feels too isolated [there] and would prefer an institution that was more in contact with the public life of the state." Indeed, as Ferguson later wrote Edwin Alderman, "I felt that the University was aiming at just such work of social service through scientific education," and he yearned for inclusion. Ferguson's dissertation—completed while he

worked at Columbia with the eugenicists James McKeen Cattell and Thorndike—underscored his desire to use scientific knowledge to solve Virginia's
"race question."[27]

Ferguson's magnum opus, "The Psychology of the Negro," appeared in April
1916. It drew immediate attention from the eugenics community. Written in
the even, dispassionate tones of the objective scientist, it set the pattern for all
subsequent hereditarian studies in comparative racial intelligence. Ferguson
believed intelligence testing could gauge the "fitness" of Virginia's "human
capital." Then, a rational allocation of the state's educational resources, based
on the inborn educability of blacks and whites, could increase social efficiency.
Tuning education to the innate capacities of blacks and whites would foster
social harmony by smoothly fitting individuals into the social machine.[28]

Ferguson compared black and white schoolchildren's results on four intelligence tests. By pairing groups of children with similar social and scholastic
backgrounds, Ferguson believed he had eliminated environment as a cause of
interracial difference. Moreover, he claimed to have conducted the first study
to establish the intraracial difference between "mulattos" and "pure negroes."
The results allowed him to construct a racial hierarchy of intelligence that
placed whites on top, mulattoes in the middle, and blacks on bottom. Within
the mulatto group, Ferguson concluded that intelligence varied directly with
the "amount" of white blood.[29]

Ferguson's methodology rested on a number of assumptions. According to
Ferguson, black students who persisted in school represented the "superior
strain" within the black population, "those who by reason of their . . . inheritable traits . . . are best fitted to make progress in academic work." Black
students entered high school because of inborn "ability and determination."
White students, in contrast, attended high school "by reason of social pressure, custom, or the tradition of [their] race." Absenteeism and truancy represented heredity for blacks and environment for whites. Ferguson ignored
the qualitative differences between black and white socioeconomic status and
segregated school facilities, treating black and white schools as equivalent
educational environments. This allowed him to ignore that black educational
achievement amidst harsh circumstances implied *stronger* hereditary stock
than that among white students. Instead, Ferguson argued that since his results indicated "that the correlation between skin color and racial purity is
high," it followed that "there was apparently nothing except native racial ability that could bring about the results found herein for the different classes
of negroes." Rather than evaluating intelligence, the study underscored

Ferguson's desire to establish the existence of an unbridgeable gap between blacks and whites.[30]

The presence of white blood explained the intraracial differences between "mulattos" and "pure" blacks. Ferguson emphasized the logical effects of this distinction: "it does not seem possible to raise the scholastic attainment of the negro to an equality with that of the white. . . . [N]o expenditure of time or of money would accomplish this end, since education cannot create mental power, but can only develop that which is innate." Only two options remained, since most African Americans lacked higher mental capacities: training in the manual arts or, borrowing Jordan's thesis, increasing the interbreeding between "pure" blacks and mulattoes. Further miscegenation was out of the question—it would lead, inevitably, to the racial destruction of whites.[31]

During World War I, Ferguson was chief examiner at Virginia's Camp Lee, measuring the minds of over 150,000 inductees from Virginia, West Virginia, and Pennsylvania. He wrote his mentor Harry Heck that his experience had "impressed me daily with the magnitude of the educational and psychological problems and opportunities for service in Virginia and the South." Ferguson's work convinced him that psychometrics promised to rationalize human resources allocation. Presciently, he predicted that, "there will be a much wider use of intelligence tests in schools and colleges as a result of their use in the army." In progressive fashion, Ferguson linked the academy and the marketplace in the name of efficiency. "It seems to me that an important service would be rendered by a state institution if such testing could be placed at the disposal of firms in the industrial centers as a part of the institution's extension work; in this time of industrial reorganization, such service should be especially useful." Intelligence testing would pave the way for truly scientific management: employees might be set to those tasks for which they were inherently suited. Virginia's industry would then gain a competitive edge.[32]

Edwin Alderman recognized the practical benefits of such research, especially when lobbied by other experts. John W. Ritchie, Ferguson's colleague at William and Mary, wrote that Ferguson "sees wonderful things that can be done in the public schools, industry, and the re-arrangement of some of our social programs with mental tests. . . . [Mental testing/eugenics] will effect greater social changes than anything that has come into the world in centuries, and Ferguson will doubtless have a share in it somewhere." Revealing the impact of Ferguson's conclusions, he wrote, "The whole negro race practically has proved feeble-minded by white standards, and Ferguson has a special interest in that question." Ritchie wrote: "I should like to see Ferguson kept in

Virginia. He is really scientific in his attitude of mind," making him of great use in social reform.[33]

Once at Virginia, Ferguson taught generations of students and Virginia educators that blacks were inherently intellectually inferior. In hindsight, his final comment to Alderman speaks volumes: "My shortcomings while at the University will be due to lack of knowledge and skill but not to lack of desire." Lacking the skill to see the biases inherent in his own knowledge, Ferguson taught ideas about racial difference that stemmed less from science than from prejudice. Long before the bias in Ferguson's work would be revealed, his results would be confirmed by the psychological and anthropological investigations of Dr. Lawrence Thomas Royster, Virginia's first professor of pediatrics, and a member of the American Eugenics Society.[34]

Pediatrics and Prevention

Born in Norfolk, Virginia, in 1874, Lawrence Thomas Royster rose to the heights of Virginia social philanthropy. Initially embracing the social meliorist ethos of Jane Addams, Royster adopted a hereditarian view of social pathology. By the time he became professor of pediatrics in the University of Virginia Medical School and head of the department of pediatrics in the University Hospital, Royster had abandoned environmentalist notions of reform, substituting a mainline eugenical belief in white superiority. Like many eugenicists, Royster was intensely proud of his own heritage. His membership in the Order of the First Families of Virginia made him an "Old Virginian," a living example of the "American race."[35]

A son of privilege, Royster attended Norfolk Academy and then proceeded to the University of Virginia, studying medicine under Paul Brandon Barringer. He received a healthy dose of hereditarianism before taking his degree in 1897. Royster then completed postgraduate work in the centers of American medical education: New York, Boston, and Baltimore. Royster's choice of pediatrics—then a new specialty—highlights his status as a progressive physician. Known "for years as one of the most able pediatricians of the South, not to say the country," he became chairman of the pediatrics sections of the American Medical Association and the Southern Medical Association, a Fellow of the American Academy of Pediatrics, and an elected Fellow of the American Academy for the Advancement of Science.[36]

Royster entered private practice in Norfolk in 1900. Following Barringer's emphasis on public health, Royster joined the State Board of Health. As a member of the Norfolk school board, his efforts to promote medical examination of Virginia schoolchildren brought him into contact with Harry Heck. He joined the Children's Code Commission of Virginia, founded and presided over the Norfolk Society for the Prevention of Cruelty to Children, and founded the Norfolk Association of Philanthropics' Bonney [Bon Air] Home for Girls.[37]

Using biology and scare tactics, Royster sought to prevent the adulteration of the American race. Royster wrote, "Above all, the mother must be told how to inform the child . . . about matters pertaining to sex, on a correct understanding of which and on the proper care along these lines depends the protection of the race." He also favored eugenically justified social control. Writing in the *Richmond Guardian* in 1907, Royster claimed that there were in rural Virginia "at least 300 wayward girls. Hundreds of others, inhabiting the slums of our cities, are growing up to lead vicious lives." Relying on Richard Dugdale's famous family study, *The Jukes*, Royster played on Virginians' fears of increased economic distress. He wrote that in seventy-five years the criminal and impoverished descendants of Ada Juke "cost the State of New York $1,225,000.00. Measure, if you can, the damage done to Virginia in the next generation from the host of girls now drifting to destruction." Only expeditious action to restrain and segregate "vicious girls" could protect society. The gender bias of Royster's social reforms is inescapable, as is his notion of eugenic segregation.[38]

Even when advocating environmental reforms like the pure food and milk campaign, Royster remained committed to hereditary determinism. "To be sure we are born with a definite biological pattern and that cannot be altered," Royster averred, continuing, "unfortunately in dealing with human beings we cannot force mating in accordance with a knowledge of their desirable attributes as we can with animals." Therefore "we must direct our efforts toward the making of the best possible adult out of the material presented to us at birth and I think we should regard the feeding of children as a public health measure." Royster self-consciously connected public health and eugenics: both aimed at "making the best possible adult out of the material presented to us," although eugenics sought to ensure that the "human ore" was of the purest variety.[39]

Royster continued this hereditarian theme when discussing physicians' responsibilities to poor whites. He complained that, "the influence of the University of Virginia Medical Department is felt wherever medicine is known," yet, "her light has not penetrated the darkness of the mountain cabin." Many mountain whites, Royster believed, suffered more from bad environment than heredity. Their "true genealogy" contained "the finest Anglo-Saxon blood."

The eugenic promise of some mountain whites was submerged beneath their stultifying surroundings. Isolated in "hills and hollers," their genetic genius went unnoticed for lack of an environment suitable for its expression. Worse, poor whites risked destroying that genetic potential through inbreeding, miscegenation, and other genetically ill-advised procreation.[40]

Royster's millennial tone peaked in 1930. In an oft-delivered address, "Religio Medici Recentis," Royster likened physicians to priests, medicine to religion, health to grace, and disease to sin. Royster, like many of his colleagues, collapsed science and religion into a single entity in the service of mankind: "Medicine is an outgrowth of religion. . . . Religion is a way of living; medicine is the application of scientific knowledge through the practice of an art. The practice of medicine is not a religion in itself, but there is a religion in the practice of medicine." Physicians thus occupied a special place in the physical and metaphysical lives of humanity. The physician's "sacred" responsibility was to evangelize the "religion of health," convincing patients of their eugenic responsibility to posterity—to produce "soundness of body and mind in those who are to bear the burdens of the future; those on whom will rest the responsibilities of government, education, business and parenthood, when we have ceased to labor. This is . . . in large measure a religion."[41]

Royster's eugenic goals became his secular creed because, "a belief in science and the utilization of scientific knowledge becomes a religious duty rather than an evidence of infidelity." Echoing Jefferson, Cabell, Barringer, Jordan, and Lewis, Royster announced that knowledge of man would come from "a close scanning or critical scrutiny of God himself through an investigation of His laws, i.e., the laws of Nature." Science, the study of natural law, was in fact religion—providing a greater understanding of divine purpose and governance.[42]

To spread his version of the gospel of social evolution, Royster collaborated with both Harry Heck and Robert Bean to link pediatrics, school inspection, eugenics, and social reform. Pediatrics, according to Royster "is in truth the greatest preventive medicine in the world." By attending to children, physicians could apply the laws of heredity and hygiene early and prevent the creation of social misfits. If physicians paid more attention to preventing congenital and "hereditary" transmission of tuberculosis, blindness, venereal disease, and feeblemindedness, society would improve. With a comprehensive eugenic program, "all feeblemindedness can be wiped out in one or at most two generations. Think what a difference this would be since from feeblemindedness results the bulk of dependency and criminality." Legislation should seek to "prevent marriage among the manifestly unfit, both physical and mental." Marriage restriction and sterilization would help purify the imagined American race. Concrete social policy would substantiate the existence of this imagined community.[43]

Royster's entire eugenic program devolved to schoolchildren. Since "legislation is so dependent on the education of the people as to the importance of health and virility in a nation that, in reality," Royster argued, "through education alone may be seen the ultimate solution of the problem [of social degeneration]." Royster wrote, "Our best opportunity lies manifestly in the school room, here we can implant the principle of eugenics when the mind is pliant and receptive, during the formative years of life, and so implant these principles that they will become just as inherent as honesty, patriotism, veneration and other desirable characteristics." Biology needed to be taught "as a fundamental just as the three R's are," to bring eugenics home to the schoolchild, "for only through biology can be taught the laws of nature by which the race is propagated, the conception of cells and cell plasma and that they are of two kinds—the good and the bad." Only education could impress children "with the moral wrong done in bringing unfit offspring into the world." Schools could create eugenic automatons, whose first principle would be fit procreation. "The public school system should be the pioneer in such a movement," Royster concluded, "and thus serve the cause of eugenics as it can be served in no other way." For Progressive Era physicians like Royster, eugenics offered the holy grail of efficiency, humanity, and permanence in reforming society.[44]

Orland Emile White: Reluctant Eugenicist?

The final player in the University of Virginia's band of eugenicists joined the faculty in 1927. By then, Ivey Lewis realized that Virginia's biology department required a trained geneticist if it was to remain competitive with other top-flight institutions. Lewis regarded himself as capable of teaching the genetics necessary for introductory biology and his eugenics course. He envisioned, however, upgrading the graduate program to produce students trained in this new science. A bequest from an alumnus provided Lewis with the opportunity to organize Virginia's second biological station, the Blandy Experimental Farm, around genetics. He hoped to create a successor to Harvard's fabled Bussey Institution, directed by the eugenicists Walter E. Castle and Edward M. East—who had studied under Charles B. Davenport and taught the second generation of American geneticists.[45]

Lewis succeeded in securing one of America's best plant geneticists to direct this new experimental station. A student of Edward M. East, Orland Emile White rose from obscurity to the heights of academic genetics. Out of a tiny backwater farm, housed in renovated slave quarters, White carved an institution that advanced American agricultural genetics like few others. Overshadowed by developments in animal genetics from the labs of Herman Muller and Thomas Hunt Morgan, the contributions of the Blandy Experimental Farm have been lost in the mists of memory. The links between White, the organized eugenics movement, and the Blandy Farm have been overlooked along with the institution's more laudable achievements. Nevertheless, they represent a significant chapter in Virginia's eugenic history.

White, like many first-generation American geneticists, grew up in the American heartland. Born in Sibley, Iowa, in 1885, he was reared in the Black Hills of South Dakota. Nature captivated the young White. He called Thoreau's *Walden* his "youthful Bible"; his hero was the American naturalist John Burroughs, to whom he wrote a fan letter. Burroughs's response, advising White to "keep your eyes & ears open, read the best books, practice writing whenever you have something you want to say" became one of White's most cherished possessions. Taking the great man's advice to heart, White worked his way through South Dakota State College (SDSC), earning a bachelor of science degree in 1909. Edgar William Olive, White's mentor at SDSC, had trained at the Bussey Institution and introduced White to eugenics. Olive put White in touch with East and Castle at Harvard; they brought White to Cambridge in the summer of 1910. White returned to SDSC for 1910–11, earning a master's degree in botany. His work so impressed East and Castle that they arranged scholarships for him at Harvard.[46]

White entered the Bussey in the fall of 1911 as East's first graduate student. White investigated two plants: tobacco, following the suggestion of East; and, like Gregor Mendel, peas. White also took courses in genetic psychology under Robert M. Yerkes, responding to the eugenic temper of the times. White earned his master's degree in 1912. In the spring of 1913, he earned his doctorate. In his two years at Harvard, White met many of the nation's foremost geneticists and eugenicists. His own student cohort included many men who would achieve distinction in genetics, including Albert Blakeslee, Robert Cook, and Clarence C. "Pete" Little. White also befriended Charles H. Danforth of the Washington University School of Medicine, another prominent eugenicist.[47]

Upon graduation in 1913, White became assistant curator of plant breeding at the Brooklyn Botanic Garden in New York. White's position introduced him to many of New York City's most influential people. White also established contact with Charles Benedict Davenport and the Eugenics Record Office. Always a freethinker, however, White became involved with Margaret Sanger and the birth control movement—a move Davenport would have disapproved, despite Sanger's support for eugenics. When Sanger began publishing the *Birth Control Review,* White contributed reviews of books dealing with heredity and eugenics. White maintained staunch feminist views throughout his career. After joining the University of Virginia, he took on female graduate students, many of whom earned their doctorates and achieved solid academic careers.[48]

Eugenics, for White, revolved around "better parenthood," as he made clear in a laudatory review of Major Leonard Darwin's *Eugenic Reform*. He agreed with all of Darwin's main themes, particularly the prohibition of parenthood among the "definitely deficient" as a eugenic measure. White also concurred with Darwin that, "conception control, on account of its wide possibilities, is likely to be the most powerful agency which exists for racial improvement or racial deterioration as the case may be."[49]

Although White worked alongside Davenport in the Society for Experimental Biology and Medicine, a group dedicated to the medical application of Mendelian genetics and racial anthropology, he cleaved to East's eugenic beliefs. During the 1920s, East reacted against the extreme eugenics popularized by Madison Grant and Lothrop Stoddard, popularizing "responsible" eugenics in books like *Inbreeding and Outbreeding, Mankind at the Crossroads,* and *Heredity and Human Affairs.* Rather than Stoddard's "rising tide of color," East adhered to Thomas Malthus's population thesis, predicting a rising tide of mediocrity and mouths to feed. To reduce the threat of overpopulation, East promoted birth control.[50]

Nevertheless, East was no racial equalitarian because, "the negro race as a whole is possessed of undesirable transmissible qualities both physical and mental, which seem to justify not only a line but a wide gulf to be fixed permanently between it and the white race." Medically, East argued that "there is a real inferiority in resistance to certain diseases" among blacks. East approvingly discussed George O. Ferguson's study of black intelligence, concurring that "mixed blood" African Americans tended to be socially disruptive. Thus, the only surge in the "tide of color" that worried East was the ripple in the American South. East wrote that, "the southland outpost is the post of danger." In East's view, White and scientists like him were the nation's eugenic sentinels.[51]

White's own eugenics publications echoed East. In reviewing *Inbreeding and Outbreeding* by East and Donald F. Jones, White wrote that "inherent capacity, inherited potentialities are the foundation stones" of greatness. "You can only with difficulty keep a 'good' man down, but alas for those poorly equipped with a 'fit' equipment of hereditary characters—for these, the social worker and the charity organization are often the perennial prop." Of miscegenation, White wrote, "Racial mixing of yellow and white, of black and white is in general to be deplored, from the standpoint of the 'whites.'" In reviewing East's *Mankind at the Crossroads*, White applauded East's warning about the dysgenic threat of "mulattoes" passing into the white population through intermarriage.[52]

Eugenical sterilization also seemed a sound policy to White. The *Birth Control Review* dedicated the March 1928 issue to sterilization, one year after the Supreme Court upheld Virginia's sterilization law. By this time, Margaret Sanger had added the subtitle "Fewer but Fitter Children" to the *Review's* masthead. White contributed to a symposium on sterilization, citing his own personal contacts and the Eugenics Record Office's Harry Hamilton Laughlin as his sources. White declared that, "for feeble-minded and insane, whether at large or in institutions liable to turn them out into the population again, I believe in compulsory sterilization." Sterilization was also warranted for "*chronic criminals.*" White closed with a call to action: "But no such laws should be put on the statute books of any state unless they are ready to use them." Eugenics was meant to be an applied science.[53]

White supported the American eugenics movement through his teaching, professional and personal friendships, and monetary donations. In October of 1941, White ordered a hundred pamphlets on eugenic sterilization, and another hundred on California's eugenic sterilization program, from the Human Betterment Foundation. He intended to distribute the pamphlets to his medical genetics class. The remaining syllabus for his extension division course, "Heredity, Variation and Environment in Plants and Animals Including Man," includes eugenic texts like Popenoe and Johnson's *Applied Eugenics*, East's *Heredity and Human Affairs*, and Herbert Spencer Jennings's *The Biological Basis of Human Nature*.[54] He also contributed money to the Second and Third International Congresses of Eugenics in 1921 and 1932, evincing his persistent commitment to racial improvement and his colleagues—Robert Bean presented a paper at the 1932 conference. At Virginia, White became fast friends with Harvey Jordan and Robert Bean, as well as the other eugenicists on the faculty.

Virginia's Other White Colleges

If the University of Virginia represented the epicenter of eugenic teaching in the state, the shock waves emanating from Charlottesville registered at virtually every other institution of higher education. At the College of William and Mary, the professional training of the biologist Donald W. Davis at Harvard, Berkeley, London, and Woods Hole convinced him that hereditarian science offered the remedy for society's ills. In 1920, Davis offered "a six weeks course in eugenics . . . for the summer session—meeting five hours per week." In the summer of 1921, Davis offered "Genetics and Eugenics" to Virginia schoolteachers. By 1934, the biology department was offering a course, "particularly intended for those not concentrating in Biology . . . [covering] human races . . . human heredity and capacities for training; eugenics." Davis corresponded with the Human Betterment Foundation of California—a mainline eugenics organization—as late as 1938. His eugenics course remained in the curriculum until 1946, the year after the world learned of Nazi eugenic atrocities.[55]

Professor Davis immersed himself in Virginia's applied eugenics program. In September 1920, Governor Westmoreland Davis appointed Davis to the "Governor's Advisory Board on Criminal Mental Hygiene," which performed a eugenic survey of the state's prison inmates. Davis served alongside the Medical College of Virginia's Beverly R. Tucker and two of the state's eugenic pioneers—the mental hospital superintendents Dr. William Drewry and Dr. Joseph DeJarnette. The committee followed Davis's recommendation and used the ERO's "Individual Analysis Card" as their survey instrument. A friend of Henry Herbert Goddard, the man who coined "moron" to describe the "highest grade" of feeblemindedness, Davis lobbied for legislation facilitating the commitment of feebleminded individuals, and a law banning marriage between the feebleminded.[56]

Davis outlined his eugenic creed in an address with the unlikely title "Genetics and Orthodontia." "We have only to notice the circumstances surrounding our herds of scrub cattle, our flocks of mongrel fowls, to realize how much is accomplished by even a little care in the selection of breeding individuals," Davis began, invoking the eugenic metaphor. "Can anyone doubt what would be the effect of selecting for breeding purposes the weakest. . . . Can there be any doubt that the result would be strains of weak, disease susceptible, deformed incapables?" Humanity, too, needed eugenics.[57]

Davis's views on interracial crossing mirrored those of Harvey Jordan. While some crosses might create desirable combinations, the majority were "from the social if not from the biological point of view highly undesirable." Potential biological disharmonies warranted marriage and immigration restriction—particularly with regard to the feebleminded. America faced race suicide because "the lower grades, mentally as well as physically, are increasing at a greater rate than the higher." Instructors in Virginia's other colleges agreed with Davis that eugenics must be brought home to intelligent people to reverse this trend.[58]

Hereditarianism infused the curriculum of Virginia Polytechnic Institute, an institution dedicated to the improvement of crops and domestic animals. Professor Harvey Lee Price offered eugenics through his genetics course, required for all biology majors, until he retired in 1950. Beginning in 1926, "Physical Education 221: Human Biology" covered "heredity and eugenics, as well as social hygiene." The pairing of eugenics and "social hygiene"—that is, sex education with particular reference to venereal disease—reflects the close association academics made between the two subjects. In 1947–48, the biology department began offering "Advanced Genetics and Eugenics." References to eugenics disappeared in 1950, the year of Price's retirement. Curricular changes depended on faculty turnover.[59]

It took changes in faculty to expunge eugenics from Harrisonburg State— now known as James Madison University. George W. Chappelear began teaching genetics and eugenics to students at Harrisonburg-Madison in 1919. Chappelear, a descendant of pioneering Old Virginian/Old American stock, dedicated a quarter of his course in advanced biology to heredity and eugenics in 1929; the entire course focused on heredity and eugenics in 1934–35. During the summers between 1935 and 1939, he taught eugenics to Virginia high school teachers through the University of Virginia's summer school. Chappelear asked Charles Benedict Davenport's advice in selecting a good eugenics text for undergraduates. Chappelear died in 1944, and his successor, Dr. Ruth K. Phillips, dropped eugenics from the course description in 1945. The skeptical Dr. Phillips moved the curriculum away from eugenics, attempting to "assist students in distinguishing between biological theories and laws." One memorialist recalled, "As one of the College's first female Ph.D.s, she helped awaken the community to a realization of the strides in learning accomplished by her sex." Perhaps she felt that "fit" women's lives could encompass more than being the nation's womb.[60]

Randolph-Macon College began its association with eugenics in 1925 with the hiring of Dr. Walter Edward Bullington. During the summers of 1921 through 1924, Bullington worked at the Long Island Marine Biological Laboratory (LIBL) in Cold Spring Harbor, Long Island. There, Charles Davenport introduced Bullington to eugenics. In his first year at Randolph-Macon, Bullington taught "Biology III: Evolution and Genetics." Three years later, the course description changed to "Evolution the first term and Eugenics the second and third terms." The year 1929 saw another change to "Evolution, Genetics, and Eugenics." The class encompassed "a study of the possibility of the application of [genetic] principles to man" until 1975.[61]

The University of Richmond's eugenics course was as durable as Bullington's. Beginning a genetics course in 1927—the year Justice Oliver Wendell Holmes declared Virginia's eugenic sterilization statute constitutional—the course blossomed into "Genetics and Eugenics," which addressed "the origin of new races; the influence of heredity and environment; applications to animal breeding and human society." Taught by two Harvard-educated Mississippians, "Genetics and Eugenics" most likely reflected the beliefs of the instructors' mentors, the Harvard geneticists Edward M. East and William E. Castle. East's eugenic and racial views comported well with these men's regional background. Eugenics remained in Richmond's curriculum until 1970. By that time, the biology faculty had expanded, including many younger members who might well have questioned the racial precepts of mainline eugenics.[62]

Responding to the ERO's 1920 survey, Washington and Lee's Professor William Dana Hoyt noted that he covered eugenics in "Theories of Biology," where students read a slew of mainline eugenic tracts. Hoyt took his doctorate at Johns Hopkins in 1910, two years after Ivey Lewis. Hoyt also studied at the University of Heidelberg, with a subsequent stint in Naples at the Stazione Zoologica. From 1912 to 1915, he worked at Hopkins before joining Washington and Lee's faculty. A botanist who studied algae, Hoyt nevertheless joined numerous eugenics organizations. He was an instructor in botany at Woods Hole, an elected Fellow of the American Association for the Advancement of Science, and a member of the American Genetic Association and the American Eugenics Society (AES).[63]

Hoyt's response to the ERO's 1921 survey on hereditary blindness reveals his eugenic views. "While strongly endorsing the principle" of preventing hereditary blindness, Hoyt remained unsure that marriage restriction "is the proper means of accomplishing the desired end." Instead, Hoyt advocated "allowing marriage and . . . teaching the dangers to which the off-spring would be subject with methods for preventing off-spring." Economic concerns underpinned Hoyt's eugenic advocacy. He concluded, "Many of the [hereditarily blind] men, if not allowed to marry, would certainly gratify their passion in illegal ways and would tend to leave off-spring more likely to become the charge of the State than those born in wedlock." Eugenic laws without eugenic knowledge meant nothing.[64]

Hoyt joined the AES in 1925. In 1927, he volunteered as a eugenics propagandist, delivering lectures with titles like "Heredity and Environment: Nature or Nurture?" or "Is There Danger of Race Deterioration?" or "Eugenics: Some Present Conditions and Suggestions." Hoyt died in September 1945. Eugenics disappeared from the course guide for seven years, reappearing in the description of Professor Edmund Berkeley's course in genetics. The term remained in the catalog until 1965.[65]

Eugenics at Virginia's Women's Colleges

Virginia's two most prominent women's colleges, Hollins and Sweet Briar, gave substantial courses in eugenics, as did the female coordinates of Randolph-Macon College and the University of Richmond. More than "finishing schools," women's colleges used eugenics as preprofessional training for women interested in school teaching, social work, and science. More important, from the eugenicists' point of view, these schools socialized the most genetically "fit" women to accept their responsibility as mothers of the future.[66]

Eugenicists recast traditional notions of "republican motherhood" along hereditarian lines. Since women contributed genes as well as wombs to the procreative equation, eugenicists argued that having many children was the patriotic duty of the "best" women. Unfortunately, intelligence, a desire for higher education, and activity outside the home—traits that characterized the "most fit" women—delayed childbearing, decreased the number of children born to fit women, and exacerbated "race suicide." Thus eugenicists faced the conundrum of encouraging fit women to sacrifice other aspirations and accept their "destiny" as the nation's gestational repository. Training as eugenics fieldworkers, ferreting out information for eugenic family studies, might satisfy women's desire for higher education and "meaningful" work, while impressing them with their eugenic responsibility. Eugenicists thus merged reform work characteristic of settlement houses with the desire to influence private procreative decisions. Trained as fieldworkers, women attained ancillary status—nurse, research assistant, and social worker—in the emerging gendered division of labor within science and social reform.[67]

The eugenicists' focus on rational procreation offered an entering wedge for female birth control advocates like Margaret Sanger.[68] Contraception, still a taboo subject in America, gained legitimacy when coupled with eugenics, an endeavor supported by many male authorities. While Charles Davenport and some other eugenicists believed that birth control would only exacerbate "race suicide," others, like Leon F. Whitney, Edward East, Orland White, and Sanger advocated contraception as an effective negative eugenic measure if spread among the unfit.

Both Hollins and Sweet Briar offered courses in eugenics. In 1919, Hollins offered "Organic Evolution," using a text by the eugenicists David Starr Jordan and Vernon Kellogg. That same year, Norman MacDowell Grier, who trained at Cold Spring Harbor under Davenport, offered "Eugenics." The course investigated "the eugenic aspect of various reform movements such as prohibition, feminism, socialism, immigration, vocational guidance, etc." Hollins's psychology and sociology departments introduced eugenics as an explanation and solution for problems caused by "social inadequates." These courses included field trips "to visit institutions in the vicinity which minister to these classes, in order that first hand observation may be made, and in order that wiser conclusions may be drawn." Beginning in 1924, as Virginia passed its eugenic laws and the federal government passed the eugenically influenced Immigration Restriction Act, Hollins offered "Races and Immigrants," a "study of the Indian and the Negro and selected immigrant groups in relation to contemporary America," offering cutting-edge theories relevant to pressing social concerns.[69]

Sweet Briar College, founded to advance "the education of white girls and young women," began offering "Variation and Heredity" in 1903. For the next six years, Donald Walton Davis, later the leading eugenicist at William and Mary, taught "the known facts with regard to evolution of species and analyses of the factors involved in the process of evolution." By the 1920s, Sweet Briar offered eugenics in "General Biology," as well as "Genetics and Eugenics," a course dedicated to "a study of the laws of inheritance, phylogenetic development and evolution with biological problems which especially concern man."[70]

Eugenics at Sweet Briar exploded in 1920 when Ivan E. McDougle joined the faculty. McDougle had trained at Clark University under the eugenicist and pioneering sociologist Edward A. Ross. In his first course, "Economics 3: Social Problems," McDougle presented "Poverty, its causes and cures; population problems, eugenics, socialism, syndicalism; the woman problem; marriage and divorce; the negro in the United States." As texts, he used Popenoe and Johnson's *Applied Eugenics* and Davenport's *Heredity in Relation to Eugenics*, creating a class that "has proved to be one of the most popular courses among the college." Elated, ERO Superintendent Harry Laughlin drew McDougle's comment to Charles Davenport's attention.[71]

Handsome and charismatic, McDougle captivated his students with his eugenic vision. By 1922–23, he was offering "Sociology 2: Dependency and Delinquency," "a study of the socially inadequate." This course included field-work; students visited nearby unfortunates to compile eugenic pedigrees. That same year, Sweet Briar students organized a "Better Babies Contest." McDougle's infant daughter Louise won the blue ribbon. The student maga-zine quipped, "Personally, we are all for such improving and eugenic contests and we trust that in future years much may be accomplished by this campaign for Better Babies!" Although McDougle left Sweet Briar in 1925, eugenics ap-peared in course descriptions until 1943, when the "reform eugenics" rhetoric of "bio-sociology" and "psycho-sociology" replaced eugenics. The latter field persisted as an interdisciplinary major until 1963.[72]

Women from both Hollins and Sweet Briar trained as eugenics fieldwork-ers under Davenport and Laughlin. Professor McDougle deployed his ERO-trained students in his own investigations. Ultimately, the relationship be-tween the ERO and Sweet Briar brought to fruition Harvey Jordan's quest to study the "lost tribe" of Virginia Indians in Amherst County.[73]

Genetics or Eugenics? Black Institutions Confront Segregation's Science

Virginia's African American students who desired higher education had four local choices: the Hampton Institute, Howard University, Virginia Union University, and Virginia State University. Historically black colleges faced difficult decisions regarding the hereditarian doctrines emerging during the Progressive Era. Whether and how these ideas would be taught strained each school; how each institution resolved these tensions reveals much about the nature of "uplift" and the construction of black identity during the early twen-tieth century.[74]

Howard University housed the nation's most famous African American biologist, Dr. Ernest E. Just. Beset by financial difficulties, Just's painstaking efforts to build a comprehensive biology department took many years to bear fruit. By 1912, however, Howard officials were able to report that eugenics was offered in the "Sex Hygiene," "Biology and Education," and "Social Biol-ogy" courses.[75]

The ERO's 1920 questionnaire, however, indicates Howard's continuing difficulties. President J. Stanley Durkee (a white administrator) apologized that, because of financial limitations "there has, as yet, been no department organized in Eugenics." Nevertheless, Durkee added hopefully, "one of our

Thomas Wyatt Turner, Ph.D., advanced "assimilationist" eugenics. (Courtesy of the Moorland-Springarn Research Center, Howard University)

former students is specializing in that subject and I hope will return here in a couple of years prepared to put in a department of Eugenics." The dean of Howard's medical school noted that E. E. Just was the faculty member most interested in eugenics, but commented that the medical school had no plans for work in eugenics because its curriculum was "too crowded and funds too limited." Despite these reports, Thomas W. Turner had been teaching eugenics at Howard since at least 1912.[76]

Thomas Wyatt Turner was born in 1877, the son of former slaves in Charles County, Maryland. Turner's devout Roman Catholic parents ensured his confirmation in the "Mother Church." Turner seemed an unlikely eugenicist. His Catholic faith put him at odds with the mainline positions regarding procreation and sterilization. His racial heritage seemed to debar him from the eugenics movement. Nevertheless, Turner developed a well-articulated eugenic sensibility that harmonized his race, religion, and reformist tendencies. He created a scientific ideology for black racial uplift—a black analog to the white American race.[77]

Turner's hardscrabble beginnings prepared him for a life of fighting racial injustice with scientific knowledge. After years of country schooling and two years as a scholarship student at an Episcopalian school in southern Maryland, the eighteen-year-old Turner walked fifty miles to Washington, D.C., to attend Howard University Preparatory School. Graduating in 1897, Turner then took a bachelor's degree at Howard in 1901. He began graduate studies at Catholic University that year, but left when Booker T. Washington called him to teach biology at the Tuskegee Institute. For a decade, from 1902 to 1912, Turner taught biology and sought to advance his own graduate training. It was during this period that he encountered eugenics.

Turner met Charles Davenport and learned incipient genetics and eugenics at the Long Island Biological Laboratory (LIBL) in the summer of 1904. A single photograph survives documenting Turner's summer in Cold Spring Harbor. In the photograph, the white male and female investigators are mixed together on the verandah of the laboratory's main building. Davenport is photographed with his daughter on his lap. Tightly bunched, this portrait evokes the intimacy of a family reunion—except for one striking exception. Toward the right-rear of the photograph, Turner stares solemnly at the camera, alone in a crowd. There is a space of slightly more than a body's width separating him from those in front and to the side of him. Nobody stands to his rear. While all the other fifty-one faces seem comfortable and relaxed, Turner's face is taut and anxious.[78]

On his one hundredth birthday, seventy-three years after that photograph was taken, Thomas Turner remarked: "I was one of the first black people to do a lot of things, I didn't get up and start cussing people out. But I said things." During the summer of 1904, he apparently did or said something to earn the lasting displeasure of Charles Davenport. Nine years later, when Harvey Ernest Jordan suggested that Davenport admit a "mulatto to the course next summer," Davenport replied that the last "colored" man, "a professor from a colored college," had displayed "a scandalously erotic nature. The example he set for the young people here was frightful." While it is unlikely that Turner could have avoided Davenport's racism, the fact that Turner was intelligent, outspoken, and a devout Catholic increased the chances that Davenport would dislike him intensely. Nevertheless, the work in genetics and eugenics captivated Turner, and he continued his dogged pursuit of an advanced degree, eventually taking his doctorate from Cornell in 1921.[79]

Turner returned to Howard in 1912 as dean of the school of education. He began teaching applied biology in 1914. Notes and examinations from his courses "Sex Hygiene" and "Biology and Education" reveal his belief in Mendelian genetics and eugenics. He assigned articles by the British "sexologist" and eugenicist Havelock Ellis, drawing on Ellis's work for his lectures. He also assigned Davenport's work, and Popenoe and Johnson's *Applied Eugenics.* His second examination in "Biology and Education" instructed students: "Describe three types of feebleminded persons. Explain applications of Mendel's law to the problem of Feeblemindedness and its control," and "Explain the application of Mendelism to Eugenics." Examining his sex hygiene students in 1915, Turner asked them to "define Eugenics. Explain how society may be helped by applying eugenic laws." Similar questions appeared on his sex hygiene final examination in 1920.[80]

Turner taught mainline beliefs regarding feeblemindedness in a way that undercut the racist notions of "reversion to type" and "atavism" that purportedly afflicted African Americans. "Defectiveness is not a reversion but direct inheritance," Turner wrote, agreeing with the eugenic convention that the feebleminded person was "incapable of competing on equal terms with his normal fellows, etc." While many white eugenicists argued that this inability to compete characterized all black/white relationships, implying inherent black defectiveness, Turner contended that the feebleminded and "fit" classes of each race were perfectly analogous. Qualitative differences existed between individuals, not races.[81]

Turner's publications underscore his belief in the "gospel of social evolution." In "The Biological Laboratory and Human Welfare," Turner outlined biology's role in progressive reform. He measured the biologist's success by asking: "To what extent has he contributed to making men better, to giving greater respect for their fellows, to making them more useful in improving the condition of mankind?" Biology prevailed only if it advanced all these reformist goals.[82]

Turner's ideology remained rooted in a hereditarian conception of life, rather than the environmentalism of earlier black reform. Turner wrote that reform must "look to the improvement of the individual as well as to the improvement of the race. . . . It must aim not only at ameliorating the conditions of life but also at bettering life itself." Just as white Virginian eugenicists distrusted sociology's environmental analysis, Turner believed that, "the sociologist . . . must be primarily a biologist." Social problems must be dealt with as "problems intimately associated with the life, strength and health of the race." Fixing the environment only alleviated symptoms, without addressing the root cause: the quality of the individuals who comprised society. Biologically informed social policy, particularly eugenics, offered the best hope for lasting social reform.[83]

Turner, like most mainline eugenicists, argued that, "the legislator who would make laws concerning [social problems] without a due appreciation of their biological significance, may do much that is worthless and even positively harmful." Like most progressives, Turner remained convinced that scientific training prepared people to approach social problems dispassionately, uninfluenced by personal prejudice. Ethical behavior would emerge from scientific inquiry. Ultimately, Turner believed in "the value of the methods of science in fitting one for sound citizenship." The dangerous syllogism—science is objective, objective things are moral, therefore science is moral—remained as attractive to Turner, who sought to liberate people from oppression, as it did to his ideological opponents, who invoked it to legitimate repression.[84]

Turner built on the Jeffersonian tradition of a universal "moral faculty" in describing how biology might create a more humane society. He believed that "ethics and the springs of human conduct may be . . . extensively bound up with our bodily structure and functions." Biological study of "lower" organisms could "impart ethical values" and "contribute to building of better individuals and better communities." If, in examining a toad, the biology student realized that the animal manifested "the same type of vital functions as himself," then, Turner believed, "it will sooner or later dawn upon him that it is an act of savagery, wantonly, to destroy toads, unless they are found to imperil human welfare. Genuine respect for the living among lower forms will go far in reinforcing one's respectful reverence of personality among men." Turner's logic inverted the usual rationale for studying nonhuman life-forms. Instead of being expendable material, toads became objects of ethical and moral reflection. In what was perhaps an antilynching plea, Turner implicitly analogized biology students' sacrifice of animals to whites' wanton killing of blacks. He clearly disagreed with the mainline eugenic sentiment that blacks' mere presence in society constituted a menace that imperiled human welfare. Instead, Turner remained convinced that the positive march of science would conquer all error, social or scientific. "A universal ethical conduct which must be the same to all men will surely follow as the ignorance and superstition of former days shall be supplanted by the truths of the laboratory," he asserted.[85]

Like white eugenicists, Turner believed that biology could "establish the true relationship of races and nations to each other." Responding to the passage of Virginia's eugenically justified Racial Integrity Act (RIA), which banned interracial marriages, Turner wrote "some of the so-called inferior peoples have forged ahead to the front ranks of civilized nations, while some so-called superior ones have become apparently decadent." In his desire to advance racial uplift, Turner pressed, "We are nearer the goal of universal brotherhood, I feel, today than we were a century ago, largely, because the pursuit of science has developed a larger sympathy among men, by teaching them that they are truly of one flesh, with a common parentage." It would be another quarter century before most biologists agreed to a statement affirming the fundamental similarity of all human beings. The 1950 UNESCO "Statement on Race" held that "race" is a social construction that aids categorization without expressing anything about the innate biological essence of individuals. Even then there would be holdouts—biologists still influenced by segregation's science.[86]

In "The Curriculum and Aims in Biological Teaching," Turner accused schools of "playing a rather backward role in preparing the youth of the country to cope with the innumerable problems, mostly biological, with which they and the whole populace are brought into daily contact." Race was the crucial biological problem confronting society. The problem was exacerbated by "false biology." Turner cited the works of Madison Grant, Lothrop Stoddard, Edward M. East, and Virginia's own Earnest Sevier Cox with their "flaming titles and their no less inflammatory contents," decrying the racist use of biology. Although forced to acknowledge East's eminence as a scientist, Turner lambasted the others as "writers who have not had even a smattering of biological training in any formal manner." Identifying ignorance as the root of all evil, Turner sought to wrest control of the eugenical impulse from white racists and turn it to the advantage of all "fit" people, white and black.[87]

Turner challenged the racist biology pervading popular textbooks, hoping to reclaim hereditarianism as a tool for African American and human social uplift. Turner quoted the five-tiered racial taxonomy presented in a popular textbook, *Essentials of Biology*, that ran from black, brown, red, and yellow to "the highest type of all, the Caucasians." Indignant, Turner commented: "This is a fair sample of the material to which our youth are exposed. One sees at a glance that while biologists in other fields are spending their lives in trying to find relationships and compatibilities among . . . living things, when [considering humans] he is content to emphasize and present to his youth only the differences, the incompatibilities, the contrasts." Turner cited the harm done to black students' self-esteem in encountering these racist dicta in their textbooks. More significantly, however, Turner unveiled the professional hypocrisy of biologists writing in support of segregation's science. By articulating a vision of biology that highlighted the continuities and harmonies among living things, Turner posited a novel model for understanding human social organization. Difference became an artifact of prejudice. Biology taught him the interdependence of all life, not its separate and independent existence. As a result, appeals to racial superiority seemed antibiological and ahistorical because "whatever this age or the dominant people of the present have accomplished rests surely and firmly on the foundation of all that has gone before."[88]

Inverting the "race suicide" thesis, Turner denounced cultural superiority in a fashion that would have alarmed white readers even as it gave African Americans hope:

> The proud, haughty, domineering people of today may be the cringing, begging, sycophantic paupers of tomorrow. Within the brief span of man's authentic history, we have record of the rise to power and the decadence of various human tribes—black, yellow, and white; we do not know and probably cannot know what characteristics or lines of conduct have the greatest survival value and are the most enduring, but it should be the chief aim of courses in Human Biology to seek out and stress every factor which makes for peaceful, harmonious, cooperation among races and among nations.

Turner refocused the eugenic quest. Instead of attempting to cement the superiority of any group or civilization, Turner aimed at creating tolerance. Thus, he escaped the trap of biological superiority while preserving the biologically determined basis of life. Turner prepared to destroy racial hierarchies by teaching the "gospel of social evolution"—how black uplift, eugenic and euthenic, could allow African Americans to equal whites in every way. Turner's "accommodationist" eugenics rejected mainline eugenicists' racism but accepted their class biases, aligning black and white eugenicists over fitness, while acknowledging the unfitness of some blacks and whites.[89]

References in Turner's lecture notes and essays suggests that he taught eugenics during this period. In 1929, Turner offered "The History of Life," covering "the origin and development of life (Organic Evolution)." In 1933, he began offering embryology, another venue for incidental instruction in eugenics. Finally, in 1942, "Biology 106" began covering "heredity at work in man." In 1945–46, after the revelation of the Holocaust, the course description dropped notice of human heredity. Turner retired the following year.[90]

———

Thomas Turner, like the "second wave" cohort at Virginia, accepted the promise of eugenics. Eugenics was the "lingua franca" of science from about 1910 to at least 1929. These men were not cranks, enthusiasts, or "corrupted" scientists. They represented mainstream scientific opinion. Most were elected Fellows of the American Association for the Advancement of Science; some held positions in the National Academy of Science; and all served in executive roles for societies governing their specific disciplines. Their thinking reflected then-current notions of eugenics, the relation of science to social policy, and social prejudice.

Teasing out the strands of scientific commitment, the desire for social control, and the influence of social prejudice from the university eugenicists' beliefs presents a formidable task. Whatever the individual strength of each of these three factors, eugenics provided the ideological loom weaving them together. For everyone but Turner, the resulting belief system reified the imagined community of the American race and cloaked the hidebound hierarchies of the South in scientific garb as natural extensions of biology. White educators converted to the "gospel of social evolution" because it secured their sense of self as members of a superior race. They proselytized as many students, professional, and laypeople as possible. Education socialized white Virginia elites to believe in the power of heredity over environment, buttressing their faith that the social order reflected the laws of nature.

Education remained crucial to the cultural heavy lifting performed by eugenics. All the academic eugenicists believed this; as a result they all sought to inculcate eugenics and the eugenic creed through their courses. Eugenics instruction was nearly ubiquitous in Virginia's colleges and universities, white and black, for men and women. In the aggregate, the scope and durability of hereditarian thinking in Virginia colleges and universities is impressive. Even in its most benign form, this instruction consigned many people to the "unfit," writing them out of the American race and drumming them out of citizenship. As the African American eugenicist Thomas W. Turner trenchantly observed, "Sound citizenship in a democracy depends in large measure upon the way in which information has become socialized, as it were, and utilized for the physical and spiritual development of the people." Turner recognized that teaching—the transmission of knowledge—could easily be used for antidemocratic purposes. Eugenic instruction in Virginia reinforced the segregated, stratified society marred by the inequity, disfranchisement, and bigotry that evolved after the Civil War.[91]

Mainline eugenics remained in the curriculum of Virginia colleges for one long professional generation. As the professors who had learned it as cutting-edge science during the first two decades of the twentieth century retired, no new generation rose to take their place. Although many scientists continued to believe that qualitative, genetic differences separated human races, few remained willing to champion these ideas in public. The leading edge of genetic inquiry swung away from human genetics, which was too complex to yield quick results. Fruit flies and plant hybrids offered rapid rates of reproduction and readily interpretable results that fueled investigation. With the retirement of Charles Davenport in the mid-1930s and the closing of the ERO in 1940, organized mainline eugenics lacked a viable institutional base. Even as the vanguard passed from the scene, however, eugenic ideology, operating through the hosts of nonspecialists who learned eugenics as part of their collegiate training, continued to affect public policy and the lives of tens of thousands of Virginians.

4

"STERILIZE THE MISFITS PROMPTLY"

Virginia Controls the Feebleminded

T HE "ROARING TWENTIES" PROMPTED massive social dislocations in American life. The economy soared as industries transformed from war-time production to creating consumer goods for the masses. Mass production and mass consumption engendered "mass amusements" that prompted cul-tural homogenization as people consumed identical entertainment. Charles Lindbergh became the first truly national celebrity, idolized as the epitome of American technical ingenuity and rugged individualism. Despite all these signs of progressivism's triumph, tensions strained American prosperity. Many people suspected that women voting, changing moral codes, social-ism, communism, and increased militancy among African Americans were all symptoms of American declension. Europe, devastated by the "Great War," embodied modern, progressive technology run amok, the bane rather than the savior of Western civilization. Nativists and eugenicists had warned of im-pending doom both before and during the war. With the best of Europe's ge-netic endowment lying dead on the battlefields of France—thanks, many eu-genicists claimed, to the fateful shot of an unfit, deranged anarchist—healthy Nordic immigration would give way to hordes of degenerate stock fleeing the desolation. The rise of socialist and communist revolts made some fear that the United States was next, inciting the postwar Red Scare. Eugenicists used the Red Scare itself to prove that the very "type" of people who started the war had emigrated to America. These immigrants' genetic proclivity toward anarchism threatened the republic; their genes harbored the seeds of future revolt, an indirect threat one or more generations removed. Eugenicists argued for immigration restriction and selective breeding among "Old Stock" Americans as the only bulwarks protecting civilization.[1]

Especially for many southerners, the 1920s struck one sustained, ominous social and political note. New South boosterism had urbanized the South. Urbanization was blamed for crime, insanity, and "feeblemindedness." The "Great Migration," an exodus of rural southern blacks to urban areas and the North, drained millions of African American workers from the South between 1915 and 1940. White elites decried the loss of labor, even as they feared waves of unfamiliar, itinerant blacks passing through their communities. Black-white contact threatened the white gene pool through miscegenation, crime, and disease. The jumble on southern city streets—mixing men and women, whites, blacks, and other people of color, the wealthy and the poor—discomfited elites who took pride in maintaining an ordered and predictable lifestyle. Disorder threatened the Jeffersonian maxim that the South nurtured the best type of American citizen, the yeoman farmer. When a stricken Woodrow Wilson left office in 1921, many southerners wondered if the region would ever again mount such political heights.[2]

Economically "backward," many southerners also felt the region labored under a false stigma of social retardation. The withering screeds of Henry Louis Mencken, writing from Baltimore, the gateway to the South, rent the cultural and intellectual fabric of southern society. In response, the second Ku Klux Klan, refounded on Stone Mountain, Georgia, in 1915, rose to its greatest strength in the early 1920s. Although it was national in membership and scope, its southern origins and racial intolerance branded it as an institution of "southern" reaction. Rooted in the popular imagination, the image of the "benighted South" increased with the fall of the Klan and the rise of fundamentalist religion. The 1925 anti-evolution trial of John T. Scopes reinforced stereotypes of anti-intellectual, antimodern southern provincialism. As the decade closed, twelve southerners, known as the "Vanderbilt Agrarians," penned their famous manifesto, I'll Take My Stand, extolling the virtue of a mythic Jeffersonian Southland, providing intellectual ballast to overdrawn caricatures.[3]

Instead of rising to the bait of the Klan, the hysteria of the fundamentalists, or the recalcitrance of the Agrarians, progressive Virginia eugenicists articulated an attractive alternative to the mythic Lost Cause. Eugenicists' rational, dispassionate program emphasized social "management," racial "adjustments," public health, and education as the four pillars of social harmony. Promising economic liberalism and urbanization without the negative consequences of social blight or racial equality, eugenics maintained traditional social hierarchies within the changing environment. Elite guidance was crucial to this new ideology that merged the racial culture of the past with the technology, wealth, and progressivism of the future.

Progressives blamed various groups of "problem" people for social and economic malaise. The so-called "feebleminded," the criminal, and the "delinquent"—whether black or white—all came under attack, regardless of race or gender. Control of the feebleminded became paramount since they were "responsible in large degree for pauperism, crime, prostitution, and other evils which burden society." By the 1920s, the fear of the "menace of the feebleminded" peaked, eliding distinctions between white and black unfit, creating a single category targeted for repression. Mental health specialists, criminologists, and sociologists all began to follow the lead of eugenicists, who claimed that the only way to solve social problems was to eliminate the individuals who caused them. While euthanasia remained beyond the pale, negative eugenics gained great currency.[4]

Alongside Virginia's reformers and educators, the state's medical community popularized the "eugenic metaphor" for public health, hoping to uplift the South and prevent disease through reproductive control rather than therapeutic intervention. Standard public health programs like quarantine, fumigation, and eradication became rhetorically paired with eugenic nostrums like segregation, sterilization, and euthanasia. Eugenicists argued that preventing the birth of those hereditarily predisposed to disease and antisocial behavior would decrease the need for expensive therapy. Many eugenically minded progressives advocated the institutional segregation of problem individuals in penitentiaries, reformatories, asylums, and "colonies" where inmates worked at trades to sustain themselves. By the 1920s, however, institutionalizing the increasing numbers of "defectives" seemed prohibitively expensive. Some Virginians believed that institutional care was "actually encouraging the anti-social classes to continue in their anti-social habits." Progressive eugenicists thought sterilization would solve this problem. Sterilizing defectives allowed them to be paroled back into society without the threat of creating "more of their kind." The impulse toward economic efficiency spurred a biological recategorization, collapsing racial, class, and gender distinctions into the feebleminded—a new "other" targeted for reform.

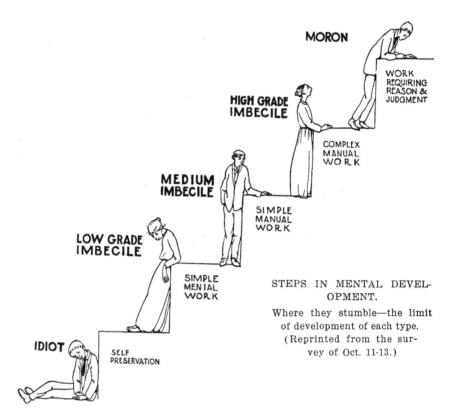

STEPS IN MENTAL DEVEL-
OPMENT.

Where they stumble—the limit
of development of each type.
(Reprinted from the sur-
vey of Oct. 11-13.)

Illustrations such as this, from a 1915 report of the Virginia State Board of Charities and Corrections, graphically presented the "menace of the feebleminded" that threatened to swamp
society with their inferior genes and economic dependency. (Courtesy of Special Collections,
University of Virginia)

The definition of the feebleminded shifted during the early twentieth century, but by the 1920s the concept of feeblemindedness exhibited consistent
race, class, and gender biases. The results of the Army Alpha and Beta intelligence tests purported to reveal a rising tide of mental defect. Virginia
led the southern states in intelligence, yet its conscripts averaged in the "moron" range. Although this disheartening result could be ascribed to the effect of lower class "mountain whites," it still undercut the traditional Jeffersonian notion of yeomen farmers as the backbone of democracy. The tests
depicted African Americans—the favored southern labor pool, and roughly
one-quarter of Virginia's population—as predominantly feebleminded. The
tests compounded stereotypes about black hypersexuality, criminality, and
disease, stigmatizing blacks as Virginia's most dysgenic population.[5]

Poor whites, and especially poor white women, were threatening, too. Dr. H. W. Dew of Lynchburg, Virginia, asserted that, "feeble-minded women are notoriously immoral," often giving birth out of wedlock, including one woman who "had two illegitimate children by her own father." Virginians found further support for this contention in the records of 120 Richmond prostitutes, 86 of whom were deemed feebleminded. The report of the State Board of Charities and Corrections concluded: "Feeblemindedness is responsible in large degree for the waywardness of these women. They should not be punished for doing what their heredity made almost sure, but society should segregate them where they will be protected from licentious men and lewd, avaricious women." Progressive Virginians lobbied to pass eugenic laws to control socially pathological people.[6]

Virginia witnessed the rise of devoted nonacademic eugenics enthusiasts between 1900 and 1920. Building on the hereditary doctrines propounded by nationally recognized eugenicists and supported by state educators, Virginia's would-be social engineers identified the genes of some Virginians as the source of problems ranging from pellagra to unwed motherhood. The collusion between legal, medical, and educational professionals in the passage of Virginia's sterilization act reveals the similarity between Virginian and national responses to fears of a rising feebleminded population.

The Virginia eugenics movement, like other states' movements, began to achieve its legislative ends between 1916 and 1930. Virginia's eugenics laws—one permitting the sterilization of the feebleminded, the other banning interracial marriage—have rarely been analyzed as part of a more coherent effort. Common roots link each act's principal proponents and the larger eugenics community. The adoption and implementation of these laws placed Virginia in the forefront of progressive social engineering, matching and in many cases exceeding initiatives in progressive northern states like Connecticut, Michigan, and New York. Ironically, many Virginia blacks joined in the racial purity crusade, making strange bedfellows of Pan-Africanists and white supremacists.[7]

From 1910 through the 1920s, Virginia progressives used eugenics to catalyze a political reaction that they hoped would be copied nationally. Indeed, other state legislatures—notably those of Alabama and Georgia in the South and of California in the West—sought to emulate the Old Dominion's example. Watched with interest by the Germans, Virginia and California's experiments became part of the initial matrix for the eugenic policy that led to the Holocaust. The eugenic impulse that led to eugenic laws, while accelerated by the explosion of Jazz Age tensions, began much earlier.

Doctors and Delinquents: Early Eugenics beyond the Academy

In the early twentieth century, many Virginia physicians encountered eugenics outside the academy. Medical journal editors assumed that their readers would know and understand the basic concepts behind eugenics, and alerted them to the new science's promise. The *Virginia Medical Semi-Monthly*, Virginia doctors' professional journal, published numerous articles advocating eugenic interventions in marriage and procreation. Written by practicing and academic physicians, these essays fostered eugenic consensus among Virginia's doctors. The "preventive" ethos of Virginia's physicians, who saw a social panacea in "racial hygiene," influenced their therapeutic approach to individual patients and to groups like blacks, women, the "feebleminded," and the insane. Two major issues first attracted the doctors' attention: restricting marriage to the physically fit, and the eugenic segregation and sterilization of the "defective."

In February 1905, Dr. A. Einer of Rural Retreat, Virginia, wrote that physicians should certify the physical and hereditary health of couples contracting marriage before the state issued a marriage license. Einer lamented that "no decided effort has been made by which to control diseases and improve the race by controlling marriage," despite the fact that he knew "of no more important preventive measure" than marriage restriction. "Sentiment" should be replaced by "a commission composed of intelligent, conscientious, non-partisan physicians" who would "render the verdict" on whether a couple should marry. Only marriage restriction promised to "hold in check the procreation of diseased and degenerate progeny" who threatened "to make national degeneration perceptible and terribly real." Collapsing "nation" and "race" into the same category, Einer concluded that only eugenic marriage restriction could protect America from "defective and pauper progeny."[8]

Chicago's Dr. G. Frank Lydston followed Einer's early work. Using an economic rhetoric that Justice Oliver Wendell Holmes would echo in 1927, Lydston told Virginia physicians, "Society has the same right as an insurance company to protect itself against loss" because "taxing normal decent people for the support of degenerates is not only morally wrong, but an economic farce." He advocated applying negative eugenic measures to the most "unfit," and promoting sound marriage selection.[9]

Marriage restriction should apply to "consumptives, epileptics, insane, incurable inebriates, and criminals unless they consent to sterilization." Advocating "voluntary" (individual consent) rather than "compulsory" (state-mandated) sterilization, Lydston cast himself as conservative—he was not sterilizing all "culls," just making it a condition for marriage. Lydston left open the "loophole" of extramarital sex. Unable to regulate "fornication"—which was illegal in many states anyway—and the associated problem of "illegitimacy," eugenic marriage laws ensured that only the fit could "legally" procreate. Lydston considered "unfit babies" and incurable people "social excreta" that "should be placed beyond the possibility of contaminating the body social" through euthanasia. Incorrigible criminals should, "in extreme cases, be removed by killing [them]." The executioner became the "social surgeon" who removed the "social cancer . . . quietly, humanely, and unexpectedly . . . . with a secret pipe for the admission of deadly gas." The scope of this "social surgery" should extend beyond the executioner's chamber, to the asylum and nursery. Euthanizing the disabled seemed to Lydston to be the greatest mercy, because "not to be born is by no means always a misfortune. Being born is sometimes a calamity."[10]

While Virginia doctors moved toward a eugenic consensus, Virginia lawmakers joined their compatriots in many northern and western states—like California, Indiana, Michigan, and Vermont—and created procedures governing the identification and institutionalization of Virginia's feebleminded. Academics like Harry Heck, Harvey Jordan, and Lawrence Royster demanded eugenic interventions in their addresses to the BCC during this period. In 1908, the General Assembly charged Virginia's Board of Charities and Corrections (BCC) to cooperate with Virginia physicians and educators in surveying the nature and extent of the "dependent, defective and delinquent classes" in Virginia's population. The board grafted its survey onto Heck's ongoing eugenic studies. In 1909, the BCC sent one questionnaire to four hundred physicians and another to public schoolteachers. Physicians were asked to "report the number of 'epileptics, idiots, feeble-minded, and cripple [*sic*] children in their care.'" Teachers received a checklist for diagnosing "backward" children. Students deemed "'unfit for education in the public schools'" by reason of mental deficiency exhibited:

1. Blinking. . . .
2. Inco-ordination. . . .
3. Spasms, fits, hysterical crying and laughing.
4. Cold and clammy hands and excessive pallor or blushing.
5. Slight malformation. . . .
6. Drooling. . . .
7. Carelessness, indolence, inattention, unreliable memory, obstinacy and either passion or stolidness.

8. Incapacity for simple acts. . . .

9. Imperfections of speech, sight, hearing, etc.

10. Excessive exaggerations, falsehood, pilfering, and poor moral sense.

11. Inability to keep up in studies. . . .

A host of factors—from poverty and malnutrition to normal childhood development—could account for these conditions. Diagnosing these "hereditary" traits relied on the subjective judgments of teachers, and remained open to bias and false correlations between physical condition, mental potential, and genetic makeup. Nevertheless, the survey's results aided BCC officials and Dr. William Drewry in establishing the Virginia Colony for the Epileptic and Feeble-Minded in 1912.[11]

By 1913, concern about the menace of the feebleminded reached new heights. A six-point list of "important facts concerning mental defectives" asserted that, "from feeble-mindedness springs, by inheritance, insanity, epilepsy and all forms of neurotic degeneracy," attributing criminality and prostitution to the same source. Since "the feeble-minded reproduce about twice as rapidly as normal stock," Virginia faced a dire threat. Feeblemindedness explained a constellation of social ills, locating their etiology in heredity.[12]

Eugenics offered the only solution. Harvey Jordan advocated compulsory sterilization in *Clinical Medicine*. Dr. L. S. Foster argued for segregation, marriage restriction, and sterilization. "This is a day of prevention," Foster wrote, "and in order to stay this increasing army of defectives, which are a great care and burden upon the country . . . and to cope successfully with this menace we must lay aside sentiment." The only practical remedies, wrote Dr. H. W. Dew of Lynchburg, Virginia, were "the regulation of marriage, and the sterilization of the confirmed criminal and the mentally defective." Invoking the figment of Old Virginians, the public health physician C. P. Wertenbaker contended: "It is unnecessary in this State and before this audience, to dwell upon the value of 'good blood' in man or in animals. Probably nowhere is the truth of the maxim 'blood will tell' more firmly believed than in Virginia." He called for "a division or bureau, similar to the bureau of vital statistics, that might be called the 'marriage division,' 'eugenics bureau' or something of the kind." Echoing the eugenic crescendo in the state's medical community, the BCC's annual report announced, "the most pressing social need of our time is the *segregation of the Feebleminded*," demanding that the legislature pass marriage restriction and sterilization laws. To attain these laws, people needed to be convinced of the efficacy of eugenic intervention.[13]

Each eugenics article published in the *Virginia Medical Semi-Monthly* between 1910 and 1924 emphasized the need to educate the public regarding eugenic imperatives. As Dr. Dew wrote, "it is largely, in my opinion, a question of educating the people, and through the people the legislature, and I believe it is our duty as physicians to take upon ourselves this work of education." Dr. J. W. Williams averred: "The father is the trustee of the germ cell, and the healthy germ cell is more important to his child than 'high society' culture and refinement. Every young man should have this fact taught him at home and in school, and it should be the first article of his social creed." Children raised with the eugenics creed would demand eugenic laws from the government.[14]

In 1908, the *Journal of the American Medical Association* explicitly endorsed eugenics. Between 1910 and 1914, "general magazines carried more articles on eugenics than on the three questions of slums, tenements, and living standards combined." While novel, eugenics was not unknown among America's physicians and educated elites. A few Virginia physicians had already put it into practice. Although historians credit Indiana's Dr. Harry Sharp with performing America's first eugenic sterilizations in 1899, Virginia also had extralegal eugenic pioneers, Drs. Charles Carrington and Bernard Barrow. At the 1908 meeting of the National Prison Association, Dr. Carrington, surgeon for the Virginia Penitentiary in Richmond, announced the results of two sterilization operations. His speech was reprinted in the *Virginia Medical Semi-Monthly* and abstracted in the *JAMA*. Carrington graduated from the University of Virginia School of Medicine in 1889, studying under James Lawrence Cabell and Paul Brandon Barringer, learning hereditarian ideas regarding "fitness" and "delinquency."[15]

Carrington published three papers detailing sterilizations he had performed upon penitentiary inmates. The first "patient" was an African American man imprisoned "for an especially brutal murder" who became "so violent and homicidal in his actions that he was adjudged insane, and sent to the Colored Insane Asylum, at Petersburg, Virginia." Carrington considered the prisoner "the wildest, most violent, and the most homicidal devil I have ever dreamed of seeing." Dehumanizing the inmate, Carrington described him as a classic "black beast-rapist"—"the fiercest, most consistent masturbator I ever heard of; as strong as a bull, as cunning as a hyena, and more ferocious and quite as dangerous as a Bengal tiger." Shouldering his professional burden, Carrington "determined to tame him," and—without benefit of legal warrant—performed a vasectomy on the man in 1902. Six years after the operation, Carrington invoked barnyard imagery to report that the man had become "a slick, fat, docile prisoner, a trusty about the yard—cured by sterilization." Carrington's second patient, "a debased little negro . . . a notoriously lusty, beastful Sodomist and masturbator" was, after vasectomy, "now a strapping, healthy-looking young buck."[16]

Dr. Bernard Barrow reported on his eugenic sterilization of five black men in June 1910. Unlike Carrington, Barrow obtained the "consent" of his patients. Whether the men he sterilized understood the procedure remains questionable. His claim that vasectomy could be reversed was a massive overstatement that probably misled some of the men. Interested in safeguarding white society by sterilizing black "defectives," Barrow argued that blacks needed white paternal control because, "the negro, as a savage race, cannot solve his social and sanitary problems, and he should not be blamed for it; it is a responsibility which rests on the shoulders of the stronger race—the white man." Virginia physicians could help improve black breeding by determining which blacks "should not be deprived of this function of procreation." Sterilization would "go a long way towards solving the negro problem by eliminating the vicious, criminally inclined, disease bearing portion of the race." Carrington's and Barrow's eugenic rhetoric transformed these early experiments from an abuse of individual liberty and the doctor-patient relationship, to a rational, objective intervention for the benefit of the patient and society. No progressive Virginian could ask for anything more.[17]

Experimentation on imprisoned and institutionalized black men followed long-standing traditions. American physicians, particularly in the South, routinely performed experimental procedures upon people living at the margins of society. Poor, disfranchised, and uneducated, lower-class blacks, poor whites, and women could not mount effective defenses against powerful authorities who believed they operated in the public interest. Stigmatized as diseased threats to the moral and physical sanctity of upper-class white America, doctors viewed these patients as fitting experimental subjects. The use of imprisoned black men minimized the chance of objection, while the apparently salubrious effect nullified potential protest. This dynamic would hold true even if doctors moved on to sterilizing white criminals.

These experiments were explicitly eugenic because if sterilization was "properly enforced with habitual criminals, we would have fewer criminals." Foreshadowing later judicial opinion, Carrington suggested that three generations established the heredity of crime: "certain families, from father to son, to grandson, furnish recruits regularly for our army of criminals." Certainly, he reasoned, if the grandfather had been sterilized, "a lot of crime and suffering would have been prevented." Likening sterilization to Jenner's smallpox vaccination—again foreshadowing later judicial opinion—Carrington asked his colleagues to lobby for a sterilization statute at the 1909 annual meeting of the Medical Society of Virginia.[18]

Carrington became Virginia's first sterilization crusader. In 1910, he lobbied the General Assembly and the Tri-State Medical Association to support his bill "to prevent procreation by confirmed criminals, idiots, imbeciles, and rapists." Carrington invoked the eugenic metaphor, using the barnyard analogy first articulated by Jefferson, arguing, "We may become a nation of good animals if we direct the same intelligence to the breeding of human beings that we do to the improvement of domestic animals." Carrington drew a parallel between Richard Dugdale's *The Jukes* and "families in Virginia who have been constantly represented on our penitentiary rolls from grandfather to son, and now grandson." Every state institution must, under the provisions of Carrington's bill, make mental examinations of its inmates. Every inmate deemed an incorrigible "criminal, a rapist, an idiot or imbecile" would be liable to sterilization. To prevent surgeons from building a cottage industry in sterilization, the statute limited the consultation fee to five dollars.[19]

Carrington targeted male criminals and rapists for sterilization, betraying common gender biases. Women, however, did not escape his attention. Arguing that, "generally speaking a feeble-minded man has to find a feeble-minded woman before he can procreate; a feeble-minded woman has no such limitations," Carrington employed a sexual double standard that assumed that "normal" women, because of their innate sexual reserve, would never be duped into sexual congress with "feebleminded" men (although they might be raped by them). Subject to the vicissitudes of the "sex impulse," otherwise "honorable" men might be seduced by morally loose, feebleminded women. Less "honorable," but still "normal," men might use feebleminded women to gratify their "normal" sexual desires. Falsely equating the relative risks of vasectomy and tubal ligation (he acknowledged but downplayed the 10 percent mortality rate among women), Carrington enunciated the justification that would result in women being sterilized almost twice as frequently as men.[20]

Carrington laid the initial legislative planks in Virginia's eugenical platform. The editor of the *Virginia Medical Semi-Monthly* opined that misguided antisterilization sentiment would "give way to reason, and the prevention of procreation in selected cases will be demanded by law." Fourteen years later, in 1924, Virginia eugenicists succeeded in passing the eugenic sterilization law that led to the landmark 1927 Supreme Court case *Buck v. Bell*, which established the constitutionality of eugenic sterilization.[21]

Placed into their national context and against the background of eugenical mobilization at Virginia's flagship medical school, these Virginia physicians' efforts to obtain a sterilization law do not seem extreme. These men viewed themselves as the scions of science, the heralds of a progressive utopia. Eugenics was the preferred specific remedy for many social ills, but its real appeal lay in the preventive promise of "cutting off the supply of defective germ plasm." Physicians mobilizing for eugenic sterilization between 1910 and 1919 stood at the nexus of science and society, where cutting-edge technology slashed encrusted cultural taboos about sex, reproduction, and the body. In that decade, sterilization remained controversial, arousing "much discussion and some hostile comment" in Virginia. Eugenics enthusiasts tailored their arguments to reach other educated and "progressive" elites—policy makers, legislators, and public officials—rather than the public. Supporters of eugenics believed that only the most "altruistic" individuals would accept limitations on their personal freedoms "in the name of eugenics"; others would resist eugenic intervention—particularly sterilization.[22]

As Edward J. Larson observed, "Some time interval inevitably exists between the formation of new scientific theories and their integration into medical or mental health practices." In Virginia, academics affiliated with the national eugenics movement trained practicing physicians through the medical school and medical societies, facilitating eugenics' acceptance. The 1924 enactment of a eugenic sterilization law, however, lagged behind professional opinion in Virginia and the rest of the South. While eighteen other states, including Michigan, Pennsylvania, Indiana, and California, passed sterilization laws in the early twentieth century, six were vetoed by state governors, five were declared unconstitutional, and one was repealed by referendum. Once Virginia's law was institutionalized by a favorable Supreme Court opinion, sterilization gathered momentum across the nation, an impetus that resisted later changes in medical knowledge. Moreover, eugenic sterilization in Virginia persisted long after most national mental and public health authorities abandoned it. Eugenic sterilization's "punctuated evolution," a call and response between theory and practice, explains the delay in achieving a sterilization law while accounting for the prolonged use of sterilization in Virginia.[23]

Institutionalization presented an alternative to sterilization. Virginia's facilities for the segregation of the feebleminded emerged from eugenic criminal theory. The yearly reports of Virginia's State Board of Charities and Corrections (BCC), founded in 1908, parroted national fears about the "menace of the feebleminded" and the threat of "born criminals." Relying on circular logic, penologists and criminologists argued that criminal recidivism indicated an inborn tendency; simultaneously, they held that feeblemindedness and hereditary taints caused crime. "Correctable" inmates became the exception, not the rule, a major shift from late-nineteenth-century notions of penal rehabilitation. Under this new hereditarian paradigm, society could only protect itself from "the criminal class" through incarceration—the segregation of "deviants" from the normal. Over time, sterilization came to be seen as a preventive measure that obviated the need for incarceration by limiting the procreation of criminals.[24]

This era's approach to criminal women connected eugenics and middle-class standards of morality. Class-based fears of "race suicide," prompted by lower-class mothers allegedly "out breeding" upper-class women, compounded the stereotype of poor women as the source of "illegitimate," unfit progeny. Most eugenically minded physicians and social workers believed that sexual promiscuity and unwed pregnancy were markers of feeblemindedness. Since feeblemindedness was hereditary, and since "like begets like," then illegitimate children must be feebleminded, too. Many officials believed any young woman convicted of a crime or a moral violation (like prostitution) was hereditarily incorrigible. Such women must be segregated in institutions to protect society. They might be released only under one of three conditions: they reformed (unlikely), they aged beyond child-bearing (costly), or they underwent sterilization.[25]

Virginia's movement for penal and social reform responded to this eugenic threat by founding homes for "wayward" women. Virginia's first reformatory for girls, lobbied for by Dr. Lawrence Royster, was located in and named after Bon Air, Virginia. After attending the ERO's summer training class for fieldworkers in 1914, Ms. Anna Marie Peterson became superintendent of this workhouse seeking to reform "vicious" women by segregating them from society. While at the ERO, Peterson worked at New Jersey's storied Vineland Training School under Henry Herbert Goddard—eugenicist, pioneering psychometrician, and America's foremost authority on female mental defectives. Ms. Peterson aligned Bon Air with the eugenics movement's notion of penal reform, patrolling the line between "normal" society and "deviant" behavior. As gatekeeper, she decided which inmates might be "paroled" back into society and which were "incorrigibles" who needed indefinite segregation. During Peterson's five years at Bon Air, she trained her successor, Margaret Bair, who remained another twenty-two years, well into the period of eugenic sterilization. The Bon Air facility referred so-called "defective delinquents" to state hospitals for sterilization, setting the pattern for other homes. By 1930, the social worker at the Norfolk "rescue" home claimed, "sterilization is a wonderful blessing for the feeble-minded girl who is bound to become a repeater. . . . [J]ust this week we are sending one of these unfortunates to the hospital for the operation."[26]

The imperatives of segregation's science led Virginia to establish one of the nation's first settlement houses for African American women. Founded by Janie Porter Barrett in 1915, the state acquiesced in funding the Virginia Industrial School for Colored Girls in 1920. The school maintained ties with the Central State Hospital and Petersburg Colony—which incarcerated feeble-minded black men—that paralleled those between Bon Air and white state hospitals. These homes, both state and private institutions, funneled women to the eugenic surgeon's table.

With the effective institutional segregation of the feebleminded, criminals, and "delinquent" children, Virginia had created a formidable first-line eugenic defense against the "mongrelization" of the state's best blood. Despite its efficacy in removing the unfit from public life and limiting their procreation, institutionalization failed the Progressive Era's litmus test for efficient social intervention. Segregation saved society from tainted blood and crime, but cost the state thousands of dollars supporting inmates. Institutionalization also incurred the opportunity cost of inmates' lost labor. These concerns resonated strongly in the cash-poor and labor-dependent South. Thus, southern progressives established eugenic "colonies."

Under the "colony" system, physician-managers—known as superintendents—expected inmates to work at menial jobs in farm and basic industry to make the institution more self-sufficient. Since most inmates were deemed socially incorrigible, they spent their incarceration engaged in productive activity—ranging from subsistence farming to handicrafts and light industry—rather than treatment. These institutions also became the referral network for, and epicenter of, eugenic sterilizations.[27]

"The Shiftless, Ignorant, and Worthless Class of Anti-Social Whites of the South": Virginia's Campaign for Eugenic Sterilization

A century before James Lawrence Cabell founded the state's first public health board, colonial administrators established a public institution for the insane. Opened in October 1773, Virginia's "Publick Hospital for Persons of Insane and Disordered Mind" remained the only state-sponsored institution of its type in America until 1824. In 1828, Virginia opened a second insane asylum in the Shenandoah Valley at Staunton, Virginia. Virginia again led the South in 1868, establishing the Central State Hospital at Petersburg for the care of

Dr. John Bell and Carrie Buck, antagonists in the landmark eugenic sterilization case *Buck v. Bell* (1927). (From "The Science of Human Affairs the Most Difficult," *Journal of Heredity,* January 1932, by permission of Oxford University Press)

insane African Americans. The Old Dominion completed its push for public institutions in 1887, when the fourth mental hospital opened in the southwestern town of Marion.

Almost 154 years after the opening of Virginia's first public custodial hospital, Virginia pioneered a new intervention through its state hospitals: the constitutionally sanctioned eugenic sterilization of the "feebleminded." On October 19, 1927, Dr. John H. Bell performed a tubal ligation on a twenty-year-old female resident at the Lynchburg Colony for the Epileptic and Feebleminded. Carrie Buck, a native of Charlottesville, Virginia, was the plaintiff in the 1927 Supreme Court case *Buck v. Bell,* which established the constitutionality of compulsory eugenic sterilization. For all the notoriety attracted by *Buck,* Virginia's involvement with eugenic sterilization antedated that famous case. Carrie Buck's sterilization involved a broad cohort of Virginia progressives seeking to establish the state as a leader in scientific, social engineering.[28]

By 1916, the liberal sowing of eugenic ideology began to bear legislative fruit. Drs. Albert Priddy and Joseph DeJarnette, superintendents of the Lynchburg and Western state hospitals respectively, tapped the legislator Aubrey Strode to draft eugenics laws. Strode played a pivotal role in reforming Virginia's mental health system. His ardent support for segregation and compulsory sterilization underscores his conviction that technocratic, "efficient adjustments" of the institutions shaping daily life would achieve social harmony. In progressive fashion, the laws Strode wrote substituted the judgment of impaneled government experts for individual families, allowing the BCC "to register, examine and commit the feebleminded to institutions where they would be segregated from 'normal' citizens," and to "see that such moral, medical and surgical treatment as [superintendents] may deem proper shall be given such patients." This broad language allowed Dr. Priddy to justify his extralegal sterilization of patients as a consequence of "medical necessity." Finally, the General Assembly passed a marriage restriction statute that prohibited "habitual criminal, idiot, imbecile . . . [and] epileptic" Virginians from marrying.[29]

Following Dr. Carrington, Virginia's next major proponents of eugenical sterilization were the BCC's Reverend Joseph Mastin and three state hospital superintendents, Drs. William F. Drewry, Albert Priddy, and Joseph DeJarnette. These men were all acquainted with Paul Barringer, Harvey Jordan, and eugenics through their overlapping activities with the BCC and the Virginia Medical Society.[30]

Dr. Drewry, superintendent of the Petersburg facility, began arguing publicly for eugenics as early as 1912, citing an increase in black feeblemindedness. Drewry warned, "To the community the presence of such individuals is a perpetual menace, a constant source of trouble and danger." Given the hereditary nature of most defectiveness, Drewry argued that, "it is criminal negligence to allow such defectives to remain free in the community" propagating harm. Thus, Drewry advocated that "the power of procreating their kind should be taken from them by the relentless hand of science, under sanction and authority of law." Aware that his suggestion might seem radical, Dr. Drewry championed "a department of eugenics and experimental psychology" at the University of Virginia to help rectify the "appalling ignorance [of] and indifference" to the problem. Drewry held these beliefs until he retired in 1923, leaving his colleagues Joseph DeJarnette and Albert Priddy to shepherd the sterilization bill through the General Assembly.[31]

Dr. Joseph DeJarnette was the superintendent of Western State Hospital in Staunton, Virginia, from 1908 to 1946. Residing less than forty miles from the University of Virginia medical school, he knew Paul Barringer, Harvey Jordan, and the "second wave" of university eugenicists. DeJarnette's thirty-eight annual reports read like primers underscoring the connection between eugenics and public health, recommending sterilization as preventive medicine. "In the treatment of all diseases," he began, "it is an established fact that prevention is far better than cure. This is especially true in the treatment of the insane, as heredity has been variously estimated to be the cause of from thirty to fifty per cent. [of all affliction]." After all, "allowing these classes [the unfit] to reproduce not only multiplies the class, but makes them perpetual. It is a crime against their offspring and a burden to their State for such to reproduce." Likening sterilization to tuberculosis prevention, DeJarnette equated eugenics and public health. "A few years ago the antispitting acts and laws for the prevention of tuberculosis were ridiculed," DeJarnette contended, "while now even the most ignorant are beginning to recognize their importance and observe them." Procreation among the unfit spread "germinal contamination" among future generations just as spitting spread the tubercle bacillus among the present population. Echoing Harvey Jordan, DeJarnette called on Virginians to "bend our greatest efforts toward perpetuating the best and highest type of man from the best," in spite of individual rights.[32]

Economics, efficiency, and humanitarianism became the watchwords of DeJarnette's eugenic program. He preached the triptych of education, segregation, and sterilization "in their order of efficiency and practicability—the least efficient first." Education seemed inefficient because it required good teachers, attentive students, and great repetition of effort. "Segregation during the reproductive age is a very expensive method," DeJarnette admitted, "but it is an hundred-fold more economical than to allow the unfit to reproduce." Sterilization, however, was "cheap and effective," and also more humane than segregation because it "would not interfere with the individual's liberty, sexual gratification or pursuit of happiness but only with his power of reproduction." Sterilized patients could be released back into the work force, increasing the state's economy, without risk of procreation. "For a higher grade and more intelligent citizenship and from the standpoint of state economics," DeJarnette urged passage of a sterilization law.[33]

To drive home his argument, DeJarnette frequently published his eugenic paean "Mendel's Law: A Plea for a Better Race of Men," which echoed Rudyard Kipling's white supremacist tract "The White Man's Burden":

Oh, why are you men so foolish— / You breeders who breed our men
Let the fools, the weaklings and crazy / Keep breeding and breeding again?

The criminal, deformed, and the misfit, / Dependent, diseased and the rest—
As we breed the human family / The worst is as good as the best.

Go to the house of some farmer, / Look through his barns and sheds,
Look at his horses and cattle, / Even his hogs are thoroughbreds;
Then look at his stamp on his children, / Lowbrowed with the monkey jaw,
Ape handed, and silly, and foolish— / Bred true to Mendel's law. . . .

This is the law of Mendel, / And often he makes it plain,
Defectives will breed defectives / And the insane breed insane.
Oh, why do we allow these people / to breed back to the monkey's nest,
To increase our country's burdens / When we should breed from the good and the
    best.

Oh, you wise men take up the burden, / And make this your loudest creed,
Sterilize the misfits promptly— / All not fit to breed.
Then our race will be strengthened and bettered, / And our men and our women
    be blest,
Not apish, repulsive and foolish, / For we should breed from the good and the
    best.[34]

DeJarnette published "Mendel's Law" in the *Virginia Medical Monthly* three
times in the 1920s and 1930s, seeing it lifted by the superintendent of the
Louisiana Hospital for the Insane in his 1922 annual report.[35] Comparing
DeJarnette's poem with Paul Barringer's contemporaneous effort "Germ or
Sperm" reveals how, by the 1920s, eugenics had ossified the cultural imagina-
tion of Virginia's leading public health experts:

Old Mother Earth is sick, I wot, / The human race is spent
When almost every child begot / Starts as an accident

Go read the records, writ in blood / Of lust unloosed and fools in stud
Imbeciles were born. . . .

Blind force thus once shaped the human form / As it still drives the sea, sand and
    worm
But better days have come
Man read the scroll so early given / He who with peas fearless strove
A light to read the law was given.[36]

DeJarnette, the ERO, area colleges, and the University of Virginia School
of Medicine developed educational and clinical exchanges, bringing medical

and social work students under DeJarnette's tutelage, reinforcing classroom instruction with practical experience. By 1905, Randolph-Macon Woman's College (RMWC) in Lynchburg offered sociology students field trips to study prisons, almshouses, and other charitable institutions, including, after 1912, the Lynchburg Colony for the Epileptic and Feebleminded, Dr. Albert Priddy's facility. By 1920, RMWC offered a biology course that included discussions of eugenics. Beginning in 1930, women could take "Taxonomy and Genetics," which in 1934 became "Genetics" and covered "Biogenesis, Evolution, Genetics and Eugenics." Four years later, with its title changed to "Genetics and Eugenics," the course was described in the college catalog as discussing "the possible improvement of the human race." DeJarnette's zeal earned him the moniker "Sterilization DeJarnette."[37]

Dr. Albert S. Priddy, superintendent of the Virginia Colony for the Epileptic and Feebleminded, was DeJarnette's second in lobbying for sterilization. Priddy believed that, "of the known causes which contribute to the development of epilepsy, that of bad heredity is the most potent, and with unrestricted marriage and intermarriage of the insane, mentally defective and epileptic, its increase is but natural." Calling his charges a "blight on mankind," Priddy raised the specter of race suicide, "unless some radical measures are adopted to curb" feebleminded procreation. Otherwise, "it will be only a matter of time before the resulting pauperism and criminality will be a burden too heavy . . . to bear." Society could alleviate this burden through sterilization. Like Carrington before him, Priddy was prompted by eugenic theory to take eugenic action, without statutory warrant.[38]

In 1917 alone, Priddy sterilized thirty women for unspecified pelvic diseases, noting: "We have continued the policy of sterilizing young women and girls of the moron type. . . . In nearly all cases sterilized, the pelvic disease was found in a greater or lesser degree, such as to make the removal of the tubes necessary for the relief of physical suffering." Morons—the highest on the then-accepted clinical hierarchy of feeblemindedness—posed the greatest threat to the nation's gene pool because they looked fit to casual observers. Like light-skinned African Americans, they could pass as normal, marrying and spreading their "taint." Priddy's "therapeutic" sterilizations may really have masked eugenic procedures.[39]

The standard of care for pelvic inflammatory diseases included sterilization, providing a convenient shield for physicians operating from eugenic rather than therapeutic motives. Priddy never explicitly suggested sterilizing feebleminded men. The lack of a male analog for pelvic disease and the paucity of evidence documenting the therapeutic benefits of vasectomy marked the procedure as eugenic rather than therapeutic, making it hard to hide motives.[40]

Dr. Priddy faced prosecution for his extralegal sterilizations. *Mallory v. Priddy* reveals how policy reforms actually resulted in abuses, as eugenic rhetoric successfully justified sterilizing black male criminals, but initially failed to convince officials that sterilization was appropriate for unfit white women. Doctors rejected sterilization because they feared legal liability, not because they doubted eugenics. No African American inmate was able to sue Dr. Carrington. Mrs. Willie Mallory, a white woman, could and did sue Dr. Priddy for unlawful imprisonment.[41]

Willie Mallory was arrested in September 1916 and charged with keeping a brothel. A juvenile court turned nine of her twelve children over to the Children's Home Society for exposure "to vicious and immoral influences." Three weeks later, Mrs. Mallory and two daughters submitted to mental examinations at the behest of a "Commission on Feeble-mindedness," the lay panel empowered by Virginia law to commit people to state institutions. The Mallory women were remanded to the Virginia Colony for the Epileptic and Feebleminded. Six months and an unsuccessful escape attempt later, under the guise of "medical necessity," Priddy sterilized Mrs. Mallory and her daughter Jessie. Priddy then released Mrs. Mallory, now "safe" to reenter society. Sixteen year-old Nannie Mallory escaped sterilization but remained in the colony with her sister, segregated from fit society.[42]

In October 1917, George Mallory sued Dr. Priddy, asking for five thousand dollars for damages, back wages, and compensation for the "pain and suffering" caused Mrs. Mallory by her "imprisonment" and sterilization. Priddy mounted a tripartite defense: Mrs. Mallory requested the procedure, it was medically necessary, and without the operation she "would most probably have died."[43]

Frustrated, George Mallory demanded "to know when can I get my child home again—My family have been braked up on false pertents." Incredulous, Mallory asked:

> Dr what busneiss did you have opreateding on my wife and daughter with out my consent. . . . you ought to be shamed of your sclft. . . . please let me no for there is no law for such treatment—I have foud that out—I am a poor man but was smart anuf to find that out.

Intelligent enough to seek legal counsel and learn his rights despite being impoverished, Mr. Mallory keenly felt his social responsibilities, turning the eugenicists' economic rationale on its head: "I earn 75$ a month I dont want my child on the state—I did not put her on them," he wrote. He then threatened Priddy: "If you dont let me have her bye easy terms I will get her by bad." George Mallory's masculine responsibility, personal integrity, and sense of human rights—in others characteristics of eugenic fitness—incensed Priddy.[44]

Priddy construed Mallory's anger as impertinence, his assertions of equality as arrogance, and his quest to free his daughter as an affront to the state. Characterizing Mallory's letter as "insulting and threatening in its tone," Priddy responded in kind, "if you dare to write me another such communication I will have you arrested and brought here too." To back up his threat, Priddy boasted, "I have the full record of you and your family from the State Board of Charities and Corrections and the Juvenile Court of Richmond," implying that those documents condemned Mallory. Claiming the women had asked him to operate and alluding to venereal infections, Priddy recast his actions as therapeutic—for both the Mallorys and society.[45]

In March 1918, the jury pronounced Priddy not guilty, validating his contention that he had acted within his professional authority. Respecting Priddy's medical expertise, resenting the impertinence of "poor white trash," and sharing the conviction that the Mallorys threatened society, the jury ratified many of Priddy's judgments. The verdict confirmed Priddy's role as "social surgeon" and public health officer, suggesting that Virginians might be ready for a sterilization law. In the interim, a 1920 law declared all current and future inmates of state institutions "lawfully committed patients" if they had been committed by court order or "Commissions of Feeblemindedness." This statute shielded superintendents from suits like *Mallory v. Priddy*.[46]

Thanks to proselytizing by academic eugenicists, and the rising national support for eugenics, Virginia would pass a sterilization law and see it upheld by the U.S. Supreme Court within a decade of *Mallory v. Priddy*. Ten years was a rapid course, given the delicate lobbying necessary to pass such an invasive measure. While sterilization bills had passed easily in eighteen northern and western states, Virginia would be the first southern state to pass such a law. Virginians' self-consciously progressive identity, relatively high level of education, and relative lack of fundamentalist religion allowed the Old Dominion to adopt a sterilization law before any other southern state.

Cribbing from ERO superintendent Harry Laughlin's "Model Eugenical Sterilization Law," Strode drafted a bill that would withstand constitutional challenge. Avoiding buzzwords like "eugenics," Strode emphasized the procedural aspects of the law rather than its effect. Sterilization became a rational response to social problems rather than an experiment in social engineering.

Hereditary feeblemindedness called for a new form of "therapy." Public health doctors could kill germs, but sick germ-plasm could only be "cured" by preventing its transmission through segregation, sterilization, or euthanasia. Segregation was costly, euthanasia was inhumane and immoral, leaving sterilization the only option.[47]

Relying on the "three C's" of "careful" procedure and "competent, and conscientious authority," the bill appealed to the paternalism common to both the Progressive Era and southern social mores. Strode invoked the menace of the feebleminded and the economic burden they posed to underscore sterilization's benefits. Strode used the eugenic metaphor to remind legislators of conventional ideas about "good" and "bad" blood among their communities. His assertion that sterilization was indicated for individuals "afflicted with hereditary forms of insanity that are recurrent, idiocy, imbecility, feeble-mindedness or epilepsy," referred lawmakers to families they knew. This rhetorical shift allowed lawmakers to act on the commonsense wisdom of the stockyard and the ledger book, as well as the esoteric laws of the genetics laboratory. Strode's language familiarized lay legislators with the normal science of the day.[48]

Strode's strategy assuaged politicians' fears that the eugenicists might be out to "get" them or their families. While few lawmakers identified with the institutionalized feebleminded, they might have feared a state investigation of their own hereditary background. Procedural safeguards ensured that those with the means to pay lawyers could effectively challenge a sterilization hearing. Those without these resources had to rely upon state-appointed legal guardians, who were paid no matter the outcome. Segregation's science thus buttressed class prerogatives, placing immense discretionary power in the hands of purportedly objective professionals: the superintendent of the institution, backed by its board of directors.[49]

Combining the menace of the feebleminded with the new diagnostic category of "social inadequacy" widened the scope of the law's application. "Social inadequacy," unlike feeblemindedness, required no special training to identify. Misfits, ne'er-do-wells, transients, criminals, prostitutes, the indolent, and the poor could be shoehorned into this category. Strode's use of the capacious classification "the probable potential parent of socially inadequate offspring," which came directly from Harry Laughlin's model law, further enlarged both the power of administrators and the group liable to sterilization. Combined with the law's concluding sections, these assertions brought all Virginians under the shadow of eugenic sterilization. Priddy and DeJarnette hoped the law would establish efficient bureaucratic machinery for rotating the feebleminded through the operating room. The law's coda immunized board members who ordered sterilizations, physicians who performed them, and "any other person legally participating in [sterilizations]" from civil or criminal prosecution, revealing the lasting impact of *Mallory v. Priddy.*[50]

The law received an enthusiastic reception by the Virginia General Assembly. Strode's effort to avoid inflammatory rhetoric worked; the *Richmond News-Leader* remarked that the measure "was not as drastic as senators at first thought," and the Senate only amended the bill "so as to provide that consent of the patient's guardian or parent must be given." The Senate passed the bill 30 to 0, while the House passed it by a vote of 75 to 2. Governor Trinkle signed the bill into law on March 15, 1924.[51]

Strode ascribed the bill's success to public support, "so great had been the change of public sentiment" since Carrington's 1910 effort. Virginia's eugenical propagandists—physicians at the state's two medical schools, undergraduate teachers of eugenics, and high school teachers taught to think and instruct eugenically—had transformed public opinion. Public interest was so lax that the bill hardly merited newspaper coverage and elicited no editorial protest. Shifting social mores had normalized sterilization.[52]

After the legislature passed the law, Drs. Priddy and DeJarnette set to testing it in the courts. Affirmation of the law would cement the state's right to "adjust" the quality of its population, protecting the American race and empowering physicians like Priddy and DeJarnette with unprecedented power. To ensure this outcome, Priddy, Strode, and former member of the Colony's board Irving Whitehead worked hard to construct a "friendly" case. Priddy chose the case of eighteen-year-old Carrie Buck to test the law. With the epigram "Three generations of imbeciles are enough," America's great libertarian jurist, Oliver Wendell Holmes Jr. consigned generations of Americans to compulsory sterilization. This signal triumph for the eugenics movement represented less the self-evident truths revealed by genetics, and more the ruthless determination of eugenicists.[53]

Carrie Buck hailed from Charlottesville, seat of Virginia eugenics. Born in 1906 to her poverty-stricken mother, Emma Buck, Carrie lived a life of destitution until her death in 1983. At age three or four, Carrie became the foster daughter of Mr. and Mrs. J. F. Dobbs, until they had her committed, in January 1924, to the Virginia Colony for the Epileptic and Feebleminded. The Dobbses alleged "it was impossible for them to care for her or control her any longer," although they really turned Carrie out to hide their shame. The Dobbses' nephew had raped and impregnated Carrie. During her commitment hearings, the Dobbses noted that Carrie's mother, Emma, was in

Carrie and Emma Buck on the grounds of the Lynchburg Colony, the day before *Buck v. Priddy* was tried in 1924. Photographed by the eugenics researcher Arthur H. Estabrook. (Arthur Estabrook Papers, M. E. Grenander Department of Special Collections & Archives, University of Albany Libraries)

the Colony and that Carrie was epileptic, subject to "some hallucinations and some outbreaks of temper," dishonesty, and "moral delinquency." On the basis of the Dobbses' testimony and that of two physicians who diagnosed Carrie "feebleminded within the meaning of the law," the Juvenile Court of Charlottesville ordered Carrie's commitment.[54]

In September 1925, one month after the sterilization law went into effect, Carrie confronted the Colony's Special Board of Directors. During a perfunctory hearing, Strode asked Carrie, "Do you care to say anything about having this operation performed on you?" Trusting her foster parents, Carrie responded, "No sir, I have not, it is up to my people." With her mother already an inmate of the Colony and her foster parents trying to hide their nephew's assault, Carrie stood at the board's mercy. The panel concluded that Carrie was indeed feebleminded and a likely "parent of socially inadequate offspring," ordering that, "she may be sexually sterilized without detriment to her health, and that the welfare of the said Carrie Buck and of society will be promoted by such sterilization."[55]

Appealed to the Circuit Court of Amherst County, *Buck v. Priddy* was contested by old friends Aubrey Strode and Irving Whitehead before their mutual acquaintance Judge Bennet Gordon. Charlottesville neighbors testified that Carrie came from a "defective" family, as Carrie's mother, Emma, was "absolutely irresponsible" and constantly seeking charitable relief. Carrie's sister Doris was portrayed as a "very stormy individual . . . incorrigible." Of

Carrie Buck's infant daughter Vivian on the lap of her foster grandmother, Alice Dobbs, in Charlottesville, the day before *Buck v. Priddy* was tried (1924). Did Vivian's attention to the camera, rather than the shiny object in her foster grandmother's hand, result in her being labeled "not quite normal?" (Arthur Estabrook Papers, M. E. Grenander Department of Special Collections & Archives, University of Albany Libraries)

Carrie's passing notes to boys in grammar school, a nurse swore that "if a girl of sixteen had written that kind of note" she would be sent to a reformatory for prostitutes. This established Carrie's "moral delinquency" and precocious sexual appetite.

Mary Duke and Caroline Wilhelm, social workers for the Red Cross, supplied additional damning evidence. Mary Duke testified that Emma Buck was "of bad character" and that her daughter Carrie "simply didn't seem to be a bright girl." Ms. Wilhelm declared that Carrie and those like her were "more or less at the mercy of other people [because of their feeblemindedness and were]... very likely to have illegitimate children." In her professional opinion, Carrie represented a "distinct liability to society." Ms. Wilhelm had examined Carrie's infant child, born out of wedlock and not quite eight months old, and labeled it "not quite a normal baby" because it had "a look about it that is not quite normal" although "just what it is I can't tell."[56]

Irving Whitehead's defense of Carrie relied on anemic cross-examinations and perfunctory, but indecisive, objections against hearsay evidence. His half-hearted efforts evinced his true motives. Just seven years earlier, as director of the Colony board, Whitehead himself had urged the board to authorize Priddy's early sterilizations. Whitehead and Priddy concurred: the feebleminded should be sterilized. Rather than being an advocate for Carrie's constitutional rights, Whitehead conspired with her adversaries.[57]

Two eugenical experts testified and received gentle treatment from Whitehead. Harry Laughlin sent in a deposition from the ERO. Basing his "scientific" opinion on secondhand evidence provided by Priddy, Laughlin concluded that the Bucks "belong to the shiftless, ignorant, and worthless class of anti-social whites of the South." Arthur Estabrook, a sociologist cum eugenicist and ERO fieldworker, appeared at trial. Estabrook met Strode through his wife, Louisa Strode, who was herself a disciple of eugenics. After a cursory examination, Estabrook pronounced Carrie Buck both "feebleminded" and "socially inadequate."[58]

The testimony of Virginia's homegrown eugenics experts, DeJarnette and Priddy, underscored the emerging gender bias of Virginia eugenicists, which derived from the sexual double standard and class prejudice. DeJarnette averred that the feebleminded "are the hewers of wood and the drawers of water, and there is not very much more likelihood that they would spread venereal disease if sterilized than if they were not." Priddy concurred that the feebleminded were a labor pool. He asserted that while some eight to ten thousand Virginians might be eligible for colonization, "some of those people wouldn't come within the Virginia definition for sterilization." Priddy viewed this as "fortunate," else the state "wouldn't have any hewers of wood or drawers of water." Priddy and his colleagues envisioned a eugenically "pure" underclass, where "like breeds with like," reinforcing the social structure and providing a tractable labor force free from crime, disease, and immorality. Priddy asserted that the demand for domestic help was "so great that probably we could get rid of half of our young women of average [moronic] intelligence" if they were sterilized. "People don't care to take them when there is the constant chance of them becoming mothers," Priddy complained. Rather than supposing that these women might be coerced into sex and impregnated by male employers—branding erstwhile "respectable" men as sexually deviant and unfit—Priddy assumed the women's unfitness. He ignored that "respectable" people were embarrassed, as Carrie Buck's foster parents were, by pregnancy's mute testimony to male defectiveness expressed as sexual abuse, marital infidelity, and moral turpitude. Instead, Priddy implied it was the feebleminded woman's fault for lacking the sense to resist sexual overtures and assault. And, Priddy and DeJarnette's attitudes toward the "feebleminded" and lower class induced a particularly ironic myopia: if all the feebleminded were sterilized, who then would take their jobs once the sterile generation passed? Neither man identified the future's "hewers of wood and drawers of water."[59]

Strode and Whitehead's collusion, buttressed by expert testimony, created an ironclad case against the Bucks. Strode expressed his confidence in the outcome by writing "Sterilization of Defectives," a eugenic primer for Virginia's legal community. He hoped to establish "the limits of the police power of an American state over the liberty of persons within its jurisdiction to reproduce their kind" by defending sterilization as "advanced eugenical science" and "enlightened medical practice." Strode argued that sterilization freed individuals otherwise destined to "languish for life in custody" at state expense, allowing them to "be discharged from custody and become self supporting to the great advantage of themselves and society." Posing the rhetorical question, "May one liberty [physical freedom] be thus restored through the deprivation of another liberty [the power to procreate]?" Strode answered with a resounding "Yes." In November, Virginia's highest court concurred, clearing the way for an appeal to the U.S. Supreme Court.[60]

In April 1927, the Supreme Court heard *Buck v. Bell*, Strode's attempt to use eugenics to weld police power to public health. Priddy died before the case rose to the Supreme Court, so Dr. John H. Bell, Priddy's successor, became the named defendant. Bell, like Priddy and DeJarnette, was an ardent eugenicist. Announcing its editorial support, the *Richmond Times-Dispatch* remarked that the law was "defended by the State as medically progressive." Indeed, Strode relied on one of the most progressive technologies in medicine and public health to cinch his argument for sterilization. He introduced the precedent set by the U.S. Supreme Court in the 1904 inoculation case *Jacobson v. Massachusetts. Jacobson* affirmed the right of a state to punish individuals who refused a mandatory smallpox inoculation for public school pupils, reinforcing the state's right to safeguard the public health. Strode's use of *Jacobson* cast eugenics in its most favorable light—as preventive medicine, not experimental science. Relying on *Jacobson* appealed to the progressive beliefs of the Court's senior member, Justice Oliver Wendell Holmes Jr., who had helped to decide *Jacobson.* Strode and Justice Holmes understood the right to procreate as affecting the public health and, as such, subject to the control of the state's police power.[61]

Holmes's ringing endorsement of Virginia's eugenical sterilization statute seems foreordained, despite his belief in judicial restraint. In *Buck,* Holmes's faith in a superior American race and his sympathy with eugenics harmonized with the Virginia law, allowing him to write an opinion resounding with eugenic overtones. The ruling had both symbolic and material importance for

Virginians. If Holmes, the Court's ancient Nestor, upheld the law, certainly Virginia was on the progressive track toward utopia.

Holmes expressed his eugenical views in public writings and private correspondence. Holmes privileged biological over political interventions because he "disliked the self-righteous, but he had no sympathy for the weak." As early as 1915, lashing out against socialist utopianism, Holmes wrote, "wholesale social regeneration . . . cannot be affected appreciably by tinkering with the institution of property but only by taking in hand life and trying to build a race." Particularly the American branch of the Nordic race needed cultivation. Rather than supporting the reforms of social meliorists, Holmes felt that "while propagation is free and we do all we can to keep the products, however bad, alive, I listen with some skepticism to plans for fundamental amelioration. I should expect more from systematic prevention of the survival of the unfit."[62]

As a Civil War veteran who carried shards of shrapnel in his body, Holmes believed he knew something about inhumane social interventions. Compared to war, the sterilization statute seemed merciful. He brought all his convictions to bear in the blast he issued as the Court's opinion. The old soldier wrote: "the public welfare may call upon the best citizens for their lives. . . . It would be strange if it could not call upon those who already sap the strength of the State for these lesser sacrifices, often not felt to be such by those concerned, in order to prevent our being swamped with incompetence." In Holmes's reasoning, "It is better for all the world, if instead of waiting to execute degenerate offspring for crime, or to let them starve for their imbecility, society can prevent those who are manifestly unfit from continuing their kind." Drawing specifically on Strode's logic, Holmes averred: "The principle that sustains compulsory vaccination is broad enough to cover cutting the Fallopian tubes. Three generations of imbeciles are enough." Holmes consigned Carrie Buck, and all those society viewed as like her, to the surgeon's knife. Afterwards, Holmes wrote to a friend that eugenic sterilization "was getting near the first principal [sic] of real reform." The decision, he told another associate, "gave me pleasure."[63]

The reaction in Carrie Buck's hometown can be gauged by the editorial in the *Charlottesville Daily Progress* praising the *Buck* decision. "Over the protests of many who held up their hands in holy horror at the thought of merely discussing such a thing publicly, much less actually practicing it with the sanction of the state," the new law "placed Virginia in the front rank of the states which are committed to a progressive program of welfare legislation." The editor lauded the "obvious wisdom of this highly beneficial law" and claimed that Carrie Buck was a fit "subject for this type of treatment." The paper heaped plaudits on Holmes, "that incomparable jurist who, despite his eighty-five years, unfailingly is found in sympathy with the most progressive tendencies in our social machine," who "delivered a concise, convincing opinion, which is a genuine classic." The editors liked Holmes's prose so well that they reprinted the decision's peroration, "which bristles with the wisdom that has been nurtured by a long judicial experience, and which in Mr. Holmes, is the companion trait of a profound social insight." Seldom before the Progressive Era did southern newspapers laud the opinions held by former officers of the Grand Army of the Republic. The editor concluded, "Virginia is fortunate in having had this eminently sane and beneficial law, safely run the gamut of judicial review and permanently enrolled upon its statute books." The following October, after Whitehead filed a pro forma request for a rehearing, which the Court denied, Dr. Bell sterilized Carrie Buck, the first of some 8,300 Virginians to be so "treated" between 1924 and 1972.[64]

Five days after Bell sterilized Carrie Buck, the *Richmond News-Leader* ran a front-page article entitled "Says Eugenists Do Cause Harm." The newspaper reported the criticisms of Dr. Raymond Pearl. "Superior people do not produce superior children," the article began, quoting Pearl's statement that, "In preaching as they do that like produces like, and inferior people produce inferior children, the orthodox eugenists are going contrary to the best established facts of science, and are, in the long run, doing their cause harm." Pearl's opinion carried great weight; he was, after all, a professor of biology at Johns Hopkins University. With this statement, Pearl undercut the logic behind Holmes's "three generations of imbeciles" pronouncement that condemned Carrie Buck to sterilization. Pearl's paper and the scientific criticism of eugenics, however, came too late for Carrie Buck, her sister, and thousands of other Virginians and Americans.[65]

The convergence of Virginia's social climate, progressive reform, and eugenic theories paved the way for the enactment of a law that violated the human and civil rights of some Virginians. The noblesse oblige of the fabled Virginia Cavaliers, the scions of the First Families of Virginia, now manifested itself in the eugenic reform of mental health care. Protests for the humane treatment of the institutionalized, and the conviction that sterilization was more merciful than institutional segregation, resonated with Virginia's established patterns of paternalism.

Simultaneously, however, the image of the "feebleminded" as a "menace" to society dehumanized institutional patients. Indeed, the segregation of the mentally disabled into the subhuman categories of imbecile, idiot, and moron paralleled the developing image of the menacing, subhuman "black beast-rapist." For the good of the public, both groups needed eugenic control. The sterilization act formed one prong of Virginia's bid to lead the nation in progressive social engineering. The Racial Integrity Act—propounded by men like Earnest Sevier Cox, John Powell, and the public health department physician Walter Plecker—formed another. That the U.S. Congress passed the eugenically motivated Immigration Restriction Act *after* Virginia's bills had become law reveals the consonance between eugenic thinking in Virginia and throughout the nation in 1924.

5

"MONGREL VIRGINIANS"

Eugenics and the
"Race Question"

THE SELF-STYLED ETHNOLOGIST EARNEST Sevier Cox announced Virginia's eugenic fears regarding the race question. Introducing his book *White America*, Cox wrote: "the Negro problem is a part of the greater problem of heredity. When eugenics seeks to eliminate the unfit and establish the fit it has for its purpose not the betterment of physical types merely, but the establishment of those types of greatest value to progressive civilization." In Cox's eyes, African Americans represented "an unfit type" and were "a matter of concern for the eugenist." According to Cox: "Those who seek to maintain the white race in its purity within the United States are working in harmony with the ideals of eugenics. Asiatic exclusion and Negro repatriation are expressions of the eugenic ideal."[1]

Eugenic sterilization promised to neutralize the "menace of the feeble-minded," but it did little to alleviate fears of miscegenation. As Virginia eugenicists mobilized for the 1924 sterilization law, an allied group promoted a law to defend "racial integrity." Led by the famous pianist John Leslie Powell; Virginia's registrar of vital statistics, Dr. Walter Ashby Plecker; and Cox, Virginians organized the Anglo-Saxon Clubs of America (ASCOA) to build public policy from academic eugenics. Melding eugenic arguments with traditional negrophobia, the ASCOA secured passage of the Racial Integrity Act of 1924 (RIA).

Virginia's adoption of the RIA paralleled passage of the federal Johnson Immigration Restriction Act of 1924 (JIRA). In both composition and ideology, the ASCOA resembled the Immigration Restriction League, the principal lobbyists for the JIRA. Both groups championed racial purity and the defense of the "American race." Virginia eugenicists dreaded black/white amalgamation to the same degree that their northern counterparts feared marriage between southeastern Europeans, Jews, and Old Stock Americans. Elites in both sections lumped these marginalized groups into the "unfit," merging racial, class, and gender prejudices. Links between Powell, Cox, Plecker and national-level eugenicists highlight these Virginians' desire to cast their state as the model for "progressive race management." Despite generations of well-documented interracial liaisons, these Virginians sought to use the force of law, impelled by the logic of science, to crush interracial intimacy.[2]

Virginia's RIA resulted from a long trend of hereditarian thinking. From Jefferson forward, Virginia scientists, doctors, and educators bombarded laypeople with scientifically justified bigotry that dehumanized African Americans and poor whites. Described in animalistic imagery, black genes became subhuman genes. Virginia's medical schools taught various theories of "racial medicine," leading to the stigmatization of blacks as repositories of disease. In spite of this purportedly endemic disease, blacks failed to die off and solve the "Negro problem" through extinction. Thus eugenicists recast the racial prognosis from a terminal condition for blacks to a chronic threat to whites. This paralleled the way white elites transmogrified intraracial class tensions into the menace of the feebleminded, consigning poor whites to the unfit. In both cases, a purportedly inferior group posed a dire threat to the superior group, necessitating and justifying astringent control.

Gauged by coverage in the African American press, black Virginians paid little attention to the eugenic sterilization bill, whereas the RIA inspired both black support and protest. Articulating their own version of eugenics to secure black racial purity against white depredations, some black intellectuals accepted the principle of human improvement while denying the existence of a racial hierarchy. Only eugenics that cast all African Americans as unfit was threatening.[3]

African Americans co-opted segregation's science, creating a liberation narrative diametrically opposed to white eugenicists' efforts to constrain black agency. Ironically, by the 1920s some African Americans advanced notions of eugenic salvation that harmonized with the ideas of racist whites.

The rising popularity of Marcus Garvey's Universal Negro Improvement Association (UNIA) among black Virginians provided the basis for the political mobilization of black "separatist" eugenics.[4]

Sex, Crime, and Disease: Diagnosing Virginia's African Americans

In the decades surrounding the turn of the twentieth century, racial tensions terrified white Americans. Frequent and spectacular lynchings and race riots sparked intense debate about racial animosity. Southern whites, many old enough to remember the antebellum era, embraced the myth of black racial declension. Arguing that blacks prospered under slavery, southerners—led by physicians, scientists, and historians—asserted that African Americans' hereditary inability to compete with whites destined blacks to extinction.[5]

Despite their belief in the innate inferiority of all blacks, white Virginians maintained that their black population represented the best of the race. In 1917, Julian Street argued in *Collier's Magazine* that "only the bad ones [slaves] were 'sold South.' . . . Naturally, then, the Virginia negro of to-day, being descended from 'selected stock'—as slave dealers' advertisements used to put it—may be expected to average somewhat higher in the human virtues than the offspring of slaves of the black belt." While extolling "Virginia darkies" as the best-bred slaves and servants, Virginia physicians argued that increased crime, sexual perversion, and disease marked the new generation of blacks, born since Reconstruction.[6]

Ruminations on the "Negro problem" filled the *Virginia Medical Semi-Monthly*. In May 1893, Dr. Hunter McGuire, a Richmond physician and president of the American Medical Association, invited Dr. G. Frank Lydston, professor of genito-urinary surgery and syphilology at the Chicago College of Physicians and Surgeons, to provide "some scientific explanation of the sexual perversion in the negro of the present day." McGuire, like Paul Barringer and many other southerners, believed that before the Civil War a "rape by a negro of a white woman was almost unknown; now the newspapers tell us how common it is." Rising rates of insanity and disease all indicated to McGuire that African Americans were reverting to savagery and destined for extinction. McGuire noted that "All history . . . shows that no inferior race, without amalgamation, can exist for very many years in contact with the dominant white man, it is the frightful 'survival of the fittest.'" Both McGuire and Lydston hoped to forestall this fate, or to allow it to happen "humanely" rather than through disease or race war. Their correspondence limned the debate in familiar terms that set the groundwork for subsequent racial medicine and eugenics.[7]

Lydston believed that blacks manifested "a distinct tendency to reversion to type." He argued that "cross breeding [with whites] will never eliminate" black atavism because "the result is a degenerate type which very frequently has all the evil propensities of the negro *plus* those of the white man, associated with a physique of a much more degenerate type than either of the ancestors." The rare instances of "mulattoes" exhibiting refined traits resulted from "more intimate association with the white race as well as from white heredity"—white-controlled environment could allow white genes to express themselves in otherwise atavistic blacks. Nevertheless, Lydston concluded that the "negro question [would] . . . . be settled by the physical degeneracy and death of the negro race" and nothing could stop it.[8]

Considering black criminality, Lydston declared, "there is only one logical method of dealing with capital crimes and criminals as a habitual class— namely, *castration*." Lydston preferred castration to execution because it stopped reproduction among criminals, and, "a few emasculated negroes scattered around" would further inhibit rape. "Executed, they would be forgotten; castrated and free, they would be a constant warning and ever-present admonition to others of their race." Lydston's solution wed the ritualized violence of spectacle lynchings, which often featured the emasculation of the victim, to the modern, antiseptic rationalism of the surgical theater.[9]

A decade later, the *Virginia Medical Semi-Monthly* began publishing the findings of Dr. William F. Drewry, Virginia's leading expert on the mental health of African Americans. Drewry announced that increases in insanity and tuberculosis were "a result as well as an indication of race degeneration" among Virginia's blacks. He concluded that "depraved and immoral habits have brought about more widespread venereal diseases" among blacks, dysgenic taints "transmitted to the third or fourth generation." The publication of Drewry's work indicates that the editors believed the piece represented sound medical scholarship.[10]

Rather than prompting a reconsideration of African inferiority, African American survival redoubled white fears of "passing" and that miscegenation could rend the fabric of southern civilization. To assuage this anxiety, eugenicists used their science to support the 1924 RIA, the 1926 Public Assemblages Act that mandated segregated seating at public events, and the 1930 statute that defined whiteness. The hereditarian opinions espoused by most academics, physicians, and public health officials provided lobbyists with powerful allies when they approached the legislature.

Promoting a Pure White Race

Academic, propagandist, and moral zealot, Earnest Sevier Cox became a tireless, lifelong crusader for the "progressive" reform of race relations in Virginia. A real estate agent and self-proclaimed ethnologist, Cox wrote the scientific manifesto undergirding Virginia's eugenic RIA. His overarching concern was the repatriation of all African Americans. He leagued with reactionary politicians like Mississippi senators Theodore Bilbo and James K. Vardaman, and North Dakota's William Langer to promote a number of colonization bills between the 1910s and 1960s. His lobbying introduced him to numerous eugenicists and race supremacists. He also associated with Marcus Garvey, Amy Jacques Garvey, and the UNIA. Earnest in pursuit of repatriation, Cox acted "in the name of eugenics," agreeing with Garvey that "mongrelizing" races through racial intermixture would destroy civilization. Prohibiting intermarriage seemed an expedient stop-gap until repatriation might be achieved. Using eugenics and genetics as a foundation, Cox erected an ideological edifice that stood for fifty years.[11]

Cox attributed all his achievements to good heredity. Like most eugenicists, he was intensely proud of his heritage, claiming relation to the First Families of Virginia and the Tennessee "Volunteers," in both places the "pioneers" who "showed aptitude and leadership in beating back marauding Indians," proving their superiority. After study at Roane College, the Moody Bible Institute, and Vanderbilt University, the University of Chicago admitted him to graduate study under its famed sociologists in the summer of 1906. "But the book that gripped me powerfully," Cox recalled, "was *Social Control* by Dr. E. A. Ross." Cox's persistence and Ross's inspiration would carry him around the world, extolling the "Aryan type of man particularly the Celto-German stock."[12]

In a letter to his sister Emma, Cox revealed the spark that kindled his racial separatism: the 1906 Atlanta race riot—a racial pogrom ignited by false reports of black men raping white women. Cox unleashed a diatribe mixing chivalry, Christianity, and patriotism. He claimed "the disposal of the Negro" was more important than "the principle of representative government for which the Revolution was fought or the principle of centrilization [*sic*] of government which produced the fiercest conflict of all history—the Civil War." He believed that whites killed blacks in order "to protect those whom God has ordained that we must protect"—white women. According to Cox, "the wonder of future generations will be, not that forty brutes have been sacrificed but that the whole brute race has not in red stains been blotted from our fair civilization." There was "but one way of escape," namely, repatriation.[13]

Cox never transcended these biases, ingrained during his southern child-hood. In South Africa, Cox experienced his eugenic epiphany as he "realized that a mixture of blood is the real danger outside of America, the German possessions excepted." Repulsed by "the prevalency of rape by Natives upon European women," Cox was horrified by consensual sexual congress that re-sulted in children light enough to pass. "[The] mix-blooded, if passed [*sic*] of property, may gain entrance to white society," Cox groaned. This hybridiza-tion of genes and wealth, repugnant to Cox's southern sensibilities, seemed to explain the decline of Egyptian civilization. Just as Madison Grant was writ-ing *The Passing of the Great Race*, Cox independently struck upon the same thesis: civilizations fall as the result of interracial procreation. Cox became the South's analog to northerners like Grant and Lothrop Stoddard. Indeed, the three men would become allies in fighting America's race problem.

Cox's first book, *White America*, resulted from his five-year trek around the world. According to Cox, America needed "those who believe in and will spread the cult of Caucasianism," a secular creed similar to Galton's hopes for eugenics. America needed to "forget past differences between North and South in a common purpose to preserve a common civilization." Cox's appeal to a common patriotism, founded on a white racial identity, harkened back to Thomas Jefferson. Cox chose this rhetoric self-consciously, quoting Jefferson and Lincoln in defense of repatriation. Civilization could be saved if Ameri-cans strengthened the color line through eugenics: rigid segregation, strict antimiscegenation laws, and immigration restriction.[14]

Virginia welcomed Cox home when he returned to the United States in 1915, although Cox and his Virginia allies had difficulty finding a publisher. Putnam's rejected Cox's manuscript "Decay of Culture" in 1917. Cox's military service during World War I further delayed publication. In the aftermath of the 1919 race riots, Cox argued that "the recent violent symptoms of race dis-cord between the blacks and whites should do much in preparing the national mind" for his ideas. Putnam's disagreed, rejecting a revised manuscript. Cox contacted the powerful New York attorney Madison Grant, whose book was fueling nativist and eugenic fires. Grant suggested that Cox elaborate on the notion that Native Americans in Virginia had so thoroughly interbred with blacks as to have become blacks. This contention mirrored Grant's belief that "one race or one type or one strain replaces another and in the mixture the lower types prevail." This interchange would have tremendous ramifications for Virginia's racial minorities in the coming years. With Grant's help, Cox tightened his manuscript and met like-minded eugenicists including Cox's Virginia sponsor, John Leslie Powell.[15]

Powell, the brightest star in Richmond's social elite, recognized as one of America's greatest concert pianists and composers, was an individual of "local import" to Cox. In 1922, Powell and Cox founded the Anglo-Saxon Clubs of America (ASCOA) as an alternative to the Ku Klux Klan. The ASCOA blossomed to over four hundred members by June 1923. The chairman, president, and secretary of the Richmond Post had all been Klansmen. Cox's ties to the Klan, fostered by his association with Powell, became career-long lifelines to committed support for white supremacy.[16]

Powell circulated among the most influential Virginians, wielding a great deal of influence. He graduated from the University of Virginia in 1901, when Paul Brandon Barringer was at the height of his power. Powell's ideological program reflects Barringer's thought, as well as the ideas of Grant, Stoddard, and Cox. Correspondence between Powell, Cox, and Walter Plecker also reveals Powell's close personal friendship with Ivey Lewis. Informed by Virginia's leading academics, the ASCOA drew on the deepest pockets in Richmond.[17]

With direct ties to Virginia's academic eugenicists as well as to national eugenics propagandists, Virginia's colleges and universities hosted chapters of the ASCOA. By June 1923, the society's informational pamphlets listed twelve Virginia posts, including chapters at the University of Virginia, the University of Richmond, the College of William and Mary, Virginia Polytechnic Institute, and Hampden-Sydney College. Harvey Jordan joined the University of Virginia chapter; both Ivey Lewis and Paul Barringer were likely members. Of the student members, president John Powell Williams became a physician; vice president O. Arthur Kirkman and secretary Curtis Simpson became lawyers. Thus, the ASCOA tapped the loyalties of men destined to enter Virginia's professional elite.[18]

Eschewing the Klan's extralegal violence and inflammatory rhetoric, the ASCOA sought "the preservation and maintenance of Anglo-Saxon ideals and civilization in America" through "the strengthening of Anglo-Saxon instincts, traditions and principles among representatives of our original American stock," immigration restriction, and "the fundamental and final solutions of our racial problems in general, most especially of the Negro problem."[19]

Beginning in June 1923 with the provocatively titled newspaper essay "Is White America to Become a Negroid Nation?" John Powell mounted a blitz to advance the ASCOA cause. Mixing negrophobia, ethnology, and eugenic theory, Powell and Cox concocted dire predictions for southern white civilization. Cox and Powell shared the fears of Virginia physicians who had worried about "racial degeneration" at the turn of the century. The time lag between physicians' theorizing and the ASCOA's organizing reflects the slow dispersal of ideas from the leading edge of science to the trailing edge of society. Powell and Cox's eugenic negrophobia appealed to many other southerners, especially after the publication of *White America*.

Cox himself bore the expense of publishing the first edition of *White America*. Madison Grant and Lothrop Stoddard lavished praise on Cox's book. The Eugenics Record Office's Harry Laughlin proclaimed: "It is a stirring volume. . . . America is still worth saving for the white race, and it can be done." Harvard's William McDougall applauded Cox's separatist thesis. R. W. Shufeldt, one of America's premier naturalists, called it "the ablest book on the negro problem." Cox's personal hero, Edward A. Ross, delivered a backhanded compliment: "Your book *White America* is a staggering one and it will probably take years for me to know where I stand regarding it." The secretary of the Southern Cooperative League for Education and Social Service wrote that *White America* "points the way of salvation for both races." These reviews helped *White America* become a textbook for university professors and the handbook for southern white supremacists. Ivey Lewis read the book "with great interest and approval." Lewis assigned it regularly as a text in his eugenics course and invited Cox to speak before his class.[20]

Cox thus established himself as the ideological authority on racial integrity. The press repeatedly referred to him as an "expert ethnologist," as much because of his self-promotion and the plaudits of his supporters as because of any certified expertise. A scathing review of *White America* commented: "Now there is no doubt that Cox is a student, for he has collected a great amount of historical material and has studied the race problem on every continent. But there is plenty of doubt as to his being a scientific student. His logic . . . is faulty at every step." Despite being dismissed in the scientific press beyond the eugenics movement, Cox convinced himself and others that he was a "renowned" authority.[21]

Fingers in the Dike: John Powell, Walter Plecker, and the Racial Integrity Act

Cox, Powell, and the state registrar of vital statistics, Dr. Walter Plecker, constituted a triumvirate linking science, spectacle, and government enforcement. Cox provided the ideology, Powell's fame attracted attention, while Plecker policed and enforced racial integrity through the Bureau of Vital Statistics. In June 1923, with the formal incorporation of the ASCOA, Powell stepped up pressure for a law guarding racial integrity.

The very structure of the ASCOA and its women's auxiliary embodied the larger masculinist ideals of segregation's science—men talked, women worked. Powell relied on the suasive influence of ASCOA's women's auxiliary, headed by his wife, Louise Burleigh Powell. Debarred from full membership, ensconced on the pedestal of southern white female purity and republican motherhood, female supporters of the ASCOA conducted much of the grassroots lobbying. Unmarried women were trained as "fieldworkers" and collected observational data. The research enabled by Sweet Briar College's eugenics courses unleashed a reign of eugenic harassment that victimized Virginia's Native American and black populations for over forty years.[22]

As young women ferreted out "proof" of the eugenic threat, Powell and Cox deluged the newspaper-reading public with the eugenics of racial purity. Virginia's two leading newspapers, the *Richmond Times-Dispatch* and the *Richmond News-Leader*, published dozens of articles between June 1923 and March 1924 promoting the ASCOA. Cox and Powell's inflammatory "Is White America to Become a Negroid Nation?" illustrated their reliance on eugenic principles. Powell averred that, "the development of eugenical science" proved that "in crossing two varieties [races], the more primitive, the less highly specialized always dominates" both physically and psychologically. Only antimiscegenation law offered "a final solution" to the race problem.[23]

Cox echoed all of Powell's claims. Virginia, Cox announced, could lead America to eugenic utopia. "If after three centuries of race contact Virginia perfects rather than abandons the color line such act cannot have other than a beneficial effect upon those States which are without a legal color line," Cox wrote. Powell and Cox called Virginians to the barricades in defense of the American race, aided by powerful newspaper editors. Powell's steady stream of alarmist articles and addresses curried elite support, convincing or cowing legislators because "white politicians were not likely to risk the consequences of being portrayed as supporters of 'social equality' or opponents of white political and cultural dominance."[24]

The RIA had three salient provisions. First, it required that every Virginian file a certificate recording the individual's racial composition. Willfully misrepresenting race would be a felony punishable by a year in jail. Second, it mandated that all marriage license applicants present their racial certificates to local clerks because "it shall hereafter be unlawful for any white person in this State to marry any save a white person." Finally, the bill defined whiteness as "a person who has no trace whatsoever of any blood other than Caucasian; but persons who have less than one sixty-fourth of the blood of an American Indian and have no other non-Caucasic blood shall be deemed to be white persons." The final clause, often referred to as the "Pocahontas exception," prevented descendants of Pocahontas and John Rolfe—many of Virginia's most prominent citizens—from being labeled racially "tainted." Virginia law had banned interracial marriage since 1691; the RIA shored up old prejudices with eugenical science. Dr. Plecker would become Virginia's gatekeeper to whiteness, birth, and death. To ensure the law's passage, Powell unleashed his star power before the General Assembly.[25]

Testifying before the legislature, Powell posed as a dispassionate, scientific observer of the race problem seeking to ensure every race's integrity. Powell provided anecdotal evidence of racial amalgamation from around the state, focusing on the mountain counties of Rockbridge and Amherst—the same counties Harvey Jordan had identified in 1911 as prime locations for eugenic studies of miscegenation. Powell also read into the record testimonials from Madison Grant, Lothrop Stoddard, and the noted eugenicist Franklin H. Giddings. The *Richmond Times-Dispatch* ran a front-page article the next day, quoting Grant's assertion that "it would be living up to Virginia's great traditions if she took the lead in legislation of this character and set, once for all, the stamp of her approval upon the importance of maintaining race purity." The *Richmond News-Leader* reported that, "[Powell] painted the 'spectre of miscegenation' so clearly that he shocked and startled his hearers." Powell played on widespread apprehension about passing and its consequences to alarm Old Virginian members of the American race.[26]

Lobbyists made a number of concessions to secure ratification. Legislators, concerned about the cost of registration and the indeterminacy of old records, made registration mandatory only for those born since 1912; retroactive registration was voluntary. The Pocahontas exception was raised to "one-sixteenth"—equating to one great-great-grandparent of "pure" Native American derivation. To mollify the ASCOA, the burden of proof for racial heritage fell on the individual, since the clerks were authorized to "withhold the granting of the [marriage] license until satisfactory proof is produced that both applicants are 'white persons' as provided for in this act." The law ostensibly protected both races: "The clerk or deputy clerk shall use the same care to assure himself that both applicants are colored when that fact is claimed." Yet Powell's pronouncement that he acted in the interest of all races rang hollow, since the act did not forbid marriages between different "colored" races. The amended bill passed with token opposition. Among those voting in favor of the RIA was a young member of the House from Charlottesville, Lemuel Smith. A 1916 Virginia graduate, Smith also voted in favor of eugenic sterilization. Thirty-one years later, Assemblyman Smith would be Justice Smith of the Virginia Supreme Court of Appeals. As a member of that court in 1955, he would hear the case *Naim v. Naim,* and uphold the annulment of an interracial marriage on the basis of the RIA—he understood and approved of eugenics. Governor E. Lee Trinkle signed the bill into law on March 20, 1924, earning plaudits from the ASCOA by registering himself and his family. Trinkle also helped Walter Plecker orchestrate an effort to convince other states to pass similar bills. As Plecker wrote the ERO's Harry Hamilton Laughlin, "One of our chief desires is to influence legislation in other states."[27]

In the afterglow of passage, Dr. Plecker began a heated campaign of "eugenical education." Claiming that between ten thousand and twenty thousand "near-white people" lived in Virginia, Plecker asserted that "they have demanded admittance of their children to white schools and in not a few cases they have intermarried with white people." Thirty years before *Brown v. Board of Education,* Plecker connected the schoolroom to the bedroom.[28]

Plecker was the law's greatest champion, popularizer, and enforcer; his devotion to racial integrity approached the monomaniacal. He threatened midwives and mothers. He patrolled cemeteries, segregating graves and defending the racial integrity of the Old Dominion's corpses. His office promoted the RIA. Plecker reported to the American Medical Association that he had created a racial integrity dragnet by weaving together "6,000 midwives; 2,500 physicians; 1,300 local registrars and about 2,500 undertakers who report deaths, beside the Clerks who report marriages and divorces." Plecker had "one or more representatives in every local community within two to five miles of every person." Ubiquitous informants would ensure that no blacks "pass" as white. Plecker particularly worried about individuals in whom white "blood" predominated: "That is the class that . . . are on the borderline, and constitute the real danger of race intermixture," he cautioned.[29]

Viewing racial integrity as a matter of public health and national survival, Plecker addressed the American Public Health Association. He emphasized the public health value of pure racial stocks, the threat posed by birth control and miscegenation, and the need for eugenic segregation to maintain racial purity. Invoking the image of "Cavaliers" and "Puritans" who were "the best that the world could then offer" racially, Plecker evoked a Nordic American race, citing Cox, Grant, and Stoddard for authority. The RIA, Plecker asserted, offered hope because it was "the most perfect expression of the white ideal, and the most important eugenical effort that has been made in 4000 years." The *American Journal of Public Health* and the popular *Literary Digest* broadcast Plecker's views before a national professional and educated lay audience.[30]

At the annual meeting of the Southern Medical Association, attended by over two thousand physicians, Plecker trumpeted the new law in "Shall America Remain White?" Since the RIA was "creating a great deal of interest in the North as well as the South," Plecker outlined the threat of unchecked miscegenation. He called for physicians and public health workers "to include eugenics as a whole or a part of regular and legitimate public health work" because "the success of any such movement is said largely to depend upon the physicians, since they are in a position best to know of racial contact and its effects." Physicians present agreed that Plecker had advanced a plausible solution.[31]

While the altar and public health presented the front lines in the battle for racial purity, the captains of eugenics sought to dominate the classroom, too. Cox and Plecker addressed biology classes throughout Virginia. Ivey Lewis arranged two engagements for Cox, hoping to "make the occasion widely public throughout the student body." Cox sought to convince the students that eugenics, embodied in the RIA, provided the necessary first step toward the "final solution" of the "Negro problem." By 1925, Plecker was addressing summer schools for teachers, "endeavoring to reach the higher schools and colleges of the state on the question of Race Improvement." Ivey Lewis congratulated Plecker for trying "so effectively to do what can be done," and pledged his personal cooperation.[32]

Dr. Plecker enforced the new law with bullying, threats, and outright lies—a rigor that surprised even supporters. Plecker targeted white mothers for special intimidation, perhaps because their transgression of the color line and defilement of the southern iconography of "pure white womanhood" infuriated him most. Barely a month after the law passed, Plecker informed a new white mother that her child's father was "negro":

> This is to give you warning that this is a mulatto child and you cannot pass it off as white. . . . You will have to do something about this matter and see that the child is not allowed to mix with white children, it cannot go to white schools and can never marry a white person in Virginia.
>
> It is an awful thing.

Plecker threatened the midwife in the same case. "This is to notify you that it is a penitentiary offense to willfully state that a child is white when it is colored," he began. "You have made yourself liable to very serious trouble by doing this thing." This case set the tone for Plecker's administration. Still, some dared to challenge Plecker in court.[33]

The RIA split its first two legal decisions. Both incidents involved the attempted marriage of white men to colored women, traditionally the least stigmatized form of interracial sexuality. The same judge, Henry W. Holt, ruled in both cases. In September 1924, Judge Holt accepted Plecker's testimony and that of a corroborating witness that Dorothy Johns was a "triple mixture" of Native American, black, and white "blood." In the second case, however, Holt ruled in favor of Atha Sorrells, declaring that her heritage betrayed no evidence of racial mixture.[34]

In dismissing the Sorrells case, Judge Holt pronounced himself "in cordial sympathy with the general purpose of the statute." Nevertheless, since the burden of proof remained upon the applicant and not the state, Holt observed that no one could prove their absolute racial purity: "In twenty-five generations one has thirty-two millions of grandfathers, not to speak of grandmothers. . . . Certainly in some instances there was an alien strain." Holt also noted that the category "Caucasian" entirely lacked scientific precision, undercutting the RIA's rationale.[35]

Using the traditional southern method of "appearance" to determine an individual's race, Holt was inclined to "discard the letter of the law" and apply "the 'rule of reason' which is that there must be an appreciable amount of foreign [non-white] blood." Since he could not "see" the nonwhite blood in Atha Sorrells's face, physiognomy, or pedigree, Holt ruled that she was white. In the eugenicists' eyes, Holt fell victim to the principal danger of miscegenation: that racial intermixture—hereditary "taint"—could not be detected by the naked eye. Eugenic antimiscegenation and sterilization prohibited the propagation of "hidden taints." Although intelligence tests offered quick, scientific diagnoses for feeblemindedness, there existed no similar test for race.[36]

The Sorrells case gained immediate notoriety. The editor of the *Richmond Times-Dispatch* questioned Judge Holt's substituting "the rule of reason" for the "letter of the law." Embarrassed, Plecker challenged Judge Holt, telling the press that the ruling "would have no affect [*sic*] on the position taken by the bureau," and that "the persons recorded as colored will remain colored, so far as we are concerned." The battle raged in the newspapers for the remainder of November, with Plecker making increasingly bellicose statements. Holt's decision so horrified Powell, Cox, Plecker, and the Virginia eugenicists that they mounted an effort to create an ironclad, lily-white RIA. This lobbying outraged segments of the Virginia elite otherwise sympathetic to eugenics and racial integrity.[37]

Plecker and Powell considered a legal appeal. Assistant Attorney General Leon M. Bazile notified Powell that his office would pursue an appeal if desired. Judge Holt reiterated his support of the law's objectives, informing the Commonwealth's attorney that he would amend his ruling to facilitate an appeal. By December, Powell felt confident enough to release *A Breach in the Dike: An Analysis of the Sorrels* [sic] *Case Showing the Danger to Racial Integrity from Intermarriage of Whites with So-Called Indians* to alert Virginians to the decision's implications.[38]

A Breach in the Dike displayed the reasoning of those who hoped to enact segregation's science. Echoing Alderman, Powell claimed that, "the political cockpit is not the proper arena for this debate," which should be handled with "sternest self-control and the coolest judgment," even as he distributed a pamphlet calculated to inflame the electorate. Powell valorized the younger generation of Virginia leaders, whose opinions had formed "under the influence of modern biology, by the new ethnology, by the new philosophy of cultural history." These influentials understood "that 'one drop of negro blood makes the negro' is no longer a theory based on race pride or color prejudice, but a logically induced, scientific fact." Using the medicalized language of eugenics, Powell claimed that "the need of the time is not for opiates, but for surgery." Drastic action needed to be taken to save white civilization from the cancer of passing.[39]

Judge Holt, Powell intimated, was "imperfectly acquainted" with the "catastrophic biologic and social results of the infusion of even an infinitesimal strain of African blood." Powell hoped to strong-arm Judge Holt and other prominent Virginians with the threat of his club's ire, suggesting that, "individuals who, for personal reasons of intimate and delicate nature, would desire to oppose the law" risked the American race.

Powell's affront crossed the fine behavioral line separating "Virginia gentlemen" from arrivistes. The powerful supporters of Judge Holt cried foul. In the *Richmond News-Leader* and *Richmond Times-Dispatch*, Judge Holt's advocates affirmed his ruling and ancestry. One supporter remarked: "Judge Holt is a native of Surry County and comes of a prominent Old Virginia family . . . his judicial record has received commendation from the highest legal sources. . . . He is particularly desirous of perpetuating the spirit of the recent law to preserve racial purity." Holt's decision reflected his legal convictions, not any weakness in his allegiance to white supremacy. Fearful that the law would be declared unconstitutional, Powell and Plecker abandoned their appeal, focusing instead on enlisting local officials in the law's enforcement.[40]

Plecker sought to rally Virginia's white elites, especially physicians, behind the RIA. His 1924 pamphlet *Eugenics in Relation to the New Family and the*

Law on Racial Integrity alerted the public to racial degeneration's dangers. He hoped the pamphlet would be "read by the young people of our schools and colleges, and by others who are, or will be our leaders in thought." By March 1925, two editions totaling over sixty-five thousand copies were distributed statewide.[41]

Plecker merged the menace of the feebleminded with the menace of passing. He paired his concern that "there is nothing that may be more certainly foreseen than the disastrous results of feeble-minded individuals being permitted to marry and bear children," with the assertion that racially intermixed families "furnish nearly all of the criminals, moonshiners and women of low morals." Thus, the mixed-race population was, by definition, feebleminded. The barnyard imagery of the eugenic metaphor drove the point home: "Stock-breeders have learned that the offspring of greatly different breeds are inferior to either parent, and that it is not wise to perpetuate such strains. This is likewise true with man."[42]

Plecker also invoked masculinist nationalism. If Virginians avoided "the shameful intermixture of the races" or "marrying into a family containing members who are hereditarily defective physically, mentally, or morally," the next generation would be equipped "to fill the place as leader of the nations of the world." Like eugenicists everywhere, Plecker averred that "education of the young, in particular, and for this end, of their parents and teachers also, is necessary to secure the best and most positive eugenic results of correct selection in marriage." Paul Brandon Barringer felt that Plecker's appeals were "gentle and persuasive."[43]

In May 1925, Plecker reprised these conclusions in "Eugenics or Race Deterioration—Which?" before the Augusta County Medical Association. It was delivered with, and published alongside, pro-eugenics articles by Reverend W. E. Davis and Dr. Joseph S. DeJarnette. The Presbyterian Davis resurrected nineteenth-century arguments that "Divine revelation accounts for the threefold racial grouping that we generally recognize today" and proved "a Divine plan for racial purity." DeJarnette connected feeblemindedness and race mixing through the eugenic metaphor, noting that the "importance of good seed and well bred animals" was obvious to most thinking people. Virginia needed "an eugenic society in every county and city in the State with a secretary devoting his entire time to securing data as to the dysgenic situations in his territory, keeping records, examining school children as to mentality, and lecturing on eugenics before the students of the high schools." He called for courses in eugenics in all the colleges, to awaken students and teachers to their procreative responsibility.[44]

DeJarnette's solutions for Virginia's eugenic predicament ranged from the familiar—segregation, marriage restriction, sterilization—to the fantastic: regulating wages "according to the number of children and the mental quality of parents," establishing the eugenic "registration of family pedigrees, traits, etc.," and competition among children in crop growing and breeding that "would tend to make them more careful in selecting their own mates in later years." He argued that Mendel's laws should be exhibited at county and state fairs as a reminder to all Virginians. When Virginia's sterilization law was affirmed by the courts, he predicted, "it will sever the black thread of inheritance, give many segregated [institutionalized] people their liberty and save untold suffering, crime and expense in the years to come."[45]

Meanwhile, Plecker admonished Virginia's physicians and launched a paean to the ancestors of the American race. "America was claimed by the great Nordic race as its final and chiefest possession," and as such was destined for greatness, if racial purity was maintained. Invoking race suicide, Plecker advocated four children as the minimum for middle- and upper-class families, who must "set aside their own selfish and indolent desires, and . . . realize that it is their religious and patriotic duty to do their part in saving their race and country." Believing that they had alerted the public to the dysgenics of intermarriage, Plecker and Powell began their end game for a revised Racial Integrity Act.[46]

Standing Fast against "Miscegenation"

By 1926, Plecker and Powell supplemented Cox's book with *Mongrel Virginians,* a work resulting from research conducted by the Sweet Briar College sociologist Ivan E. McDougle and the ERO's Arthur H. Estabrook. A study of the "Win Tribe," a triracial group whose acronym Estabrook fashioned from *W*hite, *I*ndian, and *N*egro, *Mongrel Virginians* culminated over fifteen years of eugenic theorizing.

Estabrook linked the national eugenics movement to Virginia's racial integrity and sterilization acts, breathing new life into an old idea in the winter of 1923. "I have found quite a bit of data," Estabrook wrote Charles B. Davenport, concerning "an inter-mixture of Indian, negro, and white, who have lived in a segregated region for many generations," and were known locally as "Ishes," short for "issue" of racial intermarriage. Estabrook wrote, "I think this Virginia work would interest you as there is the segregation and the intermarriage and the mental defectiveness."[47]

Members of a "tri-racial isolate" or "mongrel Virginian" family from Amherst County, photographed by Arthur H. Estabrook ca. 1924. (Arthur Estabrook Papers, M. E. Grenander Department of Special Collections & Archives, University of Albany Libraries)

Harvey Jordan first told Davenport about the "Ishes" in 1911, and Davenport never forgot the "lost tribe of Indians" that had "disappeared" through racial interbreeding. Estabrook's discovery of a high incidence of "feeblemindedness" in this isolated, inbred, racially mixed group presented Davenport with the perfect eugenic experiment. A correlation between feeblemindedness and race crossing might prove whether miscegenation led to degeneration.[48]

Throughout his career, Davenport surrounded himself with sympathizers, and the Virginia project proved no different. Davenport visited Amherst County, assuring himself of the suitability of the "material" for study, developing a base of operations at Sweet Briar. Sweet Briar's all-female student body offered a pool of potential fieldworkers and ERO students near the study site, an important consideration in an era before the widespread paving of roads. Davenport applauded McDougle's "very progressive attitude (may I say for a sociologist!) . . . that in this mountain segregate there were hereditary factors, as well as environmental, that were responsible for the end result." In preparing students to collect data on the "Ishes," McDougle used Davenport's

The Hill Folk and *Nam Family* studies. He accepted Davenport's offer of Estabrook's services, remarking, "With my twenty college majors trained for the field work we ought to complete the census of the Isshy group in three or four weeks."[49]

Estabrook's preliminary findings showed "much illegitimacy and feeble-mindedness" as well as "a low social status present in practically all the huts and log cabins where these folk live." He concluded that the "social segregation" of the "Isshies" [was] caused by the 'dark skin' of the crosses," and their geographic isolation that "caused much interbreeding. . . . The intellectual level of the group is below the average for the whites and apparently about the same as the negro." Poor performance on intelligence tests was "no doubt due to the preponderance of Indian and negro blood." Of the 550 Virginians studied, "only a few can be said to be socially adequate; the great majority are a social and biological problem not only because of their low mental level but because of the presence of the negro blood in a mixed Indian-white race which claims for itself all the rights and privileges of the Indian." He advocated further study so that "data may be available upon which to build proper marriage laws for matings between races." Unlike Plecker, Estabrook did not seem to adhere to the "one drop" rule of racial "pollution."[50]

Following the Sorrells debacle, Plecker pestered Davenport and Estabrook for the final conclusions on the "Ishes." Davenport believed the report could not be issued until respondents' names were changed. Plecker complained that "the report would not be of much value to us unless the names were included," because without names the report could not be used to enforce the RIA. Estabrook knew Plecker wanted the data "to use in the various cases now appearing in the Virginia courts." Providing names "would involve us in a great deal of trouble and I fear publicity that would come back to hurt us." Estabrook noted that, "while [Plecker] says this is only 'Virginia's attempt to settle the race problem,' many people in Virginia feel that he is not attacking the problem correctly." Davenport, wary of bad publicity, hid behind a spurious excuse: "if the impression gets around that our promise of confidence is not to be relied upon that would be an end to our power to collect data." Undeterred, Plecker continued to hound Davenport.[51]

Mongrel Virginians finally appeared in 1926, a classic extended eugenic family study. Estabrook and McDougle's conclusion tried to rehabilitate their reputation as dispassionate observers of the race problem:

> Unquestionably the people covered by this study represent an ever increasing
> social problem in the South. . . . Amidst the furor of newspaper and pamphlet

publicity on miscegenation which has appeared since the passage of the Virginia Racial Integrity Law of 1924 this study is presented not as theory or as representing a prejudiced point of view but as a careful summary of the facts of history.

Despite Estabrook's distaste for Plecker's methods, he backed the goal of racial integrity enough to include the RIA as an appendix. Ideologically, eugenics remained flexible enough to gather true believers and opportunists around the same table, fighting for the same goals, albeit for different reasons.[52]

Beginning in March 1925, the ASCOA jeopardized Virginia's eugenics movement by militating for a law requiring racial separation in all public assemblies. Powell's and Cox's eugenical arguments against interracial contact elicited a mixed response. Given the passage of the RIA, many Virginians believed the new bill was a gratuitous insult to blacks. People on both sides of the color line—from local black newspapers like the *Norfolk Journal and Guide* to the NAACP's national magazine, the *Crisis;* from the white *Richmond Times-Dispatch* to Governor E. Lee Trinkle's office—decried the AS-COA for inciting racial animosity. Governor Trinkle, no enemy of eugenics or segregation, warned, "we are getting along splendidly with the colored people in Virginia and we want to meet this situation in a way that will tend to solve the problem with as little enmity between the races as possible." Some white Virginians, led by the prominent Reverend Beverly D. Tucker, opposed further legislation. While they were "desirous of preserving white racial purity and white social supremacy," they did not "wish to hurt or humiliate the negro by unnecessarily harsh legislation." The white *Norfolk Virginian-Pilot* argued against the bill, asking simply, "why do not these white people who object to mixed seating stay away?" On November 27, 1925, Alvin Massenburg, a first-term delegate, acquiesced to ASCOA pressure and introduced the segregation bill. Thanks to its eugenic underpinnings, the law "defined segregation in Virginia for four decades to come."[53]

In February 1926, John Powell released his thirteen-part series "The Last Stand" through the *Richmond Times-Dispatch,* seeking to pressure legislators who were considering amending the RIA alongside adopting the Massenburg bill. The RIA amendment proposed to increase the allowable amount of "Indian" blood to one-eighth, but restricted the definition of whiteness to the lineal descendants of John Rolfe and Pocahontas, ignoring two other important Native American/white marriages that occurred in 1644 and 1684. No one was fooled. The *Richmond News-Leader* ran two articles that reflected the popular outrage at the possibility of thousands of "whites" becoming black by law.[54]

Despite the backlash, Powell increased his journalistic effort to cinch the loophole created by the Pocahontas clause. Citing Cox, Estabrook, and Mc-Dougle, Powell's articles relied on unsubstantiated "case studies" purporting to demonstrate the deleterious effects of miscegenation. Powell's strident tone alienated many Virginians. One reader retorted that the bills "unnecessarily insult, and irritate the best negroes among us, put all non-white nations in the same category, and, chief of all, advertise on their faces both the ill-manners and the shame of Virginia whites." Other editorials supported the bills, but said they did not go far enough, and added suggestions for laws punishing interracial fornication and fathers of "illegitimate" interracial children. Amidst the confusion, state senators tabled the revised RIA by a vote of twenty to nine. The Massenburg bill, however, passed the House of Delegates and became law without the signature of the newly elected governor, Harry Flood Byrd.[55]

Powell, Plecker, and Cox's rabid commitment to mainline eugenics polarized opinion, driving away many erstwhile supporters and shattering the potential for a "mass" eugenics movement. Virginians opted for more diffuse forms of organization, and less public enforcement of the sterilization and racial integrity laws. The eugenics movement in Virginia fractured into smaller cells arrayed along a spectrum from mainline racial eugenics to what would come to be known, after 1930, as "reform eugenics." Eschewing the overtly racist dimension of the earlier movement, reform eugenics still backed policies regarding "fit" and "unfit" genes.[56]

Unable to Operate Harmoniously: Faction in the Ranks

Although the Virginia Academy of Science (VAS), the state's premier organization of academic scientists and physicians, failed to condemn the ASCOA triumvirate, Powell, Plecker, and Cox's extremism destroyed their standing among Virginia scientists. The inability of the VAS membership to articulate their objections underscores the power of University of Virginia eugenicists in shaping Virginia's culture of segregation. Ivey Lewis and Harvey Jordan colluded to keep the VAS from addressing eugenics, an action that might have undermined the RIA's scientific justification. This left the general population to infer that Virginia's most accomplished white scientists condoned the ASCOA's actions.

The William and Mary eugenicist Donald Davis and faculty members from the Medical College of Virginia (MCV) led the charge against the scientifically specious claims made by Powell, Plecker, and Cox. In January

1925, MCV doctors Edgar Calvin Leroy Miller, John Shelton Horsley, and the prominent Richmond physician John M. G. Ryland formed a group to "attend the meeting of the committee on race relations" in Richmond to defuse tensions engendered by Plecker and Powell after the Sorrells case. This committee of academic physicians and scientists aimed to wrest the debate from the crucible of public opinion. None of these experts disagreed with the RIA; they objected to the tactics of the ASCOA. Miller and his associates hoped to capture attention, to quell anger among the state's people of color, and to regain control over segregation's science.[57]

Davis had been instrumental in founding the VAS just two years earlier, helping to elect Ivey Lewis as its first president in 1923. Now Davis organized a symposium "on the subject of human genetics with special reference to Virginia problems." His conscious avoidance of the word "eugenics" underscored his tact. He believed that "more heat than light was being shed on the problem" by the ASCOA. Davis asked George Ferguson and Robert Bean for comparisons between blacks and whites in intelligence and physique, hoping that "these comparisons [offer] a reasonable basis for differential treatment of the races in the State." The effort was not to undercut the RIA, merely to strip the scientific authority from the ASCOA parvenus.[58]

Ferguson agreed to give a talk on racial differences in intelligence, and asked Bean to "arrange a paper on the Nordics from a scientific rather than the present enthusiastic point of view." Bean offered to present a paper on the anatomical differences between the races' internal organs, hedging: "Whatever we do we should avoid any Madison Grant or Stoddard stuff. Make it truly scientific, and yet of interest to the public, and it may be worth while." Bean's research conclusions buttressed white supremacy; thus his demurrers split a rather fine hair. The scientific rectitude or social desirability of eugenics, white supremacy, and the RIA were never in dispute. Eugenics promoted by active scientists was "truth." Propounded by dilettantes, it was propaganda.

Unbeknownst to Davis, Jordan and Lewis blocked the 1925 symposium and would obstruct later attempts to consider eugenics. As racial tensions began to rise in 1927, Davis again attempted to address the VAS. Jordan replied, "After conference with Dr. Lewis, I have decided that the time is not yet quite opportune for allocation of any considerable part of the program of the annual meeting of the VAS to the subject of eugenics." Lewis and Jordan had not abandoned eugenics, racial purity, or the ASCOA. They understood the political climate and sought to shield both their scientific reputations and their political agenda from censure. Despite being a member of the ASCOA, Jordan objected to open association with Plecker because it "would affiliate us rather more closely than I think desirable at present, with the race purity problem of the Anglo-Saxon clubs." Keenly aware of the animosity stirred up by Plecker, Powell, and Cox, Jordan wanted to insulate scientific eugenicists from charges of collusion with the ASCOA, writing, "My only motive is to serve the cause of eugenics, but for the present I am of the opinion that this can best be done in Virginia by steering clear of racial questions." Even before it became clear that the racist doctrines of Powell, Plecker, and Cox lacked any scientific basis, politically shrewd eugenicists understood that harping on these issues would elicit resistance. Nowhere is this more apparent than when one examines the reaction among Virginia's African Americans when confronted with eugenic social policy.[59]

Intellectual Miscegenation: Black Responses to Eugenics Legislation

Living in a state that long prided itself on being a "slave producer," Virginia's African Americans harbored visceral memories of the dehumanizing, proto-eugenic program of slave breeding. Historians have shown that slave breeding was an uncommon practice. Yet the fact that white southerners boasted of it, and that black southerners reviled its memory, reveals the lingering significance of reproductive control. One might assume that "American blacks would have been univocally opposed to any form of racism or biologically deterministic arguments." Yet, nationally prominent black intellectuals like W.E.B. Du Bois, like some of their white counterparts, denigrated racist eugenics without denying the potential eugenic improvement of humankind. Other African American leaders, like Marcus Garvey, actively embraced notions of racial purity, joining common cause with John Powell and his followers.[60]

Virginia's African Americans manifested a similarly diverse response to eugenical public policy, seeking to co-opt the movement for their own ends. Eugenics rhetoric drew upon powerful, familiar images for white and black Americans. Strong parallels between eugenic "racial improvement" and African American "racial uplift" created ideological flexibility, allowing black activists to deploy eugenic theories against white supremacists.[61]

Black intellectuals manipulated the logic of eugenics to parry white eugenicists' dismissal of individual black's success. Du Bois's "talented tenth" of black elites challenged notions of innate inferiority by achieving as much or more than their white counterparts. The "talented tenth" began their own eugenic program, extolling themselves as the "fit" model for all blacks. Du Bois argued that the "duty" of "honest colored men and women" was to breed selectively. In 1922, Du Bois lamented that African Americans failed to "breed for brains, for efficiency, for beauty," precisely the diagnosis eugenicists applied to white society. As late as 1932, Du Bois wrote, "the mass of ignorant Negroes still breed carelessly and disastrously, so that the increase among Negroes, even more than the increase among whites, is from that part of the population least intelligent and fit, and least able to rear their children properly." Education and wise mating would ensure conformity to the intellectual, social, and economic norm, "a male, often mulatto, intellectual, middle-class, Northern urbanite." African American hereditarianism did not preclude racial intermarriage, instead embracing a class-based eugenics similar to Britain's. "Respectable" blacks should procreate, whereas the defective, delinquent, and dependent should not. Despite these eugenic undertones, Du Bois openly reviled racist eugenics, calling Stoddard a "fool." Du Bois savaged the RIA and the Massenburg bill, writing, "In the future, miscegenation is going to be widely practiced in the world and that despite the likes and dislikes of present living beings."[62]

Judging from Virginia's African American press, eugenic sterilization stirred little concern. While the white press followed the passage of the sterilization law and the course of its legal challenge, the black press took no notice. Many African Americans, seeking access to all "progressive" methods for social uplift, likely embraced sterilization and institutionalization of the "feebleminded." If whites were willing to perform these operations for their race's progress, could it not help African Americans? The procedure probably seemed less threatening in its early years, since the official in charge of the state hospital for blacks, Dr. Walter F. Drewry, was a principal exponent of sterilization and considered "a friend of the race."

Resistance emerged as news spread of coercive sterilizations among "normal," noninstitutionalized African American women. In 1935, eleven years after Virginia enacted its sterilization law, the *Richmond Planet* ran a front-page story, "Sees Scientific Race Elimination in Alabama's Sterilization Bill." The *Planet* reported that "many, knowing the past record of the state of Alabama in dealing with its Negro citizens, fear that this new instrument would be used viciously against them by a public opinion that 'stomachs' lynchings—inside as well as outside the courtroom." Unlike Virginia's law, the Alabama bill provided for the sterilization of habitual criminals. Since Alabama's supreme court had recently upheld the corrupt convictions and death sentences of the "Scottsboro Boys" (nine black men falsely accused of raping two white women), the paper worried that the court would use the sterilization statute against all blacks. The *Planet* warned, "With a majority of the white population already thinking every Negro 'an habitual criminal' one imagines he can

see the end of the race in Alabama when the hundreds of thousands of strong
Negro men and women will walk the streets and highways of that State bereft
of the God-given right to propagate their kind." Virginia blacks did not voice
similar fears about their own reproductive fate, believing they received better treatment than blacks elsewhere in the South, especially given Virginia's
infrequent incidence of lynching. The RIA called this belief into question,
however, and black newspapers pounced on the issue.[63]

John Mitchell, the *Richmond Planet*'s editor, decried a *Richmond Times-
Dispatch* editorial promoting the RIA. Believing that laws already on the
books mooted further legislation, Mitchell pointedly blamed whites for miscegenation: "they lynch colored men who are criminally intimate with white
women but they do not exercise their fury upon white men who are criminally
intimate with colored women." Acknowledging repatriation as a possible alternative to the RIA, Mitchell commented that "Hon. Marcus Garvey now in
the Tombs Prison, New York advocates [repatriation]. His present location
shows just how favorable his plan was considered."[64]

From March 1924 forward, the *Planet* assiduously publicized all scientific findings adverse to the RIA's eugenical underpinnings. In May, the *Planet*
reported the meeting of America's most august learned body, the American
Philosophical Society. At this convention, which focused on race issues in
science, Charles Davenport and many mainline eugenicists received a serious blow from famed Columbia University anthropologist Franz Boas and
others. "Nordics Knocked Out at Great Science Meet," cheered the *Planet*'s
headline, continuing, "The 'Superior Race Itch' Is Carried Out on Stretch-
ers." The *Planet* bolstered blacks' self-image by presenting a counternarrative
to mainline eugenicists, the ASCOA, and the RIA. Yet whites dismissed the
meeting as wishful thinking: since Boas was a Jew, a member of a dysgenic
race, of course he would make these claims. To Boas's claims and the *Planet*'s
statement that "even the 'purest' races are a product of endless mixtures of
stocks throughout the ages," Powell and many eugenicists replied that the
superior white American race was a mixture of nearly related racial types,
ensuring "hybrid vigor." They argued that breeding among widely divergent
racial forms like whites and blacks inevitably produced enfeebled progeny.
Still, black newspapers consistently presented alternative visions.[65]

The black press mobilized in response to Walter Plecker's misuse of the
franking privilege he obtained as a special agent for the U.S. Department of
Labor, disseminating sixty-five thousand copies of his pamphlet *Eugenics
in Relation to the New Family*. The editor of the *Norfolk Journal and Guide*
fumed, "With the sanction and seal of the great State of Virginia upon his ut-

terances, Dr. Plecker, as a Virginia health officer, paid by the taxpayers of the State, Negroes included, is industriously engaged in sowing the seeds of bitterest racial discord, from one end of the country to another."[66] The newspaper called for Plecker's resignation. When Plecker refused to resign, the Labor Department, under pressure from the NAACP, terminated his appointment.

The white press defended Plecker, arguing that the Labor Department's action amounted to "federal political censorship." Plecker himself claimed that the pamphlets were "designed to be helpful to the negro," and expressed surprise that certain "supersensitive" blacks objected. Plecker answered with seventy thousand copies of *The New Family and Racial Improvement* in 1928, sounding the tocsin of white race suicide, and alerting people to the danger of "the ultimate complete intermixture of the white and colored races if they continue to live together." Black protest lacked a local power base that could challenge Plecker who, despite his extreme methods, still expressed the conventional wisdom among most white Virginians.[67]

The third time Virginia's legislature considered racial integrity, in the Price bill of 1928, leaders of Native American tribes uncovered deep divisions between blacks and the Native American minority. The Price bill attempted to resolve an internal contradiction in Virginia law. The RIA defined a white person as anyone with no trace of "non-caucasic blood" other than one-sixteenth the blood of the Native American. It did not define a colored person, other than by implication. A preexisting 1910 law defined anyone with more than one-sixteenth "Negro" blood as colored. Thus, by the laws' terms, anyone with less than one-sixteenth black blood was simultaneously colored and white. The Price bill "sought to define as colored any person having any ascertainable amount of negro blood without regard to time or generation removed," and an "Indian" would be "every person not a colored person, but having one-fourth or more Indian blood." Plecker, Cox, and Powell rehashed the usual arguments for tightening racial classification. Wah-hun-sun-a-cook of the Pamunkeys testified before the Senate, "I will tie a stone around my neck and jump in the James River rather than be classed as a Negro." After four years of persecution by Plecker, Native American groups, assisted by sympathetic whites, began to fight back. As the population being defined out of existence by the RIA, Native Americans had resisted from the outset, but their small number and weak political organization marginalized them even more than African Americans. Thus, it took far longer for Native American resistance to register in white- and black-controlled newspapers.[68]

Wah-hun-sun-a-cook's statement elicited the *Richmond Planet*'s condemnation. Responding to the Native American leader, John Mitchell Jr. adopted "race purity" rhetoric to highlight its absurdity. "Certain it is that Negroes join with him in his effort to maintain the racial integrity of his tribe and they do not want any of its mongrel members thrown over on their side of the contention." Mitchell wanted the racial matter clarified because

> the pure, unadulterated Negroes here are loaded down and held responsible for all kinds and sorts of people masquerading as Negroes when they are not Negroes. We have Chinese Negroes, Japanese Negroes, Mexican Negroes, Indian Negroes, German Negroes, French Negroes, English Negroes, Italian Negroes, Jew Negroes, Irish Negroes and last but not least, either as to quality or quantity, we have white Negroes.[69]

Mitchell pointedly asked the Native American to name the time and place of his drowning so that "all of the manufacturers and employers of Negroes will be asked to give a holiday in order that they may enjoy one day of complete and Prayerful satisfaction" in witnessing the event.

Dropping his sarcasm, Mitchell challenged the racial propagandists "to change, nullify, modify or prove to be false the following declaration of the Scriptures: 'And hath made of one blood all nations of men for to dwell on all the face of the earth.'" Alongside this affirmation of racial equality, Mitchell ironically ran an ad for Dr. Fred Palmer's Skin Whitener, a product developed to aid passing. True to form, Plecker entirely missed Mitchell's point and wrote the editor that he was "glad to know that the true negroes are becoming interested in preserving the purity of their race," hoping that they would be "wise enough to know what to do with mixed breeds who are not white and whom the negroes do not consider black. They are the problem. The true negro is no problem from the racial standpoint, so long as he remains pure." Presumably, "what to do with mixed breeds" was report them to Plecker for monitoring, shun them in marriage, and consign them to extinction.[70]

In contrast to Mitchell, many black Virginians supported the eugenic theory undergirding the RIA, led by Marcus Garvey's UNIA. Racial purity became the foundation of their personal and political identities. Garvey's belief that the mission of the NAACP and other integrationist groups represented a "dangerous race destroying doctrine" led him to proclaim: "The Universal Negro Improvement Association on the other hand believes in and teaches the pride and purity of race. We believe that the white race should uphold its racial pride and perpetuate itself, and that the black race should do likewise." Garvey's notions of racial determinism placed him squarely within the camp of Madison Grant, Lothrop Stoddard, and Earnest Cox. Garvey encouraged his followers to read the works of Cox, Grant, and Stoddard to instill a like-minded respect for racial pride and a hatred of miscegenation.[71]

By 1921, Garvey's Pan-Africanist rhetoric became so thoroughly homogenized that, in the minds of sympathetic whites and critical blacks, he represented simply a "back to Africa" movement bent on repatriating all Diaspora blacks. The apparent ideological congruence attracted white supremacists. Garvey differed in believing that a pure black race could equal or exceed the achievements of the white race. Garvey knew that disarming antiblack organizations would buy him time and room to outflank his opponents—black and white. Organizations like the UNIA and the ASCOA advanced their interests by any means, including links with erstwhile enemies. Still, Garvey's alliance with the KKK and ASCOA was not merely Machiavellian. He believed in the common cause of racial purity.[72]

Powell's fame made him familiar to both blacks and whites, and he became the public liaison between the ASCOA and the UNIA. Powell made widely publicized speeches at New York's Liberty Hall, while his associates built national support for Garvey among white supremacists. Earnest Cox became "the most important White man in this country in the dissemination of Garveyism among those who believed in the purity of the White race." As Cox wrote to the imprisoned Garvey: "I would endeavor to show white men that you were fighting the white man's battle without the white man's aid. It is my purpose to do all that I can for you and your cause." Garvey complimented Cox's work, writing, "It strikes at the root of the evil—the mulatto—who is the principal cause of nearly all the troubles of the poor Negro in America, as well as elsewhere." It was clear to Garvey who stood behind the "Negro problem" in America: "The race enemy organization the National Association for the Advancement of Colored People, is destructive to both races. They are seeking to build up a mongrel America, and those who are associated with them are either crazy or positively immoral, at least they are misguided." Garvey's crusade for race purity underscored his racialist conception of uplift.[73]

Cox corresponded with members of the UNIA in Virginia and across the country. The president of the Richmond Division of the UNIA worked to place Cox's tracts "in the hands of members of my race intelligent enough to understand." He helped Cox to secure black audiences throughout Virginia because, "in my contact with the public, I find an increased sentiment agreeing that the INTEGRITY OF THE RACES IS A FINE IDEA AND THE APPROVAL OF SAME IS GROWING." A black minister wrote, "No truer word never was spoken than when you said, the only way to have pure stock, is to separate them [races] by sending the Negroes to Africa, where they can work out their own destiny, they have the knowledge to do so." Revealing the class distinctions that divided black separatists and integrationists, he implored Cox to convince other black ministers who preached against Garvey to reconsider. "Just one word from you white People will work wonderously [*sic*], toward tearing down this so called high Negro." Professor Arnold H. Maloney of Wilberforce University wrote: "Your views as a white man are quite analogous to my views as a colored man. I am for the governmental independence and racial integrity of my race as you are for yours. Hence, it seems to me that some rapprochement can be arrived at between us. That would expedite the solution of the dogged and inveterate race problem."[74]

Despite Richard Sherman's characterization of RIA lobbyists as a "dedicated coterie of extremists," and his assertion that "few really prominent Virginians [were] among the [ASCOA's] active members," many Virginia elites embraced eugenics, particularly as it supported traditional racial hierarchies. Eugenics generally, and in Virginia specifically, never became a grassroots mass movement because it was an impulse directed by expert authorities. Scientific and medical experts hoped to educate the populace enough to ensure compliance, but not enough to engender resistance. The involvement of physicians and scientists in the ASCOA was not coincidence, since they believed they understood the science underpinning the RIA. Jordan, Bean, Royster, and Lewis, all powerful members of both Virginia's scientific and medical communities, actively supported the ASCOA program—to a point. These Virginians convinced nationally prominent eugenicists to testify in favor of the RIA, creating coalitions with overlapping memberships locally and nationally. Arthur Estabrook testified in support of both Virginia's eugenic sterilization and eugenic marriage laws. Dr. Albert Priddy, and many other Virginians, supported both laws as well. When Powell, Plecker, and Cox overstepped the mandate conferred by eugenics' academic scientific supporters, tensions fractured the coalition.[75]

Evaluating the "popularity" of eugenics in Virginia, as evinced by the passage of the Racial Integrity Act and the sterilization law, presents a number of problems. Considering each measure individually artificially isolates the efforts, wrenching them out of their larger context. Previous commentators are undoubtedly correct in observing that the RIA was not "the product of a great popular groundswell," if by popular groundswell they mean a mass, democratic, populist revolt. Rather, intellectuals created a subtle milieu that fostered endorsement. Eugenics called for propagation of the elite and the demise of other lineages, ultimately rendering popular support unnecessary. While newspapers were not swamped by letters endorsing the eugenics bills, most of those received viewed the acts favorably. The newspaper editors' support of the acts also speaks to the popularity of eugenics. Editors would not risk circulation: they played to their audience's beliefs, whether racist, eugenic, or both. Concluding that legislators and the governor "appeared to have been guided more by perceptions of public opinion than by personal conviction" also misses the point because legislators generally act in ways least likely to raise the ire of their constituents. Those actions may or may not have anything to do with their beliefs about eugenics. To deny the popularity of eugenics—and its near-universal appeal among significant segments of elite Virginia society—simply because no readily apparent "mass" membership organization arose is surely misleading.[76]

Demanding a highly visible, centrally administered organization to "prove" the popular appeal of eugenics neglects the internal logic of the eugenics movement and its relationship to traditional southern paternalism. Eugenics relied on the existing mind-set among many Virginians, engendering support without the need for overt organizing and institution building. This preserved the elitist character of the movement, merging it with extant Virginia political culture in a manner reminiscent of antebellum *herrenvolk* democracy, where all whites were "equal" because they were not black. Eugenicists viewed themselves as an enlightened elite, charged with educating members of the "best stock" to "right-thinking" positions. Since the "best stock" correlated precisely with the white upper class, eugenical education became an exercise in self-congratulation. The "unfit" were not taught that they represented human dross since, by definition, the unfit were incapable of understanding eugenics and lacked the self-control and "altruism" to limit their procreation. Although eugenic stigmatization of poor whites fueled simmering class tensions, simultaneous fear of institutionalization and sterilization kept "poor white trash," like blacks, "in their place." Eugenicists realized that their programs could elicit strong emotional responses, so they converted those people likely to enter positions of power and hoodwinked or ignored the rest. The best forms of social control—and none are hegemonic—are often those that are the least overtly visible and most reliant on cultural socialization.

Black Virginians also turned to eugenics as a potential meliorative for deep-seated social problems. Those blacks who directly contested the eugenicists' rhetoric, pointing out the internal contradictions in the logic of racial supremacy, sought to use eugenics as its own foil. Others tried to co-opt eugenics, to argue for the improvement of the black race, or to promote notions of black racial superiority. These individuals, like Professor Turner at the Hampton Institute, understood the power and flexibility of eugenic ideology, manipulating it for their own uplift.

Given its well-developed eugenic program and progressive ethos, Virginia appeared "modern" and "progressive." Ultimately, the "effectiveness" of Virginia's eugenic programs cannot be measured in the economic and medical terms proponents argued, since changing definitions of mental disease and "defect," coupled with changing forms of social intervention, make it nearly impossible to try to calculate "savings" or "defectiveness prevented." The sterilization rate provides one index of the eugenic programs' "success," particularly when one notes the persistence of sterilization and the timing of its activity. Any attempt to arrive at an accurate quantitative estimate of the impact of the Racial Integrity Act is futile because no record was kept of the number of marriages disallowed. John Douglas Smith observed, "Those who emphasize that the Anglo-Saxon movement was essentially the work of a small group of racial zealots often overlook the impact that the law wrought on the lives of hundreds of Virginians." Smith might have increased his estimate to thousands. Moreover, the legacy of suspicion and hostility toward government and public health officials among Virginia's Native American and poor population traces its roots to the actions of Dr. Plecker. Scholars have noted that Plecker is still invoked by the older members of these communities to remind people of a terrible time, or as a bogey to compel obedience from children. The pain and suffering that resulted from these communities' reluctance to access subsequent public health initiatives are incalculable, yet directly attributable to eugenic ideology and its adherents. A more accurate assessment of the social and cultural legacy of these 1924 laws emerges from tracing the continuing evolution of eugenic ideology within the state during the ensuing generations. Far from disappearing after 1932 and the Third International Congress of Eugenics, eugenics in Virginia remained in action for at least another thirty-five years, only slowly falling into disfavor.[77]

6

"A HEALTHIER AND
HAPPIER AMERICA"

*Persistent Eugenics
in Virginia*

WRITING A TERM PAPER for Ivey Lewis's eugenics course, a University of Virginia undergraduate remarked: "In Germany Hitler has decreed that about 400,000 persons be sterilized. This is a great step in eliminating the mental deficients." The student acknowledged that, "the wide scope of the law may permit it to be used politically," yet, "the eugenic result will outweigh any evil practice, if any [should occur]." This paper was written in May 1934, ten months after Adolf Hitler signed Nazi Germany's "Law for the Prevention of Hereditarily Diseased Offspring." A 1935 student paper hailed the Nazis' mass sterilization program: "such a program, carefully and conscientiously carried out in this nation, free from politics and false assumptions, would result in a few hundred years in a healthier and happier America." In a chilling missive, Dr. Hans H. Heyn, a former student of Lewis and Orland E. White, wrote: "You won your bet when you said that I would be wearing the brown shirt pretty soon; I wear it and I am proud of it. I am a member of the S.A. (Stormtroops) too." Heyn had graduated from eugenics student to eugenics supporter to fascist eugenics enforcer.[1]

Although it is difficult to gauge the "true beliefs" of students—who may have been writing to please Lewis and earn a grade—their papers reflect the tenor of Lewis's teaching in the 1930s. A decade after the passage of Virginia's sterilization bill and Racial Integrity Act (RIA), Lewis still trumpeted the value of segregation's science. Feeblemindedness and race mixing still menaced civilization, and Lewis and his students identified Hitler's eugenic program as a more aggressive version of that pursued by many American states. After all, by 1931, thirty states had passed sterilization laws. Twenty-seven of those laws remained on the books, although they were not all actively enforced.[2]

While historians have claimed that the Great Depression retarded eugenic programs, evidence from Virginia refutes this conclusion. Not only did Virginia eugenicists continue to patrol the fit/unfit, normal/feebleminded, and white/black borders of segregation during the 1930s and 1940s, they also increased their surveillance of Jew/gentile interactions. Administrators at Virginia's colleges and professional schools, particularly the University of Virginia, mounted efforts to restrict Jewish enrollment. This move reflected both long-standing anti-Semitism and a eugenic evaluation of the biological worth of Jewish students.[3]

This increased vigilance regarding Jew/gentile intermingling roughly paralleled the rise of Nazism and Nazi eugenics. Nevertheless, it would be a vast overstatement to claim that all Virginia eugenicists were fascists or Nazis. Cataloging the similarities between Virginia and Nazi eugenicists does not reduce them to identity. Instead, revealing the contact points between the two groups underscores how eugenics could be invoked to buttress each culture's social order. Eugenics sheltered elite Virginians and Germans from the Great Depression's socioeconomic turmoil. It provided them with a scientific explanation for the economic catastrophe, absolving them of guilt and identifying scapegoats. The Great Depression confirmed Virginians' deepest eugenic fears—the societal drag of the "manifestly unfit," not reckless speculation by genetically gifted members of the American race, triggered the devastating depression. Eugenic theory merged with rising antiradicalism, quashing "liberal" responses to the crisis. Rather than advocating social welfare for all, the eugenicists acknowledged the "salubrious" effects of the Depression: it skimmed human scum from society, highlighting the necessity of a vigorous eugenic program to prevent similar disasters.[4]

The rise and fall of mainline eugenics in Virginia did not precisely parallel the trajectory of mainline eugenics at the national level, nor did it occur in lockstep with the rise and fall of the Third Reich. Extremists like Cox, Plecker, and Powell—and their allies in other states like California's Charles M. Goethe and New York's Clarence G. Campbell—appreciated Nazi racial doctrines. Patriotism prompted the University of Virginia's eugenicists to admire the Nazi program's efficiency, but to eschew the totalitarian doctrines of

TABLE 1. Virginia Sterilizations, by Decade

Decade	No. of sterilizations
1920s	208
1930s	3,209
1940s	2,098
1950s	1,395
1960-64	204

Source: Compiled from J. Paul, "Three Generations of Imbeciles," 511-13.

fascism. American eugenicists, especially those in Virginia, were able to reconcile "rugged individualism" and statist intervention in the name of protecting the American race. This ideological rapprochement explains how Virginia eugenicists differentiated themselves from their Nazi counterparts. Other Virginians adopted the more moderate reform eugenics that emerged after 1940, contributing to the durability of applied negative eugenics in Virginia.

Changes internal to the science of genetics had little effect on most Virginia eugenic "practitioners"—principally doctors, public health officials, and scientists. The continuity of belief in Virginia reveals the interaction among science, social policy, and political context. By 1940, eugenics assumed a subterranean form; taught in the classrooms and enforced through the public health department, state hospitals, and courts, it was seldom discussed openly. The persistence of Virginia's eugenic impulse highlights the slow transformation of scientific belief. Within Virginia's social context, mainliners could still espouse the science they had long believed. As a result of the dynamic between culture and science, Virginia sterilized almost 8,500 individuals, and denied thousands their cultural identity, marriage rights, schooling, medical care, and other social services (see table 1).

"Shooting the Mad Stork": Eugenics Education in the 1930s

As the 1920s closed, the University of Virginia increased its offerings in eugenics. Discontinued briefly during the low point of the Depression from 1931 to 1934, eugenics extension courses resurged in 1935. Emphasizing popular rather than technical instruction, these classes focused on "race deterioration, possibilities of improving the race, individual improvement, conflict between social and germinal heredity, man's unused resources or talents, the problem of population," and, finally, "the problem of racial crosses." The instructor believed the course would "be of special interest and value to teachers, parents, physicians and all others interested in the progress of the human race." These offerings presented eugenics to a much wider audience than enrolled undergraduates.[5]

University of Virginia students continued to learn eugenics, too. Surveying America in 1931, one of Lewis's students predicted that, "the future holds the indication that the population, in relatively few years, will be poisoned [and] average intelligence will take a drop." Although twenty-seven states had active sterilization laws—and Virginia was second only to California in total sterilizations—America was not applying the eugenic remedy rigorously enough. America needed to take better aim when "shooting the mad stork" or else succumb to the "menace of the feebleminded." Lewis found this analysis so compelling that he awarded the paper a grade of A.[6]

The titles of the term papers from Lewis's course covered the full spectrum of eugenics-related topics, from "Birth Control" to "Quality as a Biological Problem: Intelligence." The papers all accepted that "good environment will give good heredity a chance to express itself; but you cannot produce greatness from poor heredity." Student authors contended that modern society, through medical intervention and humanitarian sentiment, was short-circuiting natural selection. Only by placing concern for society over concern for the individual could America avoid "race suicide."[7]

In advancing the race suicide thesis, the authors embraced mainline eugenics. According to the students, the best hereditary stock resided largely in the upper class, "proving" that success was an index of hereditary gift rather than environmental conditioning. William Bennett Bean, whose father, Robert Bennett Bean, was a leading eugenicist on Virginia's medical faculty, argued: "Sterilization is not yet general enough to be really effective. . . . [T]he lower classes and more especially the positively undesirable elements of our society are increasing more rapidly than the so called upper class. This points definitely to race extinction."[8]

Student papers, like eugenical propagandists' tracts, masked cultural value judgments as "objective" scientific analyses. Lewis's lectures and reading assignments lent the imprimatur of scientific authority and value-neutrality to students' prejudices. Thus, the students' papers remained congruent with leading eugenic theories, Lewis's opinions, and their own interest in strengthening the segregated and stratified South.

As college students in an era when higher education was far less universal than today, these students likely identified themselves as elites—whether or not their families' socioeconomic background qualified them as such. Students probably found it more comforting to believe their social position resulted from superior genetic makeup, rather than from social prejudice and class privilege. Such a teleology provided these students with a scapegoat for social problems, particularly evident in papers written during the Great Depression. Four papers strongly maintained that the economy toppled as a result of the destabilizing effect of a massive influx of inferior, European workers combined with the disproportionate procreation of indigenous lower classes and feebleminded. All the papers concerning eugenic sterilization noted its economic benefits. Without rigorously applied eugenics, the students contended, society was being dragged down by the "under-man"—a term Lothrop Stoddard coined to describe hereditary defectives who became socialist leaders or fell prey to radical appeals. The under-man was increasingly of swarthy complexion and feeble mind.[9]

Negrophobia and racism spurred students' application of eugenic theory to racial issues, which these undergraduates perceived as being "of immense importance to the future of the United States." One student argued that racial mixture "certainly injures or destroys the more specialized qualities of the white race." A number of students decided that genocide was the best solution for the "Negro problem." Bean argued for the "wide dissemination of birth control knowledge" among African Americans: "If the negro is given knowledge of contraception and access to contraceptive devices, this combined with his high death rate and present declining birth rate, aided by strict racial integrity laws as now in Virginia will cause his extinction in a comparatively short time and then insure a white America and her place in the world." These Virginia scholars deviated from Edward J. Larson's description of their Deep South neighbors. Larson avers that his subjects did not see eugenics as a panacea for the race problem, assuming that cultural racism and antimiscegenation laws operated so well that deep southerners did not fear black/white race mixing.[10]

Lewis and the other university eugenicists' effect upon southern thinking and belief is difficult to quantify. During Lewis's tenure, the biology department at Virginia consistently produced more majors than virtually any other department in the college of arts and sciences. In 1925, Lewis noted that enrollment "continues to grow at an embarrassing rate" with the classes logging 273 students, though "340 students would have registered for biology if room had been sufficient to take them." In 1952, Lewis boasted: "Biology has from fifty to eighty undergraduate majors each year. This is the largest number found in any school in the College of Arts and Sciences with the exception of economics." All majors and graduate students took Lewis's eugenics course. Moreover, 210 investigators spent the summer at Virginia's Mountain Lake

Biological Station in the 1930s, encountering Lewis, his beliefs, and teaching. More than 900 students passed through "Biology C1" alone during Lewis's thirty-eight-year career. If even half acted upon eugenical precepts, they would represent a sizeable contingent.[11]

A 1928 letter reveals the effect Lewis's course had upon his students. Citing "Biology C1" as "a wonderful course," a student gushed, "it transcends anything I have ever had or expect to have." The student expressed his praise in millennial terms: "The hope of the University of Virginia . . . and going further the salvation of religion" depended upon the "open minded" instruction in Lewis's eugenics course. Virginius Dabney, one of the South's leading "liberals," considered Lewis "one of my much admired and greatly loved teachers." While Dabney was a "racial moderate," not a virulent racist like Lewis, he championed segregation as rational management of race relations.[12]

Charles W. Clark was another of Lewis's acolytes. Writing in 1949, Clark extolled the racial theories of Lothrop Stoddard and excoriated the service record of blacks in World War II, continuing:

> In some recent article either *Time* or *Newsweek* stated that all races are "genetically equal," whatever that may mean. This is, of course, flying right in the face of experience—not to mention facts known to every cattle breeder. Truly the backswing from Mr. Hitler over to the opposite extreme is something to behold! And I know of no one to combat this foolishness except the scientist—the biologist and the psychologist, aided by the publicity man and the statistician.
>
> We are fighting with our backs to the wall and I fear that the worst is yet to come. . . . I do not pretend that the South has been wise in handling its problem. . . . But I still think we can handle it better without direction from Washington or advice from Albany, NY.[13]

Clark's letter displays an interesting blend of southern regionalism, racism, and eugenics.

In a letter written five years later, almost nine months after the Supreme Court's *Brown* decision, Clark demonstrated his eugenic convictions. Beginning, "This is partly a eugenic report, at which I hope you will be pleased," Clark described his family of five daughters, noting, "Oddly enough when there were only four, their coloration was in exact Mendelian proportion; one blond and three little pseudo-Italians." He then described his wife's heritage, remarking specifically that she was of "Irish ancestry (Protestant!), with Scottish, English, Swedish, and Polish blood." After sanitizing her Eastern European genes by claiming that "one of her D.A.R. ancestors was a Polish

Colonel, one of Koscuisko's staff," Clark affirmed her superiority by certifying her intellect: "She has a master's degree from Emory, and I consider her very intelligent." Clark's need to absolve his mate of any hereditary taint reveals his internalization of eugenics.[14]

Clark then returned to his racist diatribe. A farmer in the Mississippi Delta, Clark remarked that he was moving away from cotton production because it "simply requires too much nigger, and he is one gentleman of whom I am thoroughly sick and tired. . . . For the present, I am . . . shifting to white labor. Ten thousand dollar machines are simply not trusted to a chimpanzee!" Clark used his eugenic, racist sensibilities to navigate his changing relation to the land, reaffirming his identity as a "modern" southerner. Abandoning black labor and cotton for white-controlled machinery and crop diversification represented a repudiation of the Agrarian impulse and an acceptance of modernity, all riding on his eugenically legitimated, racist evaluation of blacks. Clark closed the letter saying: "I intend to write you at length about a certain Supreme Court decision and its possible results. Also I shall invite all the helpful suggestions you can give," presumably toward fighting desegregation. In Lewis's opinion, "it would be a major calamity to try to force racial equality, and any informed citizens who love their country must realize that the color line must be maintained in spite of hell and high water." Reinforcing the racial status quo and eliding the boundary between science and prejudice allowed educated southern white elites to avoid the choice between equally unpalatable racial liberalism and the "backward," antimodern, pseudopopulism epitomized by the traditionalist Vanderbilt Agrarians.[15]

Between Clark's letters, Lewis incited a national controversy with his professional swan song, performed before the 1951 American Association for the Advancement of Science (AAAS) annual convention. "Biological Principles and National Policy," Lewis's address as vice president of the AAAS and president of its botany section, sounded eugenical themes, outraged listeners, and caused the AAAS to break precedent and refuse to publish the speech in *Science*. Lewis argued that national policy in welfare, education, marriage, and even the provision of food all undercut biological law and threatened American civilization. Avowing in private that his intent was "to try to deflate the rosy but unrealistic ideas of the social welfare enthusiasts," Lewis knew that he "caused quite a lot of disturbance among the council" of the AAAS.[16]

Letters of support flooded in to Lewis, many of which were racist and anti-Semitic. James A. Tignor wrote, "in this day of indecision, emotional instability and general unreliability, the German and his kindred races alone seem still to be dependable, honest, reliable, and willing to work." Tignor noted ominously: "The Gestapo was only the revolt of the [fit] people and I can well visualize it, if things keep on this way, as preferable. Enough is enough! Keep up the fight." By 1951, Lewis's eugenics was no longer credible among the majority of scientists represented by the AAAS, despite the fact that many members of that body—and the public who monitored its activities—still agreed with Lewis.[17]

The Revolt against Civilization:
Eugenic Anti-Semitism and Antiradicalism

The recurring references to Hitler and the Nazi eugenic program reveal a particular formulation of eugenic anti-Semitism in operation on the campus of the University of Virginia and throughout the state. While anti-Semitism ran rampant in the United States during the first half of the twentieth century, elite colleges and universities became foci concentrating prejudice. Administrators at the University of Virginia characterized Jewish students as a necessary evil; most of them came from wealthy New York families and thus represented full tuition payments. This pecuniary interest mixed with a cultural prejudice that was reinforced by eugenic concerns to strengthen another culture of segregation—Jew from gentile. The administrative careers of Ivey Lewis and Harvey Jordan exemplify this eugenic anti-Semitism.[18]

In his 1924 speech "What Biology Says to the Man of Today," delivered to University of Virginia students under the auspices of the Anglo-Saxon Clubs of America (ASCOA), Ivey Lewis used Jews to illustrate eugenic racial purity. "It is no accident," Lewis contended, "that the culture with the longest continuous history in the world has been carried on by the race which is most jealous of its purity." Although Jews could be congratulated for their racial purity, they were demonized for their "clannishness," which made them unassimilable and a threat to the American race. Some eugenicists, like Lewis, created a taxonomy of "good" and "bad" Jews that mirrored their views about blacks. "Good" Jews, like good blacks, conformed to middle-class white norms in social deportment, yet remained within their segregated social "place," not seeking to marry into gentile/white families or enter gentile institutions. "Bad" Jews, like "uppity" blacks, "pushed" against these boundaries and sought integration and equality with gentiles, especially through sexual intercourse. Unfortunately, in the minds of most eugenicists, the "bad" Jewish trait was the dominant hereditary type. Sir Francis Galton set the pattern for this commentary when he wrote that "the Jews are specialised for a *parasitical* existence upon other nations, and that there is need of evidence that they are capable of fulfilling the varied duties of a civilised nation by themselves."[19]

Virginia eugenicists feared Jews almost as much as they did the feeble-minded or blacks. Their unease was reflected in the admissions policies of the University of Virginia and its medical school, in letters of recommendation for Jewish students, and in disciplinary actions against Jews. Just as these men used science, through eugenics, to legitimate their negrophobia, so too did they justify their anti-Semitism as scientific inquiry into the biology of the "Jewish problem."

In 1933, as Hitler assumed power, Lewis became the university's first dean of students. He immediately began to rationalize student oversight along neo-eugenic lines. He gathered "personnel information" about the students "in some detail," on a "carefully drawn information card" to be filled out at registration and filed for reference. This data would allow Lewis to investigate individual students and groups affiliated by ethnicity, religion, association, class cohort, and other variables. Creating his own small Eugenics Record Office, Lewis used this information to monitor students he suspected to be hereditarily inferior. In 1939, Lewis wrote President Newcomb, "Every so often I make a study of the percentage of Jewish students in the University so that we may be aware of the facts and the trend." Both Dean Lewis and Dean of the College George Oscar Ferguson became alarmed because the "percentage of Jews is steadily increasing, having now reached the figure 15.5 in the College and 10.87 in the University." After the college, the medical school enrolled the greatest number of Jewish students, deeply troubling Harvey Ernest Jordan.[20]

Jordan became dean of Virginia's medical school in 1939, which gave him authority over admissions. Previously, however, Jordan had been in charge of screening and recommending applicants. In December 1934, President Newcomb, under political pressure from Richmond, inquired into the status of Emmanuel Dickler's application to the medical school. Jordan complained, "I foresee considerable difficulty about admitting Mr. Dickler unless his record is really brilliant or unless you should especially wish to have him admitted" because "the pressure for admission of New York Jewish students . . . is getting to be terrific." While he would accede to political pressure, Jordan was more interested in admitting "good applicants from Southern institutions"—individuals he deemed to be superior to Jews. Regionalism, anti-Semitism, and eugenics converged to work against Jewish applicants.[21]

Jewish students who failed to recognize their professors' anti-Semitism and asked them for letters of recommendation gambled with their futures.

Lewis wrote long and effusive letters for gentile students he barely knew. For Jewish students, however, Lewis limited himself to perfunctory notes that damned with faint praise. In 1948, a young Jewish biologist who had taken a doctorate at Virginia earned this from Lewis: "[Goldstein] has a Jewy look but never shows some of the unfavorable characteristics commonly attributed to his race." Among the many stereotypical "unfavorable characteristics" Lewis attributed to the Jewish "race" was dishonesty. Lewis often alerted officials to Jewish students attempting to pass as gentile. Attempting to torpedo a Jewish student's medical school application, Lewis wrote, "H. J. Hatchfield registered at the University of Virginia as H. J. Hochfelder." Despite his "outstandingly good" academic record, Hatchfield's action in changing his name substantiated, in Lewis's mind, not only the threat of passing, but also the existence of a Jewish proclivity to subterfuge and malfeasance. In contrast, Lewis wrote of a gentile student: "He is not only a man of intelligence and efficiency but I can testify that his character is beyond reproach and his loyalty and patriotism are unquestioned. His father is Rector emeritus of Christ Episcopal Church in Charlottesville, and on both sides of his family Mr. Gibson is of old American stock."[22] Such preferential treatment inspired the university's most famous piece of dissident poetry, Karl J. Shapiro's "University," which began, "To hurt the Negro and avoid the Jew / Is the curriculum."

Dean Lewis also tracked the number of Jewish students expelled from the university for honor violations and apparently licentious behavior. Documents show that Lewis was attempting to prove that Jews were inherently dishonest and lustful—sure signs of the hereditary nature of Jewish racial acquisitiveness. From hereditary dishonesty and immorality it was only a short step, for Lewis, to hereditary radicalism.[23]

Lewis followed Lothrop Stoddard by merging his surveillance of Jews with antiradicalism. As interest in leftist politics swept across college campuses during the Great Depression and Spanish Civil War, Lewis grew uneasy about student-led political and social rallies. Acutely aware of the Popular Front's use of class and race to mobilize radical sentiment, Lewis suppressed campus discussion of these issues. In 1939, Lewis obstructed a "radical" youth conference. During this incident he first encountered David Carliner, a young law student he branded as an "extreme leftist." The Virginia Youth Conference sought to gather students of various racial, class, and gender backgrounds to discuss Virginia's Depression-induced problems. Lewis objected to "the participation of organized labor groups, which are in no sense of the word youth organizations," as well as to the participation of African Americans. Nevertheless, Lewis and Carliner hammered out a compromise mandating strict segregation in compliance with the Massenburg Act; that no resolutions would be adopted; and the exclusion of "organizations primarily of an adult membership." Lewis declared that "a genuine youth conference can be of great value, but a 'youth conference' turned into a political-racial-labor meeting is something we would not care to seem to sponsor." Within two years, Lewis would purge the University of Virginia of its "extreme leftist" firebrand, David Carliner.[24]

The "Carliner Case," as Lewis's persecution of Carliner came to be known, attracted national attention. On July 18, 1940, the summer before his final year of law school, police arrested Carliner for distributing "peace pamphlets" in Charlottesville's African American neighborhood. Frightened, Carliner gave the arresting officer a phony name and address. Carliner failed to appear in court until he was rearrested six weeks later. The police informed Dean Lewis of these transgressions. Carliner was not enrolled at the time of this off-campus infraction, so his case seemed beyond the university's jurisdiction. Lewis then learned that Carliner had borrowed university library books and signed a friend's name on the charge slip. Although Carliner's friend asked that the situation be viewed as a misunderstanding, Lewis gave no quarter.[25]

Lewis bent the university's regulations to suit his ends. He used a rule against public drunkenness to convince both the Administrative Council—comprised of eugenically minded antiradicals like Newcomb, Lewis, and Jordan—and the student senate that Carliner should be expelled from the university for "conduct reflecting serious discredit upon the University." Both groups voted for Carliner's dismissal. The liberal magazine the *New Republic* condemned these actions as traducing the ideals of another radical: the University of Virginia's founder, Thomas Jefferson. By that time, however, Lewis had won the battle.[26]

The crucial point is not that Ferguson, Jordan, and Lewis were bigots. The key distinction is that they believed their racial, religious, and political prejudices were eminently rational responses to "proven" biological axioms. The laws of genetics and eugenics had, for Virginia eugenicists, ossified into truisms with political ramifications. Despite advances in genetics and biology, these men remained wedded to decades-old ideas linking behavior—even political activism—and heredity.

Ferguson, Jordan, and Lewis were not alone in their fealty to mainline eugenics. During the 1930s, Dr. Robert Bennett Bean published research findings that remained consonant with the eugenics of the period from 1910 to 1919. Bean's 1932 book, *The Races of Man: Differentiation and Dispersal of Man*, traced the evolution of mankind. Replete with invidious distinctions separating "higher" and "lower" races and repeatedly comparing blacks to animals, the book even had one photograph that showed the "Hand of an adult Bantu Negro and the Hand of a Gorilla" side by side, leaving the reader to note the "similarity" and infer the meaning. A photo of a "Laughing Negro" supported Bean's contention that the "finely modulated expressions of the white race" were impossible for blacks. Bean's schematic "Tree of Races" depicted the ascension of humankind from its common root in Neanderthal man. The lowest limb represented the "Black Race," with an internal hierarchy of smaller branches placing the "Negro" above the "Bushman." The "Yellow-Brown Race" occupied the next-highest limb. The main trunk of the tree represented the "White Race," with an internal hierarchy placing the "Semitic" and "Hamitic-Dravidian" subgroups below the tree-topping "Nordics."[27]

Six years later, Bean published *The Peopling of Virginia*, his final paean to the "old American" stock responsible, in his mind, for the creation of American civilization. A compilation of Bean's anthropometric work, the book was a companion study to *Old Americans*, by the Smithsonian curator Aleš Hrdlička. Both men desired to prove the existence of a distinctly American race. Identifying this new American type would "set a standard of possible value as a basis for comparison with other groups of man in other parts of the world"—a way to place Americans atop the biological ladder. As an ethnographic history of Virginia, Bean's study betrayed decided eugenic biases. The book's tempered language, like that in *The Races of Man*, partially masked Bean's value judgments. Nevertheless, an insistent Teutonism informed the narrative. "Germans have been coming to Virginia ever since the first boat landed with four Germans on board," Bean wrote. Individuals of German heritage, according to Bean, "stuck better than other stocks," and this pioneering spirit led to racial advance. The book insisted that "Old Virginians," a group to which Bean belonged, represented one of the most superior physical stocks in the world. This conclusion was consonant with Hrdlička's findings about old Americans, although Bean's tone was more triumphal, redolent with mainline sentiment.[28]

The persistence of the mainline eugenics creed is undoubtedly due in part to intellectual stagnation within the American eugenics movement. Eugenics failed to attract members of the younger generation of laboratory scientists. Inculcating eugenics in generations of students who would not become scientists, however, had already succeeded in spreading the creed throughout society. Men trained in eugenic thought would rise to important posts and control key health-care, educational, and legal institutions throughout America and the South for more than another generation. It would take time for a new scientific orthodoxy to overturn the mainline paradigm, first in the scientific community and then in America at large. The time lag between changes in science and society allowed eugenics to maintain cultural force even after new knowledge reduced its scientific significance.[29]

Raising Racial Consciousness:
Virginia as Seat for a National Eugenics Institute

The national eugenics movement suffered a number of violent shocks in the 1930s that compromised the movement's solidarity. Charles B. Davenport went into semi-retirement in 1934, leaving his post as director of the Carnegie Institution's Department of Genetics at Cold Spring Harbor in 1936. Davenport abandoned the ERO in the wake of an unfavorable audit that determined that the records compiled by Davenport, Laughlin, and hundreds of eugenics fieldworkers were "unsatisfactory for the study of human genetics." Carnegie authorities allowed Harry Laughlin three more years to finish ongoing investigations in the genetics of racehorses. Laughlin, however, wasted no time in marshaling his resources and attempting to create a sinecure for himself, his much beloved records, and mainline eugenics.[30]

In January 1936, Laughlin discussed the future of eugenics with the New York textile magnate Wickliffe P. Draper. Laughlin appealed to Draper's long-standing desire to ensure the racial purity of "Old Stock" Americans. Knowing Draper's interest in preserving a pure "American race," Laughlin wrote that, to those who "look upon the American people as a definite racial stock still in the majority of the whole population and worth preserving through an active eugenical policy, perhaps the University of Virginia seems most promising" as a home. Laughlin claimed that the university "has a tradition of American aristocracy which the nation treasures very highly and which the Virginian himself holds without peer among American colleges." Moreover, Virginia had "an active and vigorous President in Dr. Newcombe [*sic*], in the Dean Dr. Lewis and the chairman of their board, Frederick Scott of Richmond." These factors should encourage Draper in "laying plans for an Institution of National Eugenics as a part of the University of Virginia." For "a very few thousand dollars a year," Draper could underwrite "a plan of organization of such an institute to outline courses of study covering the racial aspect of applied eugenics in the public school system from the Grade 1 clear through the post graduate research work." Laughlin's assumption that he would head this national institute remained unspoken throughout his appeal.[31]

Laughlin telegrammed Virginia's president, John Lloyd Newcomb, about "the desirability and possibility of work in eugenics by Virginia." Laughlin assured him that "Draper wants nothing for himself but is in position to give substantial financial support of work which he believes would definitely re- vive American racial ideals and would advance them substantially." In the midst of the Great Depression, the thought of "substantial financial support" appealed to Newcomb. That many of his faculty supported eugenics only made the meeting more likely.[32]

The Virginia summit began in secrecy and ended in obscurity. Sensitive to Laughlin's confidential tone, Newcomb replied that he would be "glad to have [Draper] come to Charlottesville for a conference about a subject which is of mutual interest." Draper believed that Dean Lewis "especially seemed inter- ested in my ideas and suggested that I meet Messr's Cox and Powell which I hope later to do." Laughlin responded enthusiastically, "It looks as though, because of its historic background and traditional racial attitude, the South will develop leadership in Americanization during the next generation." The subsequent denial of Draper's offer raises more questions than available evi- dence can answer. Nothing exists explaining why the University of Virginia, rife with eugenic belief in a state pursuing an aggressive program of applied eugenics, would reject this windfall. Lewis's actions, however, suggest some possible answers.[33]

Ivey Lewis was, first and foremost, a shrewd politician. He knew how to aggrandize influence, and was loathe to relinquish power once he held it. Bringing Draper's institute and Laughlin to the university would jeopar- dize Lewis's position a number of ways. Laughlin presented a challenge to Lewis's authority as a eugenicist. Politically, the outspoken racial extremism of Laughlin and Draper probably alarmed Lewis. In the face of increasing black civil rights agitation, outspoken mainliners like Laughlin and Draper risked creating a backlash similar to the one that hit the Anglo-Saxon Clubs of America in 1925 and 1926. Moreover, Lewis was contending with a "Jew- ish problem" at the University of Virginia. A regular reader of the *Eugenical News,* Lewis had probably detected the journal's increasingly pro-Nazi stance. Although Lewis likely agreed with Nazi eugenic and anti-Semitic policies, he understood how controversial they were in America. Lewis enjoyed his posi- tion as a prominent educator within the state and as an influential within scientific associations. He would not have wanted to jeopardize this power by picking the wrong side in a political fight, or associating with a scientist other experts viewed dubiously.[34]

Like many scientists of his generation, Lewis felt that involving himself openly in politics sullied his reputation as an "objective" investigator. Until his retirement, he did most of his political lobbying behind the scenes. He taught generations of Virginia students mainline eugenics, yet avoided being tarred with the brush of extremism. Lewis fits the model of a scientist who preferred to "retain both his public prominence and his private bigotry." While he remained convinced that science had proven that innate racial differences resulted in social inequality, in the political atmosphere of the late 1930s his views were open to attack in a way they had not been in 1924. Lewis made no public statement about eugenics similar to his 1924 address until 1951, when he was retiring from the AAAS and had nothing to lose.[35]

Virginians Meet Manhattan: The Eugenics Research Association

Following the 1932 Third International Congress of Eugenics, Dr. Walter Plecker experienced an upsurge in professional popularity among mainline eugenicists, despite Ivey Lewis's increasing chariness. Dr. Plecker achieved prominence because members of the national movement, like the most ardent Virginia eugenicists, drifted toward their most extreme position in the 1930s. The advent of Nazism convinced many eugenicists that racial purity was achievable. Plecker, as the leader of the most aggressive eugenic antimiscegenation program in the country, naturally drew attention. Using medical parlance, Harry Laughlin proclaimed: "Doubtless the best headquarters in the world for [studying racial integrity] would be Dr. Plecker's office. . . . His methods of diagnosis of 'pass-for-whites' should be studied thoroughly at first hand."[36] In 1935, Plecker's descriptions of Virginia's Racial Integrity Act and his promotion of Earnest Cox fell on receptive ears.

Laughlin had been aware of Cox since the publication of *White America*, which Laughlin reviewed favorably in the *Eugenical News*. Cox's papers preserve correspondence with Laughlin beginning in 1934, when Laughlin sought to enlist Cox's support for immigration studies to be conducted by the prominent anti-immigration activist John B. Trevor Jr. That same year, Cox's efforts to repatriate blacks brought congratulations from the honorary president of the ERA, Clarence G. Campbell. Campbell, a Nazi sympathizer and rabid eugenicist, agreed with Cox that "repatriation is the only true solution of the Negro problem." He wrote: "I have sent Doctor Plecker a short article that might possibly go a little way toward helping the cause along. And I wish that I might come to Richmond and see you and him and Major Powell, and conspire with you on what further might be done."[37]

Acting in his capacity as secretary-treasurer of the ERA, in 1936 Harry Laughlin invited Cox to address the mainline eugenics community. Campbell offered to arrange for "an intelligent negro or two to attend the meeting and speak in support" of Cox's paper, affirming that "many of the better class of negroes see eye to eye with us on this matter." He noted, "a year or two ago some of them [upper-class/intelligent blacks] wanted to start a Negro Eugenics Society which I myself think is quite a good idea." Plecker accompanied Cox to the ERA confab. While in Manhattan, Cox introduced Plecker to Madison Grant. Plecker was awed to encounter "the leader [of] the great racial integrity movement of this country." At the same time, Laughlin arranged for the Virginians to meet Wickliffe Draper, to discuss their mutual interest in eugenics, racial purity, and repatriation.[38]

Ivey Lewis wrote to Cox just days before the New York trip, suggesting a meeting with Draper. Lewis recounted his own interview with Draper. "Mr. Draper is seriously interested in the probable solution of the negro problem. . . . He seems to be a man of means who will be able and willing to help effectively in carrying out any program which seems to promise some results." Noting that the University of Virginia was "unable to accept his assistance," Lewis hoped that Powell and Cox "might meet him and direct his enthusiasm along practical lines."[39]

Cox, Plecker, and Draper's meeting had precisely the effect for which Lewis had hoped. The interchange convinced Draper to finance a printing of *White America*, for distribution to Congress and anyone else Cox should suggest. This new edition of Cox's book attracted one of the Senate's most prominent racists: Mississippi's Theodore G. Bilbo. "Your manuscript on the history of the cause of repatriation was a knock-out," Bilbo wrote. "I used it in my speech on the lynching bill. . . . I have almost made up my mind to specialize on the repatriation of the negro." Cox and Bilbo, with Draper's funding, would work together to advance repatriation, particularly as a substitute for legislation like the Dyer antilynching bill that promised genuine improvements for African Americans.[40]

Cox's appearance before the ERA split his eugenical focus. Repatriation had always dominated his consciousness, yet the influence of Grant, Stoddard, Campbell, Laughlin, and Draper rekindled Cox's interest in Nordic superiority. Always an insistent rhythm throbbing beneath his repatriationist rhetoric, Cox developed an abiding interest in his "Teutonic" heritage. He established connections with prominent Nazi racial theorists before World

War II. After the war, he would contact other former Nazi officials. With the passage of time, Cox's views became more and more extreme.

Madison Grant introduced Cox to Nazi racial scientists. Grant requested that Cox send a copy of *White America* to Professor Hans Günther, "one of the most distinguished anthropologists of Germany." Günther, a committed Nazi Nordic supremacist, had been deeply influenced by Grant's book, and had suggested that Lothrop Stoddard release a German edition of *Revolt against Civilization*. When the Nazis took control of the province of Thuringia in 1930, Hitler appointed Günther to a new chair in *Rassenkunde* (raceology) at the University of Jena. Showing his support, Hitler attended the professor's first lecture. Günther's *Brief Race-Study of the German People* sold over 272,000 copies between 1929 and 1943. Thus Cox's relatively obscure work found its way into the hands of an architect of the German eugenic program. Cox himself sought out allegiance with Reichsminister Wilhelm Frick, Nazi secretary of the interior and a prominent racial theorist. Cox sent Frick a complimentary copy of *White America*. The Nazis, it appeared to Cox and others in 1938, held the key to sustaining civilization.[41]

"Hitting Some Hard Blows": Sterilization and Antimiscegenation, 1930–1950

Virginia's eugenic juggernaut churned ahead in the 1930s, relatively unhindered by negative publicity and changing scientific standards. The impulse for sterilization gained momentum after the *Buck* case. Initially, most geneticists and physicians felt sterilization was a sound response to severe physical and mental defect. Although the leading Americans studying mental disorders moved away from eugenic sterilization in the 1930s, state hospital directors sought to prove their institutions' utility with high patient throughput statistics. Thus, the mentally retarded fell victim to ideological inertia and political expedience.[42]

The *Virginia Medical Monthly* featured articles on eugenic sterilization throughout the 1930s. Dr. H. Coles Grant of Staunton, Virginia, reminded his colleagues that "sterilization of the insane or feebleminded must necessarily be done with as little fright and inconvenience to the patient as possible, lest the patients to follow stampede and refuse to be operated [*sic*]." Doctors from the Eastern State Hospital linked surgical and eugenic therapy, noting that "sterilization seems a rational and safe method of lowering the percentage of the mentally incompetent in future generations." The authors wrote that "one patient, sterilized incidentally to an operation for acute appendicitis, was so disturbed that it was necessary to keep her restrained most of the time for three weeks after the operation to prevent her from clawing at the incision." One wonders whether her disturbed state was part of her mental pathology or a reaction to learning that she had been sterilized. The *Medical Monthly* ran illustrated articles depicting improved operations for sterilizing women and men in 1930 and 1936. In 1936, Dr. Charles Putney discussed the Nazi eugenic program and remarked, "Hitler seems to agree with Dean Inge who says that 'The state has as good a right to remove undesirable citizens as a gardener has to weed his garden.'" Clarifying his own position, Putney wrote: "Feeblemindedness, degeneracy, criminality, and diseases get so thoroughly intermingled and become such a part of the constituents of a nation that retrogression ensues. The nation itself becomes degenerated and finally crumbles and falls." Eugenic sterilization offered salvation.[43]

These physicians acted on their beliefs. Statistics document Virginia's aggressive sterilization rate (see table 2). The year after Carrie and Doris Buck were sterilized, Virginia sterilized 206 state hospital inmates. This number jumped to 395 the following year. Virginia averaged 316 sterilizations per year in the 1930s, during the height of the Great Depression when money for social services was scarce. In the 1940s, Virginia's sterilization rate dropped to approximately 196 per year. During the 1950s, the yearly average dropped to 125. This steady decrease seems to support the thesis that eugenic sterilization waned over time, particularly as Nazi abuses came to light. Put in context, however, Virginia's statistics tell another story.[44]

The vigor of Virginia's sterilization program becomes apparent when it is compared to those of the other states. Although California, Kansas, Indiana, Michigan, and North Carolina all had sterilization statutes in operation before Virginia, by 1932 Virginia had eclipsed all but California in cumulative sterilizations. After World War II, Virginia and North Carolina vied for the most sterilizations each year. Assistant Attorney General Joseph L. Kelly Jr. chastised Virginia physicians' zeal for sterilization, issuing a warning to the State Hospital Board for failure to maintain verbatim transcripts of all sterilization hearings. Kelly told the board that "any laxity in this respect . . . would endanger the continued existence of the law itself." Virginia's doctors complied with Kelly's warning and preserved their eugenic prerogative.[45]

A striking pattern emerges from the sterilization totals tallied by state institutions (see table 3). Western State Hospital and the Lynchburg Colony led all white institutions. Lynchburg, the dedicated facility for feebleminded Virginians, would logically be expected to perform the greatest number of sterilizations. The main factor accounting for Western's robust sterilization program

TABLE 2. Virginia Sterilizations, 1928 to June 30, 1964

Year	Males	Females	Total
1928		(2)[a]	2
1929			206
1930			395
1931			324
1932			309
Total through 1932[b]	431	805	1,236
1933	108	100	208
1934[c]	218	247	465
1935	134	159	293
1936	145	161	306
1937	128	136	264
1938	148	173	321
1939	143	181	324
1940	161	188	349
1941	121	168	289
1942	149	183	332
1943	94	125	219
1944	28	103	131
1945	45	92	137
1946	61	119	180
1947	31	84	115
1948	19	113	132
1949	83	131	214
1950	60	148	208
1951	95	111	206
1952	57	96	153
1953	92	77	169
1954	57	114	171
1955	50	61	111
1956	57	30	87
1957	34	79	113
1958	46	69	115
1959	22	40	62
1960	9	53	62
1961	6	33	39
1962	11	20	31
1963	10	29	39
1964	10	13	23
Total	2,863	4,241	7,104

Source: Compiled from J. Paul, "Three Generations of Imbeciles," 511-13.

[a] The two women reported in 1928 were actually Carrie and Emma Buck, sterilized the previous year, after that year's report appeared (see J. Paul, "Three Generations of Imbeciles," 511).

[b] This is the first year in which the report lists breakdowns by gender.

[c] The original lists a double entry (two figures) for 1934 that are here summed into one figure.

was Dr. Joseph "Sterilization" DeJarnette, who personally sterilized large numbers of patients. The Central State Hospital, home to Virginia's feebleminded and insane African Americans until the Petersburg Colony opened in 1939, began sterilizing blacks in 1929. Virginia, unlike the Deep South states, spent money to sterilize blacks, averaging fifty procedures a year according to one estimate. When considered as a percentage of the population, it does not appear that Virginia disproportionately targeted blacks for sterilization. Blacks comprised approximately 24 percent of Virginia's total population and accounted for approximately 26 percent of all sterilizations between 1930 and 1960 (see table 4).[46]

A number of plausible explanations exist for Virginia's willingness to sterilize blacks as well as whites. Many poor southern states saw no reason to expend scarce resources on blacks, preferring to consign "unfit" African Americans to the chain gang. Virginia was wealthy in contrast to her Deep South neighbors, and thus could extend eugenics to African Americans. White Virginians, cognizant of the Old Dominion's history as a slave-breeding state, considered their African American population to be qualitatively superior to the black population elsewhere. Nevertheless, they still believed many African Americans were criminal, diseased, and hereditarily unfit. Since Virginia would have an African American population for the foreseeable future, many whites believed they should ensure that only the best possible blacks survived. Moreover, sterilized black women would be "safe" domestic employees, unable to be impregnated by their employers, which meant fewer light-skinned babies to blur the color line. And, sterilizing blacks increased the dysgenic pressure on the race—hastening extinction.[47]

Gender dynamics reinforced the class biases inherent in eugenic sterilization, which focused on inmates of *state*, not private, institutions. State patients tended to be from the lowest socioeconomic class, the group blamed for most

TABLE 3. Virginia Sterilizations, by Hospital, 1924 to 1964

Hospital	No. of sterilizations
Central State Hospital	1,634
Eastern State Hospital	393
Southwestern State Hospital	364
Western State Hospital	1,701
Lynchburg Training School	2,781
Petersburg Training School	246
Total	7,119

Source: J. Paul, "Three Generations of Imbeciles," 512.

TABLE 4. Virginia Sterilizations, by Race and Gender

	No. of sterilizations	*Percentage of all sterilizations*
Race		
Blacks	1,880	26
Whites	5,239	74
Gender		
Males	2,863	40
Females	4,241	60

Note: The discrepancy in total numbers between the racial and gender breakdowns reflects the different totals given in tables 2 and 3.

miscegenation by elite white eugenicists. Even though most eugenicists in Virginia cast blacks as a tremendous threat, the menace of feebleminded whites mating with blacks caused even greater alarm.

With regard to the feebleminded, Virginia matched the national pattern, sterilizing women about one and one-half times as often as men (see table 4). More men were sterilized than women in only two years between 1933 and 1964 (see table 2). African American women were sterilized at an even higher rate, receiving over 70 percent of procedures. Eugenicists sought to sterilize the youngest women first, thereby cutting off a longer period of reproductive potential. A 1940 annual report from Central State Hospital indicates that 78 percent of the women sterilized were between the ages of fifteen and twenty-four, while another 18 percent were under fourteen years old.[48]

Virginia's sterilization rates belie the notion that the Great Depression and knowledge of Nazi abuses curtailed applied eugenics in the United States. Virginia's eugenic program barely dipped in 1944–45, then slowly climbed through the early 1950s. Sterilization rates plummeted in the 1960s, as social and professional norms shifted in favor of individual autonomy and bodily integrity. Virginia sterilized its last black patients in 1970 and its last white patients in 1979. The 1924 law was updated in 1974. All eugenic language was purged from the statute enabling the sterilization of mentally retarded and incompetent individuals in 1980.[49]

Even as Virginia's sterilization program accelerated, a covert effort emerged to circumvent Judge Holt's ruling in the Sorrells case. Walter Plecker had finally learned the value of discretion, writing, "We are hitting some hard blows here in our office quietly but are avoiding any display in public." He began to take increasingly extra- and illegal steps to coerce compliance with the RIA. In all correspondence, Plecker averred that all Native Americans in Virginia were of mixed, and therefore black, "blood." Plecker opened his files to any white citizen considering marriage. He counseled one father that his daughter's intended groom was of mixed race, stating, "We hope that your daughter can see the seriousness of the whole matter and will dismiss this young man without more ado." He alerted school superintendents to the racial status of "questionable" students seeking enrollment, often resulting in the denial of admission. In 1935, he complimented a Nazi official for his efforts to track and sterilize "some six hundred children born to German women by negro fathers following the stay of [French] negro troops in Germany" after World War I. "I hope that this work has been completed and that not one has been missed," Plecker wrote, sighing, "I sometimes regret that we have not the authority to put some [similar] measures in practice in Virginia."[50]

Plecker capitalized on the authority of his office to bully individuals. "We have again a certificate purporting to be the certificate for your birth, which you returned to us after we had declined to accept it," he began one letter. He then scolded the man, who claimed he was white and his name was Wynnel:

> The name of the old negro family of which you are a member . . . is spelled two ways—Winn and Wynn without the "E." . . . under no circumstances will we permit the addition of the Tom Foolery "El" which you have put after your name; we will have none of the foolishness of "Moorish American" or "Olive Moorish American" or any of this kind of stuff. If you make up a certificate and write plain negro as the race of your father and mother and it is otherwise acceptable, we will accept it.

Plecker also threatened Wynnel's mother, demanding an explanation of the name change, threatening legal action, and devolving to invective: "We notice that you put your mother, Mary Julia Brockenbrough, also as an 'Olive Moorish American.' When did she happen to change off from a plain King William negro?"[51]

Plecker confessed his extralegal activities on a number of occasions. Always "glad to find young men interested in this study [of racial integrity]," he wrote to a student at the Virginia Military Institute, to explain the difficulties in enforcing the RIA created by Judge Holt's ruling. To aid future generations, "we entirely ignore that decision which we know was made without the facts which are in our possession. We entirely ignore their [the family in question's] claims as white on their birth certificates, and place behind each of their certificates a printed sheet designated as a warning." The warning label read, "WARNING—To be attached to the backs of birth or death certificates of those believed to be incorrectly recorded as to color or race." It then listed Plecker's historical and genealogical authorities, concluding, "there are no descendants of Virginia Indians . . . who are unmixed with negro blood." Plecker had no statutory authority to take this action until 1944. His rabid commitment to eugenical racial purity provided all the warrant he needed. Plecker was so confident that he told the commissioner of the federal Office of Indian Affairs, "Your staff member is probably correct in his surmise that Hitler's genealogical study of the Jews is not more complete [than Plecker's files]." Mobilization for World War II tested Plecker's ingenuity in circumventing contrary legal precedents. Native Americans could register with their local Selective Service Board as "Indian" and then be trained with white troops—passing into the white community around Plecker's barriers. Plecker convinced the state selective service board to amend their policy. The state board made local boards responsible for determining "the ethnic origin of each individual Registrant," providing Plecker with the opportunity to present evidence against each individual at his induction hearing.[52]

In October 1942, William Kinkle Allen called Plecker's bluff. Allen requested official birth certificates for Native Americans from Amherst County (members of the "Win tribe," and therefore, in Plecker's mind, black). Plecker informed Allen that these persons would need to reregister regarding race. "Of course," Plecker intoned, "we will accept nothing except colored on these certificates." Unlike others confronted with Plecker's scare tactics, Allen hired the Richmond attorney John Randolph Tucker, a member of the prestigious family that produced the cleric Beverly D. and Dr. Beverly R. Tucker, both opponents of Plecker's methods. Tucker berated Plecker for his extralegal actions: "I find no where in the law any provision which authorizes the Registrar to constitute himself judge and jury for the purpose of determining the race of a child born." He continued that unless Plecker produced the records, he would "apply to a proper court for a mandamus to compel you to perform your duty as prescribed by the statute." Plecker was flabbergasted. "As you point out, and as the Attorney General advises, the law does not permit us to give the truth on the certificates but seems to compel me as State Registrar to certify what I know to be absolutely false," Plecker conceded. "Perhaps you do not realize the seriousness of the matter in which you are taking part," the registrar spluttered. "The purpose of these people is not simply, if possible, to establish their claim that they are Indians but to use that means of entering and marrying into the white race," a horrible dysgenic plot. A month later, Plecker reminded local registrars that passing threatened white society. Plecker claimed that he had consulted with the attorney general and prepared "a form letter to be returned to the attendant with the original certificate when the child of a colored parent is reported as Indian or white." In view of the Allen case, the attorney general would never have given such counsel. Plecker relied on subterfuge and his office's power to cow attending midwives and physicians into compliance.[53]

In 1943, Plecker sent another warning about draft registration and passing to all local registrars of vital statistics, physicians, public health officers, nurses, school superintendents, and clerks of courts. "Some of these mongrels," Plecker warned, "finding that they have been able to sneak in their birth certificates unchallenged as Indians are now making a rush to register [for the draft] as white." Plecker again threatened local registrars with "one year in the penitentiary" for making erroneous registrations. "To aid all of you in determining just which are mixed families," Plecker added, "we have made a list of their surnames by counties and cities, as complete as possible at this time." Plecker emphasized the importance of such vigilance: "One hundred and fifty thousand other mulattoes in Virginia are watching eagerly the attempt of their pseudo-Indian brethren, ready to follow in a rush when the first have made a break in the dike."[54]

Only Plecker's retirement, at age eighty-five, in May 1946 began eroding the RIA. Shortly before his death, Plecker published a pamphlet entitled *Virginia's Vanished Race*, in which he wondered, in rhetoric redolent with the imagery of the Old South and Nazism, "Is the integrity of the master race, with our Indians as a demonstration, also to pass by the mongrelisations [*sic*] route?" It would be another twenty years before the U.S. Supreme Court declared the RIA unconstitutional, consigning the notion of a eugenic master race, at least as enshrined in statutory law, to oblivion. The process of rehabilitating Virginians of color continues, as Virginia's Native Americans seek to regain sovereign status from the U.S. Congress.[55]

Reform Eugenics in Virginia

Even as eugenic anti-Semitism increased, sterilization rates mounted, and Walter Plecker's depredations reached new heights of infamy, a reform impulse emerged in eugenics teaching. Orland Emile White, a University of Virginia geneticist from 1927 to 1955, began to turn students away from the mainline creed. Notwithstanding his own well-developed racial prejudices, White's open-minded approach to genetics merged with his liberal views about women and birth control, allowing him to puncture the inflated rhetoric of mainline eugenics. His students worked in plant rather than animal genetics, further attenuating the mainline creed. White's physical isolation at Blandy Farm, removed from the main campus during the growing season, increased his autonomy. White continued to believe in the existence of "fit" and "unfit" genes, but he became more skeptical about developing public policy from genetics.

White maintained relatively close ties to the American Eugenics Society (AES) and the larger eugenics community at least through the Third International Congress of Eugenics in 1932. In 1929, White wrote an article for the magazine *Eugenics* and agreed to be one of its correspondents for Virginia (the other was Dr. Walter Plecker). Sometime between 1936 and 1945, White expunged the entries recording his membership in the AES and the Society for Experimental Biology and Medicine from his curriculum vita. He remained a lifelong member of the American Genetics Association, which espoused reform eugenics through the 1960s.[56]

During the wave of genetic discovery following Thomas Hunt Morgan's *Drosophila* experiments, White and his graduate students' botanical research revealed the complexity of genetic interactions in the expression of an organism's phenotype (its physical characteristics). These revelations tempered students' acceptance of Ivey Lewis's mainline eugenic lessons. By the 1930s and 1940s, these aspiring scientists became more authoritative sources of genetic knowledge than Lewis. Although Lewis's eugenics course remained a requirement, graduate students probably came away from it with a different residuum than did advanced undergraduates. Many of White's well-trained students achieved solid academic careers at universities across the South, at Harvard, and in Canada.

White's two surviving course booklists reveal his shifting stance. White's 1927 syllabus is replete with eugenics texts. He assigned East's *Inbreeding and Outbreeding*, Samuel J. Holmes's *The Trend of the Race*, Albert Wiggam's *The New Decalogue of Science* and *Fruit of the Family Tree*, Edward Conklin's *Heredity and Environment*, R. Ruggle Gates's *Heredity and Eugenics*, William E. Castle's *Genetics and Eugenics*, Vernon Kellogg's *Mind and Heredity*, and Popenoe and Johnson's *Applied Eugenics*, along with books covering specific topics like plant genetics. These texts hewed to the mainline eugenics orthodoxy. By 1953, the year Ivey Lewis retired, only East's *Inbreeding and Outbreeding* survived on White's list. White had also added Aldous Huxley's portrait of a eugenic dystopia, *A Brave New World*, to the reading list. Clearly, White taught a significantly different eugenic lesson than Lewis.[57]

White's sole surviving lecture began: "Genetics is the most exact and the most dangerous of the biological group of natural sciences. . . . It deals with the principles, generalizations, concepts, and groups of facts that underlie creating a better or worse kind of animal, plant, or human being." This lone, oblique reference to eugenics is telling for its cautionary and circumspect tone. Of heredity and environment, White said: "In no manner are environment and heredity to be considered as forces, and certainly not as opposing forces as is often the popular conception held by individuals in everyday life. As the geneticist views them, heredity and environment are simply phenomena, both of which are always present all the time in the life history of any animal, plant, or human being." Men like Lewis, Jordan, Bean, and Royster echoed this statement, but all of them still hedged their equanimity by stating that heredity was ultimately more significant. Moreover, White warned, "because human beings are such poor material to work with since the ability to control them experimentally is difficult and generations mature so slowly, we know relatively little about their heredity." Where the other men would have touted the heredity of pathological and mental traits, White confined his comments to hair texture and eye color. The point of his talk was that "environment and heredity are very intimately mixed up"—a position Lewis would have agreed with in theory, but rejected in teaching.[58]

White's attitudes toward gender and reproduction broadened his students' perspectives and further limited the appeal of mainline eugenics. White admitted many more women to his graduate program, and produced more female doctors, than Lewis. Like many other eugenicists, White wondered about the effect women's higher education and changing marriage customs would have on the "future of the race." White recounted a conversation with one of his former female graduate students, the unmarried "head of a big Biology Department in a women's college." The woman was "wondering about what is going to become of the race, because so many of her intelligent class are unmarried and probably will remain so. . . . [S]he advises her girls, for the most part, to get married and have at least five children" because they would "exert a great deal more influence, in all probability, in that way then [sic] if you had continued to devote yourself entirely to a scientific career." White wondered "whether to encourage [his female graduate students] to marry the science or pray for a husband. How about it?"[59]

White's correspondent, Mary Ellen Churchill, another former graduate student who had married and dropped out of the profession to raise two children, replied: "I am still a firm believer in education for girls—to the outermost limit of their capacities. It may not pay the state but it certainly pays the girl, whether she sticks to a career or marries and has five babies." In a comment as reflective of social custom as eugenic sensibility, she wrote, "The ideal arrangement, of course, is to have both, but it takes a clever woman to manage that." White agreed entirely. Churchill had married a fellow student of White's and been forced to leave academic genetics by an unplanned pregnancy. "It isn't as if we hadn't tried all the known brands of precaution which are each and every one such a pain in the neck that we have only our own carelessness to blame. I hope the pills Mr. Wiggam predicts will be on sale before I am a grandmother because otherwise I may secure my immortality with a tribe as numerous as any ignorant Italians." Churchill's invocation of the eugenicist Albert E. Wiggam, her frank discussion of birth control, and her ethnic slur all reveal both the trusting nature of her relationship with White, and the eugenic sensibilities that helped guide her life. Fourteen years later, in reporting to White that her children were "doing well in school and are full of bounce," she joked, "When a friend asked me if my training in heredity was responsible for my superior children, I assured him it was certainly partly responsible."[60]

As a result of the Blandy Farm's small scale, White taught far fewer students than Lewis. (Nevertheless, many of them married, causing one wag to write: "Really, Dr. White, I think you ought to consider the practical Eugenics possibilities of the Farm. You have a pretty good record up to the present.") In the short run, his students did little to counterbalance the beliefs taught by Lewis. In the long run, because White's students became professors of genetics across the South, teaching a moderate, reform eugenics, they accelerated the shift in popular and professional thinking away from mainline eugenics.[61]

Ultimately, the most infamous legacy of the University of Virginia's eugenic teaching was its effect on health-care provision. Many of the students who took courses in eugenics became physicians. Of the twenty-seven student term papers surviving from Lewis's eugenics class, nine belonged to students who became doctors; one belonged to a dentist; one belonged to a woman who became a nurse; and one belonged to a man who, after studying with Orland White, became a famous plant geneticist. Those students who undertook their medical training at the University of Virginia also received booster shots of eugenics in the substantive and incidental coverage the topic received from Bean, Jordan, Royster, and others—not to mention its extensive coverage in Virginia's medical press. Undoubtedly many of these physicians integrated the lessons they learned into both their personal worldviews and professional practices.[62]

———————

Segregation's science continued to exert power throughout the 1930s and 1940s. Directed by an elite cadre of Virginians, eugenic public policy affected the lives of thousands of poor, uneducated, and disabled Virginians. The acquiescence in the eugenic program of many midlevel functionaries—from local registrars of vital statistics, to public school officials, to midwives and country doctors—speaks to the power of eugenic ideology in daily life. Some of these individuals were doubtless coerced by the autocratic, extralegal behavior of men like Walter Plecker. The complicity of many more Virginians stemmed from their silent assent. They viewed commitment and sterilization of the feebleminded, and the repression of Native and African Americans, as eminently moderate and rational approaches to social problems. Eugenics offered a viable alternative to the extralegal violence used elsewhere to suppress radicals, blacks, and the poor. Elite Virginians hoped eugenics would clarify the "muddled middle" of segregated society—the boundary of the color line "where mixed-race people moved through mixed race spaces, from railroad cars to movies to department stores, neither public nor private, neither black nor white." Eugenics alleviated status anxiety, supporting belief in the superiority and "normality" of well-to-do whites.[63]

Eugenical policy sought to make real the imagined community of the American race while justifying invented traditions of racial superiority. Eugenicists constructed archetypal norms for all humanity by defining superior and inferior not just through race and sex classifications, but also "fitness" and "unfitness." Eugenics parsed humanity using the rubric of science to reify subgroups, establish norms, and dictate social behavior. By defining mixed-race and feebleminded individuals as "not white" and placing them in a permanently inferior position in the racial taxonomy, eugenics defused the dangers of interracial interaction in mixed-race space. Embodied in public policy by the sterilization act and the RIA, eugenics sought to sanctify the only space that really had to remain pure—the conjugal bedroom.

Ultimately, the eugenicists failed to achieve their goal. During the 1960s, shifting, pluralistic definitions of what it meant to be American elided the older notions of homogeneity that undergirded the eugenic conception of the American race. Changing social context and definitions of race, class, gender, and normalcy, coupled with developments internal to genetic science, undercut eugenics. A strong residue of eugenic ideology would remain in the minds of many Americans, especially whites. The dregs of mainline eugenics would recrudesce in the white response to black civil rights militancy.

7

"THEY SAW BLACK ALL OVER"

Eugenics, Massive Resistance, and Punitive Sterilization

ON MAY 17, 1954, the U.S. Supreme Court forever changed the rules governing southern society. Chief Justice Earl Warren, writing for a unanimous Court, declared that compulsory segregation of black schoolchildren "generates a feeling of inferiority" that "affects their hearts and minds in a way unlikely to ever be undone." The Court concluded that school segregation deprived African American students of the equal protection of the laws guaranteed by the Fourteenth Amendment. Henceforth black children and white children would, in theory, sit side by side in America's public schools.[1]

The culmination of the legal campaign against Jim Crow by the National Association for the Advancement of Colored People, *Brown* signaled the ascendance of environmental concerns over hereditarian notions in the scientific, legal, and public realms. The *Brown* decision was a watershed in Supreme Court jurisprudence. The Court overrode its famous ruling in *Plessy v. Ferguson* on the basis of "sociological" evidence rather than legal precedent. The Court accepted testimony presented by sociologists and psychologists that "separate but equal" treatment "damaged" the psyches of young African Americans. *Brown* created the "breach in the dike" of segregation that Virginia eugenicists had feared for so long. Previously, in the debates over the federal Immigration Restriction Act and Virginia's sterilization and racial integrity laws, legislators and courts accepted hereditarian arguments as the rationale for exercising the state's police power. Beginning with *Brown*, environmentalist logic assumed preeminence in legal discourse about individual liberties and the state's police power. Given the social and political context of the South, however, *Brown* actually allowed hereditary determinism to make its penultimate grasp for power. *Brown* revitalized racist eugenics as a justification for southern resistance to desegregation, dubbed "Massive Resistance" by Virginia governor J. Lindsay Almond. As a result, the RIA received its final reprieve from the U.S. Supreme Court in the 1955 case *Naim v. Naim*. It would take the Supreme Court's 1967 decision in *Loving v. Virginia* to overturn the RIA, ending Virginia's history of racial control through eugenical social policy.[2]

Brown had no bearing on the other wing of mainline eugenic policy, the sterilization of the "feebleminded." Virginia's sterilization rates would not plunge until the 1960s. In 1962 and 1964, state legislators battled over the punitive sterilization of "welfare mothers," once again merging race, class, and gender biases in the name of segregation's science. In 1973 and 1974, federal courts handed down decisions in *Roe v. Wade* and *Relf v. Weinberger* that established new limits on state authority over reproduction, buttressing individual autonomy and the right to privacy. These decisions, and changing mores regarding sexuality and reproduction, ended statutory eugenic public policy. Virginia performed its last eugenic sterilizations between 1972 and 1979.[3]

In the wake of *Brown*, Virginians experienced a new "crisis of modernity," a sense of instability and change similar to the New South era. Booming worldwide populations and the "green revolution" of the 1950s and 1960s presented hereditarians with a new menace. Eugenic ideology shifted from racist mainline thinking to neo-Malthusian concerns about world overpopulation, the quality of the world population, and the increasing cost of welfare programs. Thus, both colleagues and students viewed the last racist hereditarians who joined the University of Virginia's faculty in the 1960s and 1970s more as anachronistic curiosities than pathbreaking scientists. Virginia's governmental, medical, and educational institutions had little use for their ideas and programs. The end of mainline eugenics depended upon the retirement and death of its principal proponents as much as it did upon any changes internal or external to science. The law merely reflected this change in personnel.[4]

The Passing of the Great Race-Baiters:
Death of the Eugenics Old Guard

Discounting the passing of Galton himself in 1911, death began winnowing the eugenical ranks during the 1930s and 1940s. The demise of mainline stalwarts corresponded with Frederick Osborne's ascendance in the American Eugenics Society (AES) and elite geneticists' turn toward reform eugenics. Madison Grant, Harry Hamilton Laughlin, and Charles Benedict Davenport all died before the end of World War II. Lothrop Stoddard witnessed the defeat of Germany and confronted the revelations of the Nazi Holocaust, dying in 1950 before the rise of the modern civil rights movement. In Virginia, Edwin Anderson Alderman, Paul Brandon Barringer, Lawrence Thomas Royster, Robert Bennett Bean, and Walter A. Plecker all died by 1950. In 1949, Dean Harvey Jordan retired from the University of Virginia's medical school, closing a chapter in its eugenical heritage forty-two years after his hiring.

Of all the major figures in Virginia's eugenic history, only Jordan, Ivey Lewis, John Powell, and Earnest Cox would live to see the dismantling of Jim Crow. Retired from their academic positions, Lewis and Jordan still garnered local respect but had no national influence. Jordan died in 1963. Eight years later, the university named its new medical school building in his honor. Lewis died in March 1964. By then he had heard Martin Luther King Jr.'s dream and witnessed the ratification of the Twenty-fourth Amendment, harbinger of African American reenfranchisement. Powell's star dimmed slowly. In 1951, Governor John Battle, a distant relative of Ivey Lewis, declared November 5 "John Powell Day" in honor of his achievements. Powell died in August 1963, just months before President Kennedy's assassination and President Johnson's push to pass the slain leader's civil rights bill. Neither the *Charlottesville Daily Progress* nor the *Richmond Times-Dispatch* mentioned his work for the RIA in their obituaries. Earnest Cox stepped into traffic and was fatally struck by an automobile in 1964.[5]

Marginalized and largely forgotten, Cox died as he lived, advocating racial separatism. By the end, his only remaining associations were with hardbitten white supremacists. Beginning with the *Brown* decision, Cox aligned himself with the most ardent southern racists. His correspondence contains letters from various White Citizens' Councils, the Christian Party, the Southern Gentleman's Organization, the Nationalist Information Association, the American Society for the Preservation of State Government and Racial Integrity, and various other white supremacist, anti-Semitic organizations. He sent all of these groups his tracts, which they recirculated repeatedly. Cox's correspondence with Wickliffe Draper, the textile magnate who had financed many of Cox's publications, ended in 1957. In 1958, Cox wrote to the Citizens' Council of Jackson, Mississippi: "You are doing a great work. Warren and men of his mentality will not be able to mulattoize [sic] the white South." He enclosed his two-dollar membership fee.[6]

By 1955, Cox's Teutonism had taken a sinister turn. After publishing *Teutonic Unity* in 1951, he allied himself with many Nazi expatriates. In 1955, he received a letter from Dr. Johann von Leers, who was living in exile in Buenos Aires, that stated, "I think the fundamental ideas of your book should be made public and spread, either by openly publishing it or by founding a society to spread these ideas in selected and active groups of the Teutonic Nations." Von Leers had been a professor of history at the University of Jena, an epicenter of Nazi eugenics where he had "participated in the indoctrination of Hitler's Body-Guard SS, to which I belonged." Ten years later, he found himself "surprise[d] that more or less all what [sic] was the central idea of our thinking and indoctrination I find again in the book of an American writer." Von Leers, too, feared "the menace of the 'rising tide of colour,'" and concluded by giving Cox the names of other former Nazis living in America. These men, he hoped, could do more to spread Cox's ideas than "a halfjewish [sic] congressman or newspaperman in Washington." Cox's contact with von Leers precipitated his rapid slide into neo-Nazism. By July 1955, Cox was in contact with at least two more Nazis: his old associate, Dr. Hans F. K. Günther, one of the Nazi's most prolific writers on race; and Nazi officer Friedrich Kuhfuss, who was living in exile in Barcelona. Unable to save racial integrity at home, Cox looked to Europe.[7]

In 1958, Cox helped to organize a "Germanic homecoming"—to celebrate "Herman the German," the racial ancestor of all Teutons. Cox and his expatriate Nazi friends traveled to Germany for the meeting in late 1959. The address he delivered, titled "Herman's Brother," described Old Americans as the Teutonic next-of-kin to Germans. Cox called the monument erected in honor of Herman "the racial shrine of Germanic peoples."[8]

Cox spread his neo-Nazism in America, too. He put the elderly John Powell in touch with former Nazi SS officer Wilhelm Ladewig in 1956, a correspondence that continued until at least late 1961. Beginning in 1960, Cox aligned himself with the American Nazi Party (ANP), founded in northern Virginia by George Lincoln Rockwell. He sent them "Herman's Brother" and wrote, "I am in sympathy with the general ideas expressed in [Rockwell's] propaganda." Cox agreed with Rockwell's "liberal proposals for our Negroes who want to settle in their ancestral continent." In 1962, he sent the ANP several hundred copies of his repatriationist pamphlet *Lincoln's Negro Policy*. Simultaneously, Cox corresponded with Carleton Putnam, the North's most extreme segregationist and mainline eugenicist during the desegregation crises. Throughout this period, he worked on his rambling memoir, *Black Belt around the World*, published in late 1963. The next year, Cox made his fatal misstep onto a busy Richmond street.[9]

Active inculcation of mainline, racialized eugenics decreased among Virginia's university population after 1953. The movement's momentum carried on, however, in the minds and behavior of people educated throughout the early period; people who now held positions of authority in Virginia's public administration. Postwar guilt over science's complicity in the Holocaust, the firebombing of civilian populations, and nuclear weapons was not powerful enough to corrode the bonds white Virginians had forged among science, religion, and the eugenically justified social order. The *Brown* decision provided many white Virginians with an excuse to disregard the most current biological theories of heredity. Instead, they relied upon antiquated eugenics to defend their crumbling social order through Massive Resistance, the attempt to obstruct desegregation through all "lawful" means.

"Partially a Eugenic Report": The Hereditarians Respond to *Brown*

Ivey Lewis usually promoted segregation diplomatically: through well-placed articles and congratulatory remarks to others openly fighting African American civil rights. Earnest Cox sought Lewis's aid in popularizing repatriation, and in 1951 Lewis wrote of *Teutonic Unity:* "I am in hearty agreement with what you say about the Negro in the United States. . . . [Repatriation] is the only possible solution to avoid the disaster of miscegenation." Yet, Lewis's reluctance to take the stage in favor of federal repatriation bills reveals his distaste for direct political action. Just as Lewis found it politically and professionally inexpedient to address eugenics through the Virginia Academy of Sciences in the 1920s, in the 1950s he avoided public comment on Cox's most extreme measures. Asked by Cox to testify in favor of Senator William Langer's repatriation bill in 1955, Lewis replied, "At the moment I am at the mercy of my dentist, who told me not to make any public appearance for the next four weeks." Having dodged testifying, Lewis then asked Cox for a copy of the "little book so unfairly reviewed in the *Times-Dispatch*," Cox's manifesto *Unending Hatred*. While he sympathized with Cox's ideals, Lewis would not be their public face.[10]

As the Supreme Court debated the implementation of *Brown*, Cox attempted to bring public pressure to bear by distributing *Unending Hatred* to the justices, "members of the State Legislatures, Members of Congress and certain State officials of the 17 States" with segregated schools. Cox told Lewis: "More than 4,000 of the pamphlets have been mailed out. The Mississippi White Citizens Council took 1,000 at the cost of printing." Claiming that "the Communists would have given a million dollars for the Supreme Court decision integrating the races in the schools for it certainly would cause internal dissention [*sic*] in the only nation feared by the Communists," Cox rehashed his usual arguments. "The opposed ideals of segregation and integration," Cox began, "are merely social phases of the race problem which, itself, is of a biological nature and will continue through various phases until it is settled by the blood amalgamation of the races or their geographic separation." By 1955, in the wake of McCarthyism, very few scientists were willing to defend Cox's "mongrelization" thesis. One, the University of North Carolina Medical School anatomist Wesley Critz George, was roundly criticized for his segregationist stance. Mainline ideology was beginning to be seen for what it had always been: a quasi-scientific veneer for unending hatred. Lewis preferred to keep a lower profile than did Cox, and his correspondence with Cox tapered off after 1955.[11]

Nevertheless, segregationists from the North and South continued to approach Lewis for assistance. As Charles Clark's letter from 1954 shows, Lewis had a powerful effect on many of his students, and they turned to him for advice and leadership after the *Brown* ruling. Clark explicitly connected eugenics and resistance to desegregation when he described his letter as "partly a eugenic report," and then decried *Brown* as opening the gate to miscegenation and the end of civilization. In 1955, a lawyer in Blackstone, Virginia, wrote Lewis, "I feel that we need to assemble and get before the people the biological opinion which points up the evil consequences of integration of the races." In the appropriate situation, Lewis remained vocal in his agreement that "the color line must be maintained in spite of hell and high water." To Lewis, desegregation challenged not merely his culture, but his scientific belief that society ordered itself along lines delineated by natural law operating through heredity. By extension, desegregation challenged Lewis's view of God.[12]

While racist beliefs undermined the salience of eugenical theory in scientific circles, the apparently rational basis of eugenical conclusions immunized their racism from legal scrutiny. In 1954, eugenical precepts like those guiding Lewis justified the action of the Virginia Supreme Court of Appeals in *Naim v. Naim*.

David Carliner's Revenge: The *Naim* Cases

It is unlikely that the Chinese sailor Ham Say Naim ever heard the word "miscegenation" before he jumped ship in 1942. Eleven years later, Naim, still a Chinese national, sat in Judge Floyd E. Kellam's Portsmouth, Virginia, circuit courtroom. His wife of twenty months, Ruby Elaine Naim, a white woman, sought a divorce on the grounds of adultery. Choosing not to rule on the divorce action, Kellam granted Ruby Elaine Naim an annulment under the aegis of the RIA. Ham Say Naim's lawyer appealed the case, through the Virginia Supreme Court of Appeals, to the U.S. Supreme Court in the October term of 1955. In a surprising series of events, the case bounced between the Supreme Court and Virginia's highest court. The case ended in March 1956, when the Supreme Court, in a cryptic memorandum decision, ruled the case "devoid of a properly presented federal question." The U.S. Supreme Court thus let stand a state's right to restrict marriage between the races. A decade passed before the Court revoked racial classifications in marriage law, removing the last legally enforced eugenic barrier facing Americans of color.[13]

Ham Say Naim and Ruby Elaine Naim attempted to evade the RIA—which barred interracial marriage and cohabitation in Virginia—by driving to Elizabeth City, North Carolina, to be married before settling in Norfolk. Ham engaged the immigration attorney David Carliner of Alexandria, Virginia, to assist in his naturalization. In September 1953, the situation looked bleak, and Ruby asked for a divorce or annulment. The strains of separation, bureaucratic uncertainty, and financial pressure combined with cultural factors involving class, gender, and eugenics to propel the couple toward divorce.[14]

Ham Say Naim turned to Carliner for counsel. *Naim* presented Carliner with the chance of a lifetime. A member of the American Civil Liberties Union, Carliner had been involved in civil liberties activism since his college days at the University of Virginia—where his radicalism brought him under Ivey Lewis's surveillance, resulting in Carliner's expulsion. Having completed his training at National University Law Center (now Georgetown University Law Center), Carliner viewed *Naim* as his chance to enlarge the civil rights protections guaranteed by the Fourteenth Amendment.[15]

Ironically, while Walter A. Plecker had pressed for annulments under the RIA as a way of upholding the antimiscegenation statute, David Carliner needed to "achieve" such a conviction to mount his appeal challenging the act. Carliner deadlocked Ruby's divorce claim by introducing evidence of her own marital impropriety. Carliner never contested the right of the state to regulate marriage through racial classifications nor whether such racial determinations existed upon a "rational basis." He asserted that the race of the parties could not be determined with any accuracy, following the precedent set by the Virginia Supreme Court of Appeals in *Keith v. Commonwealth*. In *Keith*, the court set aside a miscegenation conviction, holding that the state failed to prove the accused's race beyond a reasonable doubt, extending Judge Holt's ruling in the Sorrells case.[16]

Class and gender issues increased the likelihood of annulment. At a time when divorces were hard to come by under the best of circumstances, Ruby Elaine Naim and Ham Say Naim fit the stereotype of candidates for eugenic reform. Ham Say Naim's occupation as a cook reinforced his presumed racial inferiority. Testimony depicted Ruby Elaine Naim as a poor woman of questionable morals—she had two children born out of wedlock; she was an adulteress; and she appeared impetuous and quick-tempered. The Naims' miscegenous marriage threatened racial purity, while the low-class status of the couple reinforced eugenical beliefs that only the socially "unfit" engaged in interracial marriage. Ruby's children bespoke a "moral delinquency" for which the state of Virginia had routinely committed and sterilized individuals. The children raised the issue of welfare—in terms of state provision of charitable support for the family. Society should not be burdened, according to Virginia eugenicists, with caring for the substandard progeny of unfit parents.

Carliner's examination of Ruby Elaine Naim elicited anger from the witness, yet it did not sway Judge Kellam. Carliner remembered, "I was trying to make a point . . . 'How do we know this woman was all white?' Her ancestry was from Indiana, and I asked her if she knew her grandparents and her great-grandparents, just to make certain that she was Caucasian. She turned to me with great hostility and yelled, 'How do I know that you're not black!'"[17] Carliner felt he could not have made the point any better. Over Carliner's objections, however, Judge Kellam allowed Ruby Elaine Naim and her witnesses to testify about both Ruby and Ham's race, based solely on their visual impressions of the two. This line of logic remained congruent with the thirty-year-old ruling of Judge Holt in the Sorrells case. Holt had vindicated Atha Sorrells because she *appeared* white, not because hereditarian science *proved* she was white.

Docketed on the same day President Eisenhower appointed Earl Warren to the Supreme Court, with Virginia newspapers wondering how Warren's appointment might affect the pending segregation cases, a ruling legitimating interracial marriage would have struck the most sensitive nerve in the collective white southern consciousness—horror at men of color sleeping with white women. Granting a divorce would signal tacit acceptance of the validity of interracial marriage and, by extension, interracial sexuality. The law dictated annulment; the social environment buttressed that conclusion. Kellam complied with both directives, writing, "It *appearing* to the court that the complainant is a member of the Caucasian race and the defendant not of the white race . . . [i]t is adjudged ordered and decreed that the marriage of the parties . . . is void."[18]

The annulment allowed Carliner to pursue his appeal to the Virginia Supreme Court of Appeals, a body that relied on eugenics to uphold Kellam's decision. Both sides had stipulated the litigants' race, dropping the earlier debate over racial "appearances." This allowed the Supreme Court of Appeals to ignore the reasonableness of scientifically justified white supremacy and Carliner's implicit challenge to the "scientific" underpinnings of the RIA. For Carliner, the issue was not whether the classification was reasonable, but whether the state had the power to make such racial classifications in the first place. By failing to address the knotty question of racial classification, however, Carliner left open the loophole through which the state, and the miscegenation law, would escape.[19]

The Court asked State Attorney General J. Lindsay Almond Jr. (later infamous as the Massive Resistance governor of Virginia) to file an *amicus curiae* brief. Almond's argument hinged upon state rights and eugenics, summarizing the Virginia and federal appellate miscegenation rulings, contending that, "though miscegenation statutes have been persistently attacked on the ground that they violate the Federal Constitution, they have been universally upheld as a proper exercise of the power of each state to control its own citizens."[20]

When *Naim* arrived before the Virginia Supreme Court of Appeals, twenty-nine states maintained miscegenation laws. The sole precedent for the unconstitutionality of a miscegenation statute came in 1948. In *Perez v. Sharp sub. nom. Lippold*, a four-to-three ruling by the California Supreme Court held that because California recognized miscegenous marriages performed in states where such marriages were legal, "it follows that [miscegenous] marriage cannot be considered vitally detrimental to the public health, welfare and morals." Virginia's attorney general sought to distinguish between *Naim v. Naim* and *Perez v. Sharp*. He argued that the RIA left no such ambiguities regarding penalties. Furthermore, the state contended that the determining question in *Perez*, the reasonableness of racial classifications, was not present in *Naim v. Naim*. Since Carliner failed to challenge to the rationale of eugenic classification, and since restraint should govern judicial review, the state believed that the Supreme Court of Appeals should uphold Judge Kellam's ruling.[21]

Forty years later, David Carliner still became angry when he recounted his time before the Virginia Supreme Court of Appeals in 1955: "I recall very vividly . . . I was never treated with such hostility anywhere as I was by that Court. The fact this was a Chinese-white marriage didn't make any difference; they saw black all over the place. And they treated me as if I were a piece of shit." Not surprisingly, the ruling went against Carliner. In the wake of *Brown II*, amidst the mounting furor over impending desegregation, the language of the ruling is highly evocative—a blend of militant state rights and eugenical theory. Justice Buchanan, writing for the court, cribbed liberally from the state's *amicus curiae* brief, riding the wave of segregationist intransigence.[22]

Noting that *Brown* held segregation in schooling unconstitutional because education "[is] the very foundation of good citizenship," Buchanan distinguished interracial marriage from desegregated education:

> by no sort of valid reasoning could [interracial marriage] be found to be a foundation of good citizenship or a right which must be made available to all on equal terms. In the opinion of the legislature of more than half the states it is harmful to good citizenship.

According to Buchanan, "The inquiry [by the court] must be whether, considering the ends in view, the statute passes the bounds of reason and assumes the character of a merely arbitrary fiat." The RIA was a reasonable law to ensure racial purity because

> the only way by which the statute could be made effective was by classification of the races. If preservation of the racial integrity is legal [which the court had just asserted it was, under the police power], then racial classification to effect that end is not presumed to be arbitrary.
>
> It does not appear from this record that the appellant questioned the reasonableness of the classification in the trial court. There is no evidence in the record suggesting that the classification made by the statute is unreasonable or that it is not reasonably related to the purpose intended to be accomplished. In the absence of all evidence to the contrary, the presumption of reasonableness is very strong.

Buchanan implied that Carliner's case might have been more substantial had he questioned racial classification directly. This is unlikely, given Carliner's recollection of the court's response to the case. Still, by failing to challenge the eugenical underpinnings of the RIA, Carliner allowed the Virginia court to hide the act behind the mask of legal doctrine, thereby maintaining the justification for eugenic social policy.[23]

The concluding paragraphs of the Virginia decision evince the tight interweaving of social and cultural issues with eugenical precepts. Justice Buchanan wrote that marriage "has from time immemorial been considered a proper subject for State regulation in the interest of the public health, morals and welfare, to the end that family life, a relation basic and vital to the permanence of the State, may be maintained in accordance with established tradition and culture and in furtherance of the physical, moral and spiritual well-being of its citizens." As a result, he could find nothing in the Fourteenth Amendment or the Constitution that would deny "the power of the State to regulate the marriage relation so that it shall not have a mongrel breed of citizens." Honing his point, Buchanan continued:

> We find there no requirement that the State shall not legislate to prevent the obliteration of racial pride, but must permit the corruption of blood even though it weaken or destroy the quality of its citizenship. Both sacred and secular history teach that nations and races have better advanced in human progress when they cultivated their own distinctive characteristics and culture and developed their own peculiar genius.

Buchanan struck the major chords of eugenic ideology and southern white supremacy, evoking Madison Grant, Lothrop Stoddard, and Earnest Sevier Cox. Championing "racial integrity" and "racial pride" against the social and cultural solvent of "mongrelization" caused by "corruption of the blood," Buchanan used eugenic rhetoric from an era before Nazi science. This is perhaps not surprising. Most of the justices on the Supreme Court of Appeals graduated from law school between 1910 and 1929, just when eugenical thought in Virginia reached its apogee. Justice Lemuel Smith actually voted for both the eugenic sterilization and the racial integrity acts as a member of the House of Delegates. In fact, Ivey Lewis had supported Smith's nomination to the court. Thus the justices, even more than Carliner, would have been familiar with the RIA's history and eugenic foundation. Virginia would not accept civil rights arguments without a direct attack against segregation's science. Carliner's final hope lay with the U.S. Supreme Court.[24]

In the end, the Court would face *Naim* twice. Carliner believed that, in the wake of the *Brown* decisions, the case was a cinch. He later confessed: "You never know for sure what the justices are going to do. I guess a more intelligent way of doing it would be to frame your arguments to reach particular justices." Had Carliner done this, Justice Felix Frankfurter would have presented the hardest sell. The Court had avoided this issue just the year before when it denied *certiorari* to Linnie May Jackson for fear of jeopardizing *Brown*. Memos from the justices' clerks, Justice Frankfurter, and docket-book votes reveal the dimensions of the debate over *Naim v. Naim*.[25]

The best evidence of the intra-Court conflict over *Naim* exists in the memoranda prepared for the justices by their law clerks. The clerks for Justices Burton, Harlan, and Warren remarked upon the poor political timing of the *Naim* case. "In view of the difficulties engendered by the segregation cases," Burton's clerk wrote, "it would be wise judicial policy to duck this question for a time." In spite of these considerations, the clerks for Burton, Douglas, and Warren recommended that the Court set the case down for argument. While the justices sought to avoid the case in order to "give the present fire [over *Brown*] a chance to die down," concerns over procedural precedents and judicial review came to the fore.[26]

On November 4, 1955, the Court split its initial vote on *Naim*: Harlan, Minton, Clark, Burton, and Frankfurter to dismiss; Douglas, Reed, Black, and Warren to note probable jurisdiction and accept the case. The Court took the rare action of holding the case over so that the justices could give it fuller consideration. One week later, the split began identical to the first vote. Justices Reed and Warren then joined the five who voted to dismiss, and vacated the lower court's decision, remanding the case to Judge Kellam for further clarification. To avoid the appearance that they were dodging the case, the justices decided to remand rather than dismiss, throwing the ball back into Virginia's court.[27]

Upon receiving *Naim* from the U.S. Supreme Court, the Virginia Supreme Court of Appeals issued a memorandum decision of its own. Virginia's high court declared that the record was clear enough for itself and the Portsmouth court. Therefore, "The decree of the trial court and the decree of this court affirming it have become final so far as these courts are concerned." In effect, the Virginia Supreme Court of Appeals nullified an order from the U.S. Supreme Court. Newspapers across Virginia trumpeted the action as the first step in the implementation of an "Ordinance of Interposition," legislation Virginia had just passed vowing to resist desegregation. Recognizing Virginia's refusal as an affront to constitutional law, David Carliner filed a motion for recall by the U.S. Supreme Court. In light of the Virginia court's open revolt, Carliner believed that the U.S. Supreme Court had to take the case or jeopardize its standing as the court of last resort.[28]

The law clerks for Justices Douglas and Warren echoed Carliner's reaction. William A. Norris advised Justice Douglas against vacating the state judgment summarily because "it will begin to look obvious if the case is not taken that the Court is trying to run away from its obligation to decide the case." Burton's and Warren's clerks reacted in similar fashion. On March 2, 1956, the justices split six to three to deny, this time with William O. Douglas in the unlikely position as the swing vote. *Naim* seemed to have died. For some indeterminate reason, however, the Court again held the question over one week. On March 9, 1956, the Court split five to four, with Douglas resuming his position in favor of hearing the case. The Court denied the motion on the grounds that the action of the Virginia Supreme Court of Appeals "leaves the case devoid of a properly presented federal question." Despite a strongly worded dissent Warren had his clerk draft, the opinion went out as another *per curiam* decision, seeming to indicate unanimity among the brethren. *Naim v. Naim*, the first substantial constitutional challenge to segregation's science, was smothered by political pressure. David Carliner would have to wait another decade for vindication.[29]

Justice Delayed: *Loving v. Virginia*

Naim v. Naim allowed Virginia to enforce the RIA for another twelve years. Three years after *Naim* ended, Richard and Mildred Loving pleaded guilty to violating the RIA, a criminal felony. White and black Virginians respectively, the Lovings attempted to avoid the RIA by marrying in the District of Columbia, then returning to the Old Dominion as man and wife. Arrested, tried, and convicted, the court imposed the maximum penalty, one year in jail. The trial judge, Leon M. Bazile, had been assistant attorney general for Virginia when Judge Holt ruled on the Atha Sorrells case and strongly supported the RIA. Bazile exercised his sentencing prerogative. He suspended the jail term "for a period of twenty-five years upon the provision that both accused leave ... the state of Virginia at once and do not return together or at the same time ... for a period of twenty-five years." Substituting banishment for imprisonment, the judge ratcheted Virginia's antimiscegenation statute back to its seventeenth-century origins.[30]

On November 6, 1963, the Lovings filed a motion before Judge Bazile, attempting to have their banishment rescinded and the judgment against them set aside. They claimed that both measures violated the Fourteenth Amendment's protection of their civil rights. Bazile finally denied their motion on

January 22, 1965. In the meantime, the Lovings had filed civil suit in the U.S. District Court for the Eastern District of Virginia. When Bazile denied the Lovings' motion, this court continued the case to allow the Lovings to appeal to Virginia's Supreme Court of Appeals in March 1966. Bernard S. Cohen and Philip J. Hirschkop represented the Lovings. In preparation for this appeal, they sought out David Carliner, both for advice and to study his strategy in *Naim*. While Cohen and Hirschkop would appear before the highest courts of Virginia and the United States, David Carliner remained in the background.[31]

Loving's legal and social environment differed from that which confronted Carliner in 1956. The Supreme Court had struck down every other legal means of enforcing racial differentiation. Congress had enacted the Civil Rights Act of 1964 and the Voting Rights Act of 1965. Although battles between segregationists and civil rights advocates continued to be waged in the streets of southern cities, the segregationists' brutality had become a national embarrassment, even for many "moderate" whites who preferred segregation. The so-called "second reconstruction" seemed almost complete. All that remained were the miscegenation statutes.

Cohen and Hirschkop identified Carliner's error in *Naim* and aimed at racial classification's weakness, its scientific basis. In dismissing the *Loving* case, the Virginia Supreme Court of Appeals relied on the logic and precedent set in *Naim*. In rejecting Cohen and Hirschkop's attack on racial science, the court excoriated sociological jurisprudence and activist adjudication. "A decision by this court reversing the *Naim* case upon consideration of the opinions of such text writers would be judicial legislation in the rawest sense of that term. Such arguments are properly addressable to the legislature . . . and not to this court." Despite the U.S. Supreme Court's ruling that allowed courts to "resort to common knowledge or other matters which may be judicially noticed, or to other legitimate proof" to find a statute unreasonable, the Virginia court would take no notice of new science. The shackles of segregation's science, forged of eugenic logic, legal precedent, and racist hatred, held fast.[32]

In the years since *Naim*, the number of states with miscegenation statutes had dropped from twenty-nine to sixteen. Nevertheless, the Virginia court's opinion concluded, "a number of states still have miscegenation statutes and yet there has been no new decision reflecting adversely upon the validity of such statutes." The court ignored that the decreasing number of miscegenation statutes may have resulted from the realization that the laws were unreasonable. Instead, it concluded that there was "no sound judicial reason" to overturn *Naim*. As a partial sop to the Lovings, the court found the sentences unreasonable and void, vacated them, and remanded the case to Judge Bazile.[33]

The Virginia court's decision, fully expected by Cohen, Hirschkop, and Carliner, set the stage for David Carliner's final triumph over the bigotry espoused by Ivey Lewis and the Virginia eugenicists. The U.S. Supreme Court accepted *Loving* on appeal without any debate. Great change had occurred since 1956 within the ranks of the brethren. Most notably, Felix Frankfurter had retired in 1962. The Court now tended toward activist positions in regard to civil liberties and, with the exception of *Naim*, had ruled consistently to strike down laws infringing personal liberty on the basis of race. Outside the Court, thirteen states had voluntarily repealed their miscegenation statutes, deeming them repugnant to the Fourteenth Amendment or unenforceable. Although Virginia had once again upheld the RIA in *Calma v. Calma* (1962), national conventional wisdom viewed interracial marriage in a different light in 1967 than in 1956. In 1958, the earliest national poll taken, 96 percent of whites disapproved of interracial marriage. In 1965, 72 percent of southern whites and 42 percent of nonsouthern whites approved of laws banning intermarriage. By 1970, those numbers had dropped to 56 and 30 percent respectively. In 1968, 34 percent of whites in their twenties approved of interracial marriage; only 13 percent of those over fifty agreed. Thus the legal environment was conducive to reconsidering miscegenation statutes. By reviewing Carliner's experience and remaining sensitive to the cultural and legal environment, Cohen and Hirschkop would win *Loving* and reduce David Carliner's historic role to a footnote.[34]

Hewing to the line of reasoning first elaborated in *Naim*, Virginia asserted that a rational basis for the RIA existed. The Supreme Court, aware of both the legislative and scientific history of the RIA, found this absurd. As in *Brown*, Chief Justice Warren wrote the opinion for a unanimous Court, again becoming the lightning rod for the reaction that followed.

The Court signaled its hostility to the RIA early in its opinion. Noting that the law was "passed during the period of extreme nativism which followed the end of the First World War," the Court chipped away the RIA's reasonableness by implying hysteria, not rationality, as its motive. Chief Justice Warren then quoted the inflammatory, eugenic language of *Naim*, calling it "obviously an endorsement of the doctrine of White Supremacy." Warren conceded the state's right to regulate marriage, but asserted that, "over the years, this Court has consistently repudiated '[d]istinctions between citizens solely because of their ancestry' as being 'odious to a free people whose institutions are founded on the doctrine of equality.'"[35]

Warren then systematically demolished the eugenic rationale underpinning the RIA. "There is patently no legitimate overriding purpose independent of invidious racial discrimination which justifies this [racial] classification," Warren began. "The fact that Virginia prohibits only interracial
marriages involving white persons demonstrates that the racial classifications must stand on their own justification, as measures designed to maintain White Supremacy." In a ringing denunciation, Warren declared marriage
"fundamental to our very existence and survival. . . . To deny this fundamental
freedom on so unsupportable a basis as the racial classifications embodied in
these statutes, classifications so directly subversive of the Fourteenth Amendment, is surely to deprive all the State's citizens of liberty without due process
of law." Paraphrasing David Carliner's contention that marriage "must rest
with the law of natural selectivity," Warren averred: "Under our Constitution,
the freedom to marry, or not marry, a person of another race resides with the
individual and cannot be infringed by the State. These convictions must be
reversed."[36]

The victory in *Loving* contributed to the erasure of eugenics from the
public consciousness. Warren's opinion never explicitly mentioned eugenics,
although it crushed the logic of segregation's science as manifested in law. In
asserting marriage as a fundamental right, Chief Justice Warren cited the
Court's 1941 decision in *Skinner v. Oklahoma*. In *Skinner*, the Court struck
down Oklahoma's eugenic sterilization law, ruling that its provisions for the
punitive sterilization of some criminals and not others violated the equal protection clause of the Fourteenth Amendment. Writing for the Court, Justice
William O. Douglas noted: "The power to sterilize, if exercised, may have
subtle, far-reaching and devastating effects. In evil or reckless hands it can
cause races or types which are inimical to the dominant group to wither and
disappear." With the example of Adolf Hitler before his eyes, Douglas was not
indulging irrational fears. In his concurring opinion, Justice Robert Jackson
felt compelled to state, "There are limits to which a legislatively represented
majority may conduct biological experiments at the expense of the dignity
and personality and natural powers of a minority—even those who have been
guilty of what the majority define as crimes." Just four years later, in 1945,
Jackson would confront the horror of Nazi eugenics when he served as a pros-
ecutor at the Nuremberg war crimes trials. Nevertheless, the Court reserved
judgment on the rationality of eugenics, in part in deference to *Buck v. Bell*.
In *Loving*, Chief Justice Warren clearly created a parallel between eugenic
sterilization and marriage restriction—both inhibited the basic right of procreation based on classifications of human worth. While *Loving* destroyed

the rational basis for eugenic racial integrity, the legacy of eugenic sterilization had not yet run its course.[37]

Punitive Sterilization in Virginia:
Carrie Buck Meets the "Welfare Mother"

During the late 1950s and the 1960s, the eugenicists' fears shifted away from
the menace of the feebleminded and toward the so-called "population bomb."
The metaphor of explosion for the rapid rate of population increase during
the postwar decades gained widespread currency in America. The precise
language used had a negative connotation for nonwhite and non–First World
countries. America experienced the positive "baby boom," invoking images
of the nineteenth-century land- or gold-rush, as Frederick Osborn and other
leaders of the reform eugenics movement "found no cause for anxiety in the
American statistics. They revealed that the middle and upper middle classes
were contributing mightily to the baby boom; educated groups appeared to
be reproducing at a rate sufficient to replace themselves." By contrast, demog-
raphers and sociologists described Indian, African, Far Eastern, and African
American populations as destructively "exploding," destabilizing the world
order by precipitating a Malthusian crisis. The language of reform eugenics jettisoned its most overtly racist expressions, but continued to emphasize
notions of inherent "fitness" and "unfitness." This revised eugenic discourse,
when combined with "population bomb" rhetoric, maintained subtle links
among fitness, race/ethnicity, class, and gender.[38]

The new eugenic rhetoric reverberated within the halls of Virginia's legislature. During the 1956, 1958, 1960, and 1962 sessions of the General Assembly, state legislators considered bills advocating the compulsory sterilization
of women receiving federal Aid to Families with Dependent Children (AFDC,
also known as "welfare") funds if they gave birth to children out of wedlock.
Virginia was not alone in this effort; officials in California, Delaware, Georgia, Illinois, Iowa, Louisiana, Maryland, Mississippi, North Carolina, Pennsylvania, and Wisconsin also considered punitive sterilization measures in
this period. Theoretically, those in sympathy with these bills felt that parents,
and particularly mothers, who gave birth to children when they lacked the
financial means to support them, should be sterilized to prevent additional
economic burdens on society. Supporters initially advanced these bills without mentioning eugenics.[39]

Representative E. Ralph James of Hampton, Virginia, proposed the state's
first punitive sterilization law in 1956. The bill authorized the superintendent

of public welfare in any county to petition the county court judge to order "any woman who has given birth to more than one illegitimate child" to appear before the court and "show cause why she should not be sexually sterilized." Thus the onus was on the mother to prove her right to remain fertile; often a treble bind because these women would most likely be black, poor, and uneducated—ill-equipped to resist the compulsion of elite, white, male authorities. During the 1958 legislature, Representative Purcell offered a revised version of the James bill. Purcell added physician review and patient consent to the provision. Although local authorities would still initiate the proceedings, judges would decide the matter upon the testimony of "two discreet and competent physicians." If the judge ruled in favor of sterilization, the patient still had to consent to the procedure. Seeing the practical difficulties this bill would encounter, legislators killed it in committee.[40]

Despite their failure, these bills prompted a number of Virginia bureaucracies to examine the "illegitimacy problem." These studies actually disputed the conventional wisdom (which extended from eugenic notions that "like produces like" and "illegitimacy and poverty go hand in hand"), revealing that most families receiving AFDC funds did not have children born out of wedlock. In 1959, the General Assembly's Commission to Study Problems Relating to Children Born Out of Wedlock presented a report that opposed compulsory sterilization, but advocated the enactment of a statute making it legal to perform voluntary sterilization operations for nontherapeutic reasons. In each of the next two legislatures, lawmakers offered compulsory and voluntary sterilization measures for consideration.[41]

The 1960 legislature considered two sterilization bills and one eugenics bill. Senate Bill 169 provided for the voluntary sterilization of anyone above the age of majority (twenty-one) who requested the procedure and had the signed consent of their spouse. This bill also provided for the voluntary sterilization of minors upon the petition of their parents, provided the county court found that the "operation is in the best interests of such minor." House Bill 494, sponsored by ten representatives, reintroduced Purcell's 1958 modification of the James bill to sterilize welfare mothers. Both the Senate and House bills provided immunity from legal liability for physicians and court officers who participated in sterilization proceedings. Neither bill passed.[42]

House Bill 495 provided for an amendment to Virginia's eugenic sterilization law "providing for sexual sterilization of certain persons who are not inmates of institutions under control of the State Hospital Board." This bill would create four-person local "Eugenics Boards," whose members—the Commonwealth's attorney, superintendent of the local board of public welfare, and two local physicians—would be appointed by the city or county court that had jurisdiction. The bill allowed superintendents of public welfare to petition the eugenics board for the sterilization of any person "who is afflicted with a hereditary form of mental illness which is recurrent, mental deficiency, or epilepsy" not committed to a state institution. This bill extended eugenical sterilization to the entire population of Virginia, circumventing legislative reluctance to target welfare mothers. Virginia was not alone in this effort—North Carolina's eugenics program had long relied on local boards that recommended the sterilization of "welfare mothers" with and without their consent.[43]

This flurry of legislation prompted the General Assembly "to study the laws relating to sexual sterilization" then in effect. The language of the legislature's Joint Resolution reveals the degree to which eugenics had fallen out of favor by 1960. The resolution announced that the "grounds for the compulsory sexual sterilization of persons" as directed by the 1924 sterilization act "do not appear to be in keeping with advances made in medical science." The legislators challenged the notion "that a person by the laws of heredity is the probable potential parent of socially inadequate offspring" by affirming that "a person may be afflicted with a mental illness which is not hereditary but which renders him or her incapable of assuming the responsibilities of parenthood." This assertion reflects a subtle shift from sterilization as strictly eugenic (aimed at improving the gene pool) to "social service sterilization"—restricting procreation to "maintain control within state institutions," reduce welfare costs, and prevent children from being born to parents unable to care for them. The Senate directed the Virginia Advisory Legislative Council (VALC) to review the sterilization law in light of the most recent medical knowledge. The time lag between changing scientific theory and public policy appeared to be closing. One might have expected radical change in Virginia's sterilization law and its application.[44]

Instead, the VALC recommended that "no change be made in the present Virginia statute providing for the sexual sterilization of a patient in a mental institution" because "there has been no substantial complaint concerning the operation of the statute in Virginia." The report noted that, "during the 36 years in which it has been in effect, only 2826 males and 4146 females have been sterilized," implying that this number was negligible. The report concluded, "We are advised that there are no medical or other scientific data indicating that a change in the basis set out in the statute for sterilization of inmates of institutions is either imperative or desirable." The law sustained thirty-four years earlier in *Buck v. Bell* was sustained again, despite the "advances in medical science" that most subsequent scholars assumed should have invalidated the law.[45]

The VALC also recommended the adoption of a voluntary sterilization law, provided the person to be sterilized, if married, obtained the consent of their spouse. Voluntary sterilization remained a nettlesome issue nationwide, but especially in Virginia, where, in 1952, a physician was sued for sterilizing a female patient without first obtaining her husband's written permission. The jury ruled in favor of the doctor, but this type of malpractice liability terrified physicians. From a legal standpoint, voluntary sterilization remained an enigmatic procedure in the 1960s. Physicians worried that operating on healthy reproductive organs would breach the Hippocratic oath. This concern, viewed historically, creates a significant irony given Virginia physicians' lack of compunction in performing eugenic sterilizations without consent. Physicians also feared lawsuits for illegally providing birth control information, until the Supreme Court protected such action in *Griswold v. Connecticut*. In 1961, lobbying by the Virginia Medical Society and the VALC succeeded in the enactment of a statute insulating physicians from liability in elective sterilization procedures, provided there was no malpractice in the technical performance of the procedure. In March 1962, Virginia adopted a law that conformed to the VALC's recommendations. This was the first voluntary sterilization law in American history; as in eugenic sterilization, Virginia led the way.

Virginia's voluntary sterilization statute had its own eugenic implications. Although voluntary sterilization responded to the felt needs and vocal demands of many men and women, it also had an unintended side effect—abuse of sterilization by physicians. The exact definition of "voluntary consent" remained murky. How voluntary are procedures consented to by patients *advised* by their doctors that sterilization is in their own best interest? The door to coercive sterilization remained open. As the *Relf* case from Alabama showed, both scrupulous and unscrupulous physicians exerted incredible power over their patients' reproductive lives.[46]

In September 1962, eleven years before the *Relf* case first drew public attention, the *Washington Post* stumbled upon the possibility of sterilization abuse. Running Gerald Grant's story "50 Indigent Mothers Sterilized in Fauquier County" and its follow-up, "Birth Control Clinic Is 'Amazed' at Popularity of Sterilization," the *Post* ignited a controversy involving religious, minority, government, and medical leaders in a week-long melee played out in the pages of the nation's newspapers. Grant's first article recounted how twenty sociologists toured the Fauquier Hospital's birth control clinic and learned about the sterilization program at the behest of the Human Betterment Foundation. His second article reported that the sponsors of the northern Virginia facility, located in the then-bucolic farming community of Warrenton, were "'floored' by the intense interest [the sterilization program] has aroused among the Virginia County's medically indigent." Defining the "medically indigent" as those unable to pay hospital costs, Dr. H. W. Stinson revealed that 63 such women had been sterilized since 1960—two years before Virginia enacted its voluntary sterilization law. This made the operations extralegal but not illegal; there was no statute outlawing voluntary sterilization. According to Stinson, these 63 women were part of 201 total patients (indigent and paying), 118 of whom were black. Stinson claimed that the women were sterilized only after a volunteer had explained "the entire range of contraceptives available to them," and after a thirty-day waiting period. On the surface, the clinic seemed to be a model of informed consent and benign medical provision.[47]

The *Post*'s article uncovered a number of alarming aspects of the sterilization program, however. The hospital began the clinic after lay volunteers suggested it. "One of the principal lay workers" behind the contraception program, Mrs. James P. Mills, the *Post* reported, "heard the warden of Sing Sing Prison say [in 1937] that 95 per cent of his inmates were there because they were the eldest child of an overcrowded family." The *Post*'s reporter immediately suspected eugenics. He asked if lay workers like Mrs. Mills helped indigent patients to decide for or against sterilization. "Oh, yes," Mrs. Mills replied, "My job is education, many of them have never heard of family planning." Grant then pushed Dr. Stinson on the directive or advisory nature of this counseling. Stinson replied that the hospital staff "isn't trying to sell anyone anything," claiming that "we educate them and let them make a choice. It's the same as an election, would you deny anyone a vote?" (Stinson's sarcasm is particularly telling, since the previous spring the U.S. Supreme Court had ruled in *Baker v. Carr*, the famous "one man, one vote" case that began to crack the South's racist political structure by protecting African American voting.) Grant asked Stinson directly about eugenics, and Stinson replied that "any effort to prevent the reproduction of certain character traits or to cut down welfare rolls was 'the furthest thing from our minds.'" This answer did not satisfy many commentators, especially those who read hospital chief Dr. James L. Dellinger's comment: "We did lots to get the law passed. Let's face it, this sort of thing is not being done in urban centers because minority groups oppose it." In rural Virginia, however, white elites could overawe or misdirect the opposition.[48]

The report of the sterilization program led to an outcry from clerics, both for and against the sterilizations. Washington's Roman Catholic archbishop,

Patrick A. O'Boyle, denounced the practice as "grossly immoral" and a "crudely selfish and materialistic" attempt to reduce the tax rate. A day later, the Reverend Billy Graham weighed in for evangelical Protestants, warning, "We are in serious danger when we take on ourselves to sterilize women, even with their permission." Clergymen with ties to the organized eugenics movement, however, saw the matter differently. New York's famed Presbyterian Reverend Harry Emerson Fosdick, who had served on the advisory council of the American Eugenics Society from 1923 to 1935, affirmed that he "believed very much that there is a place for voluntary sterilization in our society." Reverend Joseph C. Fletcher, president of the board of directors of the Human Betterment Foundation, and future professor of biomedical ethics at the University of Virginia, argued in favor of the procedures. Methodist Bishop John Wesley Lord of Washington, ignoring the potential for abuse, praised the program for providing a "beacon of hope and enlightenment" for "those thousands in our cities and rural areas who do not have the knowledge to keep from having more children than they can love, nurture and provide for."[49]

The women sterilized gave a generally positive response to mainstream journalists, with Gerald Grant reporting that of forty-four sterilized women, only one was "completely dissatisfied" and three had complaints but were generally satisfied. On the other hand, the Nation of Islam's ideologically charged *Muhammad Speaks* reported many second thoughts under provocative headlines like, "Birth Control Death Plan!" and "White Clinic Sterilizes More Negro Women!" linking the clinic to the "Nazi formula for extinction," connecting so-called voluntary sterilization and eugenic extermination. The fact that all the doctors in Fauquier County were white exacerbated the racial tensions.[50]

The sterilization of seventeen-year-old Irene Pallot, a mother of two, emphasized the discrepancies between the clinic's public statements and actual practice. Administrator C. Robert Peery claimed that the clinic required its patients to be twenty-one years old, to have spousal consent, and have three or more children. Pallot had never gone beyond the fifth grade, a "white woman doctor" had asked her if she would like to stop having children "at her age" (implying that the procedure was reversible later), and physicians had obtained the consent of the girl's poor and uneducated father. The glaring contrast pointed to the difficulties of "voluntary" sterilization among individuals who may have lacked education, remained deferential to authority, and whose poverty left them with only the clinic as a health-care option. Although hospital officials vehemently denied "pressuring" mothers to agree to sterilization, or targeting black mothers in particular, the public image was that this county hospital was operating a "sterilization mill." Despite this controversy, or perhaps in an effort to take control of the issue, in 1962 the legislature again debated eugenics boards as an alternative to the punitive and voluntary sterilization bills.[51]

Just as in the original efforts for eugenic sterilization legislation, proponents attempted to limit debates to dispassionate experts and legislators. Supporters' failure to contain the debate doomed the punitive measures and attracted negative publicity to the voluntary measure as applied in Fauquier County. In the public arena, the hereditarian explanation for "illegitimacy" had lost much of its power. Experts denied that "like begets like" as a result of biological imperatives, countering that illegitimate children tended to be born to poor mothers as a result of a complex congeries of causes, citing environmental problems as the root of unwed pregnancy. By 1962, this environmentalist orthodoxy was so well established that most lay observers saw sterilization laws and programs as racially driven efforts at social control. Eugenics had lost the day, despite the long memory of some legislators.

The Old Guard Meets the New:
Psychology and Biology Face the Past

Henry Garrett and Audrey Shuey represented a dying gasp of hereditarianism in a state beset by what many whites viewed as the catastrophe of desegregation. Hereditarian conclusions about racial intelligence, and the eugenic programs they supported, enjoyed brief resurgences in the late 1960s and the mid-1990s, but did not reclaim their influence over science or social policy. Although many whites, and many white Virginians particularly, believed studies linking intelligence, heredity, and race reflected scientific "fact," most psychologists and sociologists recognized them as biased assertions.

In the fall of 1957, the University of Virginia hired Virginia-born Henry E. Garrett as a visiting professor. The emeritus chairman of Columbia University's psychology department, he led the resurgence of hereditarian and racial psychometrics during the 1950s and 1960s. Although many scholars cite Arthur Jensen's 1969 article "How Much Can We Boost IQ and Scholastic Achievement?" as the starting point for this hereditarian recrudescence, it really began with Garrett's work on *Brown*, which culminated in his 1967 pamphlet *The Relative Intelligence of Whites and Negroes: The Armed Forces Tests*. Garrett secured his fame in 1954, when he testified on behalf of segregation before the U.S. District Court of Appeals for the Fourth Circuit in *Davis v. County School Board*, one of the five cases bundled in *Brown*. He unsuccessfully rebutted his former students, Kenneth and Mamie Clark. The Clarks' famous "doll test"—where they presented black children with dolls of different skin tones and, based on the children's preference for white dolls, inferred psychological damage—helped convince the Supreme Court that segregation damaged black self-esteem. Incensed, Garrett committed himself to resisting *Brown* by every scientific means at his disposal.[52]

Garrett supplied ammunition to the white supremacist White Citizens Councils, allowing Richmond's Citizens Council to produce a pamphlet comprised of four of his essays, including, "Heredity: The Causes of Racial Differences in Intelligence." A supporter of Carleton Putnam, the author of the controversial 1961 volume *Race and Reason: A Yankee View* (a mainline eugenic argument in favor of racial segregation), Garrett also corresponded with Jack Kilpatrick, the reactionary editor of the *Richmond News-Leader*. Both men worked to get their segregationist and hereditarian ideas before the public at every opportunity.[53]

In 1958, Professor Audrey M. Shuey of Randolph-Macon College published *The Testing of Negro Intelligence*. This long review essay condensed "380 *original investigations* of Negro intelligence," from the prominent to the obscure—including the work of Carl C. Brigham, George Oscar Ferguson, and Henry Garrett. As one commentator noted, "Only the New York City telephone book contains more numbers than Professor Shuey's 521-page" book. Predictably, Shuey concluded that, "all taken together, [the results of these investigations] inevitably point to the presence of native [genetic] differences between Negroes and whites as determined by intelligence tests." Shuey relied on the twenty-five-year-old racist conclusions in Carl Brigham's *A Study of American Intelligence*. Shuey acknowledged that Brigham had "rejected completely his own and others' findings in the field of natio-racial differences in intelligence" because he believed that the tests were biased and failed to measure intelligence. Yet Shuey dismissed Brigham's retraction because, in addition to her interpretation of the evidence, "Garrett believes that Brigham attached too much importance to test purity." Shuey's marshalling of Garrett's views to support her argument was not coincidental: she had been his student in graduate school at Columbia. Thus, the wheel turned full circle.[54]

The eugenics tide turned in the University of Virginia's biology department as well. Taking over for Ivey Lewis in 1953, Professor Ladley Husted taught relatively orthodox mainline eugenics. Yet Husted, a former student of Lewis's, focused more on research than on promoting the eugenics creed. Orland E. White retired in 1957. He was replaced by two younger plant geneticists: University of Virginia graduate Walter S. Flory and W. Ralph Singleton. With the unleashing of atomic energy, postwar geneticists like Flory and Singleton began to investigate the effects of radioactivity on genetic material. The Blandy Experimental Farm built one of the strongest Cobalt-30 point-source radiation emitters in America, and pioneered studies of genetic mutation.

At the same time, Flory and Singleton adhered to the basic tenet of the eugenic creed: humanity could be improved by better breeding. Singleton, who had been educated at Harvard's Bussey Institution under Edward M. East and William E. Castle, remained committed to the notion of reform eugenics and the gradual improvement of humanity. As secretary of the American Genetics Association in 1962, Singleton promulgated a history of the association that stated, "In the field of human race betterment . . . a solid foundation has been laid since 1903 on which a humane and democratic program may be developed." Implicitly acknowledging eugenic abuses, the association distanced itself from the strident rhetoric of earlier mainline orthodoxy, without relinquishing the eugenic grail: "It is altogether clear that a rational program of eugenics means much more than wiping out or preventing the increase of outright mental and physical defect. It is essential, somehow, to encourage the reproduction of the most highly endowed." Fifty years after the First International Congress on Eugenics, the American Genetics Society renewed the quest.[55]

———————

Although the Supreme Court's ruling in *Loving* buried the statutory support for mainline racist eugenics, elements of the old eugenics elite lingered in Virginia. The legacy of sterilization still beset Virginia's institutionalized population for fourteen years after *Loving*, until Virginia confronted its history of coercive sterilization. After the period of Massive Resistance and token desegregation, Virginia's eugenics experience again approximated that of the nation, as the North and South converged in their scientific and social views. Over the course of two decades, eugenics slowly lost its momentum, drifting to the ragged margins of politics and science until mainline eugenicists populated the nether fringe of Virginia's academic and political arena. While eugenics would crop up from time to time, its precepts no longer resonated with most Virginians' identity as either southerners or Americans. Those who continued to profess mainline positions on race looked like backward traditionalists, not apostles of the future as they had been viewed just twenty years earlier. The conflict between traditionalism and modernity reached another turning point.

*"I Never Knew What
They'd Done with Me"*

VIRGINIA'S INVOLVEMENT WITH EUGENICS continues into the present.
By the late 1960s, the rise of the counterculture and the sexual revolution moved human sexuality temporarily beyond the purview of social engineers and into the realm of individual conscience. In Virginia, after the last
attempts for a punitive sterilization law failed as part of the "Conservative
Party" platform in late 1964, all that remained was the confrontation of the
eugenic past. The "rediscovery" of eugenic sterilization would appear to end
the history of eugenics and hereditarianism in Virginia.

The final eugenic sterilizations in Virginia's state hospitals took place between 1972 and 1979. Eugenic sterilization officially ceased in 1972 following a state Board of Mental Health directive banning the practice. In 1974,
the law was amended to allow involuntary sterilization provided the hospital had a circuit court order. Sixteen "therapeutic" sterilizations occurred at
the Lynchburg Training School between 1974 and 1979. Dr. K. Ray Nelson,
director of the Lynchburg Training School (the Lynchburg Colony for the
Epileptic and Feebleminded had been renamed) helped to uncover the history of sterilization at Lynchburg in 1979, and dissociated himself from the
former practices. Nelson and other Virginia officials stated that the twenty-
one sterilizations performed under Nelson's watch occurred in the course of

"procedures performed for health purposes that also resulted in residents' sterility."[1]

In February 1980, newspapers broke the story of Virginia's eugenic sterilization program. The specter of eugenics burst forth, reconstituted after years of conscious and semi-conscious erasure from the public memory. Three days later, the Virginia Senate unanimously voted to introduce a bill repealing the sterilization law. By that December, former patients of the state hospitals filed a class action lawsuit against their former institutional homes. Aided by the American Civil Liberties Union (ACLU), the plaintiffs in the suit, *Poe v. Lynchburg*, alleged that many patients had been sterilized without properly understanding the nature of the operation, a clear violation of statutory procedure. Moreover, the suit alleged that court-appointed legal guardians had failed in their responsibility to represent these patients. Asking the federal court to declare the sterilizations an unconstitutional violation of their civil rights, the survivors demanded state notification and the provision of free medical services and mental health counseling for all surviving patients. At a preliminary hearing, District Court Chief Judge Robert Turk dismissed the charge of unconstitutionality, ruling that the fifty-four-year-old precedent in *Buck* settled the matter. Nevertheless, Judge Turk agreed that the allegations of procedural impropriety appeared substantial enough to allow the case to proceed. Ultimately, the ACLU settled *Poe* in January 1985. The state agreed to notify survivors through radio, television, and print advertisements, operate a toll-free information hotline, and train people to counsel those who had been sterilized.[2]

When *Poe v. Lynchburg* was filed, Carrie Buck still lived in Charlottesville. Carrie had married her second husband, Charles Dettamore, in 1965, and the couple lived without indoor plumbing in a cinderblock shed heated by a wood stove. Carrie's sister Doris, also sterilized at the Lynchburg Colony, had married in 1940. Neither woman knew that she had been sterilized until later; Carrie realized her condition a month after the operation; Doris did not know until Dr. K. Ray Nelson told her in 1979. She told reporters, "They [doctors at Lynchburg] told me the operation was for an appendix and rupture." When asked whether she knew what had really been done, Doris said: "My husband and me wanted children desperate—we were crazy about them. I never knew what they'd done with me." Asked by reporters about her sterilization, Carrie replied, "They just told me I had to have an operation, that was all." Both women lived the last years of their lives apprised of the truth of their condition; neither saw justice done. Doris predeceased Carrie by a few years, and Carrie died in 1983 at age seventy-five.[3]

Were any of the Bucks feebleminded? Paul Lombardo met Carrie shortly before she died and wrote, "when I met her she was reading newspapers daily and joining a more literate friend to assist at regular bouts with the cross-word puzzles. She was not a sophisticated woman, and lacked social graces, but mental health professionals who examined her in later life confirmed my impressions that she was neither mentally ill nor retarded." So much for one of Mr. Justice Holmes's famed "three generations of imbeciles." Lombardo also discovered the school records of Carrie's daughter Vivian at the Venable School in Charlottesville. Vivian disproved the prediction of social worker Caroline Wilhelm that she was "not quite a normal baby." During four school terms from September 1930 to May 1932, Vivian established herself as a normal student of average ability who earned straight As in "deportment." Vivian died at age eight of "enteric colitis," which, as one commentator noted, may indicate that "she fell victim to one of the preventable childhood diseases of poverty (a grim reminder of the real subject in *Buck v. Bell*)." With Carrie's mother long dead and records about her nonexistent, it is impossible to refute the eugenicists' and Justice Holmes's convictions about all three generations of Carrie's family, but that is unnecessary to moot Holmes's logic.[4]

On its surface, the founding of a department of medical ethics at the University of Virginia's School of Medicine, which occurred about the same time as *Poe,* seemed to promise that the abuses of the past would never happen again. Yet among the first faculty of that department was Joseph Fletcher, an Episcopalian priest and ethicist whose support for genetic screening and the termination of "defective" pregnancies continued earlier eugenic impulses.[5] In 1997, the Virginia legislature authorized the nation's first DNA databank for law enforcement use. Virginia, so rapid to embrace Francis Galton's eugenic ideas, also pioneered the genetic updating of Galton's other signal contribution: fingerprinting.

Despite these continuities, the University of Virginia also became an epicenter of scholarly activity that squarely confronted the state's eugenic legacy. Ironically, a University of Virginia medical ethicist named John Fletcher (unrelated to Joseph Fletcher) organized the effort that resulted in the 1997 presidential apology for the Tuskegee experiment. Within five years, work by other Virginia scholars, journalists, advocates for Native Americans and the disabled, and as well as Virginia politicians resulted in the Virginia General Assembly expressing "profound regret" for the state's eugenics program. Governor Mark Warner offered a forthright apology to the survivors of Virginia's eugenics program on May 2, 2002, the seventy-fifth anniversary of *Buck v.*

Bell. That day, in Charlottesville, officials unveiled a historical marker com-memorating this sad chapter in Virginia and national history.[6]

An editorial in the *Washington Post*, written five days after the "rediscovery" of eugenic sterilization in Virginia, chided the state for its backwardness. Writing that eugenics "was abandoned long ago," the editor charged that, "the state of Virginia, in its usual way, was slow to recognize that time and knowl-edge had passed its sterilization program by. As a result, not until 1972—long after eugenics had been discredited elsewhere—did this program come to an end." Technically correct, these statements underscore the troubling legacy of eugenics in America and Virginia. Virginia did indeed continue to oper-ate "in the name of eugenics" much longer than most other places. America generally, however, has hewed to eugenic ideology much longer than most early scholars considered possible. Explaining the durability of eugenic ideol-ogy in Virginia underscores the powerful role eugenic notions have played in shaping American social structure throughout the twentieth century, and why they remain seductive in the twenty-first.[7]

Sir Francis Galton wrote, "enthusiasm to improve the race is so noble in its aim, that it might well give rise to the sense of a religious obligation." Vir-ginia eugenicists shared this belief. Eugenics' power to inspire followed a pro-gression from the observation of human differences, to the systematization of those differences as expressions of innate biology, to the formulation of public policy based on biological axioms. Eugenics articulated a new secular creed of elite white progress, based on the biological subordination of blacks, the poor, the disabled, and women.[8]

Eugenics anointed elite Virginians as members of the American race, al-lowing them to valorize all the traits they liked best about themselves. Elite whites, marked by refined gentility, education, and the purported ability to keep others "in their place," cherished their birthright as the "natural" aris-tocrats who should determine Virginia and America's destiny. The best of the "Old Virginians," as Robert Bennett Bean called them, remained "pure" Anglo-Saxons, unadulterated (they believed) with the "blood" of other races. This vigorous "stock" pushed ever forward into new fields of endeavor. Their "racial" strength prevented them from the decadence that afflicted the "poor white trash" in rural backwaters and urban ghettoes. The social stultification of the impoverished betrayed their genetic backwardness through their ten-dency to "inbreeding" and miscegenation. Thus, Virginia eugenicists conflated their own cultural biases and scientific convictions in a distinctly "southern" fashion, reinforcing traditional social hierarchies.

Historical context, then as now, shaped Virginia eugenicists and their approach to science and social problems. Their efforts further defined both the scientific method and the relationship of science to society. In the process, they helped forge a new American identity predicated on whiteness. Ultimately, eugenics helped southern and northern elites to bind the festering wounds of regional antagonism. Boston Brahmins and the First Families of Virginia met in mutual admiration of each other's "pure" ancestry and eugenic genealogy. Just as northern elites began to fear the menace of the feebleminded, poor, criminals, and southeastern European immigrants, so too did white Virginians sound the alarm over their feebleminded and African American populations. Whiteness became a source of solidarity that undergirded individual identity, and preceded claims to citizenship. In the eugenic culture of Virginia and America, to be fully human and a first-class citizen one needed to be able to claim whiteness of the purest and most rarefied sort. Eugenics shaped people's relationship to the American social contract.

The durability of these beliefs is surprising. Beginning with Jefferson, branching out through Cabell and Barringer, then nurtured by the modern eugenicists, hereditarianism set deep roots in Virginia culture. The "eugenic metaphor" resonated with both the traditionalist agrarianism and the modernist impulse among the Virginia gentry. The tension between traditionalism and progressivism strained Virginia's intelligentsia, pushing them to extremes in their efforts to maintain the culture they valued within a new historical moment. As marginalized groups increasingly militated for civil rights, intransigent eugenicists shored up their crumbling position by relying on their scientific beliefs.

The similarities between the languages of eugenics and public health reinforced the apparently interchangeable efficacy of their approaches to social problems. Old words like "stock," "kin," and "blood" became closely associated in the public mind with the emerging science of race, germ plasm, and genes. This merging of ideas and concepts created a malleable ideological amalgam that appealed both to those who sought power and those who struggled against institutional powers. Elite and poor whites could walk through a eugenic exhibition at a fair and both come out believing they were "fit" members of the American race. This sense of security proved powerful enough that, when Arthur Estabrook and Ivan McDougle studied Amherst County's poor, they found it relatively easy to convince people to divulge personal information about themselves and, especially, their neighbors. Black Virginians could also adopt eugenics as a source for black "uplift," whether one supported Du Bois' notion of the talented tenth, or Marcus Garvey's Pan-Africanist bourgeois nationalism.

Eugenics influenced Virginia's social policy for over forty years, and was dismantled only when forces from outside the state (like the Supreme Court) could aid those within the state fighting against segregation's science. Over the course of its history in Virginia, hereditarianism drifted from the periphery of the intellectual and social world to its very center and then back to the margins. Slowly, as science and society beyond the borders of Virginia changed, newer concepts displaced hereditarianism. In the meantime, eugenic and hereditarian ideas justified segregation. When segregation came under fire, defenders wielded eugenics as a shield.

The persistence of eugenics within the academy helps to explain its power in Virginia's culture and politics. Tenured professors, who often had careers running in excess of thirty-five years, remained remarkably consistent in their beliefs. Their cultural loyalties skewed their scientific skepticism, creating a conservative impulse within Virginia's intellectual community. Ivey Lewis's career embodied this ossification of belief.

In 1952, a year before he retired as Miller Professor of Biology and dean of the University of Virginia, Ivey Lewis considered acquiring artifacts belonging to Gregor Mendel. Lewis wrote, "It is a rare opportunity for the University of Virginia to become a sort of shrine for the geneticist." Juxtaposing the religious imagery of a shrine and the southern traditionalism of the University of Virginia to the modern images of higher education, science, Darwinian evolution, and genetics, Lewis's rhetoric captured the tensions straining twentieth-century "southern identity": the competing desires to be both modern and traditional. Enshrining Mendel atop Virginia's ivory tower, however, rhetorically anchored the state to a ninety-year-old conception of biological destiny, cutting against the notion of the university as a locus for the steady, "modern," and "progressive" advance of knowledge. For Lewis, Mendel's artifacts embodied not just genetics, but also the dying theories of eugenics, segregation's science.[9]

Scientists like Ivey Lewis, and their students, believed that what they observed—class, gender, and, most importantly, race stratification—resulted from the unmediated operation of natural law, not from the differentiation of society based upon biased value judgments. This attitude helps to explain the reluctance of some eugenicists to repudiate their positions when faced with "more objective" scientific refutation. Lewis, like so many of America's eugenicists, traced his own roots to Old Virginians and Old Americans and profoundly believed in his and their superiority as members of the American race. Eugenicists' absolute certainty that they were objective, and their belief that objectivity somehow guaranteed morality, remains an unnerving part of present-day scientific culture: scientists today tend to dismiss the possibility of repeating the "mistakes" of early eugenicists because today's science is somehow "more objective," and hence implicitly more moral, than the "bad science" advocated by eugenicists. Present-day scientists still teach students based on their belief in the validity of their observations—which they assert result from value-neutral, objective investigations.

Today's geneticists teach about genes connected to alcoholism, breast cancer, sexual orientation, and aggression as if the experiments that "discovered" these genes occurred in a culture unconcerned with issues surrounding substance abuse, epidemiology, morality, and violence. Contemporary genetic researchers still risk the same errors made by Lewis. With the completion of the Human Genome Project, society encounters familiar ethical issues in new ways. Population genetics, recombinant DNA technology, and the emerging fields of cloning, "germinal choice," and stem cell research all propose different paths to various utopias of health and longevity. They also offer a "back door to eugenics." Who decides which genetic "traits" or pathological conditions are "debilitating" and which are liberating? At what point does society agree that a certain genetic disorder, from any standpoint, dooms an individual to an inhumane fate? The issue seems clear-cut with fatal conditions like Huntington's disease or Tay-Sachs disorder. People begin to disagree, however, over nonlethal genetic conditions like Trisomy-21 (Down's syndrome). These syndromes offer the affected individual a chance at life, albeit far shorter and with apparent cognitive and/or physical impairments. Biomedical ethicists have already demonstrated that one need not go to extremes—discussions of breeding people for their sex, hair color, or eye color—to realize that value judgments are always already operating to condition our approach to genetic and reproductive technologies. The presence of value bias is particularly evident when we make our decisions based on the explicitly value-laden notion "quality of life." What is "quality?" How should it be decided and by whom? The upwelling among America's deaf community over the cochlear implant and genetic therapy to prevent deafness shows that one group's definition of "normalcy" can, in the charged arena of "quality of life," become another group's genocide.[10]

Perhaps it is hopeful that various agencies are considering the ethical implications of genetic information, while the government is acting to restrict the disclosure and use of personal genetic information. The American

Association of Anthropologists urged the federal government to stop using the term "race" in the collection of information "because the concept of race is a social and cultural construction with no scientific basis in human biology." Geneticists were asked to use the 2000 U.S. Census as an "ideal opportunity for geneticists to reiterate that their research does not support the concept of race as a biological entity."[11]

Even more heartening is the call by a leading genetics journal to "look closer at the issues of race, populations and ethnicity in scientific discourse, which is often associated with poorly defined lay terminology." One hundred years after the eugenic metaphor came into existence, scientists appreciate the power of language in structuring lived reality. The editor of *Nature Genetics* remarked: "This is not just a matter of sloppy language, but reflects the imprecise use of racial and ethnic classifications in biomedical research. Throughout history scientists have used social and politically determined racial categories to make scientific comparisons between races—with little or no discussion about the meaning or rationale." This comment indicates the need for a new language of biology that better represents the physical beings it purports to describe. Since at least the late nineteenth century, racial designators have been invoked as fixed, immutable, and transparent to all who encountered them—to be black in America, most assumed, was the same as being black everywhere. During the period from roughly 1910 to about 1929, scientists became well aware of the blurred lines separating race and ethnicity, culture and biology in describing humanity. Investigators self-consciously debated both the meanings of these terms and the rationale behind their use. In the end, these debates ended where they began—individual investigators deployed these terms in ways that resonated with both their scientific and political outlooks, which were never separated, despite the investigators' claims to the contrary.

If *Nature Genetics'* call erodes the conviction among many "hard" scientists that they examine reality objectively, it will help to restore the closest thing to objectivity the scientific method really has: a healthy, vigorous, and deeply critical skepticism that takes nothing, not even the language in which scientific findings are conveyed, for granted. The debate does not seem likely to be settled soon. In March 2003, articles in the prestigious *New England Journal of Medicine* debated the utility of race as a meaningful category for understanding health, medicine, and human life. In June 2005, the federal Food and Drug Administration approved the heart medication BiDil for use only in African Americans. While BiDil was cast as a therapy devised to reduce health disparities between white and black Americans, it is clear that the intuitive pull of segregation's science—and the use of difference to parse humanity—continues to seduce some people.[12]

Understanding the relationship between Virginia eugenicists, their science, teaching, and the segregated culture in which they lived helps clarify our own valuation of science today, and the role it plays in determining liberating, rather than oppressive, public policy. By examining the culture created by academic scientists—both in the past and present—we can maintain the vigilance necessary to free ourselves from the lingering tendrils of segregation's science at long last.

Notes

ABBREVIATIONS

AES	American Eugenics Society	*JAMA*	*Journal of the American Medical Association*
AAUW	American Association of University Women	*JOH*	*Journal of Heredity*
BEF	Blandy Experimental Farm	PBB	Paul Brandon Barringer
CWM	College of William and Mary	WSH	Western State Hospital
ERO	Eugenics Record Office		

INTRODUCTION: "YOU *ARE* YOUR BROTHER'S KEEPER!"

1. Harvey Ernest Jordan in Aldrich et al., *Eugenics: Twelve University Lectures*, 117. See also "Dr. Jordan on 'Eugenics,'" *Charlottesville Daily Progress*, January 16, 1913.

2. Senate Bill 1203, at http://leg1.state.va.us/cgi-bin/legp504.exe?ses=071&typ=bil&val= sb1203. An earlier version of the bill allowed the court to order castration, with the patient's consent, as "an alternative to involuntary secure inpatient treatment"—in other words, parole in exchange for castration. See http://leg1.state.va.us/cgi-bin/legp504.exe?071+ful+SB1203.

3. Gossett, *Race*, 35, 82.

4. Dunn and Dobzhansky, *Heredity, Race, and Society*, 43–46.

5. Davenport, *Heredity in Relation to Eugenics*, 250.

6. Lacqueur, *Making Sex*, 70–98. See also Kuhn, *Structure of Scientific Revolutions*.

7. Duster, *Backdoor to Eugenics*.

8. In Cyprus, those with the gene for thalassemia, a disorder related to sickle-cell anemia—a painful and sometimes disabling chronic disease even with modern treatment—are under intense social pressure not to reproduce, or to abort at-risk fetuses. Many are assenting in this program, in the name of a healthier future population (see Lila Guterman, "Choosing Eugenics: How Far Will Nations Go to Eliminate a Genetic Disease?" *Chronicle of Higher Education*, May 2, 2003, A22).

9. Fullwiley, "Molecularization of Race."

10. Bederman, *Manliness & Civilization*, 200.

11. Mark R. Warner, "Statement of Governor Mark R. Warner: On the 75th Anniversary of

the Buck v. Bell Decision," at www.governor.state.va.us; "Virginia Governor
Apologizes for Eugenics Law," *USA Today,* May 2, 2002; Black, *War against the Weak,*
499 n. 51.

12. The discussion of eugenics and social control derives from the theories of Antonio
Gramsci; Samuel Bowles and Herbert Gintis; and Magali Sarfatti Larson (see Gramsci, *The
Intellectuals and Cultural Formation;* Bowles and Gintis, *Schooling in Capitalist America;*
and M. Larson, "Production of Expertise and the Constitution of Expert Power").

13. See Kevles, *In the Name of Eugenics,* ix, chap. 1; M. Haller, *Eugenics;* Ludmerer,
Genetics and American Society; and Chase, *The Legacy of Malthus.* Recent reinterpretations
include: Stern, *Eugenic Nation;* Kline, *Building a Better Race;* D. Paul, *Politics of Heredity;*
and E. Larson, *Sex, Race, and Science.*

14. Galton, *Inquiries into Human Faculty,* 17; Kevles, *In the Name of Eugenics,* 85.

15. Gould, *Mismeasure of Man,* chap. 5; Zenderland, *Measuring Minds.*

16. Gould, *Mismeasure of Man,* chap. 5; Rafter, *White Trash.*

17. See Kevles, *In the Name of Eugenics,* 75–76; Gossett, *Race,* 162–75, chap. 15; and
Selden, *Inheriting Shame,* 118–21.

18. See Woodward, *Strange Career of Jim Crow,* chap. 3; Higham, *Strangers in the Land,*
170–71; and Gossett, *Race,* 155–60. Harvard, Yale, Columbia, and Princeton Universities, and
the American Museum of Natural History in Manhattan, housed many prominent eugenicists; see Eugenics Education Society, *First International Eugenics Congress.*

19. Eugenic Record Office superintendent Harry Hamilton Laughlin quoted in Lombardo, "Three Generations," 51.

20. Grantham, *South in Modern America,* 104.

21. Pickens, *Eugenics and the Progressives,* 18; A. Link and McCormick, *Progressivism;*
Wiebe, *Search for Order,* esp. chaps. 7 and 8.

22. The author is indebted to Ronald Numbers for pointing out this fact (Numbers, *Darwinism Comes to America,* 74). See also "Evolution" folder, RG 6/2/2.291, President's Papers,
Special Collections, University of Virginia Library, Charlottesville (hereafter the President's
Papers are cited in this form: folder title, box number, President's Papers, three-digit record
group [RG] suffix, subseries number [if applicable]). For more on Darwinism generally, see
Numbers, *Darwinism Comes to America;* Caudill, *Darwinian Myths;* and Degler, *In Search
of Human Nature.* An alternative interpretation is Robert Bannister, *Social Darwinism.*

23. Grantham, *South in Modern America,* xvi.

24. For southerners' efforts to reconcile tradition and modernity, see, generally, Gaston,
New South Creed; and Hale, *Making Whiteness.*

25. Allen, "Misuse of Biological Hierarchies."

26. Southern liberalism was decidedly conservative. See Dabney, *Liberalism in the South.*

27. G. Dorr, "Defective or Disabled?" 388.

28. For similar discursive dynamics, see Foucault, *Birth of the Clinic;* Pernick, "Eugenics
and Public Health"; and Saks, "Representing Miscegenation Law."

29. Galton's works are rife with the eugenic metaphor (Galton, *Inquiries into Human
Faculty,* 198–200). American eugenicists use the metaphor throughout the *American Breeders Magazine* (later, the *Journal of Heredity*). See also Castle et al., *Heredity and Eugenics;*
and East and Jones, *Inbreeding and Outbreeding.*

30. Otis, *Membranes.*

31. The creation of southern imagined communities is traced in Brundage, *Where These Memories Grow.*

32. E. Larson, *Sex, Race, and Science,* 5–11; M. Haller, *Eugenics,* 62–63; Solomon, *Ancestors and Immigrants.* The word "cacogenic"—"bad kin"—was coined from the Greek: *kakos* (bad) and *genos* (race, descent, kin, sex).

33. Bledstein, *Culture of Professionalism,* 65–79, 90–104.

34. Stubbe, *History of Genetics,* 272.

35. See Degler, *In Search of Human Nature,* 42–43; "The Fitter Families Contest," *Eugenical News* 8 (September 1923): 88; and Selden, *Inheriting Shame,* 23–37.

36. George William Hunter and W. G. Whitman, *Science in Our World of Progress,* quoted in Selden, *Inheriting Shame,* 74. See also Holmes, *Trend of the Race.*

37. Foucault, *Birth of the Clinic,* xii, 89 (quotation 34).

38. Brechin, "Conserving the Race," 236. Frederick Winslow Taylor pioneered "scientific management"; his name became synonymous with efficiency in the Progressive Era.

39. Pernick, *Black Stork,* 23–24.

40. M. Haller, *Eugenics,* 6–7.

41. Degler, *In Search of Human Nature;* Kevles, *In the Name of Eugenics;* Ludmerer, *Genetics and American Society.* Elazar Barkan develops these tropes in *Retreat of Scientific Racism.*

42. D. Paul, "Eugenics and the Left," in *The Politics of Heredity,* by Paul, 11–35.

43. D. Paul, *Controlling Human Heredity,* 114.

44. Lombardo, "Eugenic Sterilization in Virginia," 243; Reilly, *Surgical Solution,* 108.

1. "THE SACRIFICE OF A RACE": VIRGINIA'S PROTO-EUGENICISTS SURVEY HUMANITY

1. Barringer's use of the word "generic"—from the scientific term "genera," or family—anticipated William Bateson's 1905 coining of the word "genetics" (see Paul Brandon Barringer, "The American Negro: His Past and Future" [20 February 1900]: 5, 15, 21, "Printed Material re Race Relations, 1896–1925," box 10, Barringer Family Papers; hereafter cited as PBB, "The American Negro"). See also Woodward, *Strange Career of Jim Crow,* 67–109.

2. PBB, "The American Negro," 1.

3. Ibid., 1, 15, 19. For a discussion of the "science" behind "born criminality" and its links to eugenics, see Rafter, *Creating Born Criminals,* chaps. 4, 6, 7.

4. PBB, "The American Negro," 14. The literature on the rape myth is extensive; see, particularly, Diane Miller Sommerville, *Rape and Race in the 19th Century South* (2004); and Lisa Lindquist Dorr, *White Women, Rape, and the Power of Race in Virginia, 1900–1960* (2004).

5. PBB, "The American Negro," 19–22.

6. "The Negro in the South," *Central Presbyterian,* April 11, 1900, 2; Holland Thompson to Paul Brandon Barringer, March 8, 1900; Armistead C. Gordon to Paul Brandon Barringer, March 27, 1900; Frank P. Brent to Paul Brandon Barringer, April 12, 1900; Charles F. Thwing, President of Western Reserve University, to Paul Brandon Barringer, April 6, 1900; and Paulus A. Irving to Paul Brandon Barringer, April 28, 1900, in "Correspondence,

1900–1902" folder, box 1, Barringer Family Papers, Accession #2588, -a, -b, -c, -d, -e, -g, Special Collections, University of Virginia Library, Charlottesville (hereafter cited as Barringer Family Papers). Barringer followed Jack London, Owen Wister, and Friedrich Nietzsche in valorizing the Teutonic savage, distinguishing him from the "black beast rapist" on the basis of will. Whites used their willpower to restrain their instinctual savagery, deploying it only to conquer, then suppressing it to create civilization. Inferior blacks lacked this "germinal trait" of self-restraint (see Brechin, "Conserving the Race," 234, 242 n. 21).

7. Barringer championed the "New South Creed" (see Gaston, *New South Creed*, 13, 22).

8. W. Jordan, *White over Black*, 439–40; Jefferson, *Notes on the State of Virginia*, queries VIII, IX, XIV, XVIII, XIX.

9. Kuhn, *Structure of Scientific Revolutions*, 5. John C. Green applied Kuhn to biology in "The Kuhnian Paradigm and the Darwinian Revolution," in *Perspectives in the History of Science and Technology*, ed. Duane H. D. Roller, 3–37 (1971). Social scientists, led by cultural anthropologists, arrived at this consensus by the 1930s. Biologists largely assented to the 1950 UNESCO statement declaring race a cultural construct, although debate has continued among biologists since.

10. W. Jordan, *White over Black*, 429, 455; Peter S. Onuf, "To Declare Them a Free and Independent People."

11. W. Jordan, *White over Black*, 436. Jordan wrote in 1968, but his observation holds forty years later (see Wills, *Inventing America;* and Ellis, *American Sphinx*).

12. Jefferson, *Notes*, 138–40.

13. Wills, *Inventing America*, xxiii, 110, 114–15, 118–21.

14. Jefferson, *Notes*, 143. See W. Jordan, *White over Black*, 453–57; and Boulton, "The American Paradox," 484. According to Winthrop Jordan, Jefferson's lack of experimental evidence proved that his "appeal to that highest court [science], was not the starting point for his thoughts about Negroes but a safe refuge from them" (*White over Black*, 445, 457). For an alternate explanation, see Wills, *Inventing America*, 114, 118–24.

15. Onuf, "To Declare Them a Free and Independent People," 26; Diggins, "Slavery, Race, and Equality," 225 n. 35.

16. Onuf, "To Declare Them a Free and Independent People," 12; Jefferson, *Notes*, 143.

17. Onuf notes, "The terms 'race,' 'nation,' and 'people' were not yet clearly distinguished before the era of the American Revolution." While "the American revolutionary crisis precipitated a process of conceptual definition," it by no means cleared up the discursive morass ("To Declare Them a Free and Independent People," 15). These three terms remained interchangeable into the twentieth century.

18. Ibid., 20.

19. Ibid., 24.

20. Jefferson, *Notes*, 84–85, 165; Laughlin quoted in Hassencahl, "Harry H. Laughlin," 241.

21. Jefferson, *Notes*, 146.

22. Ibid., 146–47. Jefferson and John Adams's debate over the existence of a "natural aristocracy" prefigured eugenic arguments that declared the genetically "fit" as naturally destined to lead (W. Jordan, *White over Black*, 355).

23. Jefferson, *Notes*, 139–41; W. Jordan, *White over Black*, 445–54. Similar ideas of innate intellectual inferiority appear in Herrnstein and Murray's *The Bell Curve*.

24. Onuf, "To Declare Them a Free and Independent People," 14; Jefferson, *Notes,* 138; D. Paul, *Controlling Human Heredity,* 110–14.

25. Jefferson, *Notes,* 138. See also Davenport, "The Geography of Man in Relation to Eugenics," 289–94; and Davenport, *Heredity in Relation to Eugenics,* 189–203.

26. Jefferson, *Notes,* 141, 143, 87; Jefferson to Edward Coles, August 25, 1814, quoted in Onuf, "To Declare Them a Free and Independent People," 40.

27. Gossett, *Race,* 27–28; Jefferson, *Notes,* 58–64, 96. See Virginia's Racial Integrity Act, sections 20–54 through 20–57 of the *Virginia Code of 1950.*

28. Onuf, "To Declare Them a Free and Independent People," 40; Jefferson, *Notes,* 138; Onuf, "Race, Slavery, and National Identity," 26.

29. Onuf, "To Declare Them a Free and Independent People," 25, 26, 34, 4.

30. Jefferson, *Notes,* 165, 135. Alfred E. Wiggam's *The New Decalogue of Science* enunciates ten biological "commandments" to guide human living.

31. Bruce, *History of the University of Virginia,* 1: 6.

32. Ibid., 1: 27, 31, 35; 2: 105–16. See Lombardo and Dorr, "Eugenics, Medical Education, and the Public Health Service."

33. Harvey Ernest Jordan, "A Short History of the University of Virginia Medical School," 8, typescript, MSS 4579 (catalogued as "History of Virginia School of Medicine [manuscript], 1953"), Special Collections, University of Virginia Library, Charlottesville.

34. Flannagan, "Barringer," box 1: loosely filed, 5, 10. See also Paul Brandon Barringer, Barringer Memoir, XXXIII, 323–25, box 1, "1900–1902 Correspondence" folder, Barringer Family Papers 2588 (hereafter cited as Barringer Memoir, Barringer Family Papers). (Two drafts of Barringer's memoirs exist in his papers. The manuscript is haphazardly paginated. When possible, citation will be by Roman numeral chapter heading and page number. If only a page number appears, then the citation is to the consecutively paginated, but not chapter-divided, manuscript.) Bruce, *History of the University of Virginia,* 4: 209–10. Cabell's *Testimony of Modern Science to the Unity of Mankind* is often overlooked because it appears to be a synopsis of the extant scholarship. Careful reading, however, reveals that Cabell marshaled contemporary discussions as evidence for his own argument. The timing of the book's release probably accounts for its subsequent invisibility. It appeared on the eve of the Civil War and just before Darwin's epochal *Origin of Species.* By the time American naturalists returned to their studies after the war, Darwin's work held the stage, shattering what Darwin called "the dogma of separate creations," and raising entirely new theological debates. See Ronald L. Numbers, "Darwinism and the Dogma of Separate Creations: The Response of American Naturalists to Evolution," in his *Darwinism Comes to America,* 24–48, 166–78.

35. Stanton, *The Leopard's Spots,* 194.

36. Cabell, *Testimony,* ix, 13–14, 20, 22.

37. Ibid., 243, 246–47.

38. Ibid., 33. Cabell owned one male and two female slaves in 1850, then three female slaves in 1860. Changes in names and sex-ratios indicate that Cabell engaged in slave trading (James L. Cabell household, Albemarle County, Va., population schedule, page 196, dwelling 569, 1850 U.S. Census, National Archives micropublication M432, roll 932; James L. Cabell household, Albemarle County, Va., slave schedule, St. Anne's parish, page 78, 1860 U.S. Census, National Archives micropublication M 653, roll 1386).

39. Cabell, *Testimony,* 31–32, 120, 249. Cabell also cited differential resistance to malaria and yellow fever (39).

40. Kolchin, *American Slavery,* 181–99.

41. Barringer Memoir, Barringer Family Papers.

42. For "race suicide" as a source of anxiety at the turn of the century and its links to eugenics, see M. Haller, *Eugenics,* 79–82.

43. Bruce, *History of the University of Virginia,* 4: 14–16, 295–97; 5: 177–81; Flannagan, "Barringer," 4.

44. Barringer Memoir, XV, 1; XII, 1, Barringer Family Papers.

45. Ibid., 323, 339.

46. Fleming, *William H. Welch,* 56–118 passim; Barringer Memoir, 345, Barringer Family Papers; Flannagan, "Barringer," 6.

47. Paul Brandon Barringer, "An Essay on Constitutional Syphilis" (in two parts), *North Carolina Medical Journal* 12 (1883): 89–95, 137–45.

48. Ibid., 89, 90. Similar fears were expressed in Surgeon General Thomas Parran's classic *Shadow on the Land: Syphilis,* 13–14.

49. Barringer's language reflected the imprecision of late-nineteenth-century medical knowledge. He was referring to congenital syphilis—passed from mother to child without genetic impact. In Barringer's day, however, the exact nature of transmission and the effect of syphilis on the "germ plasm" was unknown but assumed to be linked.

50. See Brandt, *No Magic Bullet,* 31–37; and Hobson, *Uneasy Virtue,* 145–46, 189.

51. Barringer, "Constitutional Syphilis," 90. Charles Davenport would remark in 1911, "Venereal diseases are disgenic [*sic*] agents of the first magnitude and of growing importance" (Davenport, *Heredity in Relation to Eugenics,* 2).

52. Blue, Clark, and Cumming took physiology and surgery under Barringer: Blue and Clark in 1889–90, and Cumming in 1891–92. Cumming took materia medica under Barringer in 1893 (University of Virginia, *Catalogue and Announcements* [1889–90], viii –ix, 28. For the years 1890–91, ix, 59, 63, 65; 1891–92, 44; 1892–93, ix, 59; 1893–94, 69). See also Hugh Smith Cumming, unpublished memoir, Hugh Smith Cumming Papers, box 6, 773; Flannagan, "Barringer," 4; Bruce, *History of the University of Virginia,* 4: 195, 295–97; 5: 270, 178; Barringer, *Cholera and Its Prevention*; and Barringer, *Natural Bent.*

53. "The Sacrifice of a Race" (May 10, 1900); "Negro Education in the South" (December 28, 1900), "1896-1925 Printed material re: Race Relations" folder, box 10, Barringer Family Papers.

54. Edgar Gardner Murphy to Paul Brandon Barringer, April 13, 1900, "1900–1902 Correspondence" folder, box 1, Barringer Family Papers.

55. Paul Brandon Barringer to Booker T. Washington, May 5, 1900, "1900–1902 Correspondence" folder, box 1, Barringer Family Papers.

56. Paul Brandon Barringer, "The Sacrifice of a Race" (May 10, 1900), 3–4, 14, "1896–1925 Printed material re: Race Relations" folder, box 10, Barringer Family Papers. The Thirteenth (abolishing slavery), Fourteenth (mandating due process and equal protection of the law; defining citizenship), and Fifteenth (forbidding voting restriction based on race) amendments are known as the Civil War amendments. They were universally reviled by white southerners until the later twentieth century.

57. Ibid., 6–7, 16.

58. Ibid., 20–22, 26.

59. Ibid., 25–29.

60. Barringer, "Negro Education" (December 28, 1900), 233, 241, 242, "1896–1925 Printed material re: Race Relations" folder, box 10, Barringer Family Papers; Nicholas Murray Butler to Paul Brandon Barringer, "1900–1902 Correspondence" folder, box 1, Barringer Family Papers.

61. J. C. Morrison to Paul Brandon Barringer, December 29, 1900, "1900–1902 Correspondence" folder, box 1, Barringer Family Papers.

62. Paul Brandon Barringer, "Race Problems in America," 1–2, 3–5, 13, 15, "1911–1912, n.d. Race Problems in America" folder, box 7, Barringer Family Papers. For Anglo-Saxonism and Aryanism, see Gossett, *Race,* chap. 13.

63. Hermon Butler to Mr. John Hannah, April 20, 1901, "1901–1909 Correspondence" folder, box 1, 5858-j, Barringer Family Papers; G. Stanley Hall to Paul Brandon Barringer, June 9, 1905, "1903–1908 Correspondence" folder, box 1, Barringer Family Papers. See Gossett, *Race,* 169–70; and G. Stanley Hall, "Eugenics: Its Ideals and What It Is Going to Do," *Religious Education* 6 (June 1911): 152–59.

64. Paul Brandon Barringer, "Teach 'Em Birth Control," "1925, n.d. Poetry" folder, box 7, Barringer Family Papers. Barringer's poem "Germ or Sperm" bemoans human inattention to breeding (see p. 124).

2. "REARING THE HUMAN THOROUGHBRED": PROGRESSIVE ERA EUGENICS IN VIRGINIA

1. Dennis, "Educating the 'Advancing' South."

2. Laurence R. Veysey discusses this focus on businesslike efficiency in *The Emergence of the American University,* 258–59, 302–17, 346–56. See also Bruce, *History of the University of Virginia,* 5: 1–66, esp. 3.

3. See, generally, George M. Frederickson, *Black Image in the White Mind;* W. Link, *Paradox of Southern Progressivism,* xii, 3–30; and Dennis, "Educating the 'Advancing' South," 1–97.

4. The Italian Marxist Antonio Gramsci opened the debate on the conservative nature of educational institutions in *The Intellectuals.* See, generally, M. Larson, "Production of Expertise."

5. Dennis, "Educating the 'Advancing' South," 30, chap. 3. See also Anderson, *The Education of Blacks in the South, 1860–1935,* 110–47; Anderson and Moss, *Dangerous Donations,* 39–62; and Kett, "Women and the Progressive Impulse in Southern Education."

6. Dennis, "Reforming the 'Academical Village,'" 58–59. Alderman quoted ibid., 66, 81–82. See also Alderman, "The University and the State in the South."

7. Gerteis, "Populism, Race, and Political Interest." See also Dennis, "Educating the 'Advancing' South," 328.

8. Alderman quoted in Dennis, "Educating the 'Advancing' South," 349. See also Bruce, *History of the University of Virginia,* 5: 177–92 (quotation 187).

9. "The University of Virginia," *Charlottesville Daily Progress,* December 29, 1916.

10. Alderman, "The Growing South"; Edwin Alderman, "Untitled Address to Commission (December 20, 1915)," folder 103, box 8, President's Papers, .472, subseries III. George

M. Frederickson termed racial moderates like Alderman "racial accommodationists" (*Black Image in the White Mind*, 283–97).

11. Alderman, "Achievement of a Generation," 239; Alderman, "The Growing South," 10378.

12. Harvey Ernest Jordan, *Publications of Harvey Ernest Jordan*, 3 vols. (collected and bound, 1940), Wilhelm Moll Rare Book and Medical Library, University of Virginia Medical School, Charlottesville; D. Jordan and H. Jordan, *War's Aftermath;* Harvey Ernest Jordan, *A Textbook of Histology*, 3rd ed. (New York, 1920); and Harvey Ernest Jordan and James E. Kindred, *Embryology* (New York, 1926). For these individuals' significance, see Maienschein, *Transforming Traditions*.

13. These men's involvement with organized eugenics is well known (see Mehler, "A History of the American Eugenics Society").

14. For similar dynamics in the Deep South, see E. Larson, *Sex, Race, and Science*, 14–17, 40–42.

15. Harvey Ernest Jordan to Charles Benedict Davenport, October 8, 1912; Jordan to Davenport, December 3, 1906, "H. E. Jordan" folder, Charles B. Davenport Papers, American Philosophical Society, Philadelphia (hereafter cited as Davenport Papers). See also Jordan's curriculum vita and his "Raven Award" address, bound in the Harvey Ernest Jordan Collected Scientific Papers, Historical Collections, Claude Moore Health Sciences Library, University of Virginia, Charlottesville, vol. 1 (hereafter cited as H. E. Jordan Collected Scientific Papers); and H. Jordan, "Relation of the Nucleolus to the Chromosomes."

16. Philip J. Pauly, "Summer Resort and Scientific Discipline"; Hiltzik, "Brooklyn Institute," esp. 144–47, 156 n. 284, 245–51; Jordan to Davenport, December 3, 1906; Davenport to Jordan, December 6, 1906; Davenport to Jordan, February 13, 1907, Davenport Papers.

17. Jordan to Davenport, March 21, 1910, Davenport Papers. Jordan's address would later be published by the American Breeders Association. See also H. Jordan, "Heredity as a Factor," 246–51.

18. Jordan to Davenport, March 21, 1910, Davenport Papers. For the AAS&PIM and eugenics, see Meckel, *Save the Babies*, 109–23, esp. 116–19. For Jordan and statistics on "defects," see Davenport to Jordan, November 21, 1911; Davenport to Jordan, December 17, 1912; Davenport to Jordan, November 22, 1911 (carcinoma, neurofibroma); Jordan to Davenport, October 11, 1912 (melancholia, tuberculosis, left-handedness); Jordan to Davenport, January 6, 1913 (twinning and left-handedness); and Jordan to Davenport, March 4, 1913, and March 8, 1913 (left-handedness), Davenport Papers. See also Jordan to Davenport, May 22, 1911; Davenport to Jordan, August 16, 1911; and Jordan to Davenport, November 21, 1911, Davenport Papers. For discussion of Jordan's paper for the eugenics congress, see Jordan to Davenport, November 14, 1911, and February 3, 1912; Davenport to Jordan, February 5, 1912, Davenport Papers. See also H. Jordan, "Place of Eugenics"; Jordan to Davenport, May 20, 1912; and Davenport to Jordan, May 25, 1912, Davenport Papers.

19. H. Jordan, "Eugenic Bearings," 121–22. See also H. Jordan, "Heredity as a Factor," 251; H. Jordan, "Eugenics," 881–82; and H. Jordan, "Eugenics: Its Data, Scope and Promise," 109–10, 115–16.

20. Jordan to Davenport, March 21, 1910; February 3, 1912; Jordan to Davenport, May 22, 1911, Davenport Papers. See also Davenport to Jordan, September 5, 1912; Jordan to Davenport, November 27, 1912; Jordan to Davenport, December 17, 1912, Davenport Papers;

Davenport to Jordan, October 7, 1912. Jordan's Wilson lecture appeared as "Eugenics: Its Data, Scope and Promise as Seen by the Anatomist," in Aldrich, *Eugenics: Twelve University Lectures,* 107–38. See Jordan to Davenport, December 17, 1912, Davenport Papers, for a discussion of this appointment. The slides, in their original case, are still held in Special Collections, University of Virginia Library, Charlottesville (see Jordan to Davenport, July 16, 1913, Davenport Papers).

21. See Jordan to Davenport, May 22, 1911; and Davenport to Jordan, August 16, 1911; for 1912, see Jordan to Davenport, May 20, 1912; and Davenport to Jordan, May 25, 1912, Davenport Papers. See also Jordan to Davenport, July 16, 1913, Davenport Papers. Established in 1911 by Mrs. Caroline Phelps Stokes, a prominent New England philanthropist, the Phelps-Stokes Fund aimed at "negro uplift" and provided $12,500 to the Universities of Virginia and Georgia for "lectures by representative Southerners on the negro and his problems," as well as an annual fellowship award of $500 for students studying southern African Americans. See Anson Phelps Stokes to Edwin Anderson Alderman, May 11, 1914; and APS to Chancellor Barrow of the University of Georgia, carbon copy, February 8, 1915, "Phelps-Stokes Fund" folder, box 20, President's Papers, .472, subseries I.

22. Davenport to Jordan, April 10, 1911, Davenport Papers. See Davenport's brief musings about Virginia in Castle et al., *Heredity and Eugenics,* 295–96, 303–5; and in Davenport, *Heredity in Relation to Eugenics,* 206–7, 228–30.

23. Most early geneticists and eugenicists assumed the hereditary basis of all these conditions. Davenport argued that pellagra was hereditary, even after Dr. Joseph Goldberger proved its dietary basis in 1915 (see Chase, *Legacy of Malthus,* 201–25). For Davenport and Jordan on Virginia, see Davenport to Jordan, April 10, 1911, Davenport Papers. Later, Davenport became interested in research on "defectives of the Ragged Mountains" conducted by the Charlottesville Civics Club (Davenport to Jordan, February 1, 1912; Jordan to Davenport, February 3, 1912, Davenport Papers). As Gray Brechin commented: "The conventional *White* Anglo-Saxon Protestant (WASP) acronym is, of course, redundant. *Wealth* even more than color, indicates worth, particularly as it becomes hereditary, and those ASPs lacking this gene frequently fell into the category of 'white trash.' As such, they were just as eligible for sterilization as any of the lower races, since poverty was taken as a symptom of hereditary weakness" ("Conserving the Race," 241 n. 14).

24. Jordan to Davenport, March 25, 1914; Davenport to Jordan, March 31, 1914; Jordan to Davenport, June 26, 1914, Davenport Papers; Davenport and Davenport, "Heredity of Skin Pigmentation in Man," 664; Davenport, *Heredity of Skin Color;* H. Jordan, "Comparative Microscopic Study"; H. Jordan, "Inheritance of Skin Color."

25. All Jordan quotations from Jordan to Davenport, May 22, 1911. Davenport quotation from Davenport to Jordan, August 16, 1911, Davenport Papers. Edwin Conklin echoed Davenport's and Jordan's racial views (see Cooke, "Gospel of Social Evolution," 28–35).

26. H. Jordan, "Biological Worth and Social Status," 576.

27. Ibid., 578, 580–81.

28. See Kevles, *In the Name of Eugenics,* 3–5, 76–79. This movement reached its apogee with the publication of Carl C. Brigham's *A Study of American Intelligence* (1923), which purported to document racial differences in intelligence. See also Jordan to Davenport, November 27, 1912; Davenport to Jordan, November 30, 1912, Davenport Papers.

29. M. Haller, *Eugenics,* 75.

30. H. Jordan, "Inheritance of Left-Handedness"; H. Jordan, "Studies in Human Hered-ity"; H. Jordan, "Hereditary Lefthandedness." For a discussion of the Italians, see Rafter, *Creating Born Criminals,* chap. 6. See also H. Jordan, "Inheritance of Left-Handedness," 121, 122–23; and H. Jordan, "Studies in Human Heredity," 304.

31. H. Jordan, "Studies in Human Heredity," 310. See also H. Jordan, "Need for Genetic Studies." This was not the first time the *JAMA* reported Jordan's eugenical ideas. In 1911, it reported his addresses before the ASS&PIM. See his "Hereditary Tuberculosis and Infant Mortality"; and "Recommendations on Eugenics." Jordan followed the path blazed by Davenport in *Heredity in Relation to Eugenics* (chap. 8 and 165) and "Eugenics and Euthen-ics" (19).

32. H. Jordan, "Need for Genetic Studies," 4.

33. H. Jordan, "The Eugenical Aspect of Venereal Disease," 156.

34. Ibid., 157. The belief that black women were vectors of infection was common in the progressive South (see Hunter, "Domination and Resistance," 347–48).

35. H. Jordan, "The Eugenical Aspect of Venereal Disease," 158, 162.

36. Jordan's eugenics essays reiterate his 1910 address before the Virginia State Confer-ence of Charities and Corrections that was published in *American Breeders Magazine* in 1911 as "Heredity as a Factor in the Improvement of Social Conditions." See Jordan's "Eugenics: the Rearing of the Human Thoroughbred" (1912); "The Eugenic Bearings of the Efforts for Infant Conservation" (1912); "Surgical Sex Sterilization: Its Value as a Eugenic Measure" (1913); and "Eugenics: Its Data, Scope and Promise, as Seen by the Anatomist" (1913; quota-tions 247, 250).

37. This phrase appears in almost every one of his eugenics tracts, one of which is titled "Eugenics: The Rearing of the Human Thoroughbred." See also H. Jordan, "Eugenics: Its Data, Scope and Promise," 108.

38. H. Jordan, "Eugenics: Its Data, Scope and Promise," 137; H. Jordan, "Surgical Sex-Sterilization," 983; H. Jordan, "The Eugenical Aspect of Venereal Disease," 160.

39. H. Jordan, "Place of Eugenics," 1: 397, 399. See also H. Jordan, "Eugenics," 885.

40. H. Jordan, "Heredity as a Factor," 253; H. Jordan, "Place of Eugenics," 396; H. Jor-dan, "Eugenics: Its Data, Scope and Promise," 138.

41. H. Jordan, "Eugenics: Its Data, Scope and Promise," 136; H. Jordan, "Heredity as a Factor," 250. See also H. Jordan, "Eugenics," 885; and H. Jordan, "Surgical Sex-Sterilization," 983.

42. H. Jordan, "Eugenics: Its Data, Scope and Promise, 135; H. Jordan, "The Eugenical Aspect of Venereal Disease," 162–63 (quotation 163); H. Jordan, "Surgical Sex-Steriliza-tion," 987.

43. H. Jordan, "Place of Eugenics," 396; H. Jordan, "Heredity as a Factor," 876, 878.

44. H. Jordan, "Surgical Sex-Sterilization," 986. Holmes's decision in the Virginia ster-ilization case *Buck v. Bell* (274 U.S. 200) relied in part on the preventive analogy between compulsory sterilization and inoculation against smallpox.

45. Tyack, *The One Best System.* See also Woodward, *Origins of the New South,* 398–406; and Tindall, *Emergence of the New South,* 256–76.

46. Heck quoted in Lewis, "William Henry Heck," 363–64.

47. Lewis, "William Henry Heck," 365, 366.

48. Heck, *Mental Discipline,* 174; Heck, "Citizenship in Southern Education," 382.

49. Heck, "Citizenship in Southern Education," 384–85. Heck invoked the concept of "social efficiency" repeatedly throughout his writing.

50. Heck, *Mental Discipline*, 120. For a discussion of the conservative implications of Thorndike's ideas, see Curti, *Social Ideas of American Educators*, 468–70. The University of Virginia's sole copy of Davenport's *Eugenics* was bequeathed to the library by Heck. All the first editions of Thorndike's work in the University of Virginia library also came from Heck's personal library. Many of the library's other eugenical works bear the bookplate of Heck's library. For Thorndike's eugenics, see M. Haller, *Eugenics*, 64, 73; and Pickens, *Eugenics and the Progressives*, 138–44. Thorndike invoked eugenics repeatedly in his book *Human Nature and the Social Order* (442, 453–59, 878, 938). While he eschewed Mendelian simplisms, he still argued that, "Improvement of the human genes, though much slower than some enthusiasts for eugenics have represented it, is the surest means of fostering the good life; it operates at the source by producing better people" (453).

51. University of Virginia, *University Record* (Charlottesville, Va.: Michie, 1911), vol. 5, *Catalogue 1911-1912* (hereafter cited as *University Record*, followed by the year and page number); University of Virginia Questionnaire, "Eugenics and Genetics in Colleges, #1" folder, Davenport Papers. See "College Courses in Genetics and Eugenics," *Eugenical News* 1 (April 1916): 27.

52. Stanley C. Moulton quoted in Lewis, "William Henry Heck," 372. The professor of secondary education Charles G. Maphis wrote of Heck, "No professor in the University left a profounder impression on his students" (Maphis quoted in Lewis, "William Harry Heck," 381). Both Merle Curti and Geraldine Jonçich Clifford noted Thorndike's dedication to "scientific truth." Although Curti saw it as a cipher for Thorndike's "own unconscious participation in the prejudices of our own time," Clifford views Thorndike as an unsentimental realist (Curti, *Social Ideas of American Educators*, 498; Clifford, *Thorndike*, 375–76).

53. *University Record*, 1919–20, 113–14; 1920–21, 26. Ferguson began his summer courses in 1921.

3. "DEFENDING THE THIN RED LINE": ACADEMICS AND EUGENICS

1. Harry Hamilton Laughlin, ed., "1919," *Eugenical News* 4 (January 1919): 4–5. See also Veysey, *The Emergence of the American University*, 269; Marchand, *Advertising the American Dream*, 70; and Wiggam, *The New Decalogue of Science*, 174–75.

2. Cravens, *Triumph of Evolution*, 53; Selden, *Inheriting Shame*, chap. 4.

3. Alderman to David Starr Jordan, January 3, 1909, "J" folder, box 6, President's Papers, .472, subseries II. Clifford Beers to EAA, February 8, 1915, "B" folder, box 1, President's Papers, .472, subseries IV. All except Blumer served on the advisory board of the American Eugenics Society. See Mehler, "A History," 307–10. For Blumer's eugenics, see Dowbiggin, *Keeping America Sane;* and Rafter, *Creating Born Criminals*, 156–59, 198–99. Pinchot's eugenic career and David Starr Jordan's eugenic teaching are detailed in Brechin, "Conserving the Race," 236, 241 n. 13. On aristogenics, see correspondence in "A (2)" folder, box 1, President's Papers, .491, subseries I.

4. Eugenics made its way into *World's Work*, a journal in which Alderman published (see M. P. Daggett, "Women: Building a Better Race," *World's Work* [December 1912]). Lothrop Stoddard, *Reforging America*, vii, 310–11, and chap. 12. For Alderman and Stoddard, see

Lothrop Stoddard to Edwin Anderson Alderman, April 23, 1927, "1925–1927 Miscellaneous" folder, box 21, President's Papers, .472, subseries VII; Lothrop Stoddard to Edwin Anderson Alderman, April 23, 1927; Edwin Anderson Alderman to Lothrop Stoddard, April 25, 1927, "1925–1927 Miscellaneous" folder, box 21, President's Papers, .472, subseries VII; and Edwin Anderson Alderman to Miss Mina Hall, 1928, "W" folder, box 3, President's Papers, .472, subseries VIII (quotation about woman's father). The eugenicist Robert Bennett Bean gave Alderman offprints of all his articles. These reside in various volumes of *Rare Virginia Pamphlets*, Special Collections, University of Virginia Library, Charlottesville.

5. G. Dorr, "Assuring America's Place in the Sun."

6. Lewis's mother was the granddaughter of the University of North Carolina president Kemp Plummer Battle. The Lewis and Battle families have distinguished histories as "founding" families of Virginia and North Carolina. Lewis's correspondence reveals his genealogical pride. See boxes 1–5 passim, Ivey Foreman Lewis Papers, RG –6/2/1.551, Special Collections, University of Virginia Library, Charlottesville (hereafter cited as Lewis Papers); and Edwin Alderman to Ivey Lewis, January 13, 1928, "L" folder, box 2, President's Papers, .472, subseries VIII. See also Higham, *Strangers in the Land*, 170–71; Woodward, *Origins of the New South*, 321–26, 355–56; and Woodward, *Strange Career of Jim Crow*, 31–109.

7. Lewis to Edwin Anderson Alderman, "Biology" folder, box 5, President's Papers, .472, subseries III. For Brooks, see Maienschein, *Transforming Traditions*, 43–47. See also Ivey Lewis to Edwin Alderman, January 5, 1914; and Ivey Lewis to Dean J. M. Page, January 12, 1914, "Biology 1908–1914" folder, box 5, President's Papers, .472, subseries I. In 1929, he was appointed to the National Research Council, chairing its division of biology and agriculture from 1933 to 1936. He became president of the American Society of Naturalists in 1939, of the American Biological Society in 1942, and of the Botanical Society of America in 1949. In 1950–51, he was president of the biology section of the AAAS. All of these positions brought him into personal contact with major figures in the American eugenics movement.

8. See collected letters in "Biology 1908–1914" folder, box 5, President's Papers, .472, subseries I, esp. Edwin Alderman to Dean J. M. Page, January 29, 1915. See also Samuel C. Hatcher to Dean J. M. Page, February 7, 1914, ibid. Quotations from Robert E. Blackwell to Dean J. M. Page, January 14, 1914; and Edwin Alderman to R.T.W. Duke, Secretary of the Miller Board, January 14, 1914, ibid. See also Edwin Alderman to Ivey Lewis, February 6, 1915, ibid.; and Ivey Lewis to Edwin Alderman, February 20, 1915, "Biology" folder, box 2, President's Papers, .472, subseries III. Impressed by Lewis, Alderman asked *him* his opinion of *other* candidates for the job (see Ivey Lewis to Dean J. M. Page, May 25, 1914; and Ivey Lewis to Dean J. M. Page, June 22, 1914, "Biology 1908–1914" folder, box 5, President's Papers, .472, subseries I).

9. Ivey Foreman Lewis, "The Last Ten Years in Biology at the University of Virginia," "Articles on University" folder, box 3, President's Papers, .491, subseries I.

10. Cooke, "Gospel of Social Evolution."

11. Ivey Lewis to V. B. Harris, Esquire, November 2, 1922, "1922 Letters" folder, box 1, Lewis Papers. See W. H. Ruffin to Ivey Lewis, February 2, 1927, "1927 Letters" folder, box 1, Lewis Papers; and Ivey Lewis to Tom H. Garth, Westminster Presbyterian Church, October 1, 1947, "1947 Letters" folder, Lewis Papers. See also, generally, boxes 1–37, Lewis Papers, Special Collections, University of Virginia Library, Charlottesville. "Moral delinquent" was a term developed to describe the feebleminded during the *Buck v. Bell* case (Lombardo, "Three

Generations," 49). Quotations from Lewis, "Address to New Students (September 3, 1940)," "Speeches" folder, box 5, Lewis Papers. See also Ivey F. Lewis, "Ancient Wisdom and Modern Knowledge (May 5, 1935)," "Speeches" folder, box 5, Lewis Papers. Lewis echoed the eugenics popularizer Alfred E. Wiggam (*New Decalogue of Science*, 110). See "1929 Letters" folder, box 1, Lewis Papers; Ivey F. Lewis, "Untitled Essay (undated)"; Ivey Lewis to Bishop W. R. Mason, March 24, 1949, loosely filed, box 24, Lewis Papers; and Ivey F. Lewis, "Address before the American Association of University Women, Wytheville, VA (April 5, 1946)," "Dean Lewis" folder, box 11, President's Papers, .581 (hereafter cited as "AAUW").

12. Lewis's speech "What Biology Says to the Man of Today" was reported in an April 6, 1924, *New York Times* article titled "Biologist Supports Curb on Immigrants." Unless otherwise noted, all quotations in the ensuing discussion are from this article. The *Times'* coverage of Lewis was reprinted in the *Virginia Teacher,* the leading professional magazine for Virginia educators. See "Environment Cannot Mold Something out of Nothing, Says Biologist," *Virginia Teacher* 5 (June 1924), 163–64. Charles Mills's *The Racial Contract* (1997) argues that all Western social contract theory stems from an underlying racial contract that privileges the race in power. The result is a society founded on racial subordination. Eugenicists sought to reveal and sustain the racial contract by legitimating it on scientific grounds.

13. Lewis, "Biologist Supports Curb."

14. Ivey Lewis to John D. Martin, Jr., Esquire, March 6, 1948, "M" folder, box 7, Lewis Papers. For Grant and Stoddard, see M. Haller, *Eugenics,* 147. Cox's books *White America* and *Teutonic Unity: A Basis for Peace* mimic Grant's *The Passing of the Great Race* and Stoddard's *Rising Tide of Color against White World-Supremacy* and *Revolt against Civilization: The Menace of the Under Man.*

15. Ivey F. Lewis, "AAUW," 1; "Address before the Roanoke Teachers Association (December 11, 1937)," 7–8, "Speeches" folder, box 5, Lewis Papers. See also Ivey Lewis to John Dale Russell, Director Division of Higher Education, U.S. Office of Education, January 14, 1948, "R" folder, box 8, Lewis Papers; Ivey F. Lewis, "Resource Use in the South (n.d.)," and "The High School Program in Relation to Success in College Work (February 8, 1946)," 3, 18, 19, "Articles and Abstracts" folder, box 2, Lewis Papers.

16. Raymond Bice, interview by the author, December 1, 1999; Franklin Bacon and Raymond Bice, interview by the author, January 25, 1999. Correspondence between Lewis and his siblings reveals Nell's condition. Anne (Lewis) Perry to Ivey Foreman Lewis April 24, 1932; Dick Lewis to Ivey Foreman Lewis, April 27, 1932; Ivey Foreman Lewis to Kemp Plummer Lewis, April 29, 1932, "1932 Letters" folder, box 1, Lewis Papers.

17. "AES Membership Campaign, Miscellany" folder, n.d., American Eugenics Society Records, American Philosophical Society Library, Philadelphia (hereafter cited as AES Records).

18. For Mall, see Flexner and Flexner, *William Henry Welch,* 211–33. For Bean, see Marquis Who's Who, *Who Was Who in America, 1943–1950,* 2: 51; William Bennett Bean, "Robert Bennett Bean, 1874–1944," *Science* 101 (April 6, 1945): 346–48 (quotation 346); and R. J. Terry, "Robert Bennett Bean, 1874–1944," *American Anthropologist,* n.s., 48, no. 1 (January 1946): 70–74.

19. William Bennett Bean, "Robert Bennett Bean, 1874–1944," *Science* 101 (April 6, 1945): 346–48 (quotation 346). Summaries of the work of these men appear in Gould, *The Mismeasure of Man* (chaps. 2–4); and Chase, *Legacy of Malthus,* 179–80.

20. Bean, "Some Racial Peculiarities," 379; Jefferson, *Notes*, 70–71, 138–42.

21. See Bean, "Negro Brain," 778, 784; and Bean, "Training of the Negro," 950–51. See also H. Jordan, "Eugenical Aspect of Venereal Disease." For the currency of these beliefs beyond Virginia, see Hunter, "Domination and Resistance," 347–49.

22. *American Medicine* quoted in Chase, *Legacy of Malthus*, 179.

23. Franklin Mall, "On Several Anatomical Characteristics of the Human Brain Said to Vary According to Age and Sex, with Special Reference to the Frontal Lobes," *American Journal of Anatomy* 9 (1909): 1–32 (quotation 9).

24. Henry Baldwin Ward, ed., *Sigma Xi Half-Century Record and History, 1886–1936* (Burlington, Vt., 1936), 773–75. The eugenicists who addressed the society were, in chronological order, Aleš Hrdlička, Ellsworth Huntington, and John C. Merriam. For these speakers' association with organized eugenics, see Mehler, "A History," 372–73, 375–76, 400–401. Bean churned out articles about racial taxonomy, including "Two European Types"; "Three Anatomic Types"; "Human Types"; and "Types of the Three Great Races of Man." In 1932, Bean compiled all his work into his book *The Races of Man: Differentiation and Dispersal of Man*. Quotations from Bean, "The Sitting Height," 372, 377; Bean and Baker, "Some Racial Characteristics of the Heart," 274; and Bean, "Anthropology," 371–73.

25. Bean, "Disease and Death Rate," 16; Bean, "Anthropology," 371–73. See also Bean and Baker, "Some Racial Characteristics of the Spleen Weight"; Bean and Baker, "Some Racial Characteristics of the Liver Weight"; and Bean and Baker, "Some Racial Characteristics of the Heart." For a discussion of racial medicine, see Jones, *Bad Blood*, chap. 2; J. Haller, "The Physician versus the Negro," 154–67; and Savitt, *Medicine and Slavery*, 149–50; 171–79. See also Bean, "Notes on the Body-Form of Man" (quotations 8–9, 12–13).

26. Bean, "Notes on the Body-Form of Man," 15–16.

27. John W. Ritchie to Charles G. Maphis, February 16, 1919, "1919 Education" folder, box 3, President's Papers, .472, subseries III. See also George Oscar Ferguson to Charles G. Maphis, February 18, 1919, ibid.

28. Ferguson, "Psychology of the Negro." The *Eugenical News* called Ferguson's work "an extremely important paper." See "Negro Efficiency," *Eugenical News* 1 (November 1916): 79; and "The Mental Status of the American Negro," *Scientific Monthly* 12 (June 1921): 533–43.

29. Ferguson, "Psychology of the Negro," 93, 111, 130, 136–38.

30. Ibid., 29, 30–33, 35 n. 104 (quotations 91, 110).

31. Ibid., 125–26, 130.

32. Quotation from George Oscar Ferguson to William Henry Heck, November 27, 1918, "1919 Education" folder, box 3, President's Papers, .472, subseries III. For the army intelligence-testing program, see John Carson, "Army Alpha, Army Brass, and the Search for Army Intelligence," *Isis* 84 (1993): 278–309.

33. John W. Ritchie to Charles G. Maphis, February 16, 1919, "1919 Education" folder, box 3, President's Papers, .472, subseries III

34. Raymond Bice recalled that Ferguson was "extremely prejudiced" against blacks and Jews. As dean of admissions, Ferguson exercised his prejudice by restricting the admission of Jewish students (Raymond Bice interviews by the author, 1999, 2000). See also George Oscar Ferguson to Edwin Anderson Alderman, May 5, 1919, "1919 Education" folder, box 3, President's Paper, .472, subseries III.

35. Correspondence with genealogical societies dominates his papers (Lawrence Thomas

Royster Papers, Accession #4198-a, Special Collections, University of Virginia Library, Charlottesville; hereafter cited as Royster Papers).

36. University Dispensary letterhead in "Notebooks LTR" folder, box 2, Royster Papers. Pediatrics was a new discipline (Meckel, *Save the Babies*, 45–46). Frank Howard Richardson, "Review," *Medical Review of Reviews*, n.d., "William Wood and Co. ca. 1925" folder, box 1, MSS 4198-a, Royster Papers; Marquis Who's Who, *Who Was Who*, 5: 624. Certificate of Election, American Association for the Advancement of Science, December 27, 1932, box 1, Royster Papers.

37. See Royster, *Preventative Medicine;* untitled essay, box 1; "clippings," box 3, Royster Papers; and Marquis Who's Who, *Who Was Who*, 5: 624.

38. Clipping, *The Medical Counselor*, n.d. (ca. 1908), box 3, Royster Papers; clipping, *Richmond Guardian*, August 12, 1907, box 3, Royster Papers. See also Royster, *The Care of the Dependent Child*. The notion of "vicious" women dominated progressive reformers' imaginations (Odem, *Delinquent Daughters*, chap. 4, esp. 96–97).

39. Royster, untitled lecture to pediatricians, n.d., box 1, Royster Papers.

40. Royster, untitled address, ca. 1923, box 1, Royster Papers.

41. Lawrence Thomas Royster, "Religio Medici Recentis," box 1, Royster Papers.

42. Royster, "School Child," 26–29. See also Royster, "The Problem of the Feebleminded" 406–8; Royster, "Custodial Care of the Feebleminded," 2192; and Royster, *The Care of the Dependent Child*.

43. Royster, "School Child," 27; Royster, "The Relation of Weight, Height, and Size"; and Royster, "A Study of the Size."

44. Royster, "School Child," 27–28.

45. On agricultural research stations, see Charles E. Rosenberg, "The Adams Act: Politics and the Cause of Scientific Research," *Agricultural History* 38 (1964): 3–12.

46. John Burroughs to Orland Emile White, December 4, 1902, "Correspondence: John Burroughs" folder, box 1, Orland E. White Papers, Accession #12767-a, Special Collections, University of Virginia Library, Charlottesville. (The papers of Orland White occupy four separate accession numbers: 12767-a, 1267-b, RG 21/66.811, and RG 21/66.832; hereafter cited as White Papers, White Papers II, White Papers III, and White Papers IV, respectively.) A copy of Olive's "Family Records" form is in Orland E. White, MSS 7095, Special Collections, University of Virginia Library, Charlottesville. See also Castle to White, August 3, 1909; White to Castle, n.d., ca. November 1909, "Correspondence, General, of O. E. White (1909–1910)" folder, box 2, White Papers II; and East to White, "Correspondence, General, of O. E. White (1911–1919)" folder, box 2, White Papers II. See also "Dr. Orland E. White" and "Academic and Professional positions held," in "Correspondence, Miscellaneous" folder, box 9, White Papers.

47. Orland E. White to Cardenas, October 27, 1953, "Correspondence, Ca-Com" folder, box 3, White Papers. His classes with Yerkes are mentioned in Edgar W. Olive to White, November 26, 1911, "Correspondence, General, of O. E. White (1911–1919)" folder, box 2, White Papers II. Little became president of the University of Maine and the University of Michigan, and then headed the Roscoe B. Jackson Cancer Research Laboratory in Bar Harbor, Maine. Cook edited the *Journal of Heredity* and was a chief organizer of the American Genetics Association. All of these men—Castle, East, Little, and Cook—maintained close ties to the American eugenics movement. See Mehler, "A History," 321–22, 324–25, 335–36, 393–94.

See also Orland E. White to Charles H. Danforth, January 15, 1912, "Correspondence, General, of O. E. White (1911–1919)" folder, box 2, White Papers II.

48. Davenport said, "I have persistently kept out of the Birth Control movement as I am not convinced that, despite their high motives, the movement will not do more harm than good" (Charles B. Davenport to Rev. John J. Burke, January 21, 1926, Davenport Papers). Sanger's eugenic views appear throughout her books *Woman and the New Race* (1920) and *The Pivot of Civilization* (1922). Davenport-White correspondence is found in "Correspondence D (1914–1952)" folder, box 3, White Papers. Margaret Sanger's "Family Limitations" is in "Miscellaneous Scientific Papers, Lists, Diagrams" folder, box 4, White Papers II; "Book Reviews" folder, box 8, White Papers II.

49. Orland E. White, review of *Eugenic Reform* by Leonard Darwin, February 6, 1928, in "Book Reviews 1927–1928" folder, box 9, White Papers (hereafter cited as Book Reviews). See also Orland E. White, review of *Know Thyself* by Julian Huxley, n.d., Book Reviews.

50. Orland E. White to Charles Benedict Davenport, May 14, 1919, re: Society for Experimental Biology meeting; White to Davenport January 22, 1920; and Davenport to White, January 26, 1920, "Correspondence D 1914–1952" folder, box 3, White Papers. See also East and Jones, *Inbreeding and Outbreeding,* 15, 227–28; East, *Mankind at the Crossroads;* and East *Heredity and Human Affairs,* vi, 295, 299.

51. East, *Mankind at the Crossroads,* 120, 133, 135–36, 145, 235.

52. O. White, "Inbreeding and Outbreeding"; O. White, "Mankind at the Crossroads" (quotation 55).

53. O. White, "Sterilization"; O. White, "Is Dementia Praecox Inheritable?" (emphasis in original).

54. See Harry Hamilton Laughlin to Orland Emile White, April 24, 1931, re: Third International Congress of Eugenics, "Correspondence I-J" folder, box 5, White Papers; Orland Emile White, "Heredity, Variation and Environment in Plants and Animals Including Man," "Writings of O. E. White" folder, box 8, White Papers II. For the White/Jordan friendship, see Orland E. White to Loto White, November 27, 1927, "Correspondence, general, of O. E. White (1927–1928)" folder, box 2, White Papers II; See also Orland E. White to Human Betterment Foundation, October 5, 1941, box 11, folder 11.1 (Virginia), E. S. Gosney Papers and Records of the Human Betterment Foundation, Archives, California Institute of Technology.

55. Further description of these schools and the Medical College of Virginia appears in G. Dorr, "Segregation's Science," 318–22. Davis worked under Castle and East at Harvard, taking the A.B. degree in 1905 and the doctorate in 1913. Davis also studied with Samuel J. Holmes, one of America's pioneering eugenicists, at the University of California from 1905 to 1908, and at Britain's John Innes Horticultural Institution with England's Mendelian eugenicists, as well as spending five summers at Woods Hole (see Donald W. Davis Papers, Special Collections, Swem Memorial Library, College of William and Mary, Williamsburg, Va. [hereafter cited as Davis Papers]); "Eugenics Instruction Questionnaires," folder #1: "A–Ham" (1920), box 1, ERO Records; College of William and Mary, *Catalog and Announcements, 1912–1913,* 59, Special Collections, Swem Memorial Library, College of William and Mary, Williamsburg, Va. (hereafter cited as *CWM Catalog*); William and Mary Questionnaire in "Eugenics and Genetics in Colleges, #1," Davenport Papers. See also *CWM Catalog, 1918–19,* 64; *CWM Catalog, 1920–21,* 106–7; *CWM Catalog, Announcement for the Summer Session, 1921,* 25; *CWM Catalog, 1923–24,* 75; and *CWM Catalog, 1934–35,* 96. Dr. Raymond Leach Taylor

(B.S., Cornell 1924; S.M., Harvard 1927; D.Sc. Harvard 1929) taught this course for the next decade (see E. S. Gosney to Donald W. Davis, November 9, 1938, "Sex Education in College—American Eugenics Society" folder, box 5, Davis Papers).

56. "War on Disease and Ignorance in States's [*sic*] Prison," *Richmond Times-Dispatch*, September 8, 1920. See also the "Criminal Mental Hygiene" folder, box 2, Davis Papers. See Davis's manuscript "Mental Defectives in Virginia" (n.d., but 1922 by internal references), "Mental Defectives in Virginia" folder, box 4, Davis Papers; Donald W. Davis to Henry Herbert Goddard, March 7, 1925; and Henry Herbert Goddard to Donald W. Davis, March 15, 1925, "Sex Education in College—American Eugenics Society" folder, box 5, Davis Papers.

57. Donald W. Davis, "Genetics and Orthodontia," *Dental Cosmos* (September 1923): 8, in "Papers by Davis" folder, box 2, Davis Papers. See also ibid., 3–4.

58. Ibid., 5, 7.

59. See Virginia Polytechnic Institute, *Catalogue of the Virginia Polytechnic Institute* (1904), 57; (1913), 99–100.

60. Chappelear published three genealogies linking him to the Old Virginians: Chappelear, *Families of Virginia: Barrett; Families of Virginia: Chappelear; Families of Virginia: The Leake Family* (Chappelear to Davenport, July 10, 1939, "Miscellaneous Questions 1939" folder, Davenport Papers). See *State Teacher's College Catalog* (1944–45), 91. For descriptions of Chappelear and Phillips, see Raymond C. Dingledine Jr., *Madison College: The First Fifty Years, 1908–1958* (1959), 194, 226.

61. Randolph-Macon College catalog (1925), 47, Special Collections, McGraw Library, Randolph-Macon College, Ashland (hereafter cited as Randolph-Macon catalog, date). See also ibid. (1928), 53; and (1929), 53.

62. University of Richmond, *Bulletin* (1927), 43; (1930), 8–9.

63. Washington and Lee University Questionnaire, March 28, 1920, "Eugenics Instruction Questionnaires Univ. Mi-Y (1920)" folder, box 1, ERO Collection. See also *Biology at Washington and Lee* pamphlet, ibid.; and the Washington and Lee catalog for that year.

64. Dr. William D. Hoyt to Lucien Howe, January 25, 1921, "Hereditary Blindness Law—Questionnaires A–H (1921)" folder 1, box 3, ERO Records. See also Black, *War against the Weak*, 147–55.

65. See member list in "AES Membership Campaign, 1925" folder, AES Records. See also American Eugenics Society, "A List of Eugenics Lecturers (1927)," "AES Printing Orders, 1926–1942" folder, AES Records. See the Washington and Lee University catalog for the years in question.

66. G. Dorr, "Segregation's Science," 327–28, 330. For Westhampton College—Richmond's coordinate women's school—see Eugenics Instruction Questionnaires, "Univ. of Mi-Y (1920)" folder 4, box 1, series X, ERO Records. See also Selden, *Inheriting Shame*, 46.

67. See Vigue, "Eugenics and the Education of Women," 51–55. See also Jon Alfred Mjoen, "The Masculine Education of Women and Its Dangers," *Eugenics* 3 (1930): 323–26; Rossiter, "'Woman's Work' in Science"; Rafter, *White Trash*, 20–22; and Hasian, *Rhetoric of Eugenics*, chap. 4.

68. See Sanger, *Woman and the New Race;* and Sanger, *Pivot of Civilization*.

69. Hollins College catalog (1919), 7, 31, 44.

70. Sweet Briar College catalog (1903), 9, 63; (1921), 47; (1925), 48–49.

71. Ibid. (1920), 46. McDougle quotation in Sweet Briar College's Questionnaire, Eugenics Instruction Questionnaires, "R–Univ. of Ma (1920)" folder, ERO Records.

72. Sweet Briar College catalog (1922), 5; "Better Baby Contest," *Sweet Briar Magazine* 14 (June 1923): 203–4.

73. Leola Elizabeth Fields to Charles Benedict Davenport, April 4, 1927, and May 11, 1927, "Department of Genetics Assistants 1927" folder, Davenport Papers.

74. See Hasian, *Rhetoric of Eugenics*, chap. 3; Mitchell, "Adjusting the Race"; and English, "Eugenics, Modernism."

75. Manning, *Black Apollo*, 35–36, chap. 2. See the Howard University questionnaire in "Eugenics and Genetics in Colleges, #5" folder, Davenport Papers.

76. Howard University and Howard University School of Medicine questionnaires in "Eugenics Instruction Questionnaires Har –P (1920)" folder, box 1, ERO Records.

77. "T. W. Turner, 101, Dies; Rights Activist, Educator," *Washington Post*, April 23, 1978; "Biographical Sketch," both in the Thomas W. Turner Papers, Hampton University Archives, Hampton, Va. (hereafter cited as Turner Papers). The author acknowledges the Hampton University Archives and its staff for permitting access to the Turner Papers. Marouf Hasian reveals the degree to which eugenics could comport with both an individual's Catholic and African American identity in *The Rhetoric of Eugenics in Anglo-American Thought*, chaps. 3 and 5.

78. Davenport had just acquired the Carnegie Institution's support for his Station for Experimental Evolution (SEE), operated in conjunction with the LIBL; six years later, the ERO would be grafted onto these organizations, all under Davenport's purview.

79. "T. W. Turner, 101, Dies; Rights Activist, Educator," *Washington Post*, April 23, 1978. See also Harvey Ernest Jordan to Charles Benedict Davenport, July 16, 1913; Charles Benedict Davenport to Harvey Ernest Jordan, August 7, 1913, "Jordan, H. E." folder, Davenport Papers. Davenport does not name Turner, but there is no other known instance of a black man attending the ERO's summer programs. Thus, Turner and the "professor from a colored college" are likely the same man.

80. See Turner's "Lecture Notes," particularly for "Breeding," "Heredity," and "Eugenics," Turner Papers. See also "Biology and Education, Second Examination [n.d.]"; "Sex Hygiene Examination (May 17, 1915)"; and "Sex Hygiene Final (March 19, 1920)," Turner Papers.

81. Turner, "Lecture X—Eugenics"; Turner, "Feeblemindedness," Turner Papers.

82. Cooke, "Gospel of Social Evolution," 5. See also Turner, "The Biological Laboratory and Human Welfare," *Howard University Record* (January 1924), 8, Turner Papers (hereafter cited as "Biological Laboratory").

83. Turner, "Biological Laboratory," 4, 5.

84. Ibid., 5.

85. Ibid., 6.

86. Ibid., 7. See also Barkan, *Retreat of Scientific Racism*, 341–43; and Kevles, *In the Name of Eugenics*, 138.

87. Turner, "Curriculum and Aims," 681–90 (quotations 681).

88. Michele Mitchell notes that, "whereas African Americans had to contend with a legion of theory which implied that all people of color came from degenerate stock, they could actually subvert racism within eugenic thought through the guise of uplift" ("Adjusting the Race," 154). See George William Hunter, *Essentials of Biology* (1911), quoted in Turner, "Cur-

riculum and Aims," 684–85; see also Selden, *Inheriting Shame*, 70–76. Despite the danger
of stigmatizing African Americans as passive victims by ascribing "damage" to the collective
black psyche from racism, Turner implied that psychological harm came from encountering
false biology. For more on the "damage thesis," see Scott, *Contempt and Pity*. Turner's theme
harmonizes with Horace Kallen's cultural pluralism, although Kallen could never quite find a
place for African Americans in his pluralistic society (see Kallen, *Culture and Democracy*,
xvi –xviii, xliii, and 117–18). See also Turner, "Curriculum and Aims," 689.

89. Turner, "Curriculum and Aims," 689–90. See G. Dorr, "Beyond Racial Purity."

90. American Eugenics Society, "A List of Eugenics Lecturers" (1927), 14, in "AES Printing Orders, 1926–1942" folder, AES Records; Hampton catalog (1929–30), 70. It is possible,
however, that Turner abandoned teaching eugenics after the appearance of the pope's encycli-
cal *Casti conubii* (on Christian marriage) in December 1930. This papal bull categorized
birth control and mainline negative eugenics as heinous sins for "losing sight of the fact that
the family is more sacred than the State and that men are begotten not for the earth and for
time, but for Heaven and eternity."

91. Turner, "Biological Laboratory," 1.

4. "STERILIZE THE MISFITS PROMPTLY": VIRGINIA CONTROLS THE FEEBLEMINDED

1. Dumenil, *Modern Temper;* A. Scott Berg, *Lindbergh* (New York, 1998), chap. 7. See
D. Jordan and H. Jordan, *War's Aftermath*, xviii –xix. The *Journal of Heredity* ran numer-
ous articles concerning the eugenic implications of the war. See, for example: "War Hurts
Scientific Breeding Abroad," *JOH* 7 (April 1916): 168; "Some Eugenic Aspects of Military
Registration," *JOH* 8 (July 1917): 298; "America's Fighting Stocks," *JOH* 8 (October 1917):
435–41; "Kaiserism and Heredity," *JOH* 9 (December 1918): 348–54. See also Lothrop
Stoddard's *Revolt against Civilization: The Menace of the Under Man* (1922). For debates
over humanity's fitness for democracy, see the symposium in the April 1919 *Journal of Heredity*, including Edwin G. Conklin, "Heredity and Democracy"; Madison Grant, "Discussion of
Article on Heredity and Democracy"; and Frederick Adams Woods, "The Racial Limitations
of Bolshevism."

2. As late as 1942 the Virginia State Planning Board correlated urbanization and feeblemindedness (quoted in Noll, *Feeble-Minded in Our Midst*, 122). See also Lemann, *Promised
Land*.

3. See Grantham, *South in Modern America*, 92–93, 97, 113–14; McLean, *Behind the
Mask;* Grantham, *South in Modern America*, 104; and Tindall, *The Emergence of the New
South*, 208–18, 576–82.

4. Trent, *Inventing the Feeble Mind*. The quotation from the Virginia Board of Charities
and Corrections (VBCC) appears in Noll, *Feeble-Minded in Our Midst*, 13.

5. VBCC quoted in Noll, *Feeble-Minded in Our Midst*, 20.

6. Dew, "Sterilization," 5; Noll, *Feeble-Minded in Our Midst*, 40 (statistics on 41; second
quotation on 115).

7. The exception is J. Douglas Smith, *Managing White Supremacy.*

8. A. Einer, "Medical Supervision of Matrimony," *Virginia Medical Semi-Monthly* 9 (February 10, 1905): 489–92.

9. G. Frank Lydston, "Some of the Difficulties in the Application of Eugenics to the Human Race," *Virginia Medical Semi-Monthly* 14 (April 9, 1909): 16.

10. Ibid., 17–19. For contemporaneous discussions of the "lethal chamber," see Black, *War against the Weak*, 247–51.

11. M. Haller, *Eugenics*, 129; Trent, *Inventing the Feeble Mind*, 75–78, 155–65; Lombardo, "Eugenic Sterilization," 87, 89–91; *Report of the State Board of Charities and Corrections* (Richmond, Va., 1909), 23.

12. *Report of the State Board of Charities and Corrections* (1913), 11, quoted in Lombardo, "Eugenic Sterilization," 93.

13. L. S. Foster, "Feeble-Minded Children," *Virginia Medical Semi-Monthly* 17 (January 10, 1913): 472; Dew, "Sterilization," 5; Wertenbaker, "Should Virginia"; Carrington, "Keep the Race Pure"; *Report of the State Board of Charities and Corrections* (1913), 11, quoted in Lombardo, "Eugenic Sterilization," 93 (emphasis in the original).

14. Dew, "Sterilization," 8; Wertenbaker, "Should Virginia"; Carrington, "Keep the Race Pure"; Williams, "Heredity," 460.

15. "Eugenics," *Journal of the American Medical Association* 50 (1908): 613 (quotation 785). The *JAMA* ran increasing numbers of eugenics-related articles up through the 1930s. See also Higham, *Strangers in the Land*, 150–51; Carrington, "Sterilization," 389–90; and "Sterilization of Criminals," *JAMA* 52 (1909): 73–74. The University of Virginia catalog for 1888 shows that Carrington attended Cabell's courses and received a "diploma" in anatomy in 1888. The 1889 catalog reveals that he took Barringer's courses and completed his medical degree in 1889. See also Crenshaw, *Directory, 1921*.

16. See Carrington, "Sterilization" (1908), 390; Carrington, "Sterilization" (1909), 422; and Carrington, "Hereditary Criminals."

17. Bernard Barrow, "Vasectomy for the Defective Negro with His Consent," *Virginia Medical Semi-Monthly* 15 (August 10, 1910): 226–28.

18. Carrington, "Sterilization" (1908); Carrington, "Sterilization" (1909), 421.

19. Carrington published the text of the bill in his third article, "Hereditary Criminals," 6. See also *Virginia Bills*, 1910 (Senate) No. 298.

20. Carrington, "Hereditary Criminals," 7.

21. Lombardo, "Eugenic Sterilization in Virginia," 107. See "To Prevent Procreation by Confirmed Criminals, Idiots, Imbeciles and Rapists," *Virginia Medical Semi-Monthly* 15 (April 8, 1910): 23.

22. Harry Hamilton Laughlin, *American Breeders Association Committee to Study and to Report on the Best Practical Means of Cutting Off the Defective Germ-Plasm in the American Population*, vol. 1, "The Scope of the Problem," published as Eugenics Record Office, *Bulletin 10A* (Cold Spring Harbor, N.Y.: ERO, 1914). See also Jordan to Davenport, March 21, 1910, Davenport Papers; Lombardo, "Eugenic Sterilization in Virginia," 109; Carrington, "Hereditary Criminals," 7; and Whitney, *Case for Sterilization*, 275. Johanna Schoen argues that some poor women used the eugenic system to access sterilization as birth control ("Between Choice and Coercion," 134–40).

23. E. Larson, *Sex, Race, and Science*, 120. For a list of states, see Reilly, *Surgical Solution*, 46, 48. The term "punctuated evolution" was inspired by the evolutionary notion of "punctuated equilibrium," wherein change occurs rapidly in short intervals separated by long periods of stasis. See Niles Eldredge and Stephen Jay Gould, "Punctuated Equilibria: An Alternative

to Phyletic Gradualism," in *Models in Paleobiology,* ed. T.J.M. Schopf, 82–115 (San Francisco: Doubleday, 1972).

24. James, *Virginia's Social Awakening,* 170–71. See also Rafter, *Creating Born Criminals.*

25. Stansell, *City of Women,* 22–27, 36–37; Odem, *Delinquent Daughters,* chap. 4, esp. 96–97.

26. Keve, *History of Corrections,* 167–70. See also Odem, *Delinquent Daughters,* 119; and Keve, *History of Corrections,* 174–79. Peterson's instructor, Harry Hamilton Laughlin, lauded her work in the *Eugenical News* (see *Eugenical News* 1 [May 1916]: 34; 1 [June 1916]: 42; and 2 [June 1917]: 43). See also Alice Jean Underwood, "Bon Air Learning Center," 107–9, 217–19; and Superintendent's Report, Florence Crittenton Home, Norfolk, Virginia (1930), quoted in Kunzel, *Fallen Women,* 53.

27. For a useful summary of the genesis of the colony system, see Noll, *Feeble-Minded in Our Midst,* 35–38.

28. Lombardo, "Eugenic Sterilization," 69, 233; Lombardo, "Three Generations."

29. Virginia General Assembly, *Acts of Assembly,* 1916, Chapters 104, 106, and 388; Virginia General Assembly, *Acts of Assembly,* 1918, Chapter 300.

30. Barringer served as a consulting physician at the Hill Crest Sanitarium in Charlottesville throughout the first two decades of the twentieth century. Doctors William F. Drewry and Joseph DeJarnette referred private-pay patients to the sanitarium. See *Virginia Medical Semi-Monthly* 11 (1907): 13, for an advertisement for Hill Crest listing these men.

31. Drewry, "Mental Defectives." His last report is replete with eugenic lobbying. See William F. Drewry, Central State Hospital, Petersburg, Va., *Report* (Richmond: Division of Purchase and Print, 1923), 25; and Drewry, "Mental Defectives," 507.

32. Western State Hospital, Staunton, Va., *Report* (Richmond: Division of Purchase and Print, 1909), 10, 17 (hereafter these annual reports will be cited as *Report, WSH*); ibid. (1913), 10–12.

33. *Report, WSH* (1915), 9; (1922–23), 11.

34. Rudyard Kipling, "The White Man's Burden," *McClure's Magazine* 12 (February 1899). DeJarnette first published the poem in the 1921 *Report, WSH.*

35. Reilly, *Surgical Solution,* 44–45.

36. See "1906–1908 General Correspondence and Related Papers," box 2, Barringer Family Papers.

37. Randolph-Macon catalog (1911), 65; (1930), 64; (1934), 50; (1938), 48; (1948), 49. For DeJarnette's sobriquet, see, "Celebration of Dr. J. S. DeJarnette's Fiftieth Anniversary of Continuous Service at the Western State Hospital," July 21, 1939, 31, DeJarnette Papers, Western State Hospital, Staunton, Va. (hereafter cited as "DeJarnette Celebration").

38. Quotations are from Priddy's annual report for the State Epileptic Colony, Lynchburg, Va. (Richmond: Division of Purchase and Print): (1910), 7; and (1915), 15–16, respectively (hereafter these reports will be cited as *Report, SEC*).

39. Gynecological surgery has long been used to "cure" women displaying "aberrant" behavior; see Lacquer, *Making Sex,* 175–81; Ehrenreich and English, *For Her Own Good,* 120–31; Priddy quoted in *Report, SEC* (1917), 13.

40. Lombardo, "Eugenic Sterilization," 118; Braslow, *Mental Ills,* 61–62.

41. Noll, "The Sterilization of Willie Mallory," 41–57.

42. Lombardo, "Eugenic Sterilization," 122–34; Noll, "The Sterilization of Willie Mallory."

43. Priddy, quoted in Lombardo, "Eugenic Sterilization," 126.

44. Lombardo, "Eugenic Sterilization," 127–28.

45. Ibid., 128–29.

46. On appeal, the Mallorys' lawyer emphasized that the Children's Home Society had illegally incarcerated the Mallorys. On June 13, 1918, the Virginia Supreme Court of Appeals agreed, ruling that the 1916 law for convening "Commissions on Feeblemindedness" had been improperly applied. The court granted Nannie Mallory's writ of habeas corpus, and she was released (Lombardo, "Eugenic Sterilization," 130 n. 51).

47. Ibid., 154–76.

48. Ibid., 169.

49. My research indicates that no inmate who challenged a sterilization order with the aid of a privately retained attorney was ever sterilized. Conversely, records at the Williamsburg Circuit Court, which had jurisdiction over the Eastern State Hospital, seem to indicate that a small number of lawyers made a cottage industry of representing patients and collecting the fifteen-dollar fee while providing meager representation. Transcripts from these hearings, made public during the 1980 case *Poe v. Lynchburg*, revealed a "rubber stamp" process that sped inmates to the operating tables.

50. Lombardo, "Eugenic Sterilization," 174; Virginia General Assembly, *Acts of Assembly*, 1924, "An Act Providing for the Sterilization of Certain Inmates," section 6. The law's reach was true in theory if not in practice. It remained difficult to sterilize individuals of the "upper" class because of their access to adequate legal representation.

51. "Committee Favors Sterilization Bill," *Richmond News-Leader*, February 13, 1924; Lombardo, "Eugenic Sterilization, 164–67. This speedy passage reflects both general agreement with the law and the intense pressure on the legislature at the end of the 1924 term.

52. Strode quoted in Lombardo, "Eugenic Sterilization," 164–65. The *Richmond News-Leader* and the *Richmond Times-Dispatch* alternated coverage, and gave scant attention to the bills. See "Sterilization Bill Reported in House," *Richmond Times-Dispatch*, February 28, 1924.

53. "Friendly" cases can amount to a shell game when the collusion of counsel for the plaintiffs and defense undercuts the usual adversarial nature of the proceedings. Sometimes this cooperation does not breach ethical boundaries; both sides merely stipulate certain facts. In Carrie Buck's case, however, the lawyers aimed at a predetermined outcome while maintaining the charade of adversarial competition. The result was a miscarriage of justice, as Carrie received inadequate representation and the court was actively misled.

54. The Buck family's story is related in Lombardo, "Facing Carrie Buck," 14–17; Lombardo, "Eugenic Sterilization," 177–90 (quotations 178–79); Lombardo, "Three Generations," 49–55; Gould, *Mismeasure of Man*, 65–66; Gould, "Carrie Buck's Daughter," *Constitutional Commentary* 2 (1985): 331–39; Bruinius, *Better for All the World*, 23–77.

55. "Oral Evidence Taken before the Special Board of Directors," in Virginia Supreme Court of Appeals, "Carrie Buck vs. Dr. J.H. Bell," 143 Va. 310, *Virginia Briefs and Records* (1925), 32–37.

56. Transcript of *Buck v. Priddy* , quoted ibid., 67.

57. Lombardo, "Three Generations," 38–39.

58. Ibid., 51. See also Arthur H. Estabrook, *The Jukes in 1915* (Washington, D.C.:

Carnegie Institution of Washington, 1916); and Lombardo, "Eugenic Sterilization," 196–97, 197 n. 47.

59. DeJarnette, quoted in "Transcript of *Buck v. Priddy*," in *Virginia Briefs and Records* (1925), 81; Priddy quoted in *Virginia Briefs and Records* (1925), 99.

60. Aubrey E. Strode, "Sterilization of Defectives," *Virginia Law Review* 11 (1925): 296–301; 143 *Virginia Reports* 310 (1925).

61. "Assails Virginia Law," *Richmond Times-Dispatch*, April 22, 1927. See also Lombardo, "Eugenic Sterilization," 218.

62. Menand, *Metaphysical Club*, 66. See also Oliver Wendell Holmes Jr., "Ideals and Doubts," *Illinois Law Review* 10 (1915), quoted in Lombardo, "Eugenic Sterilization," 221, 222, 224–25.

63. See *Buck v. Bell* 247 U.S. 207 (1927); Holmes to Frankfurter quoted in Mennel and Compston, *Holmes and Frankfurter*, 212–13; Holmes to Laski and Einstein quoted in Lombardo, "Eugenic Sterilization," 228.

64. "Safely through the Gamut," *Charlottesville Daily Progress*, May 4, 1927. The number of Virginians sterilized in institutions varies between conservative estimates of 7,500 to 8,500. Virginia sterilized approximately 1,660 African Americans, 20 percent of the total (Himstedt, "Not for Their Own Good," 27).

65. "Says Eugenists Do Cause Harm," *Richmond News-Leader*, October 24, 1927; Raymond Pearl, "The Biology of Superiority," *American Mercury* 12 (November 1927): 257–66 (quotation 266). Pearl did not reject eugenics; he demanded a stringent definition of "unfitness" (see Barkan, *Retreat of Scientific Racism*, 210–20).

5. "MONGREL VIRGINIANS": EUGENICS AND THE "RACE QUESTION"

1. Cox, *White America*, 26–27.

2. For various interpretations of the RIA, see J. Douglas Smith, *Managing White Supremacy*, chap. 3; L. Dorr, "Arm in Arm"; and Lombardo, "Miscegenation." For interracial sexuality in Virginia, see Gossett, *Race*, 286; Rothman, *Notorious in the Neighborhood*, esp. chap. 1; and Wallenstein, *Tell the Court*.

3. Hasian, *Rhetoric of Eugenics*, 64.

4. See G. Dorr, "Beyond Racial Purity."

5. Progressive historians, led by Johns Hopkins University's William A. Dunning and Dunning's student Ulrich B. Phillips, characterized slavery as a benign institution. The extinction thesis extended from the actuarial studies of Frederick L. Hoffman.

6. Street's remarks quoted in "Selection of Negroes," *Eugenical News* 2 (April 1917): 24.

7. McGuire and Lydston, "Sexual Crimes," 105–7, 123.

8. Ibid., 110–15.

9. Ibid., 122–23; emphasis in original. See also Claiborne, "The Negro," 3–6; Hodges, "The Effect of Freedom upon the Physical and Psychological Development of the Negro," 109.

10. Drewry quoted in "Increase of Insanity in the Negro, and Causes," *Virginia Medical Semi-Monthly* (December 25, 1903): 450–51.

11. Hedlin, "Earnest Cox." My analysis relies on the Earnest Sevier Cox Papers, Duke University Rare Book, Manuscript, and Special Collections Library, Durham, N.C. (hereafter cited as Cox Papers).

12. Cox, *Black Belt*, 9–32. See also Earnest Sevier Cox to Mrs. A. M. Cox, November 14, 1900, box 1, Cox Papers. E. A. Ross quoted in D. Ross, *Origins*, 233; Gossett, *Race*, 168–72.

13. Earnest Sevier Cox to Emma Cox, September 26, 1906, box 1, Cox Papers. An accurate account of the riot is David Fort Godshalk, *Veiled Visions: The 1906 Atlanta Race Riot and the Reshaping of American Race Relations* (2005).

14. Cox, *White America*, 237–38, 321–28, chap. 15.

15. G. P. Putnam's Sons to Earnest Sevier Cox, May 1, 1917; Cox to G. P. Putnam's Sons, November 20, 1919, box 1, Cox Papers. See also Madison Grant to Earnest Sevier Cox, December 14, 1920 (and appended "Notes"); Madison Grant to Earnest Sevier Cox, January 3, 1921, box 1, Cox Papers.

16. Cox, *Lincoln's Negro Policy*, 16–17. See also J. Douglas Smith, *Managing White Supremacy*, 79.

17. Sherman, "The Last Stand," 73; J. Douglas Smith, *Managing White Supremacy*, 85.

18. Jordan acknowledged his membership in Harvey Ernest Jordan to Leon Whitney, Executive Secretary, American Eugenics Society, December 13, 1927, AES Records. Lewis presented his 1924 lecture, "What Biology Says to the Man of Today," under ASCOA auspices at the university's YMCA. Virginius Dabney identified Barringer as president of the University of Virginia chapter (*Mr. Jefferson's University: A History* [Charlottesville: University of Virginia Press, 1981], 66). See also "Anglo-Saxon Clubs of America," "1896–1925 folder," box 10, Barringer Family Papers. For these men's professions, see Tilton, *Directory, 1931*, 139, 167.

19. "Post No. 1, Anglo-Saxon Clubs, Has 400 Members," *Richmond News-Leader*, June 5, 1923.

20. Cox published these testimonials at the back of the 1925 and 1937 editions of the book. See E. A. Ross to Earnest Sevier Cox, January 27, 1925, box 2, Cox Papers. See also Ivey Foreman Lewis to Earnest Sevier Cox, February 26, 1924; Ivey Foreman Lewis to Earnest Sevier Cox, April 25, 1924, box 2, Cox Papers; and Ivey Foreman Lewis to Earnest Sevier Cox, June 4, 1936, box 4, Cox Papers.

21. The anthropologist Melville Herskovits, a student of Franz Boas, wrote the review "Extremes and Means in Racial Interpretation" (*Journal of Social Forces* 2 [May 1924]: 550–51). John Powell's rebuttal, "The Search after Values" (*Journal of Social Forces* 3 [November 1924]: 3), drew a dismissive reply, "The Nordic Alarm Again" (*Journal of Social Forces* 3 [January 1925]: 317–19).

22. Bair, "Remapping," 402, 404; Sherman, "The Last Stand," 76. See also Estabrook and McDougle, *Mongrel Virginians*.

23. John Powell and Earnest Sevier Cox, "Is White America to Become a Negroid Nation?" *Richmond Times-Dispatch*, July 22, 1923.

24. Ibid.; Sherman, "The Last Stand," 77.

25. See Sherman, "The Last Stand"; and Wallenstein, "Race, Marriage," esp. 389.

26. "Powell Asks Law Guarding Racial Purity," *Richmond Times-Dispatch*, February 13, 1924. See Harvey Ernest Jordan to Charles B. Davenport, May 22, 1911; Davenport to Jordan, August 16, 1911, "Jordan, H. E." folder, Davenport Papers; see also chapter 2 above. All of these documents reside in the John Powell Papers, Accession #7284, 7284-a, Special Collections, University of Virginia Library, Charlottesville (hereafter cited as Powell Papers). See also "Powell Asks Law Guarding Racial Purity," *Richmond Times-Dispatch*, February 13,

1924; "John Powell Discusses Racial Amalgamation in Virginia before Solons," *Richmond News-Leader,* February 13, 1924.

27. See "An Act to Preserve Racial Integrity," *Virginia Acts of Assembly,* 1924, 534–35; and G. Dorr, "Principled Expediency." Quotations from Walter A. Plecker to Harry Hamilton Laughlin, March 11, 1925, Harry Hamilton Laughlin Papers, Pickler Memorial Library, Truman State University (Northeast Missouri State College), Kirksville, Mo. (hereafter cited as Laughlin Papers).

28. "To Further Aims of Racial Law," *Richmond Times-Dispatch,* March 19, 1924; "Asks Virginians to Register As to Color under 'Integrity' Law," *Richmond News-Leader,* March 20, 1924.

29. A virtually complete record of Plecker's activities is preserved in the Cox Papers. Quotation from Walter A. Plecker to American Medical Association, September 19, 1924, box 2, Cox Papers. See also Walter A. Plecker/Department of Health, "Instructions to Local Registrars and Other Agents in Administration of Law," *Virginia Health Bulletin* 16 (March 1924): 2, box 56, Powell Papers.

30. Walter A. Plecker to Earnest Sevier Cox, October 24, 1924, box 2, Cox Papers; Plecker, "Shall We All Be Mulattoes?" 23–24.

31. "State's Racial Integrity Law Will Be Discussed at Medical Men's Meet," *Richmond News-Leader,* November 20, 1924; Plecker, "Shall America Remain White?" in *The New Family and Racial Improvement,* by Plecker, 14, 23–29 (quotation in note 22).

32. See Ivey Foreman Lewis to Earnest Sevier Cox, April 25, 1924; and Ivey Foreman Lewis to Earnest Sevier Cox, May 5, 1924, box 2, Cox Papers. See also Major Ernest G. [*sic*] Cox Addresses Students," *Richmond Times-Dispatch,* November 21, 1924; Plecker to Davenport, August 17, 1925, "Plecker, W. A." folder, Davenport Papers; Walter A. Plecker to Ivey Foreman Lewis, October 29, 1926; and Ivey Foreman Lewis to Walter A. Plecker, November 9, 1926, in "1926 Letters" folder, box 1, Lewis Papers.

33. Lombardo, "Miscegenation, Eugenics, and Racism," 447–50. Quotations from Walter A. Plecker to Mrs. Robert Cheatham, April 30, 1924; Plecker to Mrs. Mary Gildon, April 30, 1924, box 56, Powell Papers.

34. Lombardo, "Miscegenation," 440–43.

35. Holt's decision appears in J. David Smith, *Eugenic Assault,* 72. See also "Woman, Listed Negroid, Wins Right to Be Called 'White,'" *Richmond Times-Dispatch,* November 18, 1924.

36. J. David Smith, *Eugenic Assault,* 73.

37. "Woman, Listed Negroid, Wins Right to Be Called 'White,'" *Richmond Times-Dispatch,* November 18, 1924; "Testing the Racial Integrity Law," *Richmond Times-Dispatch,* November 20, 1924. Plecker quoted in "Inter-racial Law Ruling is Rapped," *Richmond Times-Dispatch,* November 19, 1924. See also "Trinkle Given Facts on Racial Law Ruling," *Richmond Times-Dispatch,* November 22, 1924; "Controversy Rages Further in Racial Integrity Law Case," *Richmond Times-Dispatch,* November 24, 1924; and "Racial Integrity Case Fought Over," *Richmond News-Leader,* November 24, 1924.

38. "May Test Law on Racial Integrity," *Richmond News-Leader,* November 19, 1924; "State May Appeal from Decision of Judge Henry Holt," *Richmond News-Leader,* November 20, 1924. At least fifty members of the ASCOA's powerful Richmond post met to debate

an appeal. See "Anglo-Saxon Club May Take Appeal in Sorrells Case," *Richmond Times-Dispatch,* December 10, 1924, 1–2. See also Lombardo, "Miscegenation, Eugenics, and Racism," 442 n. 100.

39. Powell, *Breach in the Dike,* 1–3.

40. "Action of Judge Holt Defended by Friends," *Richmond Times-Dispatch,* November 21, 1924. See also "State May Lose in Racial Cases," *Richmond News-Leader,* November 21, 1924; Lombardo, "Miscegenation, Eugenics, and Racism," 442.

41. Plecker, *Eugenics in Relation,* 1.

42. Ibid., 6.

43. Plecker, "Eugenics or Race Deterioration"; Walter A. Plecker to Dr. Paul Brandon Barringer, April 22, 1925, box 2, "1915–1925 Correspondence" folder, Barringer Family Papers.

44. Reverend W. E. Davis, "The Divine Plan of Racial Integrity," *Virginia Medical Semi-Monthly* 52 (August 1925): 289–90; DeJarnette, "Eugenics in Relation to the Insane," 290–92 (quotations 291).

45. DeJarnette, "Eugenics in Relation to the Insane," 291–92.

46. Plecker, "Eugenics or Race Deterioration."

47. Exactly when and why Estabrook came to Virginia remains unclear (Lombardo, "Eugenic Sterilization," 151–52; 195–99). See Arthur H. Estabrook to Charles B. Davenport, January 28, 1923, "Estabrook, Arthur H." folder, Davenport Papers.

48. See chapter 2 of this volume.

49. For the study's origins, see Charles B. Davenport to Ivan E. McDougle, February 6, 1923; and McDougle to Davenport, March 3, 1923; Davenport to McDougle, March 5, 1923; McDougle to Davenport, September 6, 1923; Davenport to McDougle, September 12, 1923, "McDougle, Ivan" folder, Davenport Papers. On Davenport's predilection for "yes men," see Oscar Riddle, "Charles Benedict Davenport 1866–1944," in *Biographical Memoirs* 25 (Washington, D.C.: National Academy of Sciences, 1948), 87–89. Davenport's opinion of McDougle appears in Charles B. Davenport to Professor F. Stuart Chapin, January 25, 1926, "McDougle, Ivan" folder, Davenport Papers.

50. Arthur H. Estabrook to Davenport, August 4, 1923, "Estabrook, Arthur H." folder, Davenport Papers; Ivan E. McDougle to Davenport, September 6, 1923, "McDougle, Ivan" folder, Davenport Papers; Estabrook to Davenport, July 10, 1924, "Estabrook, Arthur H." folder, Davenport Papers.

51. Walter A. Plecker to Carnegie Institution, December 18, 1924; Estabrook to Davenport, January 17, 1925; Davenport to Plecker, January 19, 1925; Plecker to Davenport, August 17, August 19, and September 21, 1925, and more generally the "Plecker, W. A." folder in the Davenport Papers.

52. For others, see Rafter, *White Trash.* See also Estabrook and McDougle, *Mongrel Virginians.*

53. For the history of the Massenburg Act, see J. Douglas Smith, *Managing White Supremacy,* chap. 4. See also "Resolutions Oppose Pending Racial Bills," *Richmond Times-Dispatch,* February 17, 1926; and "The Leading White Citizens Make Protest," *Richmond Planet,* February 20, 1926.

54. Powell's articles ran between February 16 and March 2, 1926. For popular outrage at the RIA amendment, see "Integrity Act Affects 20,000 Whites, Claim," *Richmond News-*

Leader, February 8, 1926; and "Bill Brands '63 First Families' of VA. 'Colored,'" *Richmond News-Leader,* February 9, 1926.

55. "Says Integrity Bill Is Not Harsh," *Richmond Times-Dispatch,* February 21, 1926; I. F. Love, "'The Last Stand,'" *Richmond Times-Dispatch,* February 21, 1926; Mary Mabane, "An American Problem," and R. Cary Montague, "A Real Remedy," *Richmond Times-Dispatch,* February 24, 1926; W. G. Richardson, "Evading the Issue," *Richmond Times-Dispatch,* February 28, 1926; Mrs. R. J. Owen, "From a 'Grandma,'" *Richmond Times-Dispatch,* March 1, 1926.

56. On "reform" eugenics, see Kevles, *In the Name of Eugenics,* 173–76.

57. E.C.L. Miller to Donald Davis, January 28, (1925?), "Sex Education in College—American Eugenics Society" folder, box 5, Davis Papers.

58. Donald W. Davis to George O. Ferguson, March 6, 1925, box 5, Davis Papers.

59. George O. Ferguson to Donald W. Davis, March 10, 1925; Robert Bennett Bean to Donald W. Davis, March 30, 1925; Harvey Ernest Jordan to Donald W. Davis, February 15, 1928; Donald W. Davis to Harvey Ernest Jordan, July 19, 1927, and February 11, 1928, "Sex Education in College—American Eugenics Society" folder, Davis Papers; Jordan to Whitney, December 13, 1927, "Jordan, H. E." folder, AES Records.

60. On slave breeding, see Robert William Fogel and Stanley L. Engerman, *Time on the Cross* (1974); and Eugene Genovese, *Roll, Jordan, Roll: The World the Slaves Made* (1976). For black intellectuals and eugenics, see Hasian, *Rhetoric of Eugenics,* 51; and Gaines, *Uplifting the Race,* 21, 35–37, 73–83.

61. Mitchell, "Adjusting the Race," passim.

62. English, "Eugenics, Modernism," 9, 28, 93, 201–2 (Du Bois in 1922); W.E.B. Du Bois, "Black Folk and Birth Control," *Birth Control Review* 16 (June 1932): 166–67; Du Bois on Massenburg bill in Hasian, *Rhetoric of Eugenics,* 67.

63. *Richmond Planet,* February 2, 1935; Dan T. Carter, *Scottsboro: A Tragedy of the American South,* rev. ed. (Baton Rouge: Louisiana State University Press, 1979).

64. "Racial Integrity," *Richmond Planet,* July 28, 1923.

65. "Nordics Knocked Out at Great Science Meet," *Richmond Planet,* May 24, 1924, 5; "Bye, Bye, 'Highbrows,'" *Richmond Planet,* December 6, 1924; "Is There Any Pure Race?" *Richmond Planet,* October 4, 1924.

66. "Asks Removal of Dr. Plecker," *Richmond Planet,* April 4, 1925; *Norfolk Journal and Guide,* quoted in J. Douglas Smith, *Managing White Supremacy,* 118.

67. *Richmond News-Leader,* quoted in J. Douglas Smith, *Managing White Supremacy.* Plecker quoted in the *Richmond Times-Dispatch,* March 30, 1925; also quoted in "Dr. Plecker Aroused," *Richmond Planet,* April 4, 1925. See also Plecker, *New Family.* Blacks rallied again in 1926 and 1928, objecting to the ASCOA's attempts to amend the RIA. See, in the *Richmond Planet,* "The Leading White Citizens Make Protest" and "Price Racial Integrity Bill Defeated," February 18, 1928; and "Hon. W. A. Plecker Writes His Approval," February 25, 1928.

68. Sherman, "The Last Stand," 88–89; *Richmond Times-Dispatch,* quoted in *Richmond Planet,* February 18, 1928.

69. Editorial, *Richmond Planet,* February 18, 1928.

70. Ibid.; Walter A. Plecker to Editor, *Richmond Planet,* February 28, 1928.

71. M. Garvey, "Aims and Objects," 38.

72. Garvey's wife and chief lieutenant denied this, writing, "the term, back-to-Africa, was used and promoted by the newspapers, Negro newspapers mostly, to ridicule Garvey. There was no back-to-Africa movement except in a spiritual sense" (A. Garvey, *Garvey and Garveyism*, 127, 252, chap. 25). On the UNIA –ASCOA alliance, see Edwards, "Racial Purity in Black and White," 125–27; and Earnest S. Cox to Mr. John Ditto, n.d., ca. March 1925, box 2, Cox Papers.

73. Edwards, "Racial Purity in Black and White," 117; Cox to John Ditto, n.d., ca. March 1925; Earnest Sevier Cox to Marcus Garvey, May 26, 1925; Garvey to Cox, June 10, 1925, box 2, Cox Papers.

74. This correspondence is massive and scattered throughout Cox's papers. For examples, see J. J. Peters to Cox, August 17, 1925 (New Orleans); Mrs. W. C. Corbin to Cox, October 15, 1925 (New York); A. S. Connelly to Cox, November 5, 1925 (Washington, D.C.), box 2, Cox Papers; J. W. McHurst to Cox, April 10, 1926 (Chicago); S. M. Phillips to Cox, November 24, 1926 (Independence, Kansas); William Ware to Cox, May 8, 1929 (Cincinnati), box 3, Cox Papers. Correspondence between John J. Fenner and Earnest Sevier Cox, box 2, Cox Papers. Quotation is taken from Fenner to Cox, June 17, 1925, box 2, Cox Papers; see also Fenner to Cox, September 28, 1925, box 3, Cox Papers. Arnold H. Maloney to Earnest Sevier Cox, July 24, 1925, box 2, Cox Papers.

75. Sherman, "The Last Stand," 69, 76.

76. Ibid., 87; J. Douglas Smith, *Managing White Supremacy*, 97. See also Degler, *In Search of Human Nature*, 42–44.

77. J. David Smith, *Eugenic Assault*, 108.

6. "A HEALTHIER AND HAPPIER AMERICA": PERSISTENT EUGENICS IN VIRGINIA

1. HB, "Eugenical Sterilization (May 20, 1934)," box 1, Student and Alumni Papers, RG 22, Special Collections, University of Virginia Library, Charlottesville, p. 15 (hereafter cited as Student and Alumni Papers, box, page number; student authors are identified by initials). See also PH, "Sterilization and Society (June 1935)," Student and Alumni Papers, box 1, 21. Stormtrooper quotation from Dr. Hans H. Heyn to Orland E. White, February 9, 1934; and Dr. Hans H. Heyn to Orland E. White, April 1, 1946, "Correspondence: Ha–Hey (1922–1954)" folder, box 4, White Papers.

2. M. Haller, *Eugenics*, 137.

3. Ibid., 180–81; Ludmerer, *Genetics and American Society*, 127. More recent scholars debunk this myth; see D. Paul and Spencer, "Did Eugenics Rest?" 128.

4. In "The Nazis and the American South in the 1930s: A Mirror Image?" Grill and Jenkins argue that the South, as a whole, remained hostile to the Nazis.

5. See G. Dorr, "Assuring America's Place." See also the *University of Virginia Record Extension Series* (bound in the *University Record*) for 1927–30 and 1935–38.

6. HIM, "Shooting the Mad Stork: A Paper on the Present Status of Human Sterilization," Student and Alumni Papers, box 2, 2. Virginia actually expanded its sterilization program during the 1930s (Reilly, *The Surgical Solution*, 94; J. Paul, "Three Generations of Imbeciles," 511–13).

7. See untitled list of paper topics in unfiled binder "Bibliography," box 1, Lewis Papers. Quotation from WD, "Heredity v. Environment as Portrayed by Identical Twins (undated)," Student and Alumni Papers, box 1, 5–6. See also KHB, "Quality as a Biological Problem," 1–2, 4; ESH, "Birth Control (undated)," Student and Alumni Papers, box 1, 10.

8. William Bennett Bean, "Population (1930)," Student and Alumni Papers, box 1, 26. Lewis rated Bean's paper "Excellent. Excellent. @ [*sic*] 98."

9. See, for example, IB, "The Immigration Question (undated)," box 1, 12–13; ROC, "Immigration from Europe (undated)," box 1, 1–2, 5–6, 12–14; ARF, "The Immigration Problem (undated)," box 2, 5–7; and JP, "Immigration Statistics (undated)," box 2, 10–12, all in Student and Alumni Papers. These undated papers refer directly to the Depression; their authors graduated in 1935, 1936, 1934, and 1930, respectively (Tilton, *Directory, 1931;* and Alumni Association of the University of Virginia, *Alumni Directory 1981* [White Plains, N.Y., 1981]). Stoddard, *Revolt against Civilization* (quotations from preface and 151–52).

10. Quotations, in order, from Bean, "Population," box 1, 5; NZF, "Race Mixture," box 2, 1; Bean, "Population," box 1, 21–22; and TBH, "Negro Problem," box 1, 21–22, all in Student and Alumni Papers. See also RNW, "Negro Question," box 2, 8; and LPR, "The Race Problem in America (undated)," box 2, 4, both in the Student and Alumni Papers; and E. Larson, *Sex, Race, and Science*, 2, 23, 93.

11. Ivey Lewis to Judge R.T.W. Duke, June 12, 1925, Blandy Experimental Farm Papers, RG–6/9/2.831, Special Collections, University of Virginia Library, Charlottesville (hereafter cited as BEF Records); "Report of the Miller School of Biology to the President's Committee on Research," January 11, 1952, "M-1947" folder, box A8-18F, BEF Records, 1.

12. R. R. Beasely to Ivey Lewis, (?)1928, "1928 Letters" folder, box 1, Lewis Papers; Virginius Dabney to Ivey Lewis, May 10, 1948, "D" folder, box 6, Lewis Papers; and Virginius Dabney to Ivey Lewis, January 3, 1949, "D" folder, box 10, Lewis Papers.

13. Charles W. Clark to Ivey Lewis, March 11, 1949, "C" folder, box 10, Lewis Papers. See also John D. Martin, Jr., to Ivey Lewis, January 16, 1948, "M" folder, box 7, Lewis Papers.

14. Charles W. Clark to Ivey Lewis, December 29, 1954, "1954 Letters" folder, box 1, Lewis Papers.

15. Charles Clark to Ivey Lewis, December 29, 1954, 2, "1954 Letters" folder, box 1, Lewis Papers. See also Ivey Foreman Lewis to John D. Martin, March 6, 1948, "M" folder, box 7, Lewis Papers.

16. Lewis, "Biological Principles and National Policy: Address of Retiring Chairman of Section G [Lewis] American Association for the Advancement of Science (December, 1951)," 4, "Speeches" folder, box 5, Lewis Papers"; Ivey Lewis to Harcourt Parrish, esq., July 1, 1952, "R" folder, box 27, Lewis Papers (letter apparently misfiled). See also Ivey Lewis to Harcourt Parrish, May 5, 1952, "1952 Letters" folder, box 27, Lewis Papers.

17. James A. Tignor to Ivey Lewis, January 5, 1952, "T" folder, box 29, Lewis Papers. See also A. W. Wetsel to Ivey Lewis, January 4, 1952, "W" folder, box 29, Lewis Papers.

18. Franklin Bacon and Raymond Bice, interview by the author, January 25, 2000. See also G. Dorr, "Segregation's Science," 578–96.

19. Ironically, when the American Eugenics Society held a contest for the best religious sermon on eugenics, the only entry from Virginia came from the Temple Emanu-El in Roanoke. See "Benedict, George" folder; and Rabbi George Benedict, "Eugenics (1926)," typescript, "1926 Sermon Contest #1" folder, AES Records. Lewis quoted in "Biologist Supports

Curb on Immigrants," *New York Times*, April 6, 1924. See also Leon F. Whitney and William Grossman, "Some Reasons for Jewish Excellence," *Eugenics* 3 (1930): 52–57. Galton quoted in Chase, *Legacy of Malthus*, 14 (emphasis in original).

20. Ivey F. Lewis to John Loyd Newcomb, April 12, 1934, "Dean's Office 1934–36" folder, box 9, President's Papers, .491, subseries II. See also Ivey F. Lewis, "Memorandum for the President from Dean Lewis," January 31, 1939, "General Records—Dean Lewis (1939–40)" folder, box 5, President's Papers, .491, subseries III; Ivey F. Lewis to John L. Newcomb, "Jewish Students: Session 1936–1937," "Jewish Students" folder, box 3, Lewis Papers; and Ivey Foreman Lewis, "Enrollment Statistics," November 14, 1945, "Statistics" folder, box 4, Lewis Papers.

21. Harvey Ernest Jordan to John Loyd Newcomb, December 13, 1934, "Medicine, Department of –General (1934–36)" folder, box 17, President's Papers, .491, subseries II.

22. Ivey F. Lewis to Dr. J. Henry Walker, University of Alabama, March 12, 1949, "W" folder, box 13, Lewis Papers. See also Ivey F. Lewis to Paul A. Moody, University of Vermont, August 1, 1948, "M" folder, box 13, Lewis Papers; and Lewis's letters to the University of Pennsylvania, Temple, Yale, Rochester, and Vanderbilt medical schools for Mr. Dann, November 13, 1941, "1941 D" folder, box 5, Lewis Papers. See also Ivey Foreman Lewis to Boston University School of Medicine, November 25, 1941, "1941 H" folder, box 5, Lewis Papers; Ivey Foreman Lewis to the Commandant of the Fifth Naval District, November 12, 1941, "1941 S" folder, Lewis Papers; Ivey F. Lewis to Officer in Charge, Naval Reserve Headquarters, Tenth Naval District, December 1, 1942, "1942 F" folder (letter apparently misfiled), box 7, Lewis Papers. Final quotation from Karl J. Shapiro, "University," *Virginia Spectator* 102 (November 1940): 12.

23. See charts in "Jewish Students" folder, box 3, Lewis Papers. For Lewis on Jewish students' immorality, see Ivey Foreman Lewis to Rabbi Albert M. Lewis, May 24, 1941, "1941 L" folder, box 6, Lewis Papers.

24. Ivey Foreman Lewis to John Loyd Newcomb, April 21, 1936, "Dean's Office (1934–36)" folder, box 9, President's Papers, .491, subseries II; Ivey Foreman Lewis, "Memorandum to President Newcomb," January 25, 1939, "Dean Lewis" folder, box 5, President's Papers, .491, subseries IV. Quotation from Ivey Foreman Lewis to John G. Rust, April 7, 1939, appending "Statement of Agreement between President Newcomb, Dean Lewis, Mr. Carliner, and Mr. Moore"; and copy of letter, David Carliner to Ivey Foreman Lewis, April 3, 1939, "Youth Conference" folder, box 4, Lewis Papers.

25. "Administrative Council" folder, box 1, President's Papers, .491, subseries IV. See also David Carliner, interview by the author, November 3, 1995.

26. "Nursery of Republican Patriots," *New Republic*, December 16, 1940, 822.

27. Bean, *Races of Man*, 19, 37, 97.

28. Bean, *Peopling of Virginia* (quotations v, 25, 42); Hrdlička, *The Old Americans*.

29. Ludmerer, *Genetics and American Society*, 9.

30. Hassencahl, "Harry H. Laughlin," 328–36.

31. Lombardo, "American Breed"; Tucker, *Funding of Scientific Racism*. Quotations from Harry Hamilton Laughlin to Wickliffe Draper, January [?], 1936, Laughlin Papers (copy in author's possession).

32. Harry H. Laughlin to President John Loyd Newcomb or Dean Ivey F. Lewis, February 18, 1936, Laughlin Papers.

33. See also John Loyd Newcomb to Dr. H. H. Laughlin, February 18, 1936; Wickliffe Draper to John Loyd Newcomb, February 20, 1926; John Loyd Newcomb to Wickliffe Draper, February 21, 1936; and Draper to Newcomb, February 22, 1936, "D (1934–36)" folder, box 9, President's Papers, .491, subseries III (quotations from third telegram). See also Wickliffe Draper to Harry Hamilton Laughlin, March 1, 1936, box 4, Laughlin Papers (copy in author's possession).

34. See Lombardo, "American Breed," 768–74; and Hassencahl, "Harry H. Laughlin," 336–43.

35. Barkan, *Retreat of Scientific Racism,* 218–20 (quotation 218); Ludmerer, *Genetics and American Society,* 131–33.

36. Harry Hamilton Laughlin, "Outline of Proposed Researches on Race Integrity, Standards and Traits in Southern and Eastern United States," typescript, Laughlin Papers (copy in author's possession). Quotation from Harry Hamilton Laughlin to Madison Grant, September 26, 1935, ibid.

37. Cox republished part of this review on the dust jacket and flyleaf of subsequent editions. See also Harry H. Laughlin to Earnest Sevier Cox, May 28, 1934, box 4, Cox Papers. Complete quotation from Clarence G. Campbell to Earnest Sevier Cox, March 6, 1936, box 4, Cox Papers.

38. Harry H. Laughlin to Earnest Sevier Cox, March 18, 1936; Clarence G. Campbell to Earnest Sevier Cox, May 20, 1934; Walter A. Plecker to Madison Grant, June 8, 1936; Harry H. Laughlin to Earnest Sevier Cox, June 1, 1936, box 4, Cox Papers.

39. Ivey Foreman Lewis to Earnest Sevier Cox, June 4, 1936, box 4, Cox Papers.

40. Theodore G. Bilbo to Earnest Sevier Cox, February 8, 1934, box 4, Cox Papers. See also Wickliffe P. Draper to Earnest Sevier Cox, September 18, 1936 (offer to buy books); Cox to Draper, September 19, 1936; and correspondence among Draper's agents, Cox, and the printer, box 4, Cox Papers. Dr. Paul Brandon Barringer and Dean Ivey Foreman Lewis supported this repatriationist effort (see Walter A. Plecker to Paul Brandon Barringer, March 7, 1938, box 4, Cox Papers; and Ivey Foreman Lewis to Earnest Sevier Cox, box 5, Cox Papers).

41. Madison Grant to Earnest Sevier Cox, June 11, 1930 (quotation); and Madison Grant to Earnest Sevier Cox, June 24, 1930, box 3, Cox Papers. On Günther, see Proctor, *Racial Hygiene,* 27, 53, 119, 293. See also Earnest Sevier Cox to Wilhelm Frick, November 28, 1938, box 5, Cox Papers.

42. D. Paul and Spencer, "Did Eugenics Rest?" passim.

43. H. Grant, "Sterilization by Vasectomy," 683; Mickle and Holdberry, "Eugenic Sterilization," 388, 389; Putney, "Eugenic Sterilization," 705–9. For representative examples, see Gordon, "The Social Aspect of Mental Abnormalities," 469–74; and Arnold, "Eugenic Sterilization of the Epileptic," 45–47.

44. These figures are taken from J. Paul, "Three Generations of Imbeciles," 511. Virginia's statistician for the Department of Mental Hygiene and Hospitals, Edna M. Lantz, assisted Paul in compiling these statistics.

45. J. Paul, "Three Generations of Imbeciles," 503; Reilly, *Surgical Solution,* 94. Kelly quoted in J. Paul, "Three Generations of Imbeciles," 504.

46. Himstedt, "Not for Their Own Good," 27.

47. For a close comparison of Virginia and Alabama's experiences, see G. Dorr, "Defective or Disabled?"

48. All state sterilization programs manifested this gender imbalance (see Kline, *Building a Better Race,* esp. 53–56; and Reilly, *Surgical Solution,* 95).

49. The 1924 law was repealed by 1974 Virginia Acts of Assembly, Ch. 296. Senate Bill 537, February 25, 1980, stipulated that any sterilization of mental incompetents must be done "in the best interest of such incompetent person" as determined by their family, a court, and guardian ad litem.

50. Walter A. Plecker to A. H. Shannon, September 3, 1930, box 3, Cox Papers. Examples of Plecker's coercive actions are scattered throughout the Cox Papers. See, for instance, Walter A. Plecker to Mrs. Ira Crook Hopkins, December 1, 1941, box 6, Cox Papers. See also Walter A. Plecker to L. Quibell, March 10, 1934, Powell Papers (second quotation). Final quotation is from Walter A. Plecker to Dr. W. Gross, Director, Bureau of Human Betterment and Eugenics, Berlin, July 3, 1935, box 4, Cox Papers.

51. Walter A. Plecker to John W. Wynn[el], June 21, 1941, box 6, Cox Papers.

52. Walter A. Plecker to Joseph L. Savage, December 7, 1937; and "Warning Label," box 4, Cox Papers; J. David Smith, *Eugenic Assault,* 99; Walter A. Plecker to John Collier, April 6, 1943, box 6, Cox Papers (quotation about Hitler). See also Plecker's "Memorandum No. 336" from the State Headquarters of Selective Service, which instructed all local boards that approximately 170 men had registered as Indians (Mills F. Neal, "Memorandum No. 336: Procedure for Classification of Persons Registered as Indians," January 7, 1942, Frank G. Speck Papers, American Philosophical Society Library, Philadelphia).

53. J. David Smith, *Eugenic Assault,* 95–98. See also Walter A. Plecker to Local Registrars, December [?], 1942, box 6, Cox Papers. For Plecker's effect on midwives generally and African American midwives particularly, see Fraser, *African American Midwifery,* chap. 3, and 278.

54. Walter A. Plecker to Local Registrars, Physicians, Health Officers, Nurses, School Superintendents, and Clerks of Courts, January [?], 1943, box 6, Cox Papers.

55. Plecker quoted in Peter Hardin, "Documentary Genocide," *Richmond Times-Dispatch,* March 5, 2000.

56. "News and Notes," *Eugenics* 2 (August 1929): 36; Orland E. White, "Should a Victim's [of Dementia Praecox] Relatives Marry?" *Eugenics* 2 (October 1929): 23. See "Biographical Sketches of O. E. White for Publication (1936–45)" folder, box 1, White Papers II. See also "AGA 1" folder, box A8-20F, BEF Records.

57. See "untitled book list," n.d., and "Reserve Books Biology 109 Orland E. White 1953," "Biology Book Lists and Correspondence (n.d., 1951, 1953)" folder, box 9, White Papers.

58. Orland E. White, "Genetics in Relation to Heredity and Environment, November 7, 1939 [delivered before Graduate Scientific Club]" typescript, 1–2, 7, 16, "1939 Aug.–Nov." folder, box 8, White Papers.

59. Of twenty-five students who took doctorates under White, six were women. I found no evidence of any woman taking a doctorate under Lewis; a number of women took master's degrees under him. Quotation from Orland E. White to Mary Ellen Churchill, December 21, 1944, "Correspondence Ca-Com (1910–1955)" folder, box 3, White Papers.

60. Mary Ellen Churchill to Orland White, January 2, 1945; Churchill to White, February 4, 1930; Churchill to White, January 4, 1944, "Correspondence Ca-Com (1910–1955)" folder, box 3, White Papers.

61. Dr. Laurence M. Dickerson to Orland E. White, December 16, 1934, "Correspondence

D (1914–1952)" folder, box 3, White Papers I. See the graduation and employment information listed in his reports to the dean, "Annual Report to Dean (1928–1942)" folder and "Annual Report to Dean (1943–1955)" folder, box 3, White Papers.

62. Alumni directories and other correspondence indicated student professions. That Lewis produced an even larger proportion of physicians is highly likely, as his annual reports constantly note the overcrowding of biology courses with premedical students (see "Miller Professor of Biology Reports," in "Miller Professor 1915–1925" folder, box A8-18D, BEF Records). See Lombardo and Dorr, "Eugenics, Medical Education, and the Public Health Service."

63. Hale, *Making Whiteness*, 9.

7. "THEY SAW BLACK ALL OVER": EUGENICS, MASSIVE RESISTANCE, AND PUNITIVE STERILIZATION

1. *Brown v. Board of Education of Topeka Kansas, et. al.* 347 U.S. 483 (1954).

2. For the campaign to demolish segregation, see Kluger, *Simple Justice.* Judge Holt's decision in the Sorrells case is notable for its deviation from this pattern.

3. See G. Dorr, "Protection or Control?"

4. Geographers dubbed the development of disease and weather-resistant crop strains, fertilizers, and pesticides the "green revolution" because of the radically increased crop yields that resulted (Chase, *Legacy of Malthus,* esp. chaps. 16–22).

5. J. David Smith, *Eugenic Assault*, 57.

6. The Cox Papers, especially boxes 9 through 14, reveal the extent of this correspondence. Earnest Sevier Cox to Wickliffe P. Draper, September 14, 1957, box 12, Cox Papers.

7. Dr. Johann von Leers to Earnest Sevier Cox, May 21, 1955; Earnest Sevier Cox to Professor Doctor Hans F. K. Günther, May 28, 1955; Friedrich Kuhfuss to Earnest Sevier Cox, July 19, 1955; Cox to Kuhfuss, July 27, 1955; Kuhfuss to Cox, July 31, 1955, box 10, Cox Papers.

8. Earnest Sevier Cox to Wilhelm Ladewig, n.d., box 11, Cox Papers; Wilhelm Ladewig to Earnest Sevier Cox, October 31, 1955, box 10, Cox Papers. See also Earnest Sevier Cox to William Schaumann, April 9, 1958; Earnest Sevier Cox to Wilhelm Ladewig, April 11, 1958; Earnest Sevier Cox to Admiral Dönitz, September 26, 1958; Earnest Sevier Cox to Wilhelm Ladewig, February 24, 1959, box 13, Cox Papers.

9. Earnest Sevier Cox to Wilhelm Ladewig, n.d. (internal dates suggest December 1956 or January 1957), box 11; and Earnest Sevier Cox to Wilhelm Ladewig, December 27, 1961, box 14, Cox Papers. See also Earnest Sevier Cox to American Nazi Party, May 25, 1960; Karl R. Allen to Earnest Sevier Cox, September 22, 1962; and Carleton Putnam to Earnest Sevier Cox, June 22, 1962, box 14, Cox Papers. Putnam wrote *Race and Reason: A Yankee View* (1961), which rehashed antiquated mainline eugenic arguments about race mixing.

10. Ivey Foreman Lewis to Earnest Sevier Cox, January 13, 1952, box 9, Cox Papers. See Earnest Sevier Cox to Ivey Foreman Lewis, May 8, 1955; and Ivey Foreman Lewis to Earnest Sevier Cox, May 12, 1955, box 10, Cox Papers.

11. Cox, *Unending Hatred,* in "Printed Matter 1955" folder, box 405, Harold H. Burton Papers, Manuscript Division, Library of Congress, Washington, D.C. (hereafter cited as Burton Papers). See also Robert B. Patterson, Secretary of Association of Citizens' Councils

of Mississippi to Earnest Sevier Cox, April 1, 1955, box 9, Cox Papers. Cox quotation from Cox, *Unending Hatred*, 42, "Printed Matter 1955" folder, box 405, Burton Papers. Wesley Critz George, "The Biology of the Race Problem," report prepared by commission of the governor of Alabama (1962), Burton Papers.

12. Charles Clark to Ivey Forman Lewis, December 29, 1954, "1954 Letters" folder, box 1, Lewis Papers. See the discussion of this letter in chapter 6 of this volume. See also J. Segar Gravatt, esq. to Ivey Lewis, October 3, 1955, "1955 Letters" folder, box 1; and John D. Martin, Jr., to Ivey Lewis, January 16, 1948, "M" folder, box 7, Lewis Papers.

13. The following discussion is drawn from G. Dorr, "Principled Expediency."

14. See documents in the Naim v. Naim "Portsmouth Case File," Chancery Docket Number 9319: Ended Case Number 452: box 2, page 12 (hereafter Portsmouth Case File, box number, page number, if applicable); and David Carliner, interview by the author, November 3, 1995. See also Defense Exhibit No. 5, Letter REN to HSN, 17 April 1953, Portsmouth Case File, box 1, 7; Defense Exhibit No. 9, Letter REN to HSN, 29 September 1953, Portsmouth Case File, box 1; and Virginia Supreme Court of Appeals, *Records and Briefs,* 197 *Virginia Reports* 69, 2.

15. See chapter 6 of this volume; David Carliner, interview by the author, November 3, 1995.

16. See G. Dorr, "Principled Expediency," 128; Defense Exhibit No. 1, REN to Mother, August 24, 1953, Portsmouth Case File, box 1; *Keith v. Commonwealth* 181 S.E. 283 (Va. 1935).

17. See David Carliner, interview by the author, November 3, 1995; and "Partial Record, Reporter's Transcript," Portsmouth Case File, box 2, 3–4.

18. See, for example, the front and editorial pages of the *Richmond Times-Dispatch* and the *Norfolk Virginian-Pilot,* October 3, 1953. Quotation from Chancery Order Book 23 December 1953—June 1954, Portsmouth Circuit Courthouse, Portsmouth (emphasis added).

19. Carliner to Judge Floyd E. Kellam, April 8, 1954, Portsmouth Case File, box 1. See also A. A. Bangel to Judge Kellam, April 9, 1954; Carliner to Kellam, April 13, 1954, Portsmouth Case File, box 1; and Carliner, "Reply Brief," in *Records and Briefs,* 197 *Virginia Reports* 69, 12–19, esp. 18. Other contemporary commentators recognized this dimension of the case (PLD, "The Constitutionality of Miscegenation Statutes," *Howard Law Journal* 1 [1955]: 87).

20. Attorney General, "Amicus Curiae Brief," *in Records and Briefs,* 197 *Virginia Reports,* 69, 16.

21. *Perez v. Sharp sub nom. Lippold,* 198 P. 2d 17 (1948), 17–47, esp. 31, 33. See also Dorr, "Segregation's Science," 738–41.

22. David Carliner, interview by the author, November 3, 1995.

23. *Naim v. Naim,* 197 Va. 80 (1955), 88–89. See *Purity Extract & Co. v. Lynch,* 226 U.S. 192 (1912), quoted in *Naim v. Naim,* 197 Va. 80 (1955), 89. See also Sohn, "Principle and Expediency," 90.

24. *Naim v. Naim,* 197 Va. 80 (1955), 89–90. Smith graduated from the University of Virginia in 1916 and lived in Charlottesville. Lewis telegrammed Governor W. M. Tuck, "Urge favorable consideration of Judge Smith for supreme bench on basis of character, ability, experience and wide public esteem" (draft telegram, Ivey Foreman Lewis to Governor W. M. Tuck, October 16, 1947, box 7, Lewis Papers). See also *Journal of the House of Delegates of Virginia* (Richmond: Superintendent of Public Printing, 1924), 772, 774–75; and *Acts of the General Assembly* (Richmond: Superintendent of Public Printing, 1924), 834.

25. David Carliner, interview by the author, November 3, 1995. Frankfurter's discomfort with miscegenation law is detailed in Gunther, *Learned Hand,* 667. See also *Jackson v. Alabama,* 348 U.S. 888 (1954); Wallenstein, "Race, Marriage," 414–16. The justices maintained standardized docket books in which they recorded the votes during conference, other notes, and the ultimate disposition of cases. Of the six justices' papers available to the author (Black, Burton, Douglas, Frankfurter, Harlan, and Warren), only those of Burton, Douglas, and Warren contained the docket books (Burton Papers, box 279; Douglas Papers, box 1162; Warren Papers, box 369). The papers of Justices Black, Burton, Douglas, Frankfurter, and Warren reside in the Manuscript Division, Library of Congress, Washington, D.C. The Seeley G. Mudd Library, Princeton University, maintains Justice Harlan's papers. Hereafter individual justices' papers are referred to by the justice's name.

26. Four of the six justices' papers contained copies of law clerk memoranda on *Naim:* Burton, Douglas, Harlan, and Warren. See AJM (law clerk) to Justice Harold H. Burton, October 23, 1955, Harold H. Burton Papers, box 283, 3; LML (law clerk) to Justice John Marshall Harlan, undated, 1955 file, Harlan Papers. See note 29 below for the memo of Justice Warren's clerk. For a more detailed exposition, see G. Dorr, "Principled Expediency."

27. *Naim v. Naim,* 350 U.S. 891 (1955).

28. *Naim v. Naim,* 197 Va. 734 (1956), 735. The Virginia legislature based the ordinance upon James Madison's doctrine of "interposition," most fully articulated by John C. Calhoun during the Nullification Crisis of 1831–32 (see "The Measure of Redress," *Richmond News-Leader,* January 19, 1956; "Virginia Rejects Order of U.S. Supreme Court," *Richmond News-Leader,* January 18, 1956; "Virginia Bench Rejects Supreme Court's Order," *Norfolk Virginian-Pilot,* January 19, 1956; and "State's High Court Spurns U.S. Order," *Richmond Times-Dispatch,* January 19, 1956). See also David Carliner, "Motion to Recall the Mandate and the Set the Case down for Oral Argument on the Merits, or in the Alternative, to Recall and Amend Mandate," Portsmouth Case file, box 2, 2.

29. William A. Norris (law clerk) to Justice William O. Douglas, October 24, 1955, box 1164, William O. Douglas Papers. See also SAS to Chief Justice Earl Warren, undated, box 369, Earl Warren Papers; AJM to Justice Harold Hitz Burton, October 23, 1955, box 283, 3, Harold H. Burton Papers. For the vote, see Docket Book, box 279, Harold H. Burton Papers. Quotation from *Naim v. Naim,* 350 U.S. 985 (1956). See also Warren's draft memo, box 369, Earl Warren Papers.

30. The penalty under Virginia's 1691 miscegenation law was banishment. See Waddlington, "The Loving Case," 1191–92. This narrative is drawn from the opinions of the Virginia Supreme Court of Appeals, *Richard Perry Loving, et al. v. Commonwealth of Virginia,* 206 Va. 924 (1966); U.S. Supreme Court, *Loving et lux. v. Virginia,* 388 U.S. 1 (1967); and Wallenstein, *Tell the Court,* 215–52.

31. 388 U.S. 1 (1967) at 3.

32. 206 Va. 924 (1966), 929; *Borden's Farm Products Co. v. Baldwin,* 293 U.S. 194, quoted in *Naim v. Naim,* 197 Va. 80 (1955), 89.

33. 206 Va. 924 (1966), 931.

34. Romano, *Race Mixing,* 2, 191, 207; *Calma v. Calma,* 128 S.E. 2d 440 (1962); G. Dorr, "Segregation's Science," 1761–62.

35. 388 U.S. 1 (1967), at 6, 7, 11.

36. Ibid., 11–12.

37. *Skinner v. Oklahoma,* 316 U.S. 535 (1941) at 546–47.

38. See Chase, *Legacy of Malthus,* 382–85, and chaps. 16 and 17. Quotation from Kevles, *In the Name of Eugenics,* 258.

39. J. Paul, "Return of Punitive."

40. Ibid., 97; and House Bill 394, "A Bill to provide the sexual sterilization of females who give birth to certain illegitimate children . . . ," *Virginia Bills, House* (1956). See also House Bill 718, *Virginia Bills, House* (1958).

41. Department of Welfare and Institutions of the Commonwealth of Virginia, "Report on Illegitimacy in the Aid to Dependent Children and Foster Care Programs" (September 1958) and a companion study in 1961; and "State Summary of Illegitimate Children Receiving Aid to Dependent Children" (September 1958). The Department of Public Assistance, Social Service Bureau of the City of Richmond published two studies of its own: "A.D.C. Is Everybody's Business" (September 1959) and "Illegitimacy in Richmond, Virginia, 1910–1955" (April 1957).

42. Senate Bill 169, *Virginia Bills, Senate* (1960); House Bill 494, *Virginia Bills, House* (1960).

43. House Bill 495, *Virginia Bills, House* (1960). See also Schoen, *Between Choice and Coercion*; and J. Paul, "Return of Punitive," 77–106.

44. Virginia Advisory Legislative Council, "Sterilization Laws in Virginia," Senate Document No. 5 (1961), 5–7, *Virginia Senate Documents, 1961.* "Social service sterilization" is defined in Edward J. Larson and Leonard J. Nelson III, "Involuntary Sexual Sterilization of Incompetents in Alabama: Past, Present, and Future," *Alabama Law Review* 43 (1992): 403–4, 435–41.

45. Virginia Advisory Legislative Council, "Sterilization Laws in Virginia," Senate Document No. 5 (1961), 5–7.

46. Reilly, *Surgical Solution,* 144; House Bill 300, *Virginia Bills, House* (1962). That same session the General Assembly killed yet another attempt at punitive sterilization of welfare mothers (Senate Bill 37, *Virginia Bills, Senate* [1962]). On *Relf,* see G. Dorr, "Protection or Control?" passim.

47. G. Grant, "50 Indigent Mothers." All quotations in G. Grant, "Birth Control"; and Glass, "Sterilization of 'Welfare Mothers.'" The Human Betterment Foundation traced its roots to the California eugenicists Paul Popenoe and Ezra Gosney (see Kline, *Building a Better Race,* chap. 3).

48. G. Grant, "Birth Control." Stinson told the *Herald Tribune*'s reporter, "We're not selling it, they're asking for it" (Glass, "Sterilization of 'Welfare Mothers'").

49. Gerald Grant, "Archbishop Denounces Sterilization," September 10, 1962; Marshall Peck, "Sterilizing Plan Draws Protest of Billy Graham," *New York Herald Tribune,* September 11, 1962; Gerald Grant, "The Fauquier Hospital Sterilization Story," *Background Reports* [of the National Conference of Christians and Jews] (January 1963), 1. Joseph Fletcher served on Virginia's faculty until the mid-1980s, hewing to the basic eugenic tenets of fitness and unfitness (Fletcher, *Morals and Medicine*). Lord quoted in "Sterilization Program Probe Asked," *Washington Post,* September 9, 1962; and "Capital Bishop Comes Out for Sterilizing Plan," *New York Herald Tribune,* September 12, 1962. See also the symposium on sterilization in *New Medical Materia* (November 1962): 11–24.

50. Grant, "The Fauquier County Sterilization Story," 3.

51. Senate Bill 37, *Virginia Bills, Senate* (1962).

52. Arthur Jensen, "How Much Can We Boost IQ and Scholastic Achievement?" *Harvard Educational Review* 39 (1969): 1–123. See also Kluger, *Simple Justice,* 482–84, 502–4.

53. Chase, *Legacy of Malthus,* 455. See the Kilpatrick Papers, 1923–1974, Accession #6626, Special Collections, University of Virginia Library, Charlottesville (hereafter cited as Kilpatrick Papers).

54. Chase, *Legacy of Malthus,* 452–53.

55. American Genetics Association, "The American Genetics Association: A History of the Association," typescript, 3, in "American Genetics Association, 1962" folder, box A8-20D, BEF Records.

8. CONCLUSION: "I NEVER KNEW WHAT THEY'D DONE WITH ME"

1. Leo E. Kirven, Jr., to Julius Paul, July 15, 1980 (copy in author's possession); Sandra G. Boodman and Glenn Frankel, "Over 7,500 Sterilized by Virginia," *Washington Post,* February 23, 1980. Quotation from Robert Rheinhold, "Virginia Hospital Chief Traces 50 Years of Sterilizing the 'Retarded,'" *New York Times,* February 23, 1980.

2. United Press International, "Warren Told of Her Sterilization," *Charlottesville Daily Progress,* February 24, 1980. See also Senate Bill No. 537, *Virginia Bills, Senate* (1980); *Lynchburg Story,* produced and directed by Stephen Trombley; Lombardo, "Involuntary Sterilization in Virginia"; and "Va. Sterilization Suit Settlement Is Approved," *Washington Post,* January 19, 1985.

3. Ben A. Franklin, "Sterilization of Teen-Age Woman Haunting Virginia Decades Later," *New York Times,* March 7, 1980; Doris Buck Figgins quoted in Boodman and Frankel, "Over 7,500 Sterilized." See also J. David Smith and Nelson, *Sterilization of Carrie Buck,* 216 (Doris), xviii (Carrie).

4. Paul A. Lombardo, quoted in Gould, "Carrie Buck's Daughter," 14–18.

5. Many scholars consider Fletcher the founder of modern biomedical ethics. His pathbreaking book *Morals and Medicine* (1954) is replete with eugenics. His book *The Ethics of Genetic Control* (1974) also embraced eugenic ideas. See also Gillham, *Sir Francis Galton,* 24–42, 237–40.

6. *Doing Bad in the Name of Good? The Tuskegee Syphilis Study and Its Legacy,* produced by the University of Virginia, 4 parts, 206 min., Division of Continuing Education, Education and Distance Learning Technologies, 1994, videocassette. See also William Jefferson Clinton, "Remarks in Apology to African-Americans on the Tuskegee Experiment, May 16, 1997," *Weekly Compilation of Presidential Documents* 337 (1997): 847–49; Peter Hardin, "Documentary Genocide," *Richmond Times-Dispatch,* March 5, 2000; "Seeking Sovereignty: Indians Face Barriers, See Benefits in Quest," *Richmond Times-Dispatch,* March 6, 2000; "Virginia Indians Muster Support for Sovereignty," *Richmond Times-Dispatch,* March 19, 2000; "Segregation's Era of Science," *Richmond Times-Dispatch,* November 26, 2000; General Assembly, "H.D.J. Res. 607," *2001 General Assembly, Reg. Sess.* (Virginia, 2001): approved by House of Delegates, February 2, 2001; approved by Senate February 14, 2001; Dave Reynolds, "Virginia Governor Apologizes for Eugenics," *Inclusion Daily Express,* May 6, 2002, www.inclusiondaily.com/news/advocacy/vaeugenics.htm#05062. See also *Buck v. Bell* Historic Marker, 800 Preston Avenue, Charlottesville, Va., 22903.

7. "'Three Generations of Imbeciles . . . ,'" *Washington Post,* February 27, 1980.

8. Galton, "Possible Improvement," 25.

9. Ivey Foreman Lewis to Mrs. Bertha Wailes, March 4, 1952, folder 29, box 11, Lewis Papers; W. Lewis retired the following fall, after reaching the then mandatory retirement age of seventy.

10. Duster, *Backdoor to Eugenics.*

11. "President Clinton Takes Historic Action to Ban Genetic Discrimination in the Federal Workplace," news release, February 8, 2000, copy in author's possession. See also editorial, "Census, Race and Science," *Nature Genetics* 24 (February 2000), 97 (first quotation, 98).

12. Nicholas Wade, "2 Scholarly Articles Diverge on Role of Race in Medicine," *New York Times,* March 20, 2003.

Bibliography

MANUSCRIPT COLLECTIONS

American Eugenics Society Records. American Philosophical Society Library, Philadelphia.

Barringer Family Papers. Accession #2588, -a, -b, -c, -d, -e, -g, Special Collections, University of Virginia Library, Charlottesville.

Blandy Experimental Farm Records. RG-6/9/2.831, Special Collections, University of Virginia Library, Charlottesville.

Burton, Harold H., Papers. Manuscript Division, Library of Congress, Washington, D.C.

Cox, Earnest Sevier, Papers. Duke University Rare Book, Manuscript, and Special Collections Library, Durham, N.C.

Cumming, Hugh S., Papers. MSS6922, Special Collections, University of Virginia Library, Charlottesville.

Davenport, Charles B., Papers. American Philosophical Society, Philadelphia.

Davis, Donald W., Papers. Special Collections Research Center, Earl Gregg Swem Library, College of William and Mary, Williamsburg, Va.

Douglas, William O., Papers. Manuscript Division, Library of Congress, Washington, D.C.

Eugenics Record Office Records. American Philosophical Society, Philadelphia.

Frankfurter, Felix, Collection. Harvard Microfilm, Manuscript Division, Library of Congress, Washington, D.C.

Frankfurter, Felix, Papers. Manuscript Division, Library of Congress, Washington, D.C.

Gosney, E. S., Papers, and Records of the Human Betterment Foundation. Archives. California Institute of Technology, Pasadena.

Harlan, John Marshall, Papers. Public Policy Papers, Department of Rare Books and Special Collections, Princeton University Library, Princeton, N.J.

Jordan, David Starr, Papers. #SC-058, Stanford University Libraries, Department of Special Collections and University Archives, Stanford, Calif.

Jordan, Harvey Ernest, Collected Scientific Papers. Historical Collections, Claude Moore Health Sciences Library, University of Virginia, Charlottesville.

Jordan, Harvey Ernest, Papers. Accession #9079, Special Collections, University of Virginia Library, Charlottesville.

Kilpatrick, James J., Papers, 1923–1974. Accession #6626, Special Collections, University of Virginia Library, Charlottesville.

Laughlin, Harry H., Papers. Pickler Memorial Library, Truman State University (Northeast Missouri State College), Kirksville, Mo.

Lewis, Ivey Foreman, Papers. RG-6/2/1.551, Special Collections, University of Virginia Library, Charlottesville.

Powell, John, Papers. Accession #7284, 7284-a, Special Collections, University of Virginia Library, Charlottesville.

President's Papers. Special Collections, University of Virginia Library, Charlottesville.

Royster, Lawrence Thomas, Papers. Accession #4198-a, Special Collections, University of Virginia Library, Charlottesville.

Student and Alumni Papers. RG 22, Special Collections, University of Virginia Library, Charlottesville.

Turner, Thomas Wyatt, Papers. Hampton University Archives, Hampton, Va.

Warren, Earl, Papers. Manuscript Division, Library of Congress, Washington, D.C.

White, Orland E., Papers. Accession #12767-a, 12767-b, Special Collections, University of Virginia Library, Charlottesville.

INTERVIEWS

Franklin Bacon and Raymond Bice, Westminster Canterbury, Charlottesville, Va., January 25, 2000.

Raymond Bice, Westminster Canterbury, Charlottesville, Va., December 1, 1999.

David Carliner, Carliner and Rehmes Office, Washington, D.C., November 3, 1995.

COLLEGE AND UNIVERSITY COURSE CATALOGS SURVEYED (1895–1980)

College of William and Mary
Hampton University
Randolph-Macon College
Richmond College/University of Richmond
University of Virginia
Virginia Union University

JOURNALS SURVEYED

American Breeders Magazine (1910–14)
Birth Control Review (1917–40)
Eugenical News (1916–57)
Eugenics (1928–31)
Journal of Heredity (1914–63)
Journal of the American Medical Association (1895–1980)
Virginia Medical Semi-Monthly and *Virginia Medical Monthly* (1898–1980)

NEWSPAPERS SURVEYED (1900–1980)

Cavalier Daily (University of Virginia)
Charlottesville Daily Progress
New York Times
Richmond News-Leader
Richmond Planet
Richmond Times-Dispatch
Washington Post

OTHER SOURCES

Adams, Mark B. *The Well-Born Science: Eugenics in Germany, France, Brazil, and Russia.* New York: Oxford University Press, 1990.

Alderman, Edwin Anderson. "The Achievement of a Generation." *South Atlantic Quarterly* 5 (January–October, 1906): 24.

——. "The Growing South." *World's Work* 16 (1908): 10377–78.

——. "The University and the State in the South." *Rare Virginia Pamphlets* 23 (n.d.): 53–56. Special Collections, University of Virginia.

Aldrich, Morton A., et al. *Eugenics: Twelve University Lectures.* New York: Dodd, Mead, 1914.

Allen, Garland E. "Eugenics and American Social History, 1880–1950." *Genome* 31 (1989): 885–89.

——. "The Misuse of Biological Hierarchies: The American Eugenics Movement, 1900–1940." *History and Philosophy of the Life Sciences* 5 (1983): 105–28.

——. "Science Misapplied: The Eugenics Age Revisited." *Technology Review* (August–September 1996): 23–31.

Anderson, Eric, and Alfred A. Moss Jr. *Dangerous Donations: Northern Philanthropy and Southern Black Education, 1902–1930.* Columbia and London: University of Missouri Press, 1999.

Anderson, James D. *The Education of Blacks in the South, 1860–1935.* Chapel Hill: University of North Carolina Press, 1988.

Arnold, G. B. "Eugenic Sterilization of the Epileptic and the Mentally Deficient." *Virginia Medical Monthly* 67 (January 1940): 45–47.

Ayers, Edward L. *The Promise of the New South: Life after Reconstruction.* New York and Oxford: Oxford University Press, 1992.

Bailyn, Bernard. *The Ideological Origins of the American Revolution.* Enlarged ed. Cambridge and London: Belknap Press of Harvard University Press, 1992.

Bair, Barbara. "Remapping the Black/White Body: Sexuality, Nationalism, and Biracial Antimiscegenation Activism in 1920s Virginia." In *Sex, Love, Race: Crossing Boundaries in North American History,* ed. Martha Hodes, 399–422. New York: New York University Press, 1999.

Bannister, Robert C. *Social Darwinism: Science and Myth in Anglo-American Social Thought.* Philadelphia: Temple University Press, 1979.

Barkan, Elazar. *The Retreat of Scientific Racism: Changing Concepts of Race in Britain and the United States between the World Wars.* Cambridge: Cambridge University Press, 1992.

Barringer, Paul Brandon. "An Essay on Constitutional Syphilis." *North Carolina Medical Journal* 12 (1883): 89–95, 137–45.

———. *Cholera and Its Prevention: A Circular by the State Board of Health*. Richmond: Superintendent of Public Printing, 1893.

———. *The Natural Bent*. Edited by Anna Barringer. Chapel Hill: University of North Carolina Press, 1949.

Bean, Robert Bennett. "Anthropology in the Medical Curriculum." *Science* 56 (October 21, 1921): 371–73.

———. "Disease and Death Rate in Human Types." *New Orleans Medical and Surgical Journal* 69 (September 1916): 175–90.

———. "Human Types." *Quarterly Review of Biology* 1 (1926): 360–92.

———. "The Negro Brain." *Century Magazine* 72 (1906): 778–84.

———. "Notes on the Body Form of Man." In *Eugenics in Race and State: Scientific Papers of the Second International Congress of Eugenics*, 7–24. Baltimore: Williams and Wilkins, 1923.

———. *The Peopling of Virginia*. Boston: Chapman and Grimes, 1938.

———. *The Races of Man: Differentiation and Dispersal of Man*. New York: University Society, 1932.

———. *The Racial Anatomy of the Philippine Islanders*. Philadelphia and London: Lippincott, 1910.

———. "The Sitting Height." *American Journal of Physical Anthropology* 5 (October-December 1922): 349–90.

———. "Some Racial Peculiarities of the Negro Brain." *American Journal of Anatomy* 5 (1906): 353–432.

———. "The Three Anatomic Types of Africa." *American Journal of Anatomy* 33 (March 1924): 105–18.

———. "The Training of the Negro." *Century Magazine* 72 (1906): 947–53.

———. "Two European Types." *American Journal of Anatomy* 31 (March 1923): 359–71.

———. "Types of Man in the Yellow-Brown Race." *American Journal of Anatomy* 35 (March 1925): 63–80.

———. "Types of the Three Great Races of Man." *American Journal of Anatomy* 37 (1926): 237–71.

Bean, Robert Bennett, and Wilmer Baker. "Some Racial Characteristics of the Heart and Kidney Weight in Man." *American Journal of Physical Anthropology* 2 (1919): 274–81.

———. "Some Racial Characteristics of the Liver Weight in Man." *American Journal of Physical Anthropology* 2 (1919): 167–74.

———. "Some Racial Characteristics of the Spleen Weight in Man." *American Journal of Physical Anthropology* 2 (1919): 1–9.

Bederman, Gail. *Manliness & Civilization: A Cultural History of Gender and Race in the United States, 1880–1917*. Chicago and London: University of Chicago Press, 1995.

Benson, Keith R., Jane Maienschein, and Ronald Rainger, eds. *The Expansion of American Biology*. New Brunswick, N.J., and London: Rutgers University Press, 1991.

Berg, A. Scott. *Lindbergh*. New York: G. P. Putnam's Sons, 1998.

Black, Edwin. *War against the Weak: Eugenics and America's Campaign to Create a Master Race*. New York: Four Walls Eight Windows Press, 2004.

Bledstein, Burton. *The Culture of Professionalism*. New York: Norton, 1976.

Bloom, Jack M. *Class, Race, and the Civil Rights Movement.* Bloomington and Indianapolis: Indiana University Press, 1987.

Boaz, Noel T., and Linda D. Wolfe. *Biological Anthropology: The State of the Science.* Bend, Ore.: International Institute for Human Evolutionary Research, 1995.

Boulton, Alexander O. "The American Paradox: Jeffersonian Equality and Racial Science." *American Quarterly* 47 (September 1995): 467–92.

Bowler, Peter J. *The Mendelian Revolution: The Emergence of Hereditarian Concepts in Modern Science and Society.* Baltimore: Johns Hopkins University Press, 1989.

———. *Theories of Human Evolution: A Century of Debate, 1844–1944.* Baltimore: Johns Hopkins University Press, 1986.

Bowles, Samuel, and Herbert Gintis. *Schooling in Capitalist America: Educational Reform and the Contradictions of Economic Life.* New York: Basic Books, 1976.

Brandt, Allan M. *No Magic Bullet: A Social History of Venereal Disease in the United States since 1880.* New York and Oxford: Oxford University Press, 1985.

Braslow, Joel. *Mental Ills and Bodily Cures: Psychiatric Treatment in the First Half of the Twentieth Century.* Berkeley and London: University of California Press, 1997.

Brechin, Gray. "Conserving the Race: Natural Aristocracies, Eugenics, and the U.S. Conservation Movement." *Antipode* 28 (Summer 1996): 229–45.

Brigham, Carl C. *A Study of American Intelligence.* Princeton, N.J.: Princeton University Press, 1923.

Broberg, Gunnar, and Nils Roll-Hansen, eds. *Eugenics and the Welfare State: Sterilization Policy in Denmark, Sweden, Norway, and Finland.* East Lansing: Michigan State University Press, 1996.

Bruce, Philip Alexander. *History of the University of Virginia 1818–1919: The Lengthened Shadow of One Man.* 5 vols. New York: Macmillan, 1919–22.

Brundage, W. Fitzhugh, ed. *Where These Memories Grow: History, Memory, and Southern Identity.* Chapel Hill: University of North Carolina Press, 2000.

Bruinius, Harry. *Better for All the World: The Secret History of Forced Sterilization and America's Quest for Racial Purity.* New York: Vintage, 2007.

Cabell, James Lawrence. *The Testimony of Modern Science to the Unity of Mankind; being a summary of the conclusions announced by the highest authorities in the several departments of physiology, zoology and comparative philology in favor of the specific unity and common origin of all the varieties of man.* New York: Robert Carter and Brothers, 1859.

Carlson, Elof Axel. *The Unfit: History of a Bad Idea.* Cold Spring Harbor, N.Y.: CSHL Press, 2001.

Carrington, Charles V. "Hereditary Criminals—The One Sure Cure." *Virginia Medical Semi-Monthly* 15 (April 8, 1910): 4–8.

———. "Keep the Race Pure." *Virginia Medical Semi-Monthly* 17 (December 12, 1913): 434–38.

———. "Sterilization of Habitual Criminals, With Report of Cases." *Virginia Medical Semi-Monthly* 13 (December 11, 1908): 389–90.

———. Sterilization of Habitual Criminals." *Virginia Medical Semi-Monthly* 14 (December 24, 1909): 421–22.

Castle, William E., John M. Coulter, Charles B. Davenport, Edward M. East, and William L. Tower. *Heredity and Eugenics.* Chicago: University of Chicago Press, 1912.

Caudill, Edward. *Darwinian Myths: The Legends and Misuses of a Theory.* Knoxville: University of Tennessee Press, 1997.

Chase, Alan. *The Legacy of Malthus: The Social Costs of the New Scientific Racism.* New York: Knopf, 1977.

Claiborne, John Herbert. "The Negro." *Virginia Medical Semi-Monthly* 5 (April 13, 1900): 3–6.

Clifford, Geraldine Jonçich. *Edward L. Thorndike: The Sane Positivist.* 2nd ed. Middletown, Ct.: Wesleyan University Press, 1984.

Cooke, Kathy Jane. "A Gospel of Social Evolution: Religion, Biology, and Education in the Thought of Edwin Grant Conklin." Ph.D. diss., University of Chicago, 1994.

Cox, Earnest Sevier. *Black Belt around the World.* Richmond, Va.: self-published; Mitchell and Hotchkiss, Printers, 1963.

———. *Lincoln's Negro Policy.* Pamphlet. 1962. Newport Beach, Calif.: Noontide Press, 1968.

———. *Teutonic Unity: A Basis for Peace.* Richmond, Va.: self-published, 1951.

———. *White America.* Richmond, Va.: White America Society, 1923; rev. ed. 1937.

Cravens, Hamilton. *The Triumph of Evolution: American Scientists and the Heredity-Environment Controversy 1900–1941.* Philadelphia: University of Pennsylvania Press, 1978.

Crenshaw, Lewis D., ed. *Directory of the Living Alumni of the University of Virginia, 1921.* Charlottesville: Michie, 1921.

Curti, Merle. *The Social Ideas of American Educators.* New York: Scribner's, 1935.

Dabney, Virginius. *Liberalism in the South.* Chapel Hill: University of North Carolina Press, 1932.

———. *Mr. Jefferson's University: A History.* Charlottesville: University of Virginia Press, 1981.

Davenport, Charles B. *Eugenics.* New York: Holt, 1910.

———. "Eugenics and Euthenics." *Popular Science Monthly* 78 (1911): 16–20.

———. *The Feebly Inhibited.* Washington, D.C.: Carnegie Institution of Washington, 1915.

———. *Heredity in Relation to Eugenics.* New York: Holt, 1911.

———. *Heredity of Skin Color in Negro-White Crosses.* Washington, D.C.: Carnegie Institution of Washington, 1913.

———. *How We Came By Our Bodies.* New York: Holt, 1936.

———. "The Geography of Man in Relation to Eugenics." In *Heredity and Eugenics,* by William E. Castle et al., 289–312. Chicago: University of Chicago Press, 1912.

Davenport, Charles B., and Morris Steggerda. "Race Crossing in Jamaica." *Scientific Monthly* 27 (September 1928): 225–38.

Davenport, Gertrude Crotty, and Charles B. Davenport. "Heredity of Skin Pigmentation in Man." *American Naturalist* 44 (November 1910): 641–72.

Davis, Reverend W. E. "The Divine Plan of Racial Integrity." *Virginia Medical Semi-Monthly* 52 (August 1925): 289–90.

De Baecque, Antoine. *The Body Politic: Corporeal Metaphor in Revolutionary France, 1770–1800.* Translated by Charlotte Mandell. Stanford, Calif.: Stanford University Press, 1993.

Degler, Carl N. *In Search of Human Nature: The Decline and Revival of Darwinism in American Social Thought.* New York and Oxford: Oxford University Press, 1991.

DeJarnette, Joseph S. "Eugenics in Relation to the Insane, the Epileptic, the Feeble-Minded and Race Blending." *Virginia Medical Semi-Monthly* 52 (August 1925): 290–92.

Dennis, Michael A. "Educating the 'Advancing' South: State Universities and Progressivism in the New South, 1887–1915." Ph.D. diss., Queen's University, Kingston, Ontario, 1996.

——. "Reforming the 'Academical Village': Edwin A. Alderman and the University of Virginia, 1904–1915." *Virginia Magazine of History and Biography* 105 (Winter 1997): 53–86.

Dew, H. W. "Sterilization of the Feeble-Minded, Insane and Habitual Criminals." *Virginia Medical Semi-Monthly* 17 (April 11, 1913): 4–8.

Diggins, John P. "Slavery, Race, and Equality: Jefferson and the Pathos of the Enlightenment." *American Quarterly* 28 (Summer 1976): 206–28.

Dorr, Gregory Michael. "Assuring America's Place in the Sun: Ivey Foreman Lewis and the Teaching of Eugenics at the University of Virginia, 1915–1953." *Journal of Southern History* 66 (May 2000): 257–96.

——. "Beyond Racial Purity: African Americans and Integrationist Eugenics." Paper presented at the Organization of American Historians conference, Memphis, Tenn., April 3, 2003.

——. "Defective or Disabled?: Race, Medicine, and Eugenics in Progressive Era Virginia and Alabama." *Journal of the Gilded Age and Progressive Era* 5 (October 2006): 359–92.

——. "Principled Expediency: Eugenics, *Naim v. Naim,* and the Supreme Court." *American Journal of Legal History* 42 (Spring 1998): 119–59.

——. "Protection or Control?: Women's Health, Sterilization Abuse, and *Relf v. Weinberger.*" Paper presented at the Social Science History Association conference, St. Louis, Mo., October 26, 2002.

——. "Rearing Human Thoroughbreds: Eugenics, Medical Education, and Public Health." Paper presented at the American Association for the History of Medicine conference, Bethesda, Md., May 21, 2000.

——. "Segregation's Science: The American Eugenics Movement and Virginia, 1910–1980." Ph.D. diss., University of Virginia, 2000.

Dorr, Lisa Lindquist. "Arm in Arm: Gender and the Racial Integrity Act of 1924." *Journal of Women's History* 11 (Spring 1999): 143–66.

——. *White Women, Rape, and the Power of Race in Virginia, 1900–1960* Chapel Hill: University of North Carolina Press, 2004.

Dowbiggin, Ian. *Keeping America Sane: Psychiatry and Eugenics in the United States and Canada, 1880–1940.* Ithaca, N.Y.: Cornell University Press, 2003.

Drewry, William F. "The Mental Defectives." *Virginia Medical Semi-Monthly* 16 (January 26, 1912): 500–508.

Du Bois, W.E.B. *The Souls of Black Folk.* New York: Penguin Books, 1989.

Dumenil, Lynn. *The Modern Temper: America in the 1920s.* New York: Hill and Wang, 1995.

Dunn, L. C., and Theodosius Dobzhansky. *Heredity, Race, and Society.* 2nd ed. New York: New American Library of World Literature, 1952.

Duster, Troy. *Backdoor to Eugenics.* New York and London: Routledge, 1990.

East, Edward M. *Heredity and Human Affairs.* New York and London: Scribner's, 1927.

——. *Mankind at the Crossroads.* New York and London: Scribner's, 1924.

East, Edward M., and Donald F. Jones. *Inbreeding and Outbreeding: Their Genetic and Sociological Significance.* Philadelphia and London: Lippincott, 1919.

Edwards, William A. "Racial Purity in Black and White: The Case of Marcus Garvey and Earnest Cox." *Journal of Ethnic Studies* 15 (1987): 117–42.

Ehrenreich, Barbara, and Deirdre English. *For Her Own Good: 150 Years of the Experts' Advice to Women.* New York: Anchor/Doubleday, 1978.

Ellis, Joseph J. *American Sphinx: The Character of Thomas Jefferson.* New York: Knopf, 1997.

English, Daylanne Kathryn. "Eugenics, Modernism and the Harlem Renaissance." Ph.D. diss., University of Virginia, 1996.

Estabrook, Arthur H., and Ivan E. McDougle. *Mongrel Virginians: The Win Tribe.* Baltimore: Williams and Wilkins, 1926.

Eugenics Education Society. *First International Eugenics Congress: Scientific Papers and Appendices.* London: Eugenics Education Society, 1912.

———. *Problems in Eugenics: Report of Proceedings of the First International Eugenics Congress.* 2 vols. London: Eugenics Education Society, 1913.

Eugenics Record Office. "Report of the Committee to Study and to Report on the Best Practical Means of Cutting Off the Defective Germ Plasm in the American Population." *Bulletin 10a and 10b.* Cold Spring Harbor, Long Island: Eugenics Record Office, 1914.

Ferguson, George Oscar, Jr. "The Mental Status of the American Negro." *Scientific Monthly* 12 (June 1921): 533–43.

———. "The Psychology of the Negro: An Experimental Study." *Archives of Psychology* 36 (April 1916): 1–138.

"The Fitter Families Contest." *Eugenical News* 8 (September 1923): 88.

Flannagan, Roy K. "Dr. Paul Brandon Barringer." Address before the Alumni Association of the University of Virginia, June 7, 1941. Barringer Family Papers, box 1, loosely filed, pp. 5, 10.

Fleming, Donald. *William H. Welch and the Rise of Modern Medicine.* Boston: Little, Brown, 1954.

Fletcher, Joseph. *The Ethics of Genetic Control: Ending Reproductive Roulette: Artificial Insemination, Surrogate Pregnancy, Nonsexual Reproduction, Genetic Control.* New York: Prometheus Books, 1988.

———. *Morals and Medicine: The Moral Problems of: The Patient's Right to Know the Truth; Contraception; Artificial Insemination; Sterilization; Euthanasia.* Princeton, N.J.: Princeton University Press, 1954.

Flexner, Simon, and James Thomas Flexner. *William Henry Welch and the Heroic Age of American Medicine.* New York: Viking Press, 1941. Reprint, Baltimore and London: Johns Hopkins University Press, 1993.

Foucault, Michel. *The Birth of the Clinic: An Archeology of Medical Perception.* New York: Pantheon, 1973. Reprint, New York: Vintage Books, 1994.

Franklin, John Hope, and Alfred A. Moss Jr. *From Slavery to Freedom: A History of African Americans.* 7th ed. New York: McGraw-Hill, 1994.

Fraser, Gertrude Jacinta. *African American Midwifery in the South: Dialogues of Birth, Race, and Memory.* Cambridge and London: Harvard University Press, 1998.

Frederickson, George M. *The Black Image in the White Mind: The Debate on Afro-American Destiny, 1817–1914.* New York: Harper and Row, 1971.

Fullwiley, Duana. "The Molecularization of Race: Institutionalizing Racial Difference in Pharmacogenetics Practice." *Science in Culture* 16 (2007): 1–30.

Gaines, Kevin. *Uplifting the Race: Black Leadership, Politics, and Culture in the Twentieth Century.* Chapel Hill: University of North Carolina Press, 1996.

Galton, Sir Francis. *Hereditary Genius: An Inquiry into Its Laws and Consequences.* London: Macmillan, 1869.

——. *Inquiries into Human Faculty and Its Development.* London: Macmillan, 1883. Reprint, New York: AMS Press, 1973.

——. "The Possible Improvement of the Human Breed under Existing Conditions of Law and Sentiment." Chapter 1 in *Essays in Eugenics.* London: Eugenics Education Society, 1909.

Gallagher, Nancy L. *Breeding Better Vermonters: The Eugenics Project in the Green Mountain State.* Hanover, N.H.: University Press of New England, 1999.

Garrow, David J. *Liberty and Sexuality: The Right to Privacy and the Making of Roe v. Wade.* New York: Macmillan, 1994.

Garvey, Amy Jacques. *Garvey and Garveyism.* 1963. Reprint, New York: Octagon Press, 1968.

Garvey, Marcus. "Aims and Objects of Movement for Solution of Negro Problems." In *Philosophy and Opinions of Marcus Garvey,* ed. Amy Jacques Garvey, 2: 37–43. Reprint, Dover, Mass.: Majority Press, 1986.

Gaston, Paul M. *The New South Creed: A Study in Southern Mythmaking.* New York: Vintage Books, 1970.

Gerteis, Joseph. "Populism, Race, and Political Interest in Virginia." *Social Science History* 23 (2003): 197–227.

Gillham, Nicholas Wright. *Sir Francis Galton: From African Exploration to the Birth of Eugenics.* New York: Oxford University Press, 2001.

Glass, Andrew J. "Sterilization of 'Welfare Mothers': Report on Virginia Law in Action." *New York Herald Tribune,* September 9, 1962.

Goddard, Henry Herbert. *The Kallikak Family.* New York: Macmillan, 1912. Reprint, New York: Arno Press, 1973.

Gordon, Alfred. "The Social Aspect of Mental Abnormalities and the Problem of Eugenics." *Virginia Medical Monthly* 56 (October 1929): 469–74.

Gosney, E. S., and Paul Popenoe. *Sterilization for Human Betterment: A Summary of Results of 6,000 Operation in California, 1909–1929.* New York: Macmillan, 1931.

Gossett, Thomas F. *Race: The History of an Idea in America.* 2nd ed. New York and Oxford: Oxford University Press, 1997.

Gould, Stephen J. "Carrie Buck's Daughter." *Constitutional Commentary* 2 (1985): 331–39.

——. *Ever Since Darwin: Reflections in Natural History.* 4th ed. New York: Norton, 1977.

——. *The Mismeasure of Man.* 2nd ed. New York: Norton, 1996.

Gramsci, Antonio. "The Intellectuals." In *Selections from the Prison Notebooks,* translated and edited by Q. Hoare and G. N. Smith. New York: International, 1971.

——. *The Intellectuals and Cultural Formation* [*Gli intellettuali e l'organizzazione della cultua*]. Torino: Einandi, 1949.

Grant, Gerald. "50 Indigent Mothers Sterilized in Fauquier County." *Washington Post,* September 4, 1962.

——. "Birth Control Clinic Is 'Amazed' at Popularity of Sterilization." *Washington Post,* September 9, 1962.

Grant, H. Coles. "Sterilization by Vasectomy under State Law." *Virginia Medical Monthly* 57 (January 1930): 683–84.

Grant, Madison. *Conquest of a Continent: Or, the Expansion of Races in America.* New York and London: Scribner's, 1933.

——. *The Passing of the Great Race: Or, the Racial Basis of European History.* New York: Scribner's, 1916.

Grantham, Dewey W. *The South in Modern America: A Region at Odds.* New York: Harper-Perennial, 1994.

Grill, Johnpeter Horst, and Robert L. Jenkins. "The Nazis and the American South in the 1930s: A Mirror Image?" *Journal of Southern History* 58 (November 1992): 667–94.

Gunther, Gerald. *Learned Hand: The Man and the Judge.* New York: Knopf, 1994.

Guterman, Lila. "Choosing Eugenics: How Far Will Nations Go to Eliminate a Genetic Disease?" *Chronicle of Higher Education,* May 2, 2003, A22.

Hall, Jacqueline Dowd. "'The Mind That Burns in Each Body': Women, Rape, and Racial Violence." In *Powers of Desire: The Politics of Sexuality,* edited by Ann Snitow, Christine Stansell, and Sharon Thompson, 328–49. New York: Monthly Review Press, 1983.

——. *Revolt against Chivalry: Jessie Daniel Ames and the Women's Campaign against Lynching.* New York: Columbia University Press, 1974.

Hale, Grace Elizabeth. *Making Whiteness: The Culture of Segregation in the South, 1890–1940.* New York: Pantheon Books, 1998.

Haller, John S., Jr. "The Physician versus the Negro: Medical and Anthropological Concepts of Race in the Late Nineteenth Century." *Bulletin of the History of Medicine* 44 (1970): 154–67.

Haller, Mark. *Eugenics: Hereditarian Attitudes in American Thought.* New Brunswick, N.J.: Rutgers University Press, 1963.

Hammar, Lawrence. "The Dark Side to Donovanosis: Color, Climate, Race and Racism in American South Venereology." *Journal of Medical Humanities* 18 (1997): 40–47.

Harris, Jonathan Gil. *Foreign Bodies and the Body Politic: Discourses of Social Pathology in Early Modern England.* London and New York: Cambridge University Press, 1998.

Hasian, Marouf A., Jr. *The Rhetoric of Eugenics in Anglo-American Thought.* Athens: University of Georgia Press, 1996.

Haskell, Thomas L., ed. *The Authority of Experts: Studies in History and Theory.* Bloomington: Indiana University Press, 1984.

Hassencahl, Frances Janet. "Harry H. Laughlin, 'Expert Eugenics Agent' for the House Committee on Immigration and Naturalization, 1921 to 1931." Ph.D. diss., Case Western Reserve University, 1970.

Heck, William Henry. "Citizenship in Southern Education." *Alumni Bulletin* (October 1919): 20–25. This piece originally appeared in *School Review* 12 (1904): 810–19.

——. *Mental Discipline and Educational Values.* 2nd ed. New York: John Lane, 1911.

Hedlin, Ethel "Earnest Cox and Colonization: A White Racist's Response to Black Repatriation, 1923–1966." Ph.D. diss., Duke University, 1974.

Heinemann, Ronald L. *Harry Byrd of Virginia.* Charlottesville: University Press of Virginia, 1996.

Herrnstein, Richard J., and Charles Murray. *The Bell Curve: Intelligence and Class Structure in American Life.* New York: Free Press, 1994.

Higham, John. *Strangers in the Land: Patterns of American Nativism, 1860–1925.* 4th ed. New Brunswick, N.J.: Rutgers University Press, 1994.

Hiltzik, Lee Richard. "The Brooklyn Institute of Arts and Sciences' Biological Laboratory, 1890–1924: A History." Ph.D. diss., State University of New York at Stony Brook, 1993.

Himstedt, Erin. "Not for Their Own Good: African American Mental Health and Eugenic Sterilization Programs in Virginia." Master's thesis, University of Virginia, 1995.

Hobson, Barbara Meil. *Uneasy Virtue: The Politics of Prostitution and the American Reform Tradition.* New York: Basic Books, 1987.

Hodes, Martha. *White Women, Black Men: Illicit Sex in the Nineteenth-Century South.* New Haven: Yale University Press, 1997.

Hodges, James Allison. "The Effect of Freedom upon the Physical and Psychological Development of the Negro." *Virginia Medical Semi-Monthly* 5 (May 25, 1900): 106–10.

Hofstadter, Richard. *The Age of Reform.* New York: Vintage Books, 1955.

——. *Social Darwinism in American Thought.* Rev. ed. New York: Braziller, 1959.

Hollaway, Pippa. *Sexuality, Politics, and Social Control in Virginia, 1920–1945.* Chapel Hill: University of North Carolina Press, 2006.

Holmes, Samuel J. *The Trend of the Race: A Study of Present Tendencies in the Biological Development of Civilized Mankind.* New York: Harcourt, Brace, 1921.

Hrdlička, Aleš. *The Old Americans.* Baltimore: Williams and Wilkins, 1925.

Hunter, Tera W. "Domination and Resistance: The Politics of Wage Household Labor in New South Atlanta." In *We Specialize in the Wholly Impossible: A Reader in Black Women's History,* edited by Darlene Clark Hine, Wilma King, and Linda Reed, 343–57. New York: New York University Press, 1995.

James, Arthur W. *Virginia's Social Awakening: The Contribution of Dr. Mastin and the Board of Charities and Corrections.* Richmond, Va.: Garrett and Massie, 1939.

Jefferson, Thomas. *Notes on the State of Virginia.* Edited by William Peden. Chapel Hill: University of North Carolina Press, 1954. Reprint, New York and London: Norton, 1972. Page numbers are from the reprint edition.

Jennings, Herbert Spencer. *The Biological Basis of Human Nature.* New York: Norton, 1930.

Jones, James H. *Bad Blood: The Tuskegee Syphilis Experiment.* 2nd ed. New York: Free Press, 1993.

Jordan, David Starr, and Harvey Ernest Jordan. *War's Aftermath: A Preliminary Study of the Eugenics of War.* Boston and New York: Houghton Mifflin, 1914.

Jordan, Harvey Ernest. "The Biological Status and Social Worth of the Mulatto." *Popular Science Monthly* 82 (June 1913): 573–82.

——. "A Comparative Microscopic Study of the Melanin Content of Pigmented Skins with Special Reference to the Question of Color Inheritance among Mulattos." *American Naturalist* 45 (August 1911): 449–70.

——. "The Eugenic Bearings of the Efforts for Infant Conservation." *Transactions of the American Association for the Study and Prevention of Infant Mortality* 2 (1912): 117–24.

——. "The Eugenical Aspect of Venereal Disease." *Transactions of the American Association for the Study and Prevention of Infant Mortality* 3 (1912–13): 156–63.

——. "Eugenics: Its Data Scope and Promise as Seen by the Anatomist." In *Eugenics: Twelve University Lectures,* by Morton A. Aldrich et al., 107–38. New York: Dodd, Mead, 1914.

——. "Eugenics: The Rearing of the Human Thoroughbred." *Cleveland Medical Journal* 11 (1912): 875–88.

——. "Hereditary Lefthandedness, with a Note on Twinning." *Journal of Genetics* 4 (1914–15): 67–81.

——. "Hereditary Tuberculosis and Infant Mortality." *Transactions of the American Association for the Study and Prevention of Infant Mortality* 2 (1912): 144–45.

——. "Heredity as a Factor in the Improvement of Social Conditions." *American Breeders Magazine* 2 (1911): 246–54.

——. "Infant Mortality in Relation to the Hereditary Effects of Tuberculosis." *Transactions of the American Association for the Study and Prevention of Infant Mortality* 3 (1913): 154–55.

——. "The Inheritance of Left-Handedness." *American Breeders Magazine* 2 (1911): 19–29, 113–24.

——. "The Inheritance of Skin Color." *Science*, n.s., 36 (August 2, 1912): 151–52.

——. "The Need for Genetic Studies of Pulmonary Tuberculosis." *Journal of the American Medical Association* 59 (1912): 1518–19. Page numbers refer to the offprint of this paper in Jordan's Collected Scientific Papers, which is paginated differently from the journal article.

——. "The Place of Eugenics in the Medical Curriculum." In *Problems in Eugenics: Papers Communicated to the First International Eugenics Congress*, 396–99. London: Eugenics Education Society, 1912.

——. "Recommendations on Eugenics." *JAMA* 52 (December 2, 1911): 1864.

——. "Relation of the Nucleolus to the Chromosomes in the Primary Oocyte of Asterias forbesil." *Publication Number 102*, 37–72. Washington, D.C.: Carnegie Institution of Washington, 1908.

——. "Studies in Human Heredity." *Bulletin of the Philosophical Society, University of Virginia* 1 (July 1912): 293–317.

——. "Surgical Sex-Sterilization: Its Value as a Eugenic Measure." *American Journal of Clinical Medicine* 20 (1913): 983–87.

Jordan, June. "Mississippi 'Black Home': A Sweet and Bitter Bluesong." *New York Times Magazine*, October 11, 1970, 64–65, 67, 70, 72, 74, 77, 80, 82, 85, 87.

Jordan, Winthrop D. *White over Black: American Attitudes toward the Negro 1550–1812*. Chapel Hill and London: University of North Carolina Press, 1968.

Kallen, Horace M. *Culture and Democracy in the United States*. New York: Boni and Livright, 1924. Reprint, New Brunswick, N.J.: Transaction, 1998.

Kamrat-Lang, Debora. "Healing Society: Medical Language in American Eugenics." *Science in Context* 8 (1985): 175–96.

Kelley, Robin D. G. *Race Rebels: Culture, Politics, and the Black Working Class*. New York: Free Press, 1994.

Kett, Joseph F. *The Formation of the American Medical Profession: The Role of Institutions, 1780–1860*. New Haven and London: Yale University Press, 1968. Reprint, Westport, Ct.: Greenwood, 1980.

——. "Women and the Progressive Impulse in Southern Education." In *The Web of Southern Social Relations: Women, Family, & Education*, edited by Walter J. Fraser Jr., R. Frank Saunders Jr., and Ron L. Wakelyn, 166–80. Athens: University of Georgia Press, 1985.

Keve, Paul W. *A History of Corrections in Virginia*. Charlottesville: University Press of Virginia, 1986.

Kevles, Daniel J. *In the Name of Eugenics: Genetics and the Uses of Human Heredity.* New York: Knopf, 1985.

Kevles, Daniel J., and Leroy Hood, eds. *The Code of Codes: Scientific and Social Issues in the Human Genome Project.* Cambridge and London: Harvard University Press, 1992.

Kline, Wendy. *Building a Better Race: Gender, Sexuality, and Eugenics from the Turn of the Century to the Baby Boom.* Berkeley and Los Angeles: University of California Press, 2001.

Kluger, Richard. *Simple Justice: The History of Brown v. Board of Education and Black America's Struggle for Equality.* New York: Vintage Books, 1975.

Kolchin, Peter. *American Slavery 1619–1877.* New York: Hill and Wang, 1993.

Kraut, Alan M. *Silent Travelers: Germs, Genes, and the "Immigrant Menace."* New York: Basic Books, 1994.

Kuhn, Thomas S. *The Structure of Scientific Revolutions.* 3rd ed. Chicago and London: University of Chicago Press, 1996.

Kunzel, Regina G. *Fallen Woman, Problem Girls: Unmarried Mothers and the Professionalization of Social Work, 1890–1945.* New Haven and London: Yale University Press, 1993.

Lacqueur, Thomas. *Making Sex: Body and Gender from the Greeks to Freud.* Cambridge and London: Harvard University Press, 1990.

Ladd-Taylor, Molly. "Eugenics, Sterilization and Modern Marriage in the U.S.A.: The Strange Career of Paul Popenoe." *Gender and History* 13 (2001): 298–327.

———. *Mother-Work: Women, Child Welfare, and the State, 1890–1930.* Urbana: University of Illinois Press, 1994.

Larson, Edward J. *Sex, Race, and Science: Eugenics in the Deep South.* Baltimore and London: Johns Hopkins University Press, 1995.

———. *Summer of the Gods: The Scopes Trial and America's Continuing Debate over Science and Religion.* New York: Basic Books, 1997.

Larson, Magali Sarfatti. "Production of Expertise and the Constitution of Expert Power." In *The Authority of Experts: Studies in History and Theory,* edited by Thomas L. Haskell, 28–80. Bloomington: Indiana University Press, 1984.

Laughlin, Harry H. *Eugenical Sterilization in the United States: A Report of the Psychopathic Laboratory of the Municipal Court of Chicago.* Chicago: Psychopathic Laboratory of the Municipal Court, 1922.

Lederer, Susan E. *Subjected to Science: Human Experimentation in America before the Second World War.* Baltimore and London: Johns Hopkins University Press, 1995.

Lemann, Nicholas. *The Promised Land: The Great Black Migration and How It Changed America.* New York: Vintage Books, 1995.

Lewis, Ivey Foreman. "Biologist Supports Curb on Immigrants." *New York Times,* April 6, 1924.

———. "William Henry Heck 1879–1919." *University of Virginia Alumni Bulletin* (October 1919): 357–79.

Link, Arthur S., and Richard L. McCormick, *Progressivism.* Arlington Heights, Ill.: Harlan Davidson, 1983.

Link, William A. *The Paradox of Southern Progressivism, 1880–1930.* Chapel Hill and London: University of North Carolina Press, 1992.

Lombardo, Paul A. "'The American Breed': Nazi Eugenics and the Origins of the Pioneer Fund." *Albany Law Review* 65 (2002): 743–830.

——. "Eugenic Sterilization in Virginia: Aubrey Strode and the Case of *Buck v. Bell.*" Ph.D. diss., University of Virginia, 1982.

——. "Facing Carrie Buck." *Hastings Center Report* (March-April 2003): 14–17.

——. "Involuntary Sterilization in Virginia: From Buck v. Bell to Poe v. Lynchburg." *Developments in Mental Health Law* 3 (1983): 13–14, 18–21.

——. "Medicine, Eugenics, and the Supreme Court: From Coercive Sterilization to Reproductive Freedom." *Journal of Contemporary Health Law and Policy* 13 (1996): 1–25.

——. "Miscegenation, Eugenics, and Racism: Historical Footnotes to *Loving v. Virginia.*" *University of California, Davis, Law Review* 21 (1988): 421–52.

——. "Three Generations, No Imbeciles: New Light on *Buck v. Bell.*" *New York University Law Review* 60 (April 1985): 30–62.

Lombardo, Paul A., and Gregory Michael Dorr. "Eugenics, Medical Education, and the Public Health Service: Another Perspective on the Tuskegee Syphilis Experiment." *Bulletin of the History of Medicine* 80 (2006): 291–316.

Love, Rosaleen. "'Alice in Eugenics Land': Feminism and Eugenics in the Scientific Careers of Alice Lee and Ethel Elderton." *Annals of Science* 36 (1979): 145–58.

Ludmerer, Kenneth M. *Genetics and American Society: A Historical Appraisal.* Baltimore and London: Johns Hopkins University Press, 1972.

Lydston, G. Frank. "Some of the Difficulties in the Application of Eugenics to the Human Race." *Virginia Medical Semi-Monthly* 14 (April 9, 1909): 15–19.

The Lynchburg Story. Produced and directed by Stephen Trombley. 55 min. Worldview Pictures Production, 1993. Videocassette.

MacDowell, E. Carleton. "Charles Benedict Davenport, 1866–1944: A Study of Conflicting Influences." *Bios* 17 (March 1946): 3–50.

Maienschein, Jane. *Transforming Traditions in American Biology, 1880–1915.* Baltimore and London: Johns Hopkins University Press, 1991.

Mall, Franklin P. "On Several Anatomical Characters of the Human Brain, Said to Vary According to Race and Sex, with Especial Reference to the Weight of the Frontal Lobe." *American Journal of Anatomy* 9 (1909): 1–32.

Manning, Kenneth R. *Black Apollo of Science: The Life of Ernest Everett Just.* New York: Oxford University Press, 1983.

Marchand, Roland. *Advertising the American Dream: Making Way for Modernity, 1920–1940.* Berkeley and Los Angeles: University of California Press, 1985.

Marquis Who's Who, Inc. *Who Was Who in America.* Vol. 5, *1969–1973.* Chicago: A. N. Marquis, 1975.

McGuire, Hunter, and G. Frank Lydston. "Sexual Crimes among the Southern Negroes—Scientifically Considered—An Open Correspondence." *Virginia Medical Monthly* 20 (May 1893): 105–25.

McLean, Nancy K. *Behind the Mask of Chivalry: The Making of the Second Ku Klux Klan.* New York: Oxford University Press, 1995.

Meckel, Richard A. *Save the Babies: American Public Health Reform and the Prevention of Infant Mortality, 1850–1929.* Baltimore and London: Johns Hopkins University Press, 1990.

Mehler, Barry Alan. "A History of the American Eugenics Society, 1921–1940." Ph.D. diss., University of Illinois at Urbana-Champaign, 1988.

Menand, Louis. *The Metaphysical Club: A Story of Ideas in America*. New York: Farrar, Strauss, and Giroux, 2002.

Mennel, Robert M., and Christine L. Compston, eds. *Holmes and Frankfurter: Their Correspondence, 1912–1934*. Hanover: University Press of New England, 1996.

Mickle, E. R., and C. E. Holdberry. "Eugenic Sterilization." *Virginia Medical Monthly* 57 (September 1930): 387–89.

Mills, Charles W. *The Racial Contract*. Ithaca, N.Y., and London: Cornell University Press, 1997.

Mitchell, Michele. "Adjusting the Race: Gender, Sexuality, and the Question of African-American Destiny, 1877–1930." Ph.D. diss., Northwestern University, 1998.

———. *Righteous Propagation: African Americans and the Politics of Racial Destiny after Reconstruction*. Chapel Hill: University of North Carolina Press, 2004.

Murray, Pauli, ed. *States' Laws on Race and Color*. Athens and London: University of Georgia Press, 1997.

Noll, Steven. *Feeble-Minded in Our Midst: Institutions for the Mentally Retarded in the South, 1900–1940*. Chapel Hill and London: University of North Carolina Press, 1995.

———. "The Sterilization of Willie Mallory." In *"Bad" Mothers: The Politics of Blame in Twentieth-Century America*, edited by Molly Ladd-Taylor and Lauri Umansky, 41–57. New York: New York University Press, 1988.

Numbers, Ronald L. *Darwinism Comes to America*. Cambridge and London: Harvard University Press, 1998.

Odem, Mary E. *Delinquent Daughters: Protecting and Policing Adolescent Female Sexuality in the United States, 1885–1920*. Chapel Hill and London: University of North Carolina Press, 1995.

Onuf, Peter S. "'To Declare Them a Free and Independent People': Race, Slavery, and National Identity in Jefferson's Thought." *Journal of the Early Republic* 18 (Spring 1998): 1–46.

Ordover, Nancy. *American Eugenics: Race, Queer Anatomy, and the Science of Nationalism*. Minneapolis: University of Minnesota Press, 2003.

Osborn, Frederick. *Preface to Eugenics*. New York: Harper and Brothers, 1940.

Otis, Laura. *Membranes: Metaphors of Invasion in Nineteenth-Century Literature, Science, and Politics*. Baltimore and London: Johns Hopkins University Press, 1999.

Parran, Thomas. *Shadow on the Land: Syphilis*. New York: Reynal and Hitchcock, 1937.

Pascoe, Peggy. "Miscegenation Law, Court Cases, and Ideologies of 'Race' in Twentieth-Century America." *Journal of American History* (June 1996): 44–69.

Pastore, Nicholas. *The Nature-Nurture Controversy*. New York: Kings Crown Press, 1949. Reprint, New York and London: Garland, 1984.

Paul, Diane B. *Controlling Human Heredity, 1865 to the Present*. Atlantic Highlands, N.J.: Humanities Press International, 1995.

———. *The Politics of Heredity: Essays on Eugenics, Biomedicine, and the Nature-Nurture Debate*. Albany: State University of New York Press, 1998.

Paul, Diane B., and Hamisch G. Spencer. "Did Eugenics Rest on an Elementary Mistake?" In *The Politics of Heredity: Essays on Eugenics, Biomedicine and the Nature-Nurture Debate*, by Paul, 117–32. Albany: State University of New York Press, 1998.

Paul, Julius. "The Return of Punitive Sterilization Proposals: Current Attacks on Illegitimacy and the AFDC Program." *Law and Society Review* 3 (August 1968): 77–106.

——. " . . . Three Generations of Imbeciles Are Enough . . . ": State Eugenic Sterilization
Laws in American Thought and Practice, 1965." Typescript, Historical Collections,
Wilhelm Moll Rare Book and Medical History Room, University of Virginia School of
Medicine, Charlottesville.

Pauly, Philip J. "Summer Resort and Scientific Discipline: Woods Hole and the Structure of
American Biology." In *The American Development of Biology*, edited by Ronald Rainger,
Keith R. Benson, and Jane Maienschein, 121–50. New Brunswick, N.J.: Rutgers Univer-
sity Press, 1988.

Pearl, Raymond. "The Biology of Superiority." *American Mercury* 12 (November 1927):
257–66

Pernick, Martin S. *The Black Stork: Eugenics and the Death of "Defective" Babies in American
Medicine and Motion Pictures since 1915*. New York and Oxford: Oxford University Press,
1996.

——. "Eugenics and Public Health in American History." *American Journal of Public
Health* 87 (November 1997): 1767–72.

Pickens, Donald K. *Eugenics and the Progressives*. Nashville, Tenn.: Vanderbilt University
Press, 1968.

Plecker, Walter A. "Birth Registration and Racial Integrity Law." *Virginia Journal of Education* 18 (September 1924): 13.

——. *Eugenics in Relation to the New Family and the Law on Racial Integrity*. Richmond,
Va.: Bureau of Vital Statistics, 1924.

——. "Eugenics or Race Deterioration—Which?" *Virginia Medical Semi-Monthly* 52 (August
1925): 282–88.

——. *The New Family and Racial Improvement*. Richmond, Va.: Bureau of Vital Statistics,
1928.

——. "Racial Improvement." *Virginia Medical Monthly* (November 1925): 486–90.

——. "Shall We All Be Mulattoes?" *Literary Digest* 23 (March 7, 1925): 23–24.

Popenoe, Paul, and Roswell Hill Johnson. *Applied Eugenics*. 1st, 2nd, and 3rd eds. New York:
Macmillan, 1918, 1926, 1931.

Powell, John. *A Breach in the Dike: An Analysis of the Sorrels Case Showing the Danger to
Racial Integrity from Intermarriage of Whites with So-Called Indians*. Richmond, Va.:
Liberty Printing Press, n.d. (ca. 1925).

Proctor, Robert. "Eugenics among the Social Sciences: Hereditarian Thought in Germany
and the United States." In *The Estate of Social Knowledge*, edited by JoAnne Brown and
David K. van Keuren, 175–208. Baltimore and London: Johns Hopkins University Press,
1991.

——. "From *Anthropologie* to *Rassenkunde* in the German Anthropological Tradition." In
Bones, Bodies, and Behavior: Essays on Physical Anthropology, edited by George W.
Stocking Jr., 138–79. Madison: University of Wisconsin Press, 1988.

——. *Racial Hygiene: Medicine under the Nazis*. Cambridge: Harvard University Press,
1988.

Provine, William B. "Geneticists and the Biology of Race Crossing." *Science* 182 (November
1973): 790–96.

Putney, Charles W. "Eugenic Sterilization." *Virginia Medical Monthly* 63 (March 1936):
705–9.

Quantz, Richard. "Founding of the University of Virginia School of Education." *Occasional Paper Series in the Social Foundations of Education* 3 (April 1979): 1–15.

Radford, John P. "Sterilization versus Segregation: Control of the Feebleminded, 1900–1938." *Social Sciences and Medicine* 33 (1991): 449–58.

Rafter, Nicole Hahn. "Claims-Making and the Socio-Cultural Context of the First U.S. Eugenics Campaign." *Social Problems* 39 (1992): 17–34.

——. *Creating Born Criminals.* Urbana and Chicago: University of Illinois Press, 1997.

——, ed. *White Trash: The Eugenic Family Studies, 1877–1919.* Boston: Northeastern University Press, 1988.

Reilly, Philip R. *The Surgical Solution: A History of Involuntary Sterilization in the United States.* Baltimore and London: Johns Hopkins University Press, 1991.

——. "The Virginia Racial Integrity Act Revisited: The Plecker-Laughlin Correspondence: 1928–1930." *American Journal of Medical Genetics* 16 (1983): 483–92.

Riddle, Oscar. "Biographical Memoir of Charles Benedict Davenport 1866–1944." *National Academy of Sciences Biographical Memoirs,* vol. 25. Washington, D.C.: National Academy of Sciences, 1948.

Robitscher, Jonas. *Sterilization.* Springfield, Ill.: Thomas, 1973.

Romano, Renee C. *Race Mixing: Black-White Marriage in Postwar America.* Cambridge: Harvard University Press, 2003.

Rosen, Christine. *Preaching Eugenics: Religious Leaders and the American Eugenics Movement.* New York: Oxford University Press, 2004.

Rosen, Ruth. *The Lost Sisterhood: Prostitution in America, 1900–1918.* Baltimore and London: Johns Hopkins University Press, 1982.

Ross, Dorothy. *The Origins of American Social Science.* Cambridge and New York: Cambridge University Press, 1991.

Rossiter, Margaret. "'Woman's Work' in Science, 1880–1910." *Isis* 71 (1980): 381–89.

Rothman, Joshua D. *Notorious in the Neighborhood: Sex and Families across the Color Line in Virginia, 1787–1861.* Chapel Hill: University of North Carolina Press, 2003.

Royster, Lawrence Thomas. *The Care of the Dependent Child.* Richmond: Frank H. Evory, ca. 1920. Special Collections, University of Virginia Library, Charlottesville.

——. "Custodial Care of the Feebleminded." *Journal of the American Medical Association* 65 (December 18, 1915): 2192.

——. *Preventative Medicine: A Study in Education.* Richmond: W. Wood, 1905. Special Collections, University of Virginia Library, Charlottesville.

——. "The Problem of the Feebleminded—A Plea for Adequate State Custodial Care." *Virginia Medical Semi-Monthly* (November 26, 1915): 406–8.

——. "The Relations of Weight, Height, and Age in Negro Children." Reprinted from *American Journal of Diseases of Children* 38 (December 1929), not paginated. Special Collections, University of Virginia Library, Charlottesville.

——. "The School Child in Its Relation to Eugenics." *Transactions of the Fourth International Congress on School Hygiene* 4 (1914): 26–35.

——. "A Study of the Size of the Sella Turcica in White and Colored Males and Females between the Eighth and Ninth Years, as Measured on Flat X-ray Films." *American Journal of Physical Anthropology* 14 (July-September 1930): 452–58.

Saks, Eva. "Representing Miscegenation Law." *Raritan* 8 (1988): 39–69.

Sanger, Margaret. *The Pivot of Civilization.* New York: Brentano's, 1922.

———. *Woman and the New Race.* New York: Brentano's, 1920.

Savitt, Todd. *Medicine and Slavery: The Diseases and Health Care of Blacks in Antebellum Virginia.* Urbana: University of Illinois Press, 1981.

Schoen, Johanna. "Between Choice and Coercion: Women and the Politics of Sterilization in North Carolina, 1929–1975." *Journal of Women's History* 13 (Spring 2001): 132–56.

———. *Choice and Coercion: Birth Control, Sterilization, and Abortion in Public Health and Welfare.* Chapel Hill: University of North Carolina Press, 2005.

Scott, Daryl Michael. *Contempt and Pity: Social Policy and the Image of the Damaged Black Psyche 1880–1996.* Chapel Hill and London: University of North Carolina Press, 1997.

Second International Congress of Eugenics, Harry H. Laughlin Chairman of Exhibits. *The Second International Exhibition of Eugenics.* Baltimore: Williams and Wilkins, 1923.

Selden, Steven. "Educational Policy and Biological Science: Genetics, Eugenics, and the College Textbook, c. 1908–1931." *Teachers College Record* 87 (Fall 1985): 42–51.

———. *Inheriting Shame: The Story of Eugenics and Racism in America.* New York and London: Teachers College Press, 1999.

Sherman, Richard. "The Last Stand: The Fight for Racial Integrity in Virginia in the 1920s." *Journal of Southern History* 54 (1988): 69–92.

Smith, J. David. *The Eugenic Assault on America: Scenes in Red, White and Black.* Fairfax, Va.: George Mason University Press, 1993.

Smith, J. David, and K. Ray Nelson. *The Sterilization of Carrie Buck.* Far Hills, N.J.: New Horizon Press, 1989.

Smith, J. Douglas. *Managing White Supremacy: Race, Politics, and Citizenship in Jim Crow Virginia.* Chapel Hill: University of North Carolina Press, 2002.

Smith, Shawn Michelle. "'Baby's Picture Is Always Treasured': Eugenics and the Reproduction of Whiteness in the Family Photograph Album." *Yale Journal of Criticism* 11 (1998): 197–220.

Smith, Susan L. *Sick and Tired of Being Sick and Tired: Black Women's Health Activism in America, 1890–1950.* Philadelphia: University of Pennsylvania Press, 1995.

Sohn, Chang Moon. "Principle and Expediency in Judicial Review: Miscegenation Cases in the Supreme Court." Ph.D. diss., Columbia University, 1970.

Solomon, Barbara Miller. *Ancestors and Immigrants: A Changing New England Tradition.* Cambridge: Harvard University Press, 1956.

Soloway, Richard A. *Demography and Degeneration: Eugenics and the Declining Birthrate in Twentieth-Century Britain.* 2nd ed. Chapel Hill and London: University of North Carolina Press, 1995.

Sommerville, Diane Miller. "The Rape Myth in the Old South Reconsidered." *Journal of Southern History* 61 (August 1995): 481–518.

Spencer, Frank, ed. *A History of American Physical Anthropology 1930–1980.* New York: Academic Press, 1982.

Stansell, Christine. *City of Women: Sex and Class in New York, 1789–1860.* Urbana and Chicago: University of Illinois Press, 1986.

Stanton, William. *The Leopard's Spots: Scientific Attitudes toward Race in America 1815–1859.* Chicago: University of Chicago Press, 1960.

Stern, Alexandra Minna. *Eugenic Nation: Faults and Frontiers of Better Breeding in Modern America*. Berkeley and Los Angeles: University of California Press, 2005.

Stoddard, Lothrop. *Clashing Tides of Colour*. New York and London: Scribner's, 1935.

——. *Re-Forging America: The Story of Our Nationhood*. New York and London: Scribner's, 1927.

——. *Revolt against Civilization: The Menace of the Under Man*. New York: Scribner's, 1922.

——. *The Rising Tide of Color against White World Supremacy*. New York: Scribner's, 1920.

Strode, Aubrey E. "Sterilization of Defectives." *Virginia Law Review* 11 (1925): 296–301.

Stubbe, Hans. *The History of Genetics: From Prehistoric Times to the Rediscovery of Mendel's Laws*. Cambridge: MIT Press, 1972.

Third International Congress of Eugenics, Committee on Publication. *A Decade of Progress in Eugenics: Scientific Papers of the Third International Congress of Eugenics*. Baltimore: Williams and Wilkins, 1934. Reprint, New York and London: Garland, 1984.

Thorndike, Edward Lee. *Educational Psychology*. 2nd ed. New York: Teachers College, 1910.

——. *Human Nature and the Social Order*. New York: Macmillan, 1940.

Tilton, McLane, ed. *Directory of the Living Alumni of the University of Virginia, 1931*. Charlottesville, Va.: Michie, 1931.

Tindall, George B. *The Emergence of the New South 1913–1945*. Baton Rouge: Louisiana State University Press, 1967.

Trent, James W., Jr. *Inventing the Feeble Mind: A History of Mental Retardation in the United States*. Berkeley and London: University of California Press, 1994.

Tucker, William H. *The Funding of Scientific Racism: Wickliffe Draper and the Pioneer Fund*. Urbana: University of Illinois Press, 2002.

Turner, Thomas W. "The Curriculum and Aims in Biological Teaching," *School Science and Mathematics* 27 (October 1927): 681–90. Also published in *Morehouse Journal of Science* (January 1928): 10–17.

Twelve Southerners. *I'll Take My Stand: The South and the Agrarian Tradition*. New York: Harper and Brothers, 1930.

Tyack, David B. *The One Best System: A History of American Urban Education*. Cambridge: Harvard University Press, 1974.

Underwood, Alice Jean. "Bon Air Learning Center: 1910–1970, Historical Perspectives on Institutional Policy." Ph.D. diss., University of Virginia, 1984.

University of Virginia. *Catalogue and Announcements*. Richmond: Everett Waddey, 1889–90.

Veysey, Laurence R. *The Emergence of the American University*. Chicago: University of Chicago Press, 1965.

Vigue, Charles L. "Eugenics and the Education of Women in the United States." *Journal of Educational Administration and History* 19 (1987): 51–55.

Waddlington, Walter A. "The Loving Case: Virginia's Anti-Miscegenation Statute in Historical Perspective." 52 *Virginia Law Review* (1966): 1189–1255.

Wallenstein, Peter. "Race, Marriage, and the Law of Freedom: Alabama and Virginia, 1860s-1960s." *Chicago-Kent Law Review* 70 (1994): 371–437.

——. *Tell the Court I Love My Wife: Race, Marriage, and Law—An American History*. New York: Palgrave Macmillan, 2002.

Walters, Ronald G. ed. *Scientific Authority and Twentieth-Century America*. Baltimore and London: Johns Hopkins University Press, 1997.

Washington, Joseph R., Jr. *Marriage in Black and White*. Boston: Beacon Press, 1970.

Wertenbaker, C. B. "Should Virginia Have a Marriage Law Based on Eugenics?" *Virginia Medical Semi-Monthly* 17 (December 12, 1913): 420–23.

White, G. Edward. "The Evolution of Reasoned Elaboration: Jurisprudential Criticism and Social Change." *Virginia Law Review* 59 (1973): 279–302.

White, Orland Emile. "Inbreeding and Outbreeding." *New Republic*, November 10, 1920, 279–80.

———. "Is Dementia Praecox Inheritable? Should a Victim's Relatives Marry?" *Eugenics* 2 (October 1929): 23.

———. "Mankind at the Crossroads." *Birth Control Review* 8 (February 1924): 55–56.

———. "Sterilization: A Symposium." *Birth Control Review* 12 (March 1928): 89–90.

White, Robert M. "Unraveling the Tuskegee Study of Untreated Syphilis." *Archives of Internal Medicine* 160 (March 13, 2000): 585–98.

Whitman, Mark. ed. *Removing a Badge of Slavery: The Record of Brown v. Board of Education*. Princeton, N.J., and New York: Markus Wiener, 1993.

Whitney, Leon F. *The Case for Sterilization*. New York: Stokes, 1934.

Wiebe, Robert H. *The Search for Order 1877–1920*. New York: Hill and Wang, 1967.

Wiggam, Alfred E. *The Fruit of the Family Tree*. 3rd ed. Indianapolis: Bobbs-Merrill, 1922. Reprint, New York: Blue Ribbon Books, 1926.

———. *The New Decalogue of Science*. 3rd ed. New York: Bobbs-Merrill, 1922. Reprint, New York: Garden City Publishing, 1926.

Williams, J. W. "Heredity—Eugenics." *Virginia Medical Semi-Monthly* 17 (December 26, 1913): 460–63.

Williamson, Joel. *The Crucible of Race: Black-White Relations in the American South since Emancipation*. New York and Oxford: Oxford University Press, 1984.

Wills, Garry. *Inventing America: Jefferson's Declaration of Independence*. New York: Doubleday, 1978. Reprint, New York: Vintage Books, 1979.

Woodward, C. Vann. *Origins of the New South 1877–1913*. Baton Rouge: Louisiana State University Press, 1951.

———. *The Strange Career of Jim Crow*. 3rd ed. New York: Oxford University Press, 1974.

Zenderland, Leila. *Measuring Minds: Henry Herbert Goddard and the Origins of American Intelligence Testing*. Cambridge: Cambridge University Press, 1998.

Index

Italicized page numbers refer to illustrations.

ability, 5

African Americans: artistic talent, 79; as black-beast rapists, 22, 79, 115; co-opt eugenics, 158–59, 162–64, 165–66, 226, 248n88; criminality, 45, 60, 140; deny white supremacy, 104, 160, 162; as depicted by eugenicists, 138; and disease, 110; domestics, as threat, 41, 61–62, 80; educability, 44–45, 80, 85; eugenics, 138; feebleminded, 122, 140; intelligence, 30, 80, 83–84, 110, 234n23; as menace, 80, 151, 186; mulattoes, as threat, 125, 147, 151; as "problem," 8, 24, 38, 49, 59, 109, 138–39; projected extinction of, 44, 81, 139–40; quality of, in Virginia, 139; and racial purity, 111, 160, 161, 162–64; response to eugenics legislation, 158–64; reversion of, 12, 21, 101, 139–40; sexuality, 139–40; and sterilization, 115, 159–60, 186; wayward women, home for, 120; women, 79. *See also* Garvey, Marcus; Turner, Thomas Wyatt; Mitchell, John

agrarianism, 49, 108

Aid to Families with Dependent Children (AFDC). *See* "welfare mothers"

Alderman, Edwin Anderson, 11, 42; as educational reformer, 50–52, 66; and eugenic metaphor, 71–72; and eugenics associations, 71; on race, 52, 71; and Lothrop Stoddard, 71. *See also* Lewis, Ivey Foreman

American Association for the Advancement of Science (AAAS), 73, 86, 95, 105, 173

American Public Health Association, 34, 147

"American race" ("Old Americans," "Old Virginians"), 14, 27, 28, 61, 67, 147, 225, 234n17; black analog to, 99; defined, 12–13; eugenics as justification for, 49, 75, 194. *See also* Bean, Robert Bennett

Amherst County, 58, 146

Anglo-Saxon, 10, 24, 87. *See also* Anglo-Saxon Clubs of America; whites: as Teutonic savages

Anglo-Saxon Clubs of America (ASCOA), 137; alliance with Marcus Garvey, 163; college chapters of, 143; goals of, 143; jeopardize Virginia eugenics movement, 155–58; links to Ku Klux Klan, 143; women's auxiliary, 145

anti-evolution, 11, 108

anti-Semitism, 168, 174–77

Bair, Margaret, 119

Banneker, Benjamin, 26, 30

Barrett, Janie Porter, 120

Barringer, Paul Brandon, 18, 50, *23;* on African American criminality, 21, 44; on African American educability, 23, 43, 44–45; on African American recapitulation, 21–22; on African American reversion, 21–22, 26, 44; and ASCOA, 143, 254n18; background of, 24–25, 39–40; on "Negro problem," 44; persistent influence of, 42, 47; and Walter Ashby Plecker, 151; poetry of, 47, 124; and public health, 42; retirement of, 46–47; on science and religion, 47; and slavery, 39, 43–44; supporters of, 24, 42, 46; on syphilis, 40–41, 236n49; and traditionalism, 39

Barrow, Bernard, 116

Bateson, William, 14

Bazile, Leon, 149, 207

Bean, Robert Bennett: on African Americans, 79–80, 81, 82; and "American race" (Old Americans, Old Virginians), 78, 82, 83, 178; background of, 78; brain studies of, 78–79; on disease susceptibility, 81–82; eugenics affiliations, 82–83; in 1930s, 178; similarity to Thomas Jefferson, 79; on syphilis, 80; and Virginia Academy of Science, 157

Bean, William Bennett, 170, 171

Bell, John, 121, *121;* replaces Priddy in *Buck v. Bell,* 133

"Better Babies Contest," 98

bias: in William Bennett Bean's studies, 81, 82; in eugenics, 5, 6, 15, 225, 226; in George Oscar Ferguson's work, 84–85, 86; in student papers, 170–71

biology: field stations, 54–55; overlap with eugenics 4, 54; underlying sociology of, 21, 74, 75, 101

birth control, 10, 96–97, 193

Blandy Experimental Farm, 89, 90, 190, 193, 219

blood: as genetic material, 13, 15, 59, 114, 187, 205; responsible for intelligence, 84, 85, 128

Blumenbach, Johann Friedrich, 31

Bon Air Home, 119–20

Brown v. Board of Education of Topeka, 195

Bryan, William Jennings, 6

Buck, Carrie, 121, *121, 130;* background of, 129–31; feeblemindedness debated, 129–32; feeblemindedness debunked, 223; later years and death of, 222; and sterilization hearing, 130; sterilized, 135

Buck, Doris, 222

Buck, Emma, 129, *130,* 131

Buck, Vivian, 131, *131,* 223

Buck v. Bell, 9, 117, 121. *See also Buck v. Priddy*

Buck v. Priddy, 130–31; decision, 134; as "friendly" case, 129, 132, 252n53; as historical marker, 223–24; as inspiration for other laws, 118; reaction to, 134–35

Bullington, Walter Edward, 94; eugenics course of, 95; relationship with Charles B. Davenport, 94–95

Burroughs, John, 90

Butler, Nicolas Murray, 45, 66

Cabell, James Lawrence, 18, 235n34; background of, 34; influence on Paul Brandon Barringer, 38, 40, 42; on permanent varieties, 35; and public health 33, 34; and reversion, 37; on science and religion, 35; and slavery, 36, 37, 235n38

California, 9

Campbell, Clarence G., 181–82

Carliner, David, 177, 201, 206, 208; flawed approach to *Naim,* 203, 204; and *Naim v. Naim,* 201–6. *See also under* Lewis, Ivey Foreman

Carrington, Charles: background of, 115, 250n15; as sterilization advocate, 117; sterilization operations of, 115–17

castration, 2, 140, 231n1

Catholic church, criticizes eugenics, 6, 215–16, 249n90

Central State Hospital, 120

citizenship. *See* race

Civil War amendments (to Constitution), 43, 236n56

Clark, Charles, 172–73
crime: "born criminals," 9, 22, 118; convict-lease system (chain gang), 12
College of William and Mary, 93
Conklin, Edwin Grant, 5, 53, 54, 73; and "gospel of social evolution," 74, 88, 101
Cox, Earnest Sevier, 76, 103, 137; background of, 141–42; and Theodore G. Bilbo, 182, 261n40; death of, 199; and ERA, 181–82; and Marcus Garvey, 163–64; and Madison Grant, 142, 183; lectures to students and teachers, 148; lobbies for Racial Integrity Act, 145; on miscegenation, 142; and neo-Nazism, 198–99; reaction to Sorrells case, 149; *Unending Hatred,* 200; and James K. Vardaman, 141; *White America,* 143, 144; *See also under* Nazis
Cumming, Hugh Smith, 42

Dana, William Hoyt, 95; eugenic beliefs of, 95–96
Darwin, Charles, 9, 25
Davenport, Charles B., 5, 53, 71, 74, 78; and birth control, 96–97, 246n48; correspondence with Walter Ashby Plecker, 154; and Mendelian segregation 4; and miscegenation, 57–58; retirement of, 179; on syphilis, 236n51; and Virginia faculty, 53, 71, 74, 78; and Virginia research, 153. *See also under* Jordan, Harvey Ernest
Davis, Donald Walton: background of, 93, 246n55; eugenic beliefs of, 93–94; eugenics creed of, 93; eugenic metaphor and, 93; and miscegenation, 93–94; at Sweet Briar, 97; and Virginia Academy of Science, 156–57; and Virginia feebleminded survey, 93
Deep South versus Upper South, 11
defect. *See* ability
DeJarnette, Joseph: background of, 122–23; equates feebleminded and mulattos, 151; and eugenic metaphor, 152; nickname, 125, 186; publication of "Mendel's Law," 123–24; testimony in *Buck v. Bell,* 132

disability. *See* ability
DNA fingerprints, 9
Draper, Wyckliffe P., 179–80
Drewry, William, 114; on menace of African American feebleminded, 122, 140
DuBois, W. E. B., 158–59

East, Edward M., 89, 95, 103; and birth control, 97; eugenic beliefs of, 91–92
education, 7, 105, 108; as cultural conservation, 50–51; and eugenics, in colleges outside Virginia, 232n18; and southern reform, 46, 49–51; survey of schoolchildren, 113; teachers and eugenics, 71, 76, 94, 113–14, 148; tracking, 67, 77, 84. *See also under* "efficiency"; eugenics; physicians
"efficiency," 16, 56, 123; and education, 84, 85; and God, 12
Estabrook, Arthur, 58; research for *Mongrel Virginians,* 153, 154–55, 225; testimony in *Buck v. Bell,* 132
eugenic metaphor: Edwin Anderson Alderman and, 71–72; and bias, 15; Charles Carrington's use of, 117; Donald Walton Davis's use of, 93; defined, 12; Joseph DeJarnette's use of, 151, 152; and education, 18; Sir Frances Galton's use of, 232n29; Thomas Jefferson's use of, 31–32; and medicine, 15–16; and memory, 14; Walter Ashby Plecker's use of, 151; for public health, 109; and social control, 15
eugenics: academic support for, 105; apologies for, 2, 9, 19; "back door to," 7; college courses in, 67–69, 70, 93–98, 100–101, 169–72; creed of, 12, 26, 62, 88, 177, 219, 224; critics of, 6; and Deep South, 17; defined, 1; demise of, 17, 19, 106, 194, 199, 226; economic efficiency of, 16, 61, 87, 109, 123; and education, 63–64, 70, 89, 105, 115, 124; erased from public memory, 210; eugenic segregation, expense of, 120, 123; explains social problems, 3, 69, 97; history of, 9–10; as lingua franca of

eugenics (*continued*)
science, 104; magazine coverage of, 115; "mainline eugenics," 17, 102, 105, 160, 168; maintains hierarchies, 7, 49; and medicine, 53; and morality, 12, 75; negative, 10, 63, 109; non-academic eugenics, 111; organizations, 54; as penal solution, 2, 16; persistence of, 7, 105, 118, 166, 178, 183, 219, 224; popularity of, in Virginia, 164–66; positive eugencis, 10, 62–63; as public health, 63, 148; reform eugenics, 17, 156, 190–93; as social control, 49; and social mobility 10; in states other than Virginia, 111, 113, 118, 184; time lag in adoption/rejection of, 6, 17–18, 19, 106, 118, 144, 213. *See also* hereditarianism

Eugenics Record Office (ERO), 53, 91, 92, 93, 147, 152; audit of, 179; closing of, 106; students of, 57, 98, 119, 153; surveys of, 95, 87, 98

Eugenics Research Association (ERA), 53, 83, 181–82

"Eugenics Tree," *13*

euthanasia, 10, 43, 109, 113

evolution, 25; academics defense of, 74

"false biology," 103

feebleminded, the, 18, 101, *110*, 249n2; "colony" system for, 120; defined, 17, 110; equated with mulattoes, 151; eugenic eradication of, 88; menace of, 8, 19, 108, 114, 117, 122, 136; segregation of, 114, 120; sexuality of, 117; and social inadequacy, 128; as source of criminality, 88, 108, 114; sterilization of, 92, 128, 183–84; threat of high-grade feebleminded (morons), 125; treatment of male feebleminded, 125–26; treatment of women feebleminded, 111, 119–20, 132

Ferguson, George Oscar: and anti-Semitism, 175; background of, 83; bigotry of, 244n34; opinion on miscegenation, 84, 85; studies of African American intelligence, 84, 218; and Virginia Academy of Science, 157

"final solution," 60, 61

fitness/unfitness, 12, 16, 75, 194; as bias, 5; defined by class, 234n22; defined by disability, 6

"Fitter Families Contests," 15, 49,

Fletcher, Joseph C., 216, 223

Galton, Sir Francis, 9, 174, 224

Garrett, Henry, 217–18

Garvey, Marcus, 160, 162–64; and "back to Africa" myth, 163, 258n72

genetics, heredity, 6; blending and, 4; term coined, 14

genetics, discrete (particulate genetics, "hard" genetics), 4, 8, 52; and disease, 57, 239n23; equivalent to environment, 56, 192; overpowered by environment, 67, 196; overpowers environment, 22, 27, 56, 67, 72, 75, 87, 101

genetic therapy, 7

germ (germ plasm), 12–14, 33

Goddard, Henry Herbert, 65

gonorrhea, 8

"gospel of social evolution." *See under* Conklin, Edwin Grant

Grant, Madison, 71, 103, 142; *Passing of the Great Race*, 76

Great Depression, 168, 169, 187, 259n9; dysgenics as cause of, 170

Haeckel, Ernst, 22

Hall, G. Stanley, 46

Hampton Institute, 98, 104

Heck, William Henry "Harry", 18, 65, 113; background of, 66; death of, 68; and educational tracking, 67; and education and public health, 68; first eugenics course of, 66, 67–68, 240n50; on heredity, 67; mentors Ferguson, 83, 85; and normal science, 68; as teacher, 68; and Edward Lee Thorndike, 66–67

hereditarianism, 8, 16, 27, 42, 67; and college courses, 93, 94; in education, 71, 75, 77; as religion, 26; and sectional rapprochement, 25, 49, 138, 225 heredity. *See* genetics, hereditary

historically black colleges. *See* Hampton Institute; Howard University

Hollins College, 97

Holmes, Oliver Wendell, Jr., 2, 65, 95; decision in *Buck v. Bell,* 133–34; eugenic beliefs of, 134

Holt, Henry W., 149–50; 202

Howard University, 98–99, 100–101

Human Genome Project, 17, 227

imagined community, 12, 14, 49. *See also* "American race"

immigration: college courses about, 97; menace of, 8, 49, 107–8; restriction, 10, 75

intelligence (IQ), 57, 59, 65, 239n28. *See also under* African Americans

intelligence tests, 10, 59, 66, 83–85; and *Mongrel Virginians,* 154; army alpha and beta tests, 85, 110

International Congress of Eugenics: First Congress, 63, 82, 238n18; Second Congress, *13,* 82, 92; Third Congress, 92, 181, 191

interracial marriage, public opinion polls on, 209

Jacobsen v. Massachusetts, 133

James Madison University, 94

Jefferson, Thomas, 18, 26–32; and "American race," 27, 28; on black inferiority, 27; and education, 29; as foundational thinker, 25, 27–28, 75, 79; on human origins, 25; and immigration, 28–29; links to later eugenicists, 28, 31, 32; and science, 27–28, 234n14; and science and religion, 32; slaves of, 27; and yeomen farmers, 108, 110. *See also under* eugenic metaphor; miscegenation

Jordan, David Starr, 53, 71, 97

Jordan, Harvey Ernest, *53,* 18, 113; anti-Semitism of, 175; and ASCOA, 143, 254n18; background of, 47, 54; dean of medical school, 175; and economic efficiency of eugenics, 63; and eugenic

metaphor, 60, 240n36; and eugenics, 55–57, 60; eugenics creed of, 60, 62, 64–65; and eugenics and medicine, 61; hiring of, 47; links to Paul Brandon Barringer, 47, 54; on left-handedness, 60; on miscegenation, 58–59; and normal science, 56; and prominent eugenicists, 53–54; and public health, 63–64; relationship with Charles B. Davenport, 53, 55–59; and sterilization, 55, 63, 114; suggests eugenic studies in Virginia, 57–58, 98, 153; suggests students for ERO, 57, 100; on syphilis, 61, 62, 65; on tuberculosis, 60; and Virginia Academy of Science, 156–58; on women, 64

Jukes, The (Dugdale), 87, 117

Just, Ernest E., 98, 99

Ku Klux Klan, 108, 143

Lacquer, Thomas, 6

Laughlin, Harry Hamilton, *5,* 70, 127, 128; deposition in *Buck v. Bell,* 132; on immigration, 28; and University of Virginia, 179–80, 182; on *White America,* 144

language: blurring of biological, 13–14; medicalized, 15–16, 32; of public health, 16, 109, 225

Lewis, Ivey Foreman, *73;* anti-radicalism of, 176–77; anti-Semitism of, 174–76; and ASCOA, 143, 254n18; background of, 72–74, 242n6, 246n7; and Carliner case, 177; as dysgenic father, 77; effect of teaching on, 167, 171–72, 191, 193, 263n62; eugenic beliefs of, 75, 76–77; eugenics courses and, 69, 170–72, 191; final lecture of, 173; introduces Earnest Sevier Cox to Wyckliffe P. Draper, 182; on Thomas Jefferson, 76–77; and Mendel artifacts, 226; on miscegenation, 76; opinion of sociology, 76; political discretion of, 157–58, 180, 181, 199–200; relationship with Edwin Anderson Alderman, 72, 74; relationship with Earnest Sevier Cox, 144, 148; relationship with Charles B.

Lewis, Ivey Foreman (*continued*)
Davenport, 74; relationship with Harry
Hamilton Laughlin, 180; on religion and
science, 72, 74–75; retirement of, 218; on
segregation, 76; supporters of, 172–74;
and Virginia Academy of Science, 156–57
Lewis, Nell Battle, 77
Linnaeus, Carolus, 3
Lippmann, Walter, 6
Loving v. Virginia, 9, 207–10
Lydston, G. Frank, 112–13; on African
American inferiority, 140; on miscegena-
tion, 140; rhetoric like Holmes's, 112
lynching, 11, 102, 140, 160

Mall, Franklin, 78; refutes Robert Bennett
Bean, 80–81
Mallory v. Priddy, 126–27, 252n46
marriage restriction, 10, 89; law, 8, 75,
114; physicians and, 112. *See also* Racial
Integrity Act; *Loving v. Virginia*
Massive Resistance, 19, 172, 173, 200;
defined, 199; scientific supporters of,
217–18; term coined, 203
Mastin, Joseph, 122
McDougle, Ivan E.: daughter wins better
babies contest, 98; at Sweet Briar, 97–98,
225
McGuire, Hunter Holmes, 34
melting pot, 8
Mendel, Gregor, 3, 90
Mendel's Law. *See* segregation: Mendelian
"Mendel's Law" (DeJarnette), 123–24
Miller School of Biology. *See* University of
Virginia: biology department
miscegenation, 22, 57–58; defined, 10–11;
as gauged by "appearances," 149, 202–3;
Thomas Jefferson on, 30–31; states with
laws against, 203, 204
Mitchell, John, 160, 161–62
modernism (modernity), 5; crisis of, 196;
in shift from Old South to New South,
48–49; versus tradition, 7, 11, 25
Mongrel Virginians (Estabrook), 153,
154–55, 225

monogenism: defined, 35; and slavery, 35
moral delinquent, 242n11
morality, inborn, 25, 36, 102
Murphy, Edgar Gardner, 42

Naim v. Naim, 19, 147; class and race in,
202; eugenics and racism in, 205; intra-
court conflict over, 206; U.S. Supreme
Court and, 205–6, 207; Virginia Su-
preme Court and, 204–5, 206
Native Americans, 58, 97, 166, 187, 223; Paul
Brandon Barringer on 45–46; Thomas
Jefferson on, 31; and Racial Integrity Act,
161–62, 188–90
Nazi Germany, 19, 167, 172, 174, 210
Nazis, 167, 205; Earnest Sevier Cox and,
182–83, 198; Walter Ashby Plecker and,
181, 188, 189; John Leslie Powell and,
198; sterilization program of, 168–69,
174, 184, 187, 216
"Negro problem." *See* African Americans: as
"problem"
Nelson, K. Ray, 221
Newcombe, John Lloyd, 179–80
New South boosterism, 25; Paul Brandon
Barringer and, 38–39
normal science, 38, 128; defined, 26
North Carolina, 50, 66, 72, 213

"Old Stock." *See under* Virginians; *see also*
"American race"
"Old Virginians." *See under* Virginians; *see
also* "American race"

Petersburg Colony, 120
Peterson, Anna Marie, 119
Phelps-Stokes Fund, 57, 239n21
physicians, 193; call for eugenics education,
81–82, 89, 115, 122–23, 151; eugenic
reporting of, 113; and eugenics, 112–14,
115; immunized from prosecution for
sterilization, 127, 129; sterilization practices of, 115, 125, 169, 183–88
physician's gaze. *See under* language,
medicalized

Plecker, Walter Ashby, 137; on "American
race," 147, 152; calls for resignation of,
160–61; enforcement of Racial Integrity
Act, 187–90; and ERA, 182; eugenics
pamphlets of, 150–51, 161; on miscegenation, 151, 161; and *Mongrel Virginians*,
152–53, 154; popularizes Racial Integrity
Act, 147–48, 150–51; racial integrity
"dragnet" of, 147; reaction to Sorrells
case, 149; retirement of, 190
"Pocahontas clause." *See under* Racial Integrity Act
Poe v. Lynchburg, 9, 19, 221
policy: institutional policy, 8; public policy,
8, 9, 11, 106; social policy, 8, 9, 74, 105,
226
polygenism: defined, 35; slaveholder's resistance to, 35
Powell, John Leslie, 137; antagonizes
Virginia elites, 150, 155–56; background
of, 143; lobbies for Racial Integrity Act,
145–47; reaction to Sorrells case, 149
Priddy, Albert, 122; and extralegal sterilization, 125–26; on race suicide, 125;
testimony in *Buck v. Bell*, 132. *See also*
Mallory v. Priddy
Progressive Era, 8, 16, 25, 52, 65, 98, 120,
135
progressivism, 39, 85, 101, 134–35, 166;
boosters of, 41; education and, 11, 18, 50,
52, 65, 66; and "efficiency," 16; eugenicists and, 108, 109; language and, 16;
medicine and, 34, 63, 86; racism and,
49; race relations and, 51, 138; reformers
and, 11, 38, 42, 48, 61, 74, 118; southerners and, 49, 50, 75; technology and, 107,
133; Virginians and, 111, 116
public health, 33–34, 63, 68, 108; physicians
cast eugenics as, 123; resistance to, 166;
surgeons general and, 42, 236n52. *See*
also under language

race: "appearance" of, 149; calls to abandon
use of, in scientific papers, 228; and citizenship, 12, 28, 30, 59, 75, 105; and civilization, 36, 76; and inferiority/superior-
ity (hierarchy), 3, 7, 10, 26, 85, 177–78;
molecularization of, 7; one drop rule for,
31, 154; permanent varieties of, 33, 35;
problem of, 49; as social construct, 103;
UNESCO statement on, 103, 234n9. *See*
also "American race"
race suicide, 38, 59, 96, 103–4, 119; defined, 8
racial contract, 75, 243n12
racial integrity (purity), 8, 10, 11, 75; and
intelligence, 84; as response to miscegenation, 140, 160; student opinions
regarding, 171, 172–73. *See also* African
Americans: and racial purity; Racial
Integrity Act
Racial Integrity Act, 19, 76, 102; amendments to, 149, 161; defended and upheld,
204; effect of, 166; enforcement of,
148, 187–89; parallels immigration
restriction, 138; provisions of, 145–46;
"Pocahontas clause" of, 146, 148, 156, 161;
popularity of, among whites, 164–65;
and Sorrells case, 149. *See also Naim v.*
Naim; Loving v. Virginia
racism. *See* scientific racism
Randolph Macon Women's College, 94–95,
125
rape: black on white, 22; as cause of race
war, 22
recapitulation, defined, 22. *See also* Barringer, Paul Brandon: on African American
recapitulation
Reed, Walter, 34, 42
Relf v. Weinberger, 196, 214
reversion. *See* Barringer, Paul Brandon: on
black reversion
Roosevelt, Theodore, 24, 65
Ross, Edward Alsworth, 24, 97, 144
Royster, Lawrence Thomas, 83, 113, 119;
background of, 86; eugenics and, 87,
88–89; and eugenics creed, 88; and
public health, 86, 87; reform efforts of,
87; work with William Henry "Harry"
Heck, 86–87

Sanger, Margaret, 91, 96

science: morality of, 6, 47, 49, 102; objectivity of, 4, 7, 68, 226–27; public perception of, 51–52; reinforces imagined community, 49; as religious faith, 1, 4, 25, 32, 62, 177, 224; and social context, 1, 4, 27, 225; as syllogism, 6, 47, 102, 227

scientific racism: origins of, 26; shift in, in early twentieth century, 25, 49

segregation, 3, 18, 82; in education, 50; eugenic segregation, 3, 87, 111, 112, 118–20; institutional segregation, 10, 109; legal segregation, 25; Mendelian segregation, 3, 4, 8, 10, 101; racial segregation, 11; as rational race relations, 52. *See also* feebleminded, the: segregation of

segregation's science, 7, 19, 103, 120; buttresses class prerogatives, 128; co-opted by African Americans, 102, 104, 138–39; impact of, 194; and Racial Integrity Act, 150, 208

Sharp, Harry, 115

Shuey, Audrey, 218

Singleton, Ralph, 218–19

slavery, 27, 37; slave breeding and, 44, 139, 158, 186

Smith, Lemuel, 146–47, 205

social control, 14, 105

Social Darwinism, 32

Sorrells, Atha, 149

Spencer, Herbert, 32

sterilization, 10, 112; abuse of, 159, 214–17; in Alabama, 159–60; challenges to, 252n49, 252n50; consent to, 214; of criminals, 92, 115–17; ends in Virginia, 222; eugenic sterilization, 109–36; extralegal sterilization, in Virginia, 115–16; law, in states other than Virginia, 118, 127, 184; law, in Virginia, 8, 114, 121–22, 127–29; in 1930s Virginia, 183–87; punitive sterilization, 196, 211–13; as "social service," 213; statistics on, 2, 9, 125, 135, *169*, 184–87, *185*, *186*, *187*, 253n64, 261n44; student opinion of, 167, 170, 171;

voluntary sterilization, 9, 214; of women, 186, 262n48. *See also Buck v. Bell*

Stoddard, Lothrop, 71, 76, 103. *See also under* Alderman, Edwin Anderson

Strode, Aubrey: background of, 122; drafts sterilization law, 127–28; tries *Buck v. Bell,* 133

students, 9, 64; on African Americans, 172–73; and anti-Semitism, 175–76; eugenic papers of, 167, 169–71; and fears of "Negro problem," 171; Jewish, numbers in eugenics classes, 70, 171–72

Sweet Briar College, 97–98;

syphilis, 8, 22, 44, 80; as dysgenic force, 40–41; and Tuskegee experiment, 34; and Tuskegee experiment apology, 223. *See also under* Barringer, Paul Brandon; Jordan, Harvey Ernest

taxonomy, 3, 57, 82

thalassemia, 7, 231n8

Thorndike, Edward Lee, 65, 83. *See also under* Heck, William Henry "Harry"

tradition. *See under* modernism (modernity)

Trinkle, E. Lee, 147

tuberculosis, 8, 22, 44, 60; prevention of, likened to sterilization, 123

Turner, Thomas Wyatt, *99;* background of, 99–100; criticizes racist biology, 103, 249n88; eugenic beliefs of, 101–2, 104; on eugenic propagandists, 103; on race suicide, 103–4; relationship with Charles B. Davenport, 100, 248n79; and science as religion, 102–3

Universal Negro Improvement Association (UNIA). *See* Garvey, Marcus

University of Richmond, 95

University of Virginia, 33, 48; 179–80; aspirations to policy power, 74; biology department, 89, 171–72; Jewish quotas at, 174–75; medical ethics at, 223; medical school, 33, 39, 51, 223; progressive reform of, 50–51, 52–53, 66, 90

Upper South. *See* Virginia; North Carolina

Virginia, 7; as eugenics exemplar, 111, 138, 146, 147, 166; eugenics movement in, 111, 156–58, 164–65, 199; and Industrial School for Colored Girls, 120; institutions in, 120–21; and rediscovery of eugenics history, 221–22, 224. *See also* physicians

Virginia Academy of Science, 156–58

Virginia Bureau of Charities and Corrections, 55, 56, 113, 118, 122

Virginia Colony for the Epileptic and Feebleminded (Lynchburg Colony, Lynchburg Training School), 114, 121, 221

Virginia General Assembly, 2, 9; and marriage restriction, 122, 127, 146–47; and segregation of feebleminded, 113, 120–21; and sterilization, 129

Virginians: average intelligence of, 110; educated Virignians, 8, 74; elite Virginians, 8, 9, 12; Old Stock Virginians (Cavaliers), 18, 19, 49–50; proposed state eugenics boards, 212, 217; quality of African American Virginians, 139; react to *Buck v. Bell*, 134–35, 138. *See also* physicians

Virginia Polytechnic Institute, 94

Washington, Booker T., and Paul Brandon Barringer, 43, 45, 46

Washington and Lee University, 95

"welfare mothers," 19, 196

White, Orland Emile: background of, 90–91; and birth control, 97; eugenics affiliations of, 191; eugenic beliefs of, 92, 191–92; female students of, 192–93, 262n59; and prominent eugenicists, 90, 92, 245n47; reform eugenics of, 190–93; relationship with Charles B. Davenport, 91; relationship with Edward M. East, 91; relationship with Harry Hamilton Laughlin, 92; relationship with Margaret Sanger, 91; retirement of, 218; on sterilization, 92

Whitehead, Irving, 129, 130, 131–32

whites: class tensions among, 49; elite whites, 8, 9, 11, 49, 165, 224; elite political control of, 51, 109; poor whites, 11, 49, 87, 111; sterilization of poor whites, 116; as "Teutonic savages," 234n6; university students as elite whites, 170–71

women, 64, 79, 94, 145, *187;* as criminals, 119; as genetics students, 192–93; homes for wayward women, 119–20; poor women, 111; and race suicide, 96; republican motherhood and eugenics, 96; and sexual double standard, 64, 117, 132; and sterilization, 116, 186–87, 215, 216–17, 250n22. *See also under* feebleminded

women's colleges: send students to ERO, 98; student fieldworkers at, 154. *See also* Hollins College; Randolph Macon's Women's College; Sweet Briar College

CARTER G. WOODSON INSTITUTE SERIES

Michael Plunkett
Afro-American Sources in Virginia: A Guide to Manuscripts

Sally Belfrage
Freedom Summer

Armstead L. Robinson and Patricia Sullivan, eds.
New Directions in Civil Rights Studies

Leroy Vail and Landeg White
Power and the Praise Poem: Southern African Voices in History

Robert A. Pratt
The Color of Their Skin: Education and Race in Richmond, Virginia, 1954–89

Ira Berlin and Philip D. Morgan, eds.
Cultivation and Culture: Labor and the Shaping of Slave Life in the Americas

Gerald Horne
Fire This Time: The Watts Uprising and the 1960s

Sam C. Nolutshungu
Limits of Anarchy: Intervention and State Formation in Chad

Jeannie M. Whayne
A New Plantation South: Land, Labor, and Federal Favor in Twentieth-Century Arkansas

Patience Essah
A House Divided: Slavery and Emancipation in Delaware, 1638–1865

Tommy L. Bogger
Free Blacks in Norfolk, Virginia, 1790-1860: The Darker Side of Freedom

Robert C. Kenzer
Enterprising Southerners: Black Economic Success in North Carolina, 1865–1915

Midori Takagi
"Rearing Wolves to Our Own Destruction": Slavery in Richmond, Virginia, 1782–1865

Alessandra Lorini
Rituals of Race: American Public Culture and the Search for Racial Democracy

Mary Ellen Curtin
Black Prisoners and Their World, Alabama, 1865–1900

Philip J. Schwarz
Migrants against Slavery: Virginians and the Nation

Armstead L. Robinson
Bitter Fruits of Bondage: The Demise of Slavery and the Collapse of the Confederacy, 1861–1865

Francille Rusan Wilson
The Segregated Scholars: Black Social Scientists and the Creation of Black Labor Studies, 1890–1950

Gregory Michael Dorr
Segregation's Science: Eugenics and Society in Virginia

CPSIA information can be obtained
at www.ICGtesting.com
Printed in the USA
LVHW020324231121
704135LV00010B/2068